Level G

Developing Math & Thinking Skills

Mathematical Reasoning™ Series

📖 Beginning 1 📖 Beginning 2
📖 Level A 📖 Level B 📖 Level C 📖 Level D
📖 Level E 📖 Level F 📖 Level G 📖 Understanding Geometry
📖 Grades 2-4 Supplement 📖 Grades 4-6 Supplement
📖 Middle School Supplement (Grades 7-9)

Written by
Carolyn Anderson

Graphic Design by
Chip Dombrowski • Annette Langenstein • Karla Garrett

Edited by
Patricia Gray • Judith Wicks • Joe Walker

© 2013
THE CRITICAL THINKING CO.™
(Bright Minds™)
www.CriticalThinking.com
Phone: 800-458-4849 • Fax: 831-393-3277
P.O. Box 1610 • Seaside • CA 93955-1610
ISBN 978-1-60144-314-4

Printed in China by Shanghai Chenxi Printing Co., Ltd. (July 2013)

About the Author

Carolyn Anderson holds graduate degrees in mathematics and education. She taught for more than 20 years in the North Kansas City School District and is currently an Associate Professor of Mathematics at Park University. There she teaches mathematics and math method courses for early childhood and elementary teachers.

Carolyn spent nearly ten years as managing editor of Math Magic, a national math magazine and math-enrichment developer. She has written educational material for whole numbers, decimals, money, metric system, geometry, and trigonometry. Carolyn has authored a book of math mazes and several math puzzle books. She has been a speaker at numerous conferences on integrating technology into math curriculum and developing summer enrichment programs.

Carolyn has been nominated numerous times for the North Kansas City School District teacher of the year. In 1993 she won the KCI/Northland Regional Chamber Excellence in Education Award. Also, she was recognized as the outstanding math alumni of the year at Central Missouri State University. In 1999 she was the winner of the Larry Markt "above and beyond" award.

Carolyn believes it is important to structure classes for success and good material is a key component of that.

Table of Contents

NCTM Standards

Skills	Number and Operations	Algebra	Geometry	Measurement	Data Analysis and Probability
Absolute Value	237, 307, 334				
Angle		92, 93, 232	13, 25, 232, 233, 235, 271	26, 27, 92, 93, 232, 393, 394	
Area		79		51, 74, 75, 76, 180, 349, 350, 351, 352, 395, 402, 403	
Capacity customary, metric				268, 269, 270, 310, 311, 312	
Circles			38, 260, 261	177, 260, 261, 262, 263, 264, 265, 289, 348, 351, 402	
Combinations					67, 136, 191, 380
Congruence			171, 201		
Coordinate System			15, 158, 159, 160, 161, 162, 330, 331, 332		
Count	21, 83				
Critical Thinking	4, 94, 109, 403	12, 24, 37, 58, 79, 81, 82, 90, 91, 94, 102, 104, 112, 122, 133, 134, 139, 168, 174, 178, 179, 187, 200, 213, 238, 248, 252, 302, 306, 324, 336, 364, 375, 376, 378, 379, 381	61, 82, 201, 234, 271, 273, 392	79, 270	87
Data Analysis bar graph, line graph, survey, table, picture					53, 54, 87, 88, 89, 175, 274, 362, 363, 382, 384, 385

NCTM Standards (Cont.)

NCTM Standards

Skills	Number and Operations	Algebra	Geometry	Measurement	Data Analysis and Probability
Decimals concept, add, subtract, multiply, divide	124, 125, 126, 127, 141, 142, 143, 144, 145, 146, 147, 148, 149, 151, 290, 291, 292, 293, 294, 295, 296, 297, 298, 299, 337, 338, 339, 340, 341, 370, 371, 372, 373, 404				
Draw			15, 38, 180, 181, 182, 346, 392	79, 180, 181, 182	
Equations Expression	69, 334	163, 333			
Equivalence	40, 95, 96, 123, 242, 335, 365	63, 215, 375			
Estimation addition, subtraction, multiplication, division	83, 86, 360, 361				
Exponents	72, 73, 388				
Factors	17, 39, 70, 71, 97, 276, 313, 320, 321, 366, 367	112, 378			
Fractions form/vocabulary, add, subtract, multiply, divide	40, 41, 44, 95, 96, 98, 99, 106, 107, 108, 110, 111, 114, 115, 116, 117, 118, 119, 120, 121, 123, 239, 242, 243, 244, 245, 246, 247, 250, 251, 253, 254, 255, 256, 257, 258, 259, 278, 279, 280, 281, 282, 283, 284, 285, 286, 287, 365, 366, 367, 370, 404	288		45, 46, 342, 343	42, 43
Graph, Table, Chart, Figure analyze, represent	278	364	15, 159, 160, 161, 162, 180, 181, 182, 331, 332	180, 181, 182, 262	16, 42, 43, 53, 54, 87, 88, 175, 176, 274, 325, 362, 363
Inequalities	123, 335	200			
Integers	152, 153, 154, 155, 156, 157, 326, 327, 328, 329				
Length customary, metric				45, 46, 47, 48, 49, 103, 130, 177, 236, 342, 343, 344, 345, 403	
Likelihood, Probability					135, 136, 192, 193, 194, 377
Lines parallel, perpendicular, slope			100, 101, 103, 132, 161, 162, 332, 346, 403		

NCTM Standards (Cont.)

NCTM Standards

Skills	Number and Operations	Algebra	Geometry	Measurement	Data Analysis and Probability
Mean, Median, Mode					65, 66, 205, 383
Money add, subtract, multiply, divide	55, 56, 57, 137, 138, 139, 140, 150, 184, 198, 199, 281, 291, 301, 386	56, 87, 139, 200, 275			
Multiple	105, 113, 249, 315, 317, 322, 323	316			
Negative Numbers	152, 153, 154, 155, 156, 157, 326, 327, 328, 329				
Notation	69, 237, 307, 334				
Order	5, 126, 144, 335, 337				
Order of Operations	62, 63, 214, 215, 335, 389				
Patterns geometric, numeric	70, 313, 372, 373, 387	28, 59, 187, 213, 324, 336, 397			
Percent	195, 196, 197, 198, 199, 374, 386	375			
Perimeter		79		50, 77, 347, 352, 402	
Place Value expanded notation, number form, word form	1, 2, 3, 5, 124, 125, 206, 207, 337				
Polygons			13, 14, 52, 74, 75, 76, 77, 78, 234, 272, 273, 392	92, 93, 232, 347, 349, 350, 394, 395	
Prime/Composite	71, 97, 307, 314, 318, 319, 320, 321	112, 379			
Properties	17, 22, 23, 68, 70, 313, 319				
Reflection, Translation, Rotation			170, 305, 403		
Ratio rates, proportion	183, 184, 185, 186, 187, 188, 189, 190, 300	187, 188, 189, 190, 300			377
Rounding	84, 85, 358, 359				
Shapes 2 dimensional, 3 dimensional			131, 234, 303, 304		
Symmetry			171		

NCTM Standards (Cont.)

NCTM Standards

Skills	Number and Operations	Algebra	Geometry	Measurement	Data Analysis and Probability
Temperature customary, metric				64, 103, 266, 267, 403	
Time				21, 128, 129	
Variable as Unknown in addition, in subtraction, in multiplication, in division		122, 163, 164, 165, 166, 167, 168, 169, 216, 217, 218, 219, 220, 221, 222, 223, 224, 225, 226, 227, 228, 229, 230, 231, 333, 398, 399, 400, 401			
Vocabulary	202, 307, 403	202, 203, 204, 258, 397	80, 103, 304	103	103
Volume				353, 396	
Weight customary, metric				172, 173, 308, 309	
Whole Numbers addition, subtraction, multiplication, division	6, 7, 8, 9, 10, 11, 17, 18, 19, 20, 21, 29, 30, 31, 32, 33, 34, 35, 36, 59, 60, 62, 63, 68, 69, 70, 71, 73, 109, 208, 209, 210, 211, 212, 214, 215, 277, 313, 354, 355, 360, 361, 368, 369, 387, 404				
Word Problems	7, 11, 21, 36, 109, 140, 150, 199, 338, 340, 356, 357, 390, 391	90, 178, 179, 189, 259, 275, 288, 381		236, 267, 311, 312, 344, 348, 352, 402	

About This Book

Teaching and practicing sixth grade math concepts and skills has never been easier! This unique all-in-one book allows the teacher to learn right along with the student—no lesson preparation needed! This will save you hours of time. Each section introduces a specific topic, followed by appropriate practice and application activities. Students enjoy the colorful, engaging challenges of the varying activities!

How to Use This Book

This book is designed to foster a cooperative experience between you and your student. The highly effective activities teach sixth grade math skills and concepts—and some seventh grade math standards. The skills and concepts presented spiral throughout the book. This means that you will see a topic dealt with for a few pages and then a gap before it is covered again. We do that so the student has multiple opportunities to think about and apply the skill/concept.

Our suggestion is that you proceed through the book page by page. A student who successfully finishes *Mathematical Reasoning™ Level G* will know and be able to apply the mathematics skills and concepts taught to most sixth-graders and some skills not typically taught until seventh grade.

Most activities in this book are designed to include space for students to do their work. Some activities, however, may require additional paper.

All the books in this series are designed to make students think critically. Students who have worked in one or more of the previous books are likely to find this book challenging, but not too challenging. Students who have not used the previous books are likely to find this book more challenging, but should eventually catch up and benefit from the exposure to mathematical reasoning.

Teaching Suggestions

Important: Keep learning fun and you will have an energetic student who looks forward to each lesson. Work around a student's attention span.

There is no one correct way to teach the skills presented in this book. Have fun figuring out different ways to relate the skills to the student's daily life.

The activities in this book are written to the standards of the National Council of Teachers of Mathematics (NCTM).

General Comments

NCTM-suggested strands of Number and Operations, Algebra, Geometry, Measurement, and Data Analysis and Probability are the main categories represented at this level. These strands are subdivided into related skills that can be seen in the left-hand column of the Table of Contents beginning on page iii. We encourage you to look carefully at each area and find innovative ways to strengthen the connection between the various strands and the everyday life of the child.

Mathematical knowledge and its application is becoming an increasingly critical requirement for successful participation in our society. The foundations for this success are embedded within the activities in this book. These are the stepping-stones upon which each child's future will be built. Each skill is important and deserves careful consideration by parents, teachers, and students.

To aid in reading, a comma is placed to separate groups of three place values, called periods. When reading, the name of the period is said after the amount in it.

Five million, nine hundred fifty-three thousand, five hundred

Write in the missing word below for each problem.

1. 6,014,014 = six million, fourteen thousand, __________

2. 359,205 = three hundred fifty-nine thousand, two __________ five

3. 9,245,050 = nine million, two hundred forty-five __________, fifty

4. 1,001,100 = one __________, one thousand, one hundred

5. 47,803 = forty-seven __________, eight hundred three

6. 2,604,019 = two million, six __________ four thousand, nineteen

Approximately 540 peanuts are used to make a 12 ounce jar of peanut butter. To make 11,025 jars, 5,953,500 peanuts are needed.

Write each problem in number form in the crossword puzzle below.

1) twenty-seven thousand, fourteen

2) four million, seven hundred thousand, three

3) five hundred four thousand, thirty

4) ten thousand, three

5) seven hundred thirty thousand, seven hundred thirty

6) three hundred thirty-three thousand, three hundred three

7) one million, seven hundred forty-two thousand, five hundred sixty-one

8) thirty-two thousand, one hundred four

9) six million, twenty thousand, four

10) five thousand, five

									7.		9.	
						5.	6.					
		1. 2		4.								
	2.	7										
		0							10.			
		1										
3.		4					8.					

Earth travels around the sun at the speed of sixty-seven thousand miles per hour (67,000 mph).

number form	5,046
word form	five thousand, forty-six
expanded notation	5,000 + 40 + 6

Four of the following five problems contain equal amounts in different forms. Circle the problem that does not have all equal amounts.

1. 21,200

   twenty-one thousand, two hundred

   20,000 + 1,000 + 200

2. 5,500,050

   five million, five hundred thousand, fifty

   5,000,000 + 500,000 + 50

3. 103,013

   one hundred three thousand, thirteen

   100,000 + 3,000 + 10 + 3

4. 8,080,800

   eight million, eighty thousand, eight hundred

   80,000,000 + 80,000 + 800

5. 407,704

   four hundred seven thousand, seven hundred four

   400,000 + 7,000 + 700 + 4

Number Sense?

Do you have a sense about number size?

Choice Box

1,500	60
2,016	7,500,000
~~3,661~~	897

Match the statements below to the appropriate number in the choice box.

The height of the Statue of Liberty from the ground to the tip of the flame in inches is 3,661.

2. The cost to build the Titanic in 1912 was $__________.

3. The length of the White House in inches is __________.

4. The number of steps to the top of the Washington Monument is __________.

5. The approximate number of active volcanoes located around the world is __________.

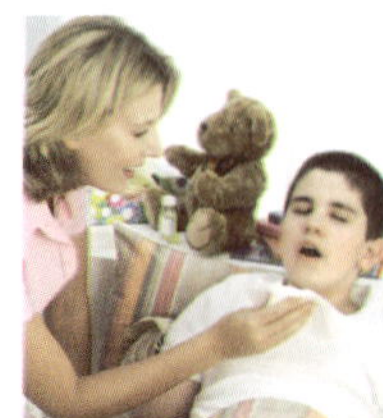

The approximate speed of a cough in miles per hour is __________.

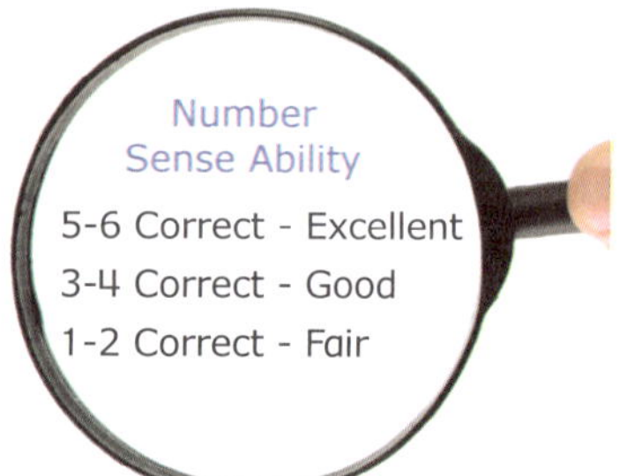

Write the answers in the ten spaces on the ropes in increasing order (ascending).

Write each problem in number form on the climbing wall below.

1. 5,000 + 10 + 3

2. six thousand, six

3. 1,000,000 + 5,000

4. seventeen thousand, one hundred

5. 5,200

6. 100,000 + 50 + 9

7. fifty thousand, twenty

8. 8,000 + 80 + 8

9. 12,047

10. nine hundred thousand, one

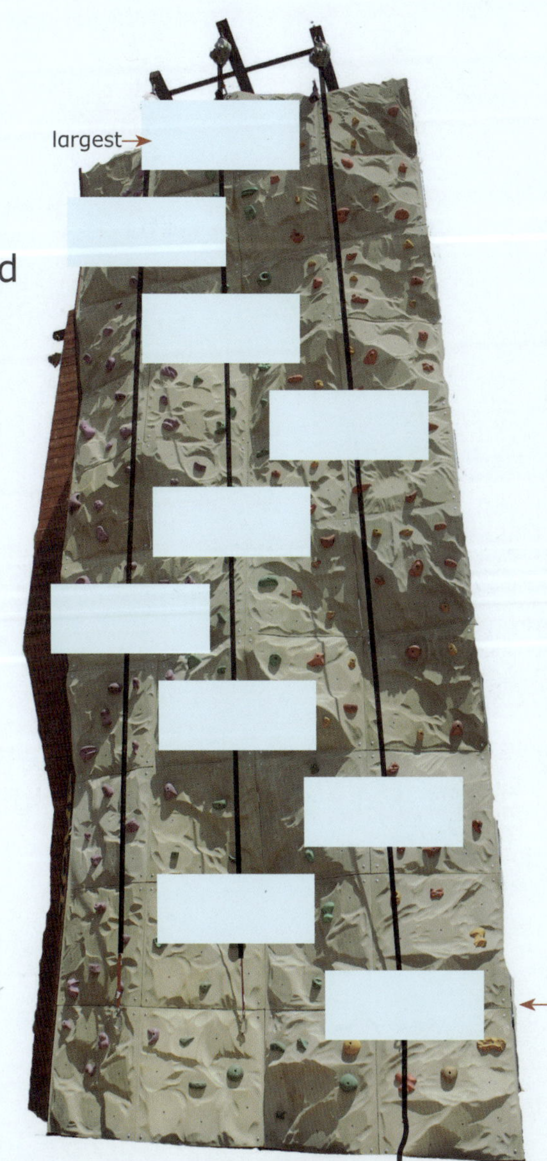

Add – Sum – Total ALTOGETHER!

The answer to an addition problem is called the sum.
The numbers to be added are called addends.

$125 + 16 + 7 = \longrightarrow$

$$\begin{array}{r} 125 \\ 16 \\ +\quad 7 \\ \hline 148 \end{array}$$

Before adding, line up like place values. Regroup when needed.

Find each sum; then cross out the correct answers below to find the false answer.

1. $\begin{array}{r} 34 \\ 87 \\ +\ 231 \\ \hline \end{array}$

2. $\begin{array}{r} 5 \\ 234 \\ +\ 55 \\ \hline \end{array}$

3. $\begin{array}{r} 57 \\ 68 \\ +\ 126 \\ \hline \end{array}$

4. $\begin{array}{r} 143 \\ 559 \\ +\ 16 \\ \hline \end{array}$

5. $\begin{array}{r} 134 \\ 358 \\ +\ 236 \\ \hline \end{array}$

6. $\begin{array}{r} 65 \\ 452 \\ +\ 15 \\ \hline \end{array}$

7. $\begin{array}{r} 602 \\ 301 \\ +\ 37 \\ \hline \end{array}$

8. $\begin{array}{r} 7 \\ 47 \\ +\ 573 \\ \hline \end{array}$

9. $\begin{array}{r} 104 \\ 93 \\ +\ 580 \\ \hline \end{array}$

10. $\begin{array}{r} 142 \\ 491 \\ +\ 323 \\ \hline \end{array}$

11. 69 + 57 + 7 = ____

12. 38 + 8 + 32 = ____

13. 375 + 17 + 8 = ____

14. 307 + 263 + 13 = ____

400	627	728	532	352
294	820	133	718	251
777	583	956	78	940

Find the sum for each question.

1 

Approximately how fast can a quarter horse run?

25 + 17 + 8 + 3 + 2 = _____ miles per hour

2 

Approximately how fast can a tiger run?

2 + 5 + 8 + 7 + 4 + 9 = _____ miles per hour

3 

Approximately how fast can a race car go?

96 + 45 + 16 + 5 + 38 = _____ miles per hour

4 At Allen Middle School there are two 5th grade classes, one with 21 students and the other 25; two 6th grade classes, one with 19 students and the other 23; and two 7th grade classes, one with 18 students and the other 26. What is the total number of students at the school? Complete the equation.

___ + ___ + ___ + ___ + ___ + ___ = ______

5 How many miles from Los Angeles to Tampa? ______ miles

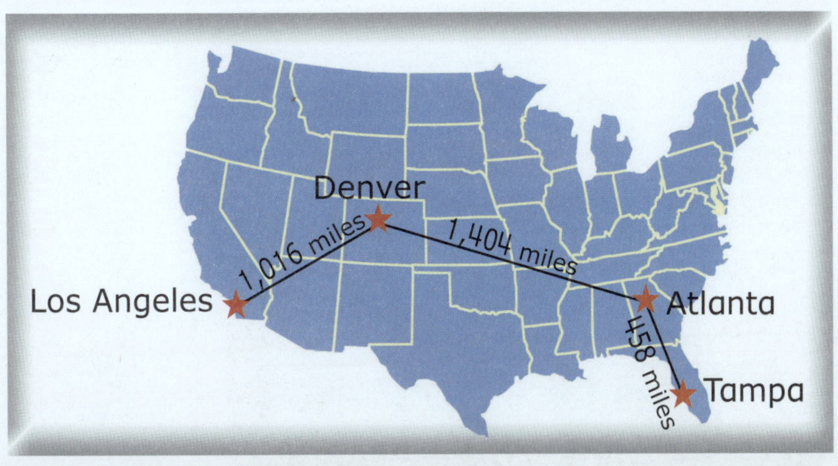

Write each answer in the crossword puzzle below. You may need a piece of paper to do your work.

Across

1. 59 + 29 = ____
3. 43 + 183 + 21 = ____
6. 492 + 888 + 7 = ____
10. 28 + 47 = ____
11. 2,096 + 4,134 = ____
12. 23 + 4 + 561 = ____
13. 2,408 + 6,743 = ____
14. 67 + 24 = ____
15. 34 + 283 + 6 = ____
20. 42 + 63 + 458 = ____
21. 483 + 369 = ____
23. 812 + 57 + 39 = ____
24. 5,246 + 2,907 = ____

Down

1. 733 + 146 = ____
2. 7,658 + 859 = ____
3. 2,046 + 521 + 46 = ____
4. 19 + 23 = ____
5. 53,995 + 19,041 = ____
7. 172 + 50 + 129 = ____
8. 43 + 45 = ____
9. 493 + 291 = ____
14. 58 + 38 = ____
16. 109 + 142 = ____
17. 95 + 60 = ____
18. 49 + 40 = ____
19. 69 + 9 = ____
21. 100 − 19 = ____
22. 50 − 27 = ____

1. 8	2. 8	■	3.	4.	5.	■	6.	7.	8.	9.
10.		■	11.				■	12.		
13.				■		■	14.		■	
■		■	15.	16.		■		■	17.	■
18.	■	19.	■	20.			■	21.		22.
23.			■		■	■	24.			

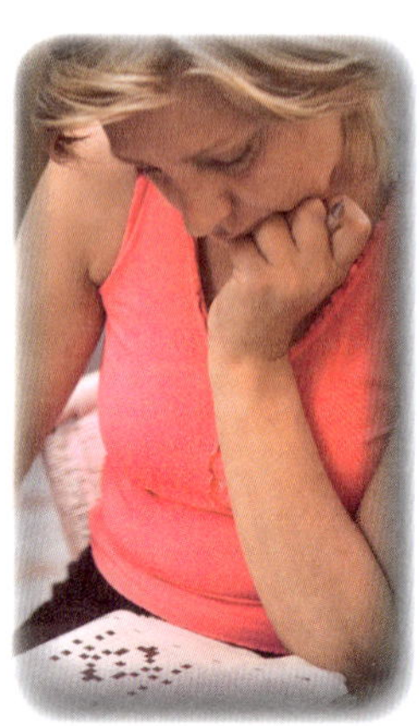

Subtracting finds the difference between two numbers.

503 − 17 = →

```
  4 9 1
  5̸0̸3
−  17
  486
```

- Line up like place values.
- Start subtracting with the ones.
- Regroup when needed.

Find each difference; then cross out the correct answers below to find the false answer.

1. 751 − 190
2. 506 − 142
3. 946 − 79
4. 200 − 104
5. 317 − 288
6. 2,109 − 649
7. 1,690 − 716
8. 3,121 − 2,719
9. 5,638 − 4,999
10. 8,037 − 3,408
11. 24,875 − 5,928
12. 69,493 − 59,412
13. 30,030 − 29,106
14. 10,459 − 9,273

1,186	18,947	402	10,081	1,236
364	974	924	561	29
96	639	4,629	1,460	867

A subtraction problem can be worded many ways.

- Find the difference between 137 and 48.
- Find 137 minus 48.
- Find 48 less than 137.
- Find 137 decreased by 48.

$$\begin{array}{r} \overset{12\,17}{\cancel{1}\cancel{3}7} \\ -\ 48 \\ \hline 89 \end{array}$$

Subtract each problem; then use the letters to solve the riddle below.

a	823 − 41	h	245 − 129	w	300 − 127	s	568 − 21
i	5,832 − 1,493	n	6,218 − 1,919	o	5,240 − 1,489	l	2,137 − 1,428
g	6,201 − 1,192	u	2,083 − 1,221	t	3,264 − 2,496	p	58,493 − 9,295

Where did the pig go to heal from a fall?

___	___	___	___	___	___	___	___	___
116	3,751	5,009	547	49,198	4,339	768	782	709

Subtract to find the answer to each question.

1. 

In what year did the Wright brothers fly the first powered airplane?

2,101 − 198 = ________

2. 

In what year was the first television developed?

2,851 − 927 = ________

3. 

In what year was the first microwave created?

2,000 − 54 = ________

4. 

In what year did the first DVD players appear?

4,455 − 2,458 = ________

5. The New York Empire State Building is 1,250 feet high and the Seattle Space Needle is 605 feet high. What is the height difference? Fill in the equation.

________ − ________ = ________ feet

Complete the tables below.

1) Place the numbers 0, 2, 4, 6, 8, 10, 12, 14, and 16 in the nine squares to make a magic square.

			= 24
			= 24
	8	12	= 24
			= 24
= 24	= 24	= 24	= 24

2) Place the numbers 1, 4, 7, 10, 13, 16, 19, 22, and 25 in the nine squares to make a magic square.

			= 39
			= 39
	13		= 39
22			= 39
= 39	= 39	= 39	= 39

point A ● denoted → $\dot{\mathbf{A}}$	A point or location is denoted (labeled) by a capital letter.
line segment 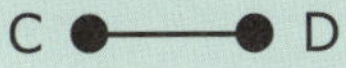 denoted → $\overline{\mathbf{CD}}$	A line segment connects two points.
polygon 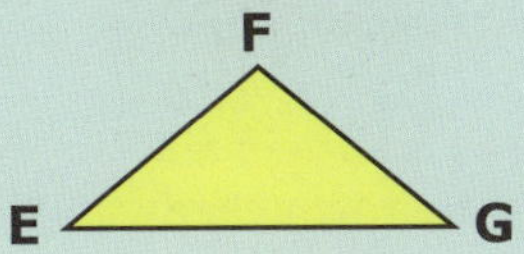 denoted → triangle **EFG** or Δ**EFG**	A polygon is a closed figure made from line segments.
vertices 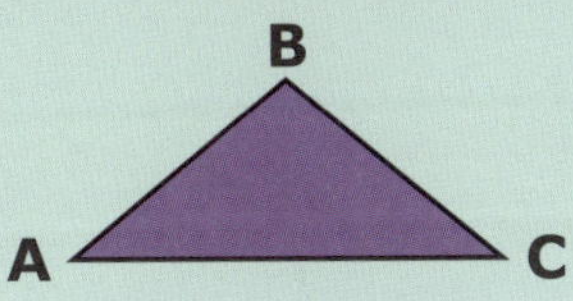	The points where the sides of a polygon meet are called the vertices. Polygons are named by their vertices. This triangle has vertices **A**, **B**, and **C**.

Name the sides and vertices.

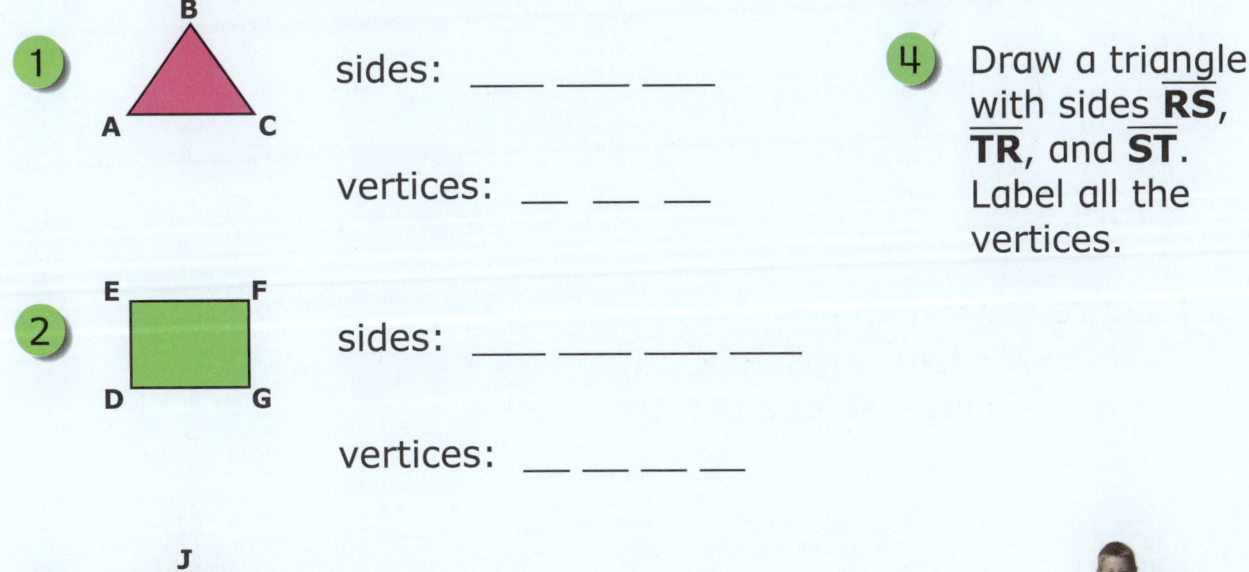

1 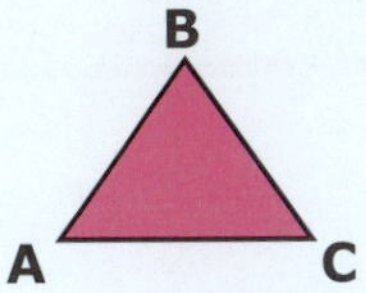

sides: ____ ____ ____

vertices: __ __ __

2 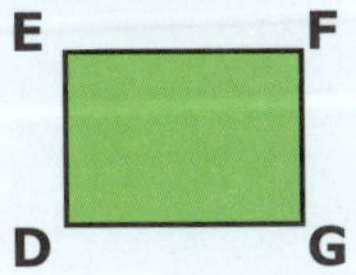

sides: ____ ____ ____ ____

vertices: __ __ __ __

3 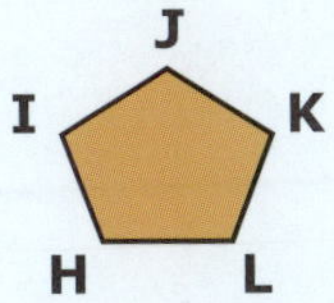

sides: ____ ____ ____ ____ ____

vertices: __ __ __ __ __

4 Draw a triangle with sides $\overline{\mathbf{RS}}$, $\overline{\mathbf{TR}}$, and $\overline{\mathbf{ST}}$. Label all the vertices.

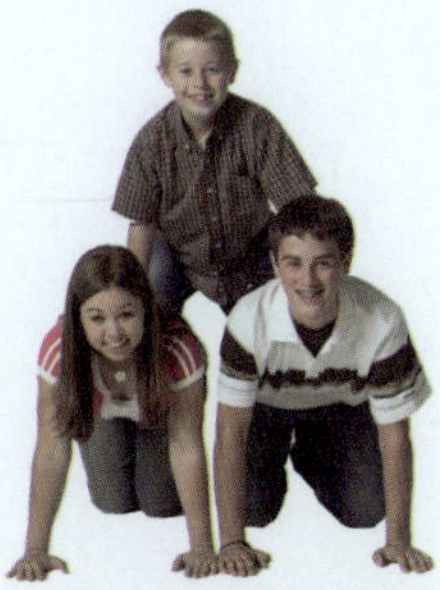

A triangle with two sides of equal length is called an isosceles triangle.

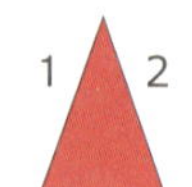

A triangle with two sides forming a right (90°) angle is called a right triangle.

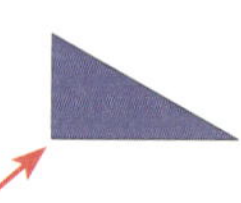

A triangle with three sides of equal length is called an equilateral triangle.

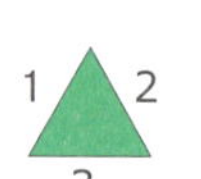

A triangle with all three sides having different lengths is called a scalene triangles.

Name each triangle.

1. Triangle **ABC**, $\overline{\mathbf{AB}}$ = 2 cm, $\overline{\mathbf{BC}}$ = 5 cm, and $\overline{\mathbf{AC}}$ = 2 cm.

   ABC is a/an ______________________ triangle.

2. In triangle **RST**, $\overline{\mathbf{RS}}$ = 9 cm, $\overline{\mathbf{ST}}$ = 9 cm, and $\overline{\mathbf{RT}}$ = 9 cm.

   RST is a/an ______________________ triangle.

3. In triangle **EFG**, $\overline{\mathbf{EF}}$ = 11 cm, $\overline{\mathbf{FG}}$ = 10 cm, and $\overline{\mathbf{EG}}$ = 8 cm.

   EFG is a/an ______________________ triangle.

4. Draw a triangle with a right angle and two equal length sides.

5. Let one square = 1 cm by 1 cm. Draw a right triangle with sides of 3 cm, 4 cm, and 5 cm.

3 cm
4 cm
5 cm

An **ordered pair** of numbers inside a parenthesis (2,12) locates a point (•) on a grid.

- The first number indicates how many units to the right (→).
- The second number indicates how many units up (↑).

In order, use the ordered pairs to locate each point on the grid below. Connect the points to see a picture. The star (★) is located at (2,12).

1 (5,7)	2 (6,8)	3 (5,9)	4 (5,7)	5 (4,8)
6 (3,8)	7 (1,6)	8 (1,4)	9 (4,1)	10 (7,1)
11 (10,4)	12 (10,7)	13 (8,8)	14 (7,8)	15 (5,7)

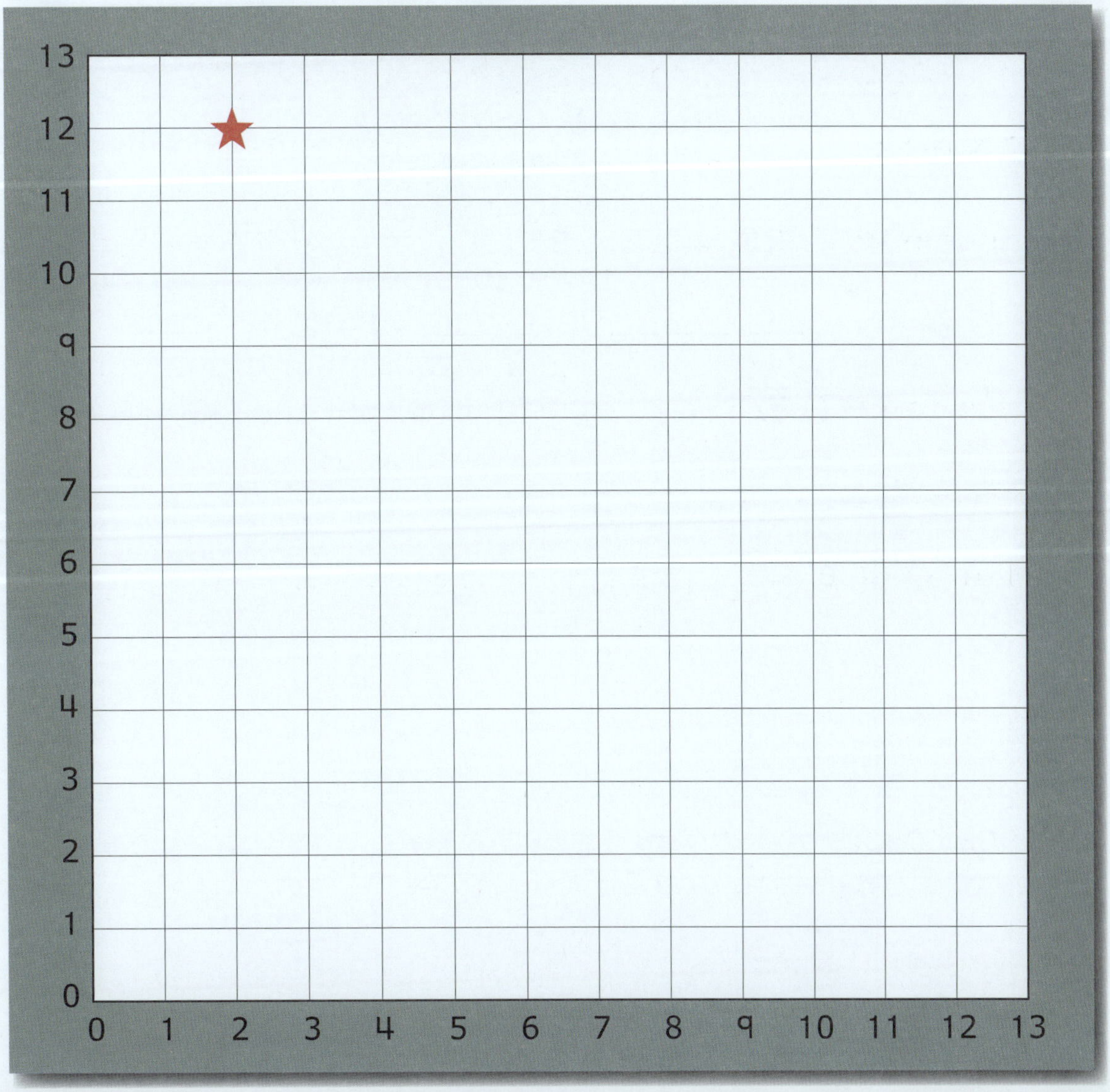

13
12 ★
11
10
9
8
7
6
5
4
3
2
1
0
0 1 2 3 4 5 6 7 8 9 10 11 12 13

Mr. Well listed his 8 students as boy, girl, boy, girl, boy, girl, girl, and girl. He showed this information as a table, bar graph, and circle graph.

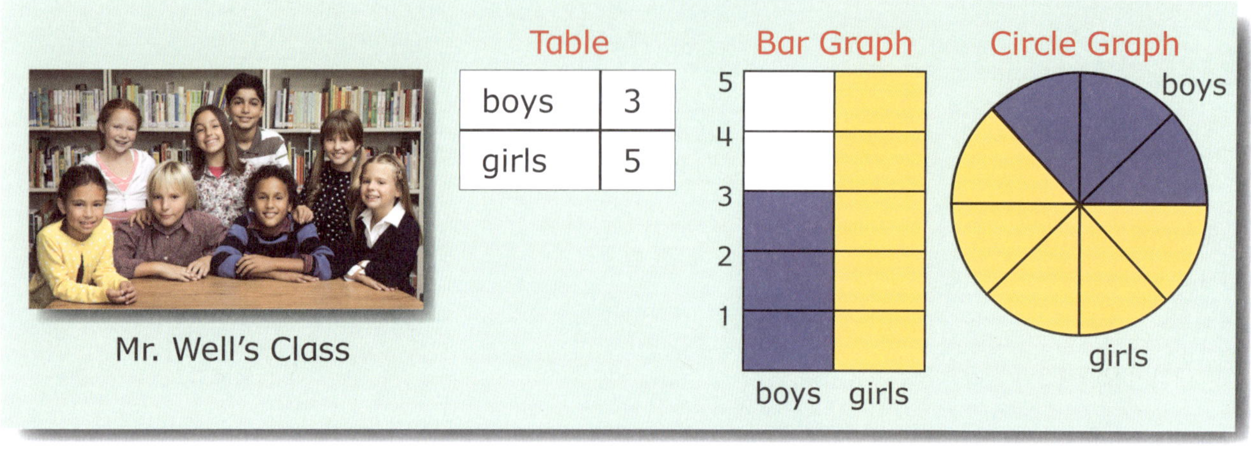

Table

boys	3
girls	5

Mr. Well's Class

Mrs. Jona's class played Mr. Well's class at baseball and recorded the wins and losses. She listed win, win, loss, win, win, loss, loss, win, loss, win, loss, and win for her class. Make a table, bar graph, and circle graph for this information.

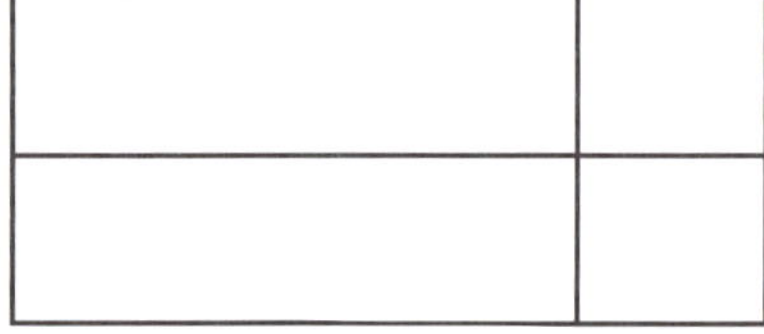

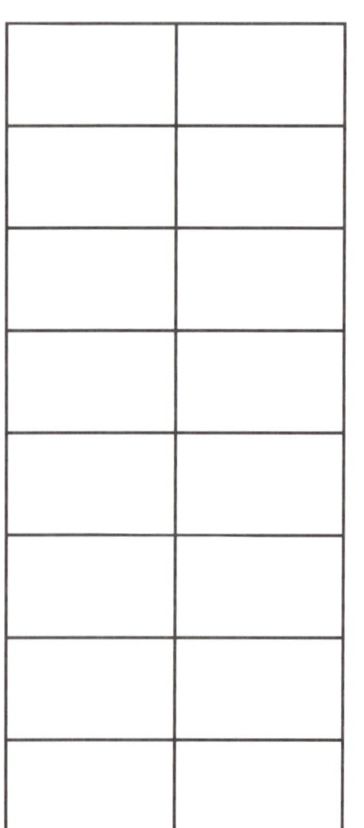

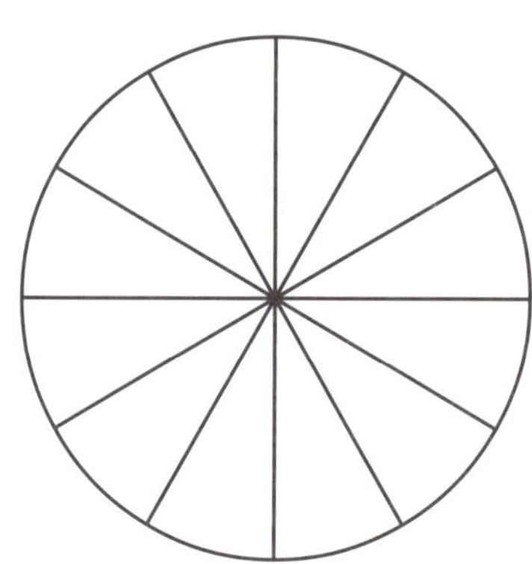

Multiplication allows for fast addition of the same number.

$3 \times 8 = 24$
(eight summed three times)
$8 + 8 + 8 = 24$

$5 \times 14 = 70$
(fourteen summed five times)
$14 + 14 + 14 + 14 + 14 = 70$

The numbers used in multiplication are called factors and the answer is called the product.

$3 \times 8 = 24$

factors product

Fill in the following multiplication chart.

Notice
4×6 equals 6×4.
In multiplication, the order of the factors does not matter. This is called the commutative property.

×	1	2	3	4	5	6	7	8	9
1	1								
2									
3									
4									
5									
6									
7									
8									
9									

How many tomato plants are in 5 rows with 15 plants in each row?

5 × 15 = 75 plants

$$\begin{array}{r} \overset{2}{1}5 \\ \times\ \ 5 \\ \hline 75 \end{array}$$

How many tomato plants are in 12 rows with 28 plants in each row?

12 × 28 = 336 plants

$$\begin{array}{r} \overset{1}{2}8 \\ \times\ 12 \\ \hline 56 \\ +\ \overset{1}{2}80 \\ \hline 336 \end{array}$$

Insert zero placeholders where needed.

Find each product; then cross out the correct answers below to find the two false answers.

1. $\begin{array}{r} 36 \\ \times\ 4 \\ \hline \end{array}$

2. $\begin{array}{r} 83 \\ \times\ 9 \\ \hline \end{array}$

3. $\begin{array}{r} 74 \\ \times\ 5 \\ \hline \end{array}$

4. $\begin{array}{r} 69 \\ \times\ 8 \\ \hline \end{array}$

5. $\begin{array}{r} 46 \\ \times\ 23 \\ \hline \end{array}$

6. $\begin{array}{r} 79 \\ \times\ 36 \\ \hline \end{array}$

7. $\begin{array}{r} 68 \\ \times\ 45 \\ \hline \end{array}$

8. $\begin{array}{r} 95 \\ \times\ 87 \\ \hline \end{array}$

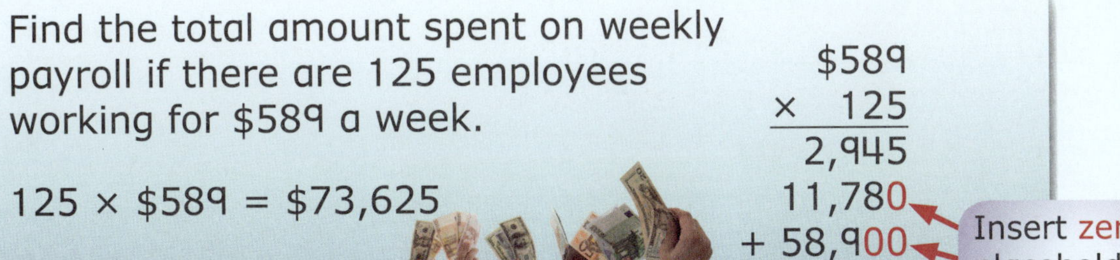

Find the total amount spent on weekly payroll if there are 125 employees working for \$589 a week.

$125 \times \$589 = \$73,625$

$$\begin{array}{r} \$589 \\ \times\ \ 125 \\ \hline 2,945 \\ 11,780 \\ +\ 58,900 \\ \hline \$73,625 \end{array}$$

Insert zero placeholders where needed.

Find each product; then use the letters to solve the riddle below.

h	c	a
214×321	417×234	129×362

o	r	n
513×124	728×356	104×832

What do you throw out when you need it and take it in when you do not need it?

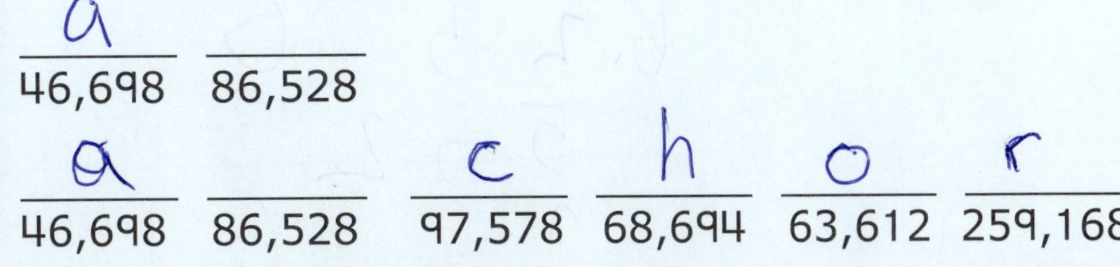

___ ___
46,698 86,528

___ ___ ___ ___ ___ ___
46,698 86,528 97,578 68,694 63,612 259,168

Write each answer in the crossword puzzle below. You may need a piece of paper to do your work.

Across

1. 4 × 22 = 88
3. 17 × 28 = ______
6. 46 × 96 = ______
10. 9 × 9 = ______
11. 74 × 29 = ______
12. 6 × 84 = ______
13. 59 × 73 = ______
14. 7 × 9 = ______
15. 25 × 25 = ______
20. 19 × 28 = ______
21. 33 × 26 = ______
23. 12 × 12 = ______
24. 37 × 246 = ______

Down

1. 4 × 221 = ______
2. 15 × 542 = ______
3. 4 × 1,069 = ______
4. 1 × 71 = ______
5. 9 × 7,117 = ______
7. 3 × 151 = ______
8. 2 × 5 = ______
9. 24 × 27 = ______
14. 4 × 15 = ______
16. 18 × 14 = ______
17. 2 × 75 = ______
18. 3 × 7 = ______
19. 6 × 14 = ______
21. 9 × 9 = ______
22. 2 × 41 = ______

1. 8	2. 8		3.	4.	5.		6.	7.	8.	9.
10.			11.					12.		
13.							14.			
			15.	16.					17.	
18.		19.		20.				21.		22.
23.							24.			

Find the product for each question.

1. There are 60 minutes in an hour and 24 hours in a day. How many minutes are in a day?

$$\begin{array}{r} 24 \\ \times 60 \\ \hline \_\,\_ \\ +\_\,\_\,\_\,\_ \end{array}$$

__________ minutes in a day

2. If you take on average 14 breaths a minute, how many breaths would you take in an hour?

____

3. If you take on average 14 breaths a minute, how many breaths would you take in a day?

____

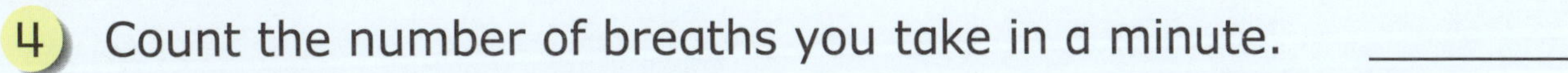

4. Count the number of breaths you take in a minute. __________

5. Count how many breaths you take in an hour.

____

6. How many breaths do you take in a day?

____

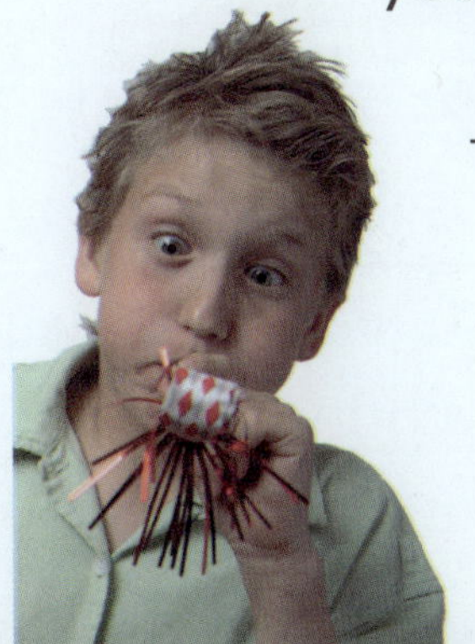

Numbers have certain ways you can expect them to behave. These ways are called properties.

Let a, b, and c represent numbers.

The **Commutative Property of Addition and Multiplication** states that in addition and multiplication, order does not matter.

$a + b = b + a$ $a \times b = b \times a$

$3 + 4 = 4 + 3 = 7$ $3 \times 4 = 4 \times 3 = 12$

The **Associative Property of Addition and Multiplication** states that in addition and multiplication if you have three numbers, you may figure the first two or last two and then the other.

$a + (b + c) = (a + b) + c$ $a \times (b \times c) = (a \times b) \times c$

$3 + (4 + 5) = (3 + 4) + 5 = 12$ $3 \times (4 \times 5) = (3 \times 4) \times 5 = 60$

The **Distributive Property of Multiplication** states you may multiply by the sum of two numbers or multiply each number separately, and then add.

$a \times (b + c) = a \times b + a \times c$

$3 \times (4 + 5) = 3 \times 4 + 3 \times 5 = 27$

The **Zero Property for Multiplication** states that any number times zero is always zero.

$a \times 0 = 0$

The **Identity Property for Addition** states that when zero is added to any number, the value does not change.

$a + 0 = a$

The **Identity Property for Multiplication** states that when multiplying any number by one, the value does not change.

$1 \times a = a$

Which property is shown?

1. $17 \times 0 = 0$ ______________________

2. $895 \times 25 = 25 \times 895$ ______________________

3. $12 + (8 + 9) = (12 + 8) + 9$ ______________________

4. $10 \times (3 + 9) = 10 \times 3 + 10 \times 9$ ______________________

5. $1 \times 3{,}604 = 3{,}604$ ______________________

6. $5 \times (4 \times 7) = (5 \times 4) \times 7$ ______________________

7. $(842 - 115) \times 0 = 0$ ______________________

8. $5{,}167 + 0 = 5{,}167$ ______________________

9. $2 \times (5 + 9) = 2 \times (9 + 5)$ ______________________

10. $3 \times (8 + 9) = 24 + 27$ ______________________

Name the property that makes each of the steps true.

11. Given: $81 + (19 + 30)$
    Step 1: $81 + (30 + 19)$ ______________________
    Step 2: $(81 + 30) + 19$ ______________________
    Step 3: $3\times(27 + 10) + 19$ ______________________

12. Given: $11 \times 23 \times 0$
    Step 1: $23 \times 11 \times 0$ ______________________
    Step 2: 0 ______________________

Balance Benders™

Circle the correct answer for each balance puzzle.

1

a. 

b. 

c. 

2

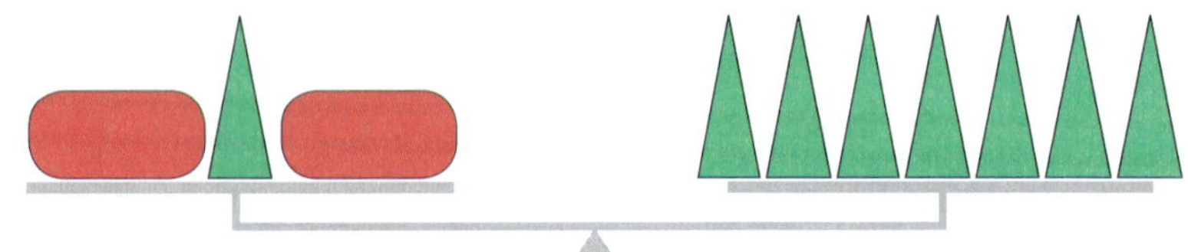

a. 

b. 

c. 

d. 

For more activities like this, please see our *Balance Benders™* series.

ray A B This ray can be denoted (labeled) as $\overrightarrow{AB}$	A **ray** starts at an endpoint and extends forever in one direction.
angle 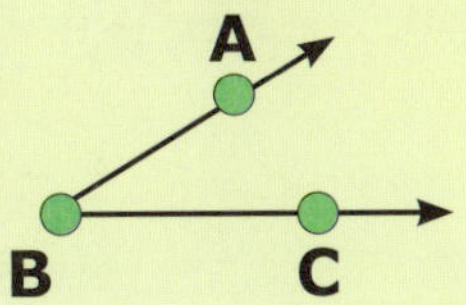 This angle can be denoted (labeled) as ∠**ABC**, ∠**CBA,** or ∠**B**.	An **angle** is made when two rays have the same endpoint. The shared endpoint is called the vertex. The angle is denoted by a **point** on one ray, the **vertex**, and a **point** from the other ray.

Use the table above to fill in the answers.

1 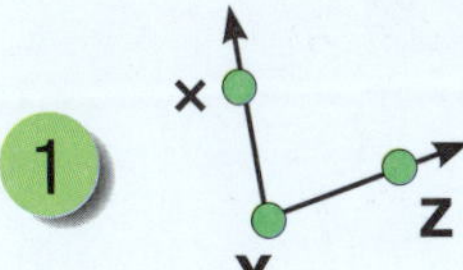

rays: ________ ________

vertex: ________

angle: ________ ________ ________

2 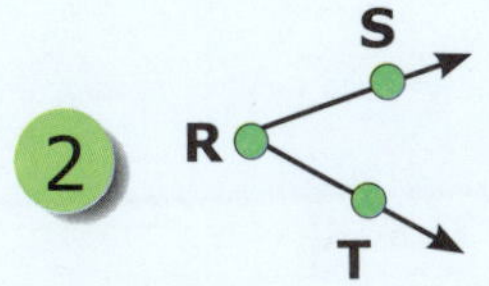

rays: ________ ________

vertex: ________

angle: ________ ________ ________

3 Draw ∠**RCP** in **black**.

4 Draw ∠**BMC** in blue.

5 Draw ∠**RWP** in red.

C

W

B

P

A protractor measures angles in degrees (°).

To measure an angle, place the 0° edge of the protractor on the lower ray of the angle with the center of the protractor on the vertex. Then record where the other ray hits the numbers.

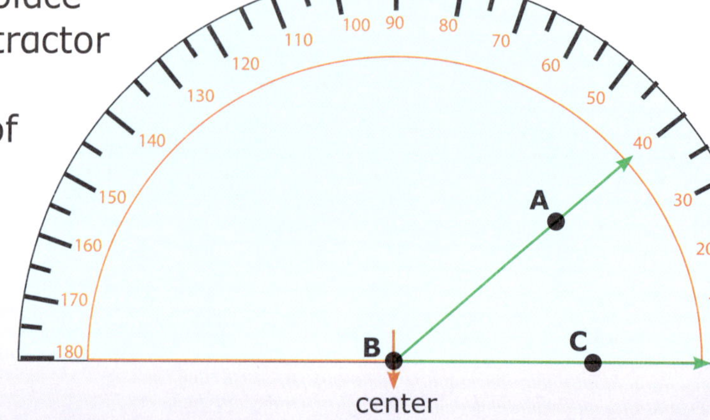

∠ABC = 40°

A right angle ( ) measures 90°.

An acute angle ( ) measures less than 90°.

An obtuse angle ( ) measures between 90° and 180°.

Use a protractor to measure each angle. Then write the measure below and state if the angle is a right, an acute, or an obtuse angle. If the sides are not long enough, extend them with a ruler.

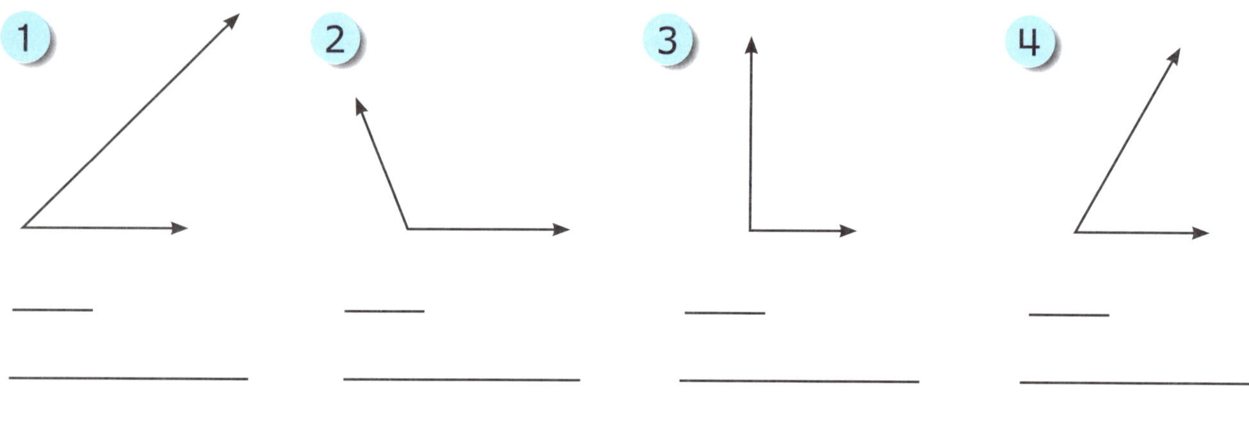

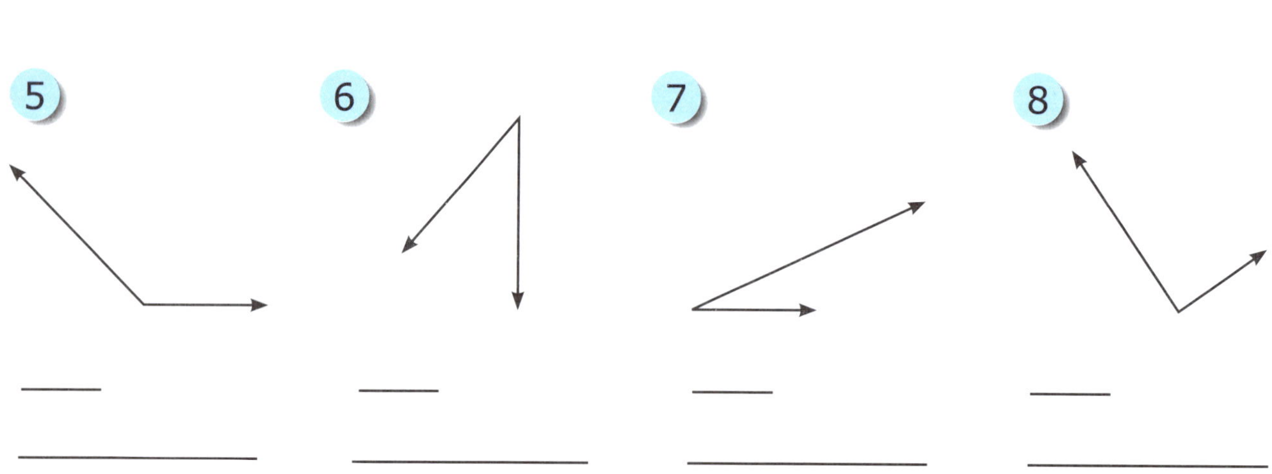

Determine the degree of each angle.

1) ∠AGF = 160°
2) ∠BGF = ________
3) ∠CGF = ________
4) ∠DGF = ________
5) ∠EGF = ________
6) ∠CGD = ________
7) ∠DGE = ________
8) ∠AGC = ________

9) Draw the listed angles and see a picture.

∠BDH

∠BAC

∠HCB

∠EFG

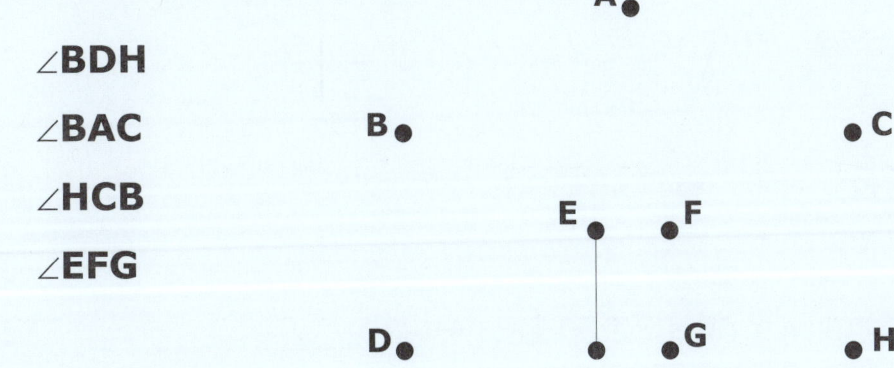

10) Write the measure of each angle.

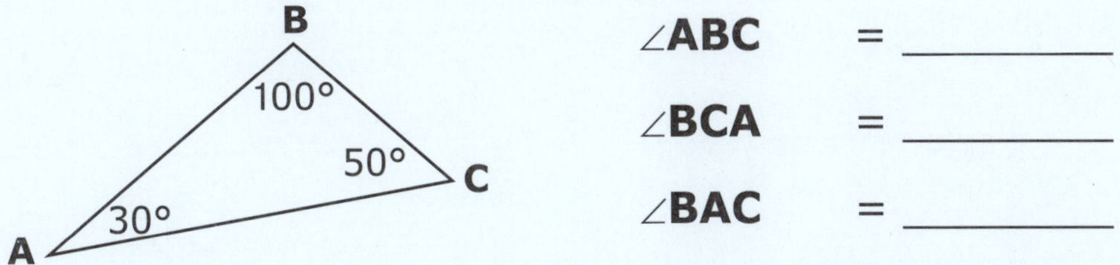

∠ABC = ________

∠BCA = ________

∠BAC = ________

Complete the next two terms of each pattern.

1) 1, 4, 16, 64, _______, _______, ...

2) 100, 88, 76, 64, _______, _______, ...

3) 12, 25, 38, 51, _______, _______, ...

4) 217, 336, 455, 574, _______, _______, ...

5) 1,000, 901, 802, 703, _______, _______, ...

6) 144, 72, 36, 18, _______, _______, ...

7) 15, 20, 19, 24, 23, 28, 27, _______, _______, ...

8) 8, 32, 16, 64, 32, 128, 64, _______, _______, ...

9) $\frac{1}{4}$, 1, $1\frac{3}{4}$, $2\frac{1}{2}$, _______, _______, ...

10) └, ┌, ┐, ┘, _______, _______, ...

Division (÷) is the **inverse operation** of multiplication (×).

Division is used to find how many equal sized groups (divisor) are in an amount (dividend). The result is called the quotient.

$$\text{divisor}\overline{)\text{dividend}}\quad \text{quotient}$$

How many groups of 6 can be formed from 162 people?

162 ÷ 6 = ?

$$\begin{array}{r} 2 \\ 6\overline{)162} \\ -12 \\ \hline 4 \end{array}$$

The answer from the subtraction must always be smaller than the divisor.

$$\begin{array}{r} 27 \\ 6\overline{)162} \\ -12\downarrow \\ \hline 42 \\ -42 \\ \hline \end{array}$$ groups

check

$$\begin{array}{r} 27 \\ \times\ 6 \\ \hline 162 \end{array}$$

Find each quotient; then cross out the correct answers below to find the two false answers.

1. $5\overline{)130}$
2. $7\overline{)294}$
3. $8\overline{)520}$
4. $9\overline{)171}$
5. $6\overline{)222}$
6. $4\overline{)264}$
7. $3\overline{)138}$
8. $8\overline{)224}$
9. $5\overline{)85}$
10. $9\overline{)162}$
11. $6\overline{)402}$
12. $7\overline{)483}$

65 38 28 46 42 66 69 37 18 67 19 26 25 17

On average, a person laughs about 420 times in 4 weeks. How many times does the average person laugh in a week?

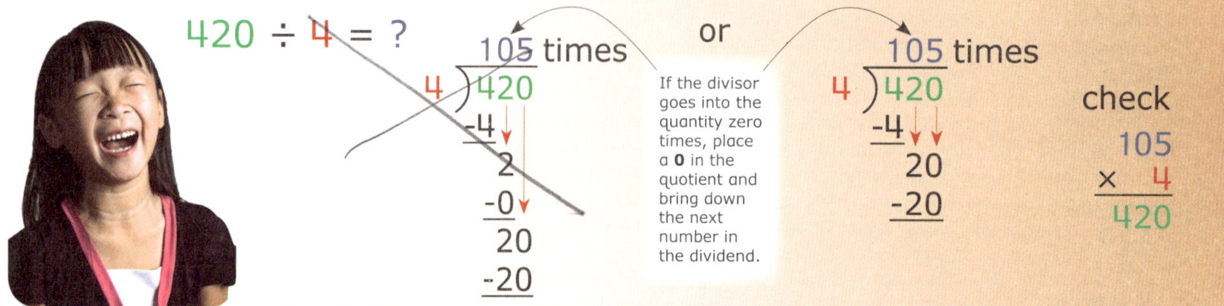

Find each quotient; then use the letters to solve the riddle below.

u $4\overline{)512}$

t $3\overline{)1{,}692}$

n $6\overline{)5{,}154}$

b $9\overline{)4{,}518}$

i $5\overline{)4{,}170}$

a $8\overline{)1{,}096}$

h $7\overline{)2{,}905}$

m $2\overline{)1{,}016}$

What nail does a carpenter not want to hit?

___ ___ ___ ___ ___ ___ ___ ___ ___

564 415 128 508 502 859 137 834

Write each answer in the crossword puzzle below. You may need a piece of paper to do your work.

Across

1. 176 ÷ 2 = 88
3. 372 ÷ 3 = ______
6. 1,635 ÷ 1 = ______
10. 846 ÷ 9 = ______
11. 9,264 ÷ 4 = ______
12. 2,034 ÷ 3 = ______
13. 1,555 ÷ 1 = ______
14. 288 ÷ 8 = ______
15. 651 ÷ 3 = ______
20. 3,066 ÷ 7 = ______
21. 4,655 ÷ 5 = ______
23. 5,004 ÷ 6 = ______
24. 7,182 ÷ 7 = ______

Down

1. 4,455 ÷ 5 = ______
2. 8,456 ÷ 1 = ______
3. 2,504 ÷ 2 = ______
4. 92 ÷ 4 = ______
5. 41,573 ÷ 1 = ______
7. 4,662 ÷ 7 = ______
8. 111 ÷ 3 = ______
9. 4,688 ÷ 8 = ______
14. 259 ÷ 7 = ______
16. 1,314 ÷ 9 = ______
17. 1,188 ÷ 9 = ______
18. 232 ÷ 4 = ______
19. 148 ÷ 2 = ______
21. 810 ÷ 9 = ______
22. 80 ÷ 5 = ______

1. 8	2. 8	■	3.	4.	5.	■	6.	7.	8.	9.
10.		■	11.				■	12.		
13.				■		■	14.		■	
■		■	15.	16.		■		■	17.	■
18.	■	19.	■	20.			■	21.		22.
23.			■		■	■	24.			

Fast Multiplication of Whole Numbers by 10, 100, or 1,000

Multiply by 10 Place 1 zero to the right of the number.	42 × 10 = 420
Multiply by 100 Place 2 zeros to the right of the number.	42 × 100 = 4,200
Multiply by 1,000 Place 3 zeros to the right of the number.	42 × 1,000 = 42,000

Complete each problem; then cross out the correct answers below to find the four false answers.

1) 2 × 100 = ________

2) 24 × 10 = ________

3) 240 × 10 = ________

4) 20 × 1,000 = ________

5) 20 × 100 = ________

6) 40 × 100 = ________

7) 4 × 10 = ________

8) 40 × 10 = ________

9) 400 × 1,000 = ________

10) 100 × 100 = ________

11) 24 × 1,000 = ________

12) 10 × 100 = ________

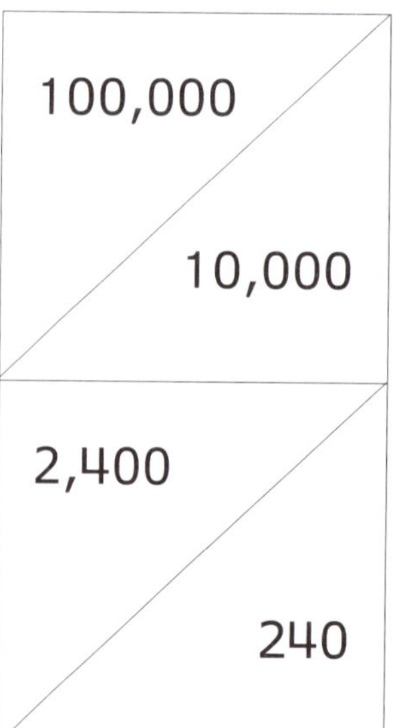

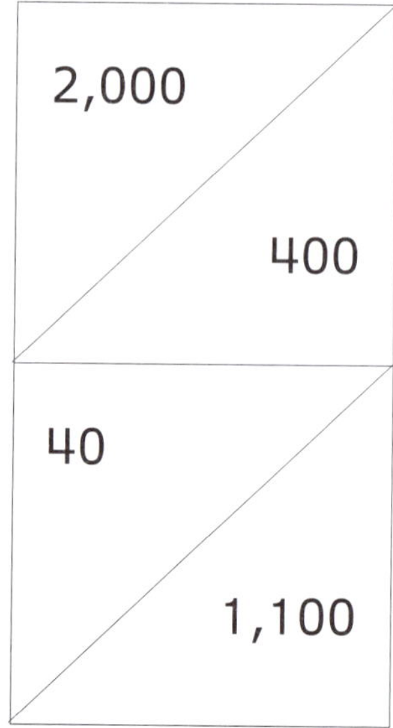

Fast Whole Number Multiplication of Multiples of 10

Multiply the multiples without the zeros on the right, then add the zeros on the right to the result.

$20 \times 30 = 600$	$420 \times 700 = 294{,}000$
$2 \times 3 = 6$	$42 \times 7 = 294$

Find each product the fast way; then use the letters to solve the riddle below.

e $50 \times 70 =$ _____

t $60 \times 20 =$ _____

n $23 \times 20 =$ _____

p $15 \times 30 =$ _____

g $42 \times 30 =$ _____

c $9 \times 700 =$ _____

w $140 \times 20 =$ _____

r $210 \times 300 =$ _____

l $200 \times 310 =$ _____

o $42 \times 60 =$ _____

a $40 \times 700 =$ _____

s $80 \times 90 =$ _____

What are the plumber's favorite shoes?

___	___	___	___	___
6,300	62,000	2,520	1,260	7,200

If Alva sent 120 text messages in a 30 day month, how many sent messages was she averaging a day? $120 \div 30 = ?$

$$\begin{array}{r} 4 \\ 30\overline{)120} \\ -120 \\ \hline \end{array} \qquad \begin{array}{r} 30 \\ \times\ 4 \\ \hline 120 \end{array}$$

Multiply the quotient 4 by the divisor 30 and place it under the dividend before subtracting. When subtracting, the difference must be less than the divisor (0 < 30).

Find each quotient.

1. $34\overline{)102}$
2. $53\overline{)265}$
3. $41\overline{)369}$
4. $92\overline{)368}$
5. $73\overline{)511}$
6. $65\overline{)260}$
7. $81\overline{)486}$
8. $93\overline{)651}$
9. $55\overline{)330}$
10. $86\overline{)344}$
11. $75\overline{)675}$
12. $16\overline{)48}$
13. Joe bought 48 doughnuts. How many dozen is that?

____

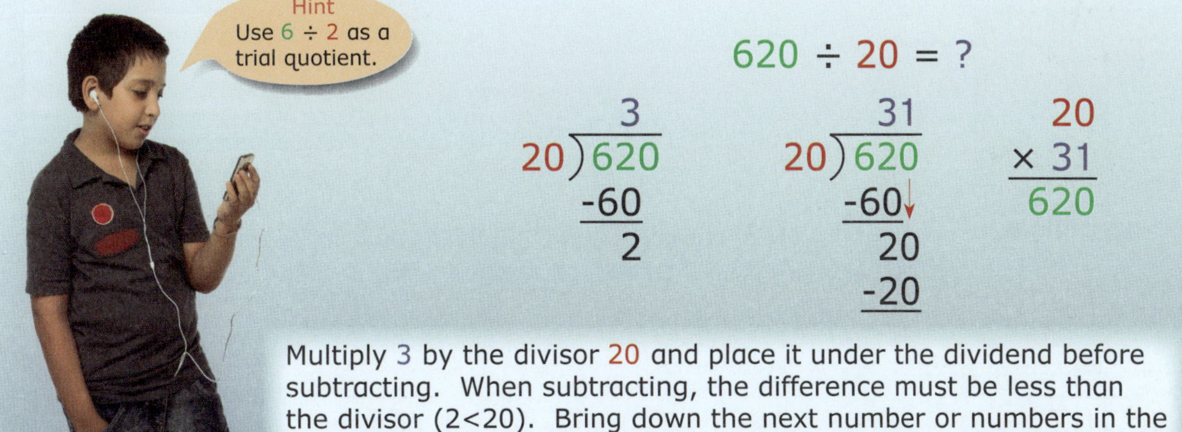

Find each quotient.

1) $50\overline{)1{,}600}$ 2) $40\overline{)1{,}800}$ 3) $70\overline{)4{,}480}$ 4) $30\overline{)2{,}490}$

5) $10\overline{)970}$ 6) $80\overline{)4{,}560}$ 7) $60\overline{)5{,}760}$ 8) $20\overline{)1{,}740}$

Write an equation for each problem, then solve.

1. Cal spent $108 for 9 movie tickets. How much was each ticket?

_______ ÷ _______ = _______

2. In 20 hours, the Jones family drove 1,040 miles. What was the average distance per hour?

_______ ÷ _______ = _______

3. The school spent $39 for socks for the 13 basketball players. How much did they spend per player?

_______ ÷ _______ = _______

4. Jim built 7 identical houses using 1,183 toy building blocks. How many blocks did he use on each house?

_______ ÷ _______ = _______

5. The average person reads about 200 words a minute. How many words can an average person read in half a minute?

_______ ÷ _______ = _______

6. How many words can you read in half a minute or 30 seconds? ______

Balance Benders™

Circle the correct answer for each balance puzzle.

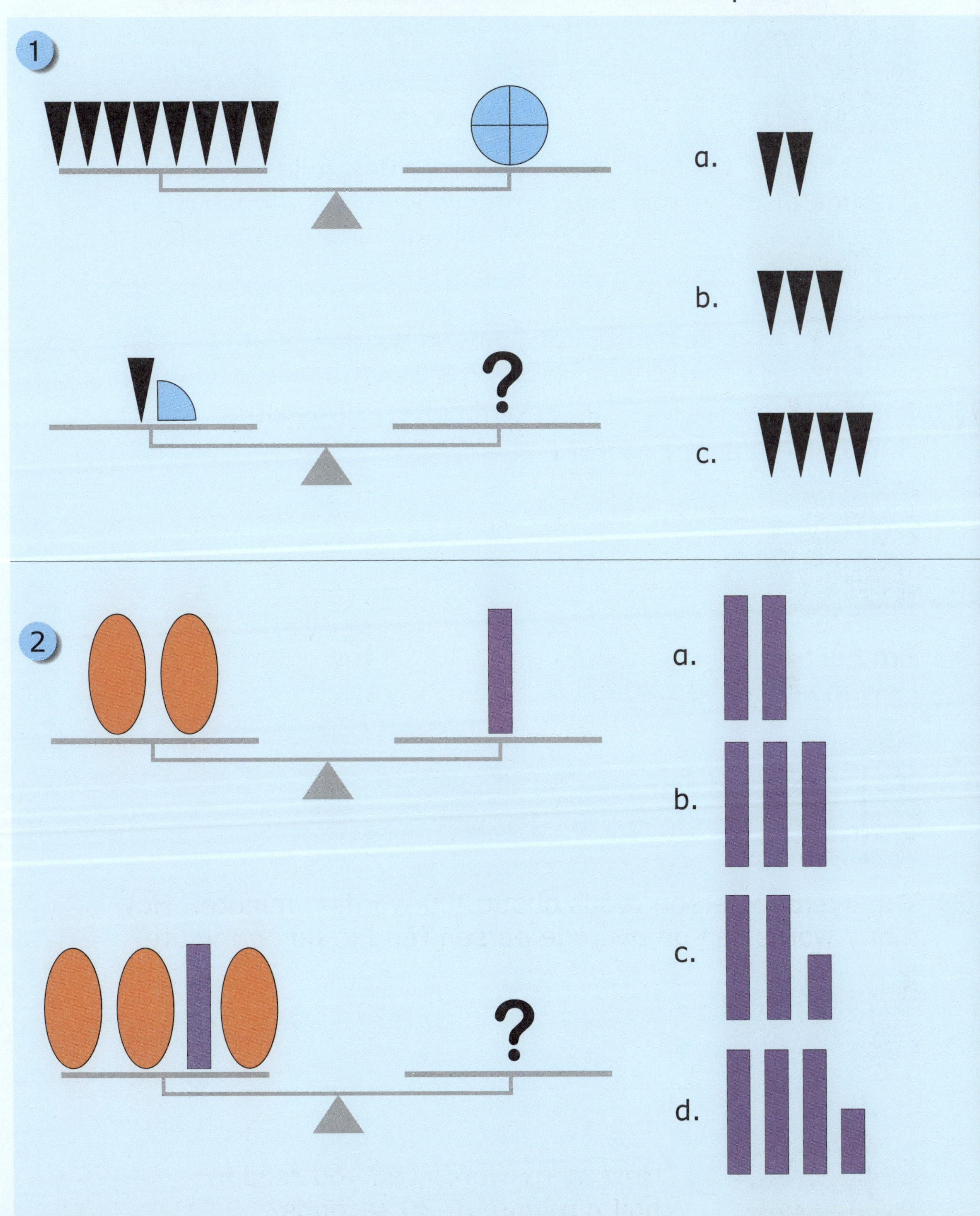

For more activities like this, please see our *Balance Benders*™ series.

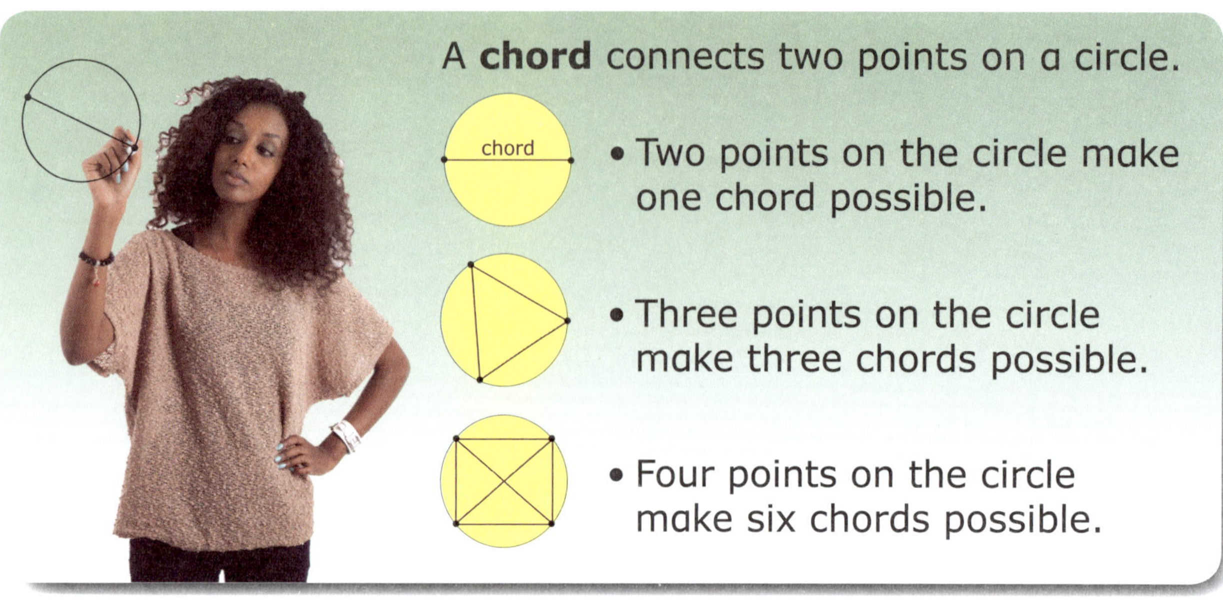

Draw the possible chords for five and six points on a circle and complete the table. Discover the pattern that relates points to chords.

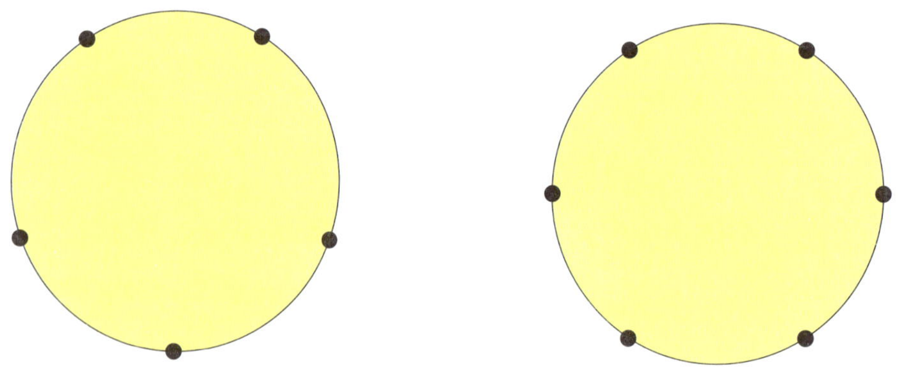

Points on a Circle	Number of Possible Chords
2	1
3	3
4	6
5	
6	
7	
8	

The factors of a number are those numbers that divide into that number evenly.

Factors for 18: 1, 2, 3, 6, 9, 18
Factors for 7*: 1, 7

*If the only factors of a number are 1 and itself, the number is called prime. All other numbers are called composite.

1. The factors of 16: ___, ___, ___, ___, ___
2. The factors of 24: ___, ___, ___, ___, ___, ___, ___, ___
3. The factors of 28: ___, ___, ___, ___, ___, ___
4. The factors of 35: ___, ___, ___, ___
5. The factors of 54: ___, ___, ___, ___, ___, ___, ___, ___

The greatest common factor (GCF) of two numbers is the largest factor that can divide evenly into each of the numbers.

Factors for 18: 1, 2, 3, 6, (9), 18
Factors for 27: 1, 3, (9), 27

The greatest common factor (GCF) for 18 and 27 is 9.

6. Factors for 8: ___, ___, ___, ___
   Factors for 12: ___, ___, ___, ___, ___, ___
   GCF for 8 and 12 is ______

7. Factors for 20: ___, ___, ___, ___, ___, ___
   Factors for 25: ___, ___, ___
   GCF for 20 and 25 is ______

8. Factors for 40: ___, ___, ___, ___, ___, ___, ___, ___
   Factors for 60: ___, ___, ___, ___, ___, ___, ___, ___, ___, ___, ___, ___
   GCF for 40 and 60 is ______

How many of all the blocks are red?

$\frac{3}{5}$ ← 3: numerator (red blocks); 5: denominator (total number of blocks)

$\frac{1 \times 2}{2 \times 2} = \frac{2}{4}$

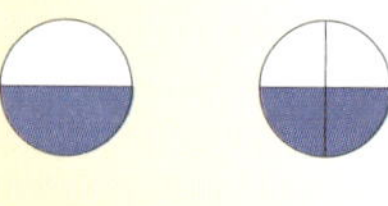

Multiplying the numerator and denominator by the same whole number greater than 1 produces an equivalent fraction.

$\frac{2 \div 2}{4 \div 2} = \frac{1}{2}$

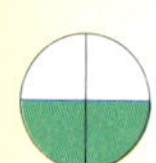

Dividing the numerator and denominator by their greatest common factor* produces the simplest form or lowest terms of the fraction.

Find the numerator that makes each fraction equivalent.

1. $\frac{2 \times 4}{3 \times 4} = \frac{\quad}{12}$

2. $\frac{3 \times}{4 \times} = \frac{\quad}{16}$

3. $\frac{5 \times}{6 \times} = \frac{\quad}{48}$

4. $\frac{5 \times}{8 \times} = \frac{\quad}{56}$

5. $\frac{1 \times}{5 \times} = \frac{\quad}{30}$

6. $\frac{4 \times}{5 \times} = \frac{\quad}{45}$

7. $\frac{2 \times}{9 \times} = \frac{\quad}{81}$

8. $\frac{3 \times}{4 \times} = \frac{\quad}{36}$

9. $\frac{5 \times}{6 \times} = \frac{\quad}{18}$

10. $\frac{2 \times}{9 \times} = \frac{\quad}{63}$

11. $\frac{1 \times}{4 \times} = \frac{\quad}{12}$

12. $\frac{9 \times}{10 \times} = \frac{\quad}{100}$

* See page 39 for the explanation of the greatest common factor.

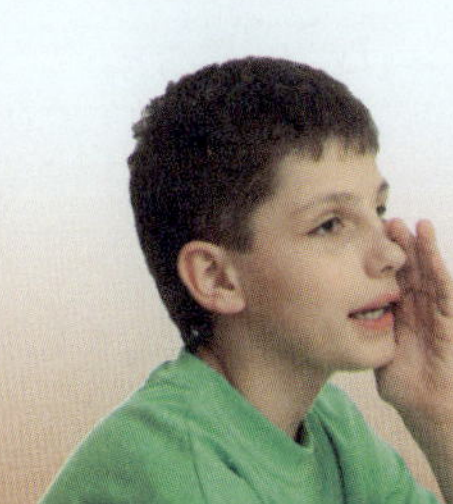

Hint: Divide each numerator and denominator by the greatest common factor to find each fraction's simplest form.

$$\frac{10 \div 5}{15 \div 5} = \frac{2}{3}$$

Write each fraction in simplest form; then use the letters to solve the riddle below.

f $\frac{2 \div 2}{4 \div 2} = \frac{\quad}{\quad}$

t $\frac{6 \div \quad}{9 \div \quad} = \frac{\quad}{\quad}$

c $\frac{2 \div \quad}{8 \div \quad} = \frac{\quad}{\quad}$

m $\frac{10 \div \quad}{12 \div \quad} = \frac{\quad}{\quad}$

a $\frac{20 \div \quad}{25 \div \quad} = \frac{\quad}{\quad}$

n $\frac{2 \div \quad}{16 \div \quad} = \frac{\quad}{\quad}$

l $\frac{10 \div \quad}{45 \div \quad} = \frac{\quad}{\quad}$

r $\frac{9 \div \quad}{12 \div \quad} = \frac{\quad}{\quad}$

e $\frac{2 \div \quad}{10 \div \quad} = \frac{\quad}{\quad}$

p $\frac{20 \div \quad}{24 \div \quad} = \frac{\quad}{\quad}$

u $\frac{20 \div \quad}{32 \div \quad} = \frac{\quad}{\quad}$

i $\frac{14 \div \quad}{49 \div \quad} = \frac{\quad}{\quad}$

Where do baby cows go to eat?

___ ___ ___ ___ ___ ___ ___ ___ ___ ___

$\frac{1}{4}$ $\frac{4}{5}$ $\frac{2}{9}$ $\frac{1}{2}$ $\frac{1}{5}$ $\frac{2}{3}$ $\frac{1}{5}$ $\frac{3}{4}$ $\frac{2}{7}$ $\frac{4}{5}$

Circle graphs are used to display information in a visual way. Below are two different game boards.

Find what fractional part of the graph is a certain color. All fractions should be in simplest form.

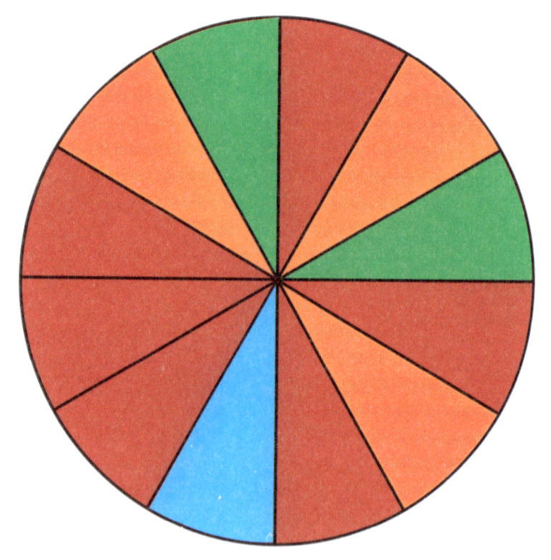

green $\frac{2}{12} = \frac{1}{6}$ orange ___ = ___

blue ___ red ___ = ___

green ___ = ___ orange ___ = ___

black ___ blue ___ = ___

red ___ = ___

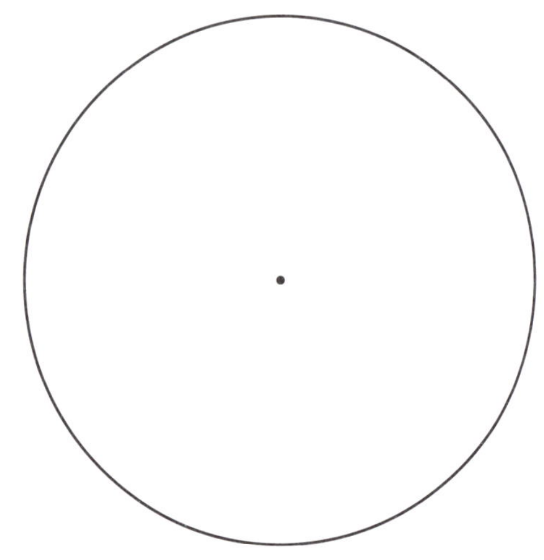

Draw a circular game board with $\frac{2}{3}$ red and $\frac{1}{6}$ blue.

Find what fractional part of the graph is a certain color. All fractions should be in simplest form.

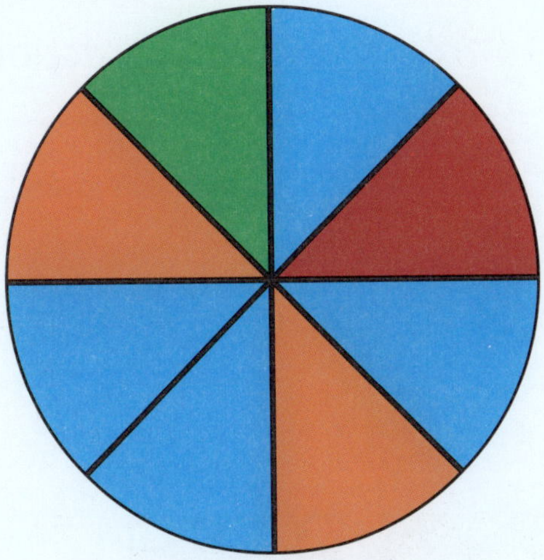

green ___

orange ___ = ___

blue ___ = ___

red ___

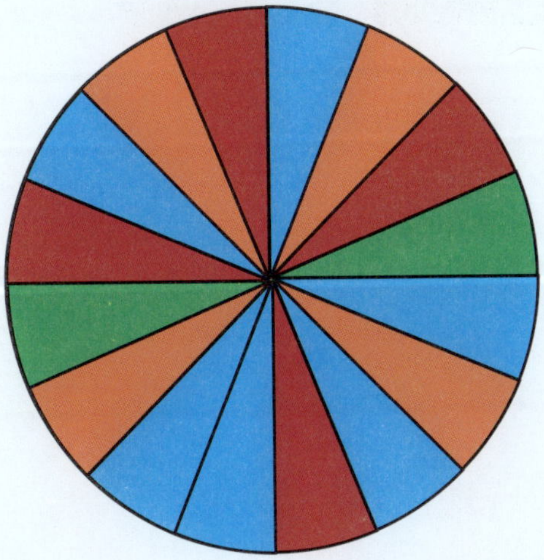

green ___ = ___

orange ___ = ___

blue ___ = ___

red ___ = ___

Draw a circular game board with $\frac{3}{8}$ blue, $\frac{1}{4}$ red, and the rest yellow.

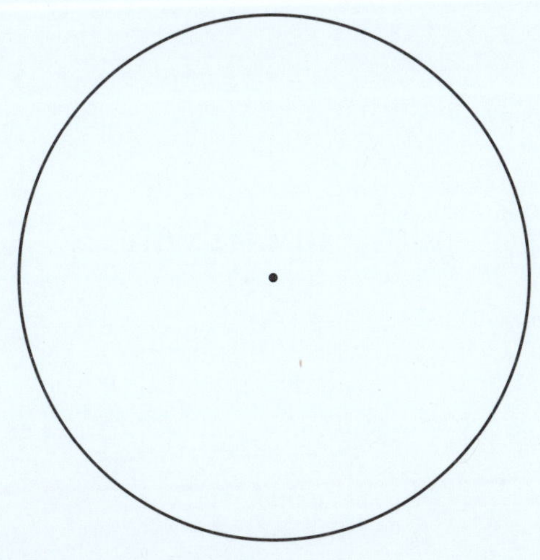

A number with a whole number and fraction is called a mixed number.

How much pizza is in the picture?

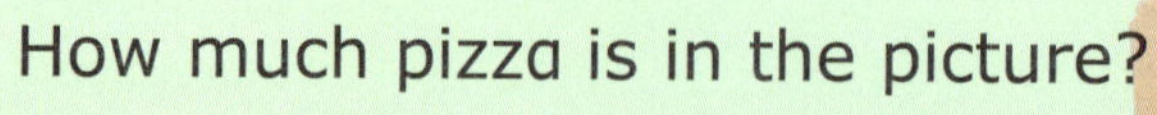

$$\frac{8}{8} + \frac{1}{8} = 1 + \frac{1}{8} = 1\frac{1}{8}$$

1. Color $2\frac{3}{4}$ candy bars.

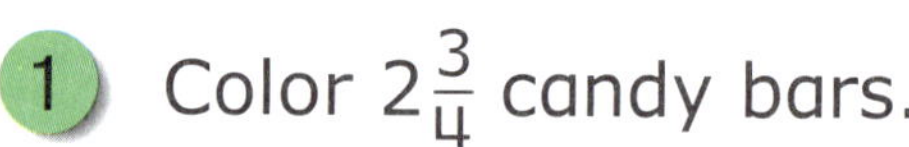

2. Color $4\frac{5}{6}$ pies.

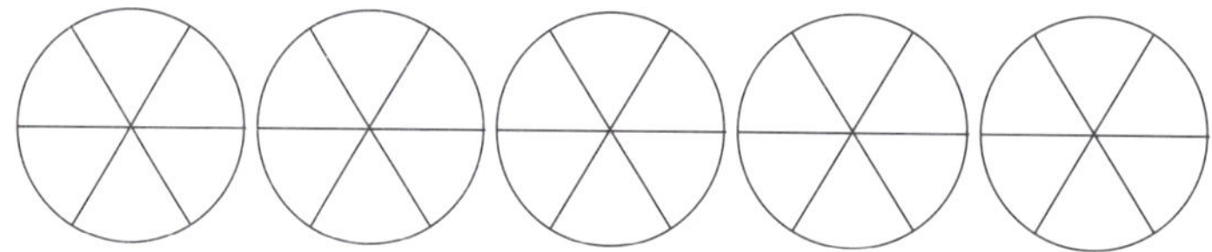

3. Color $3\frac{1}{3}$ crackers.

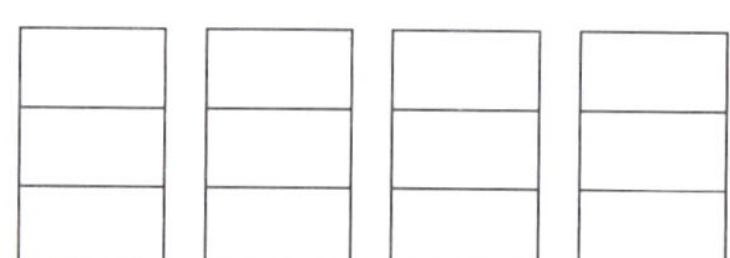

4. Color 3 triangles.

5. Color $1\frac{2}{3}$ squares.

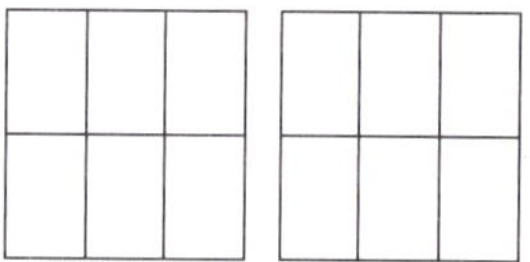

6. Color $1\frac{3}{4}$ pizzas.

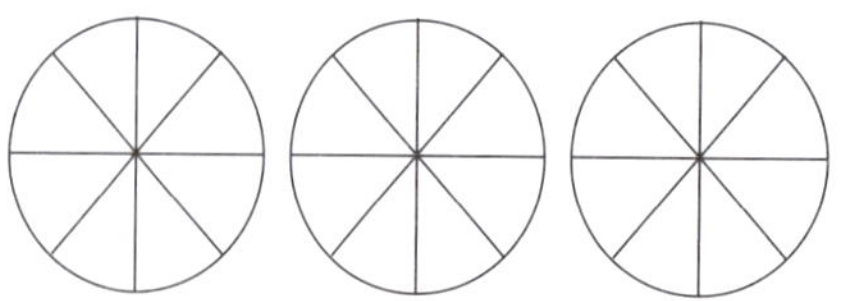

7. Draw a line $1\frac{3}{4}$ inches long below the ruler.

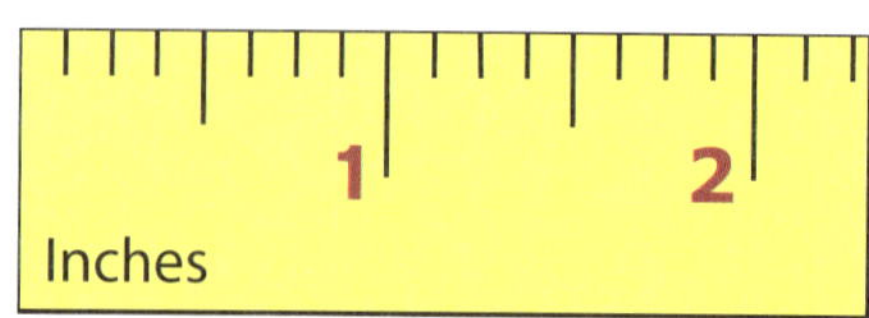

Customary Units

The rulers below show each inch cut into 8 equal parts. What is the length of each line? Write all fractions in simplest form.

$1\frac{2}{8} = 1\frac{1}{4}$ inch

1. length of red line ______

   length of blue line ______

   length of green line ______

   length of orange line ______

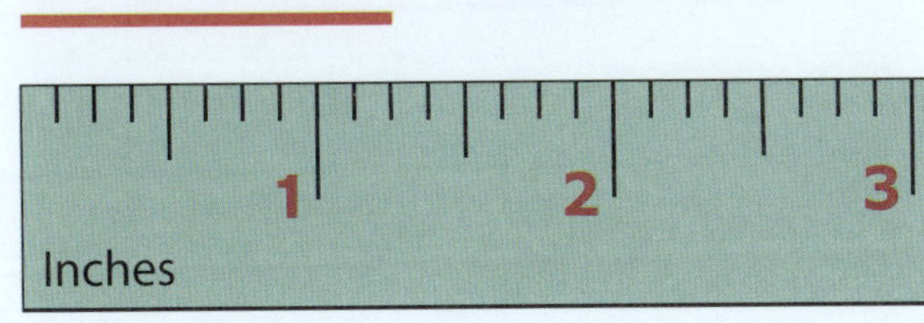

2. length of red line ______

   length of blue line ______

   length of green line ______

   length of orange line ______

   length of brown line ______

1 2 3 4 5 6

Inches

Fingernails grow an average of $\frac{1}{8}$ inch per month. Nails grow faster in the summer than any other season.

In the ruler below, each inch is cut into eight equal parts. What measurement is each arrow pointing to? Write all fractions in simplest form.

1. Use the letters of the measurements to solve the riddle below.

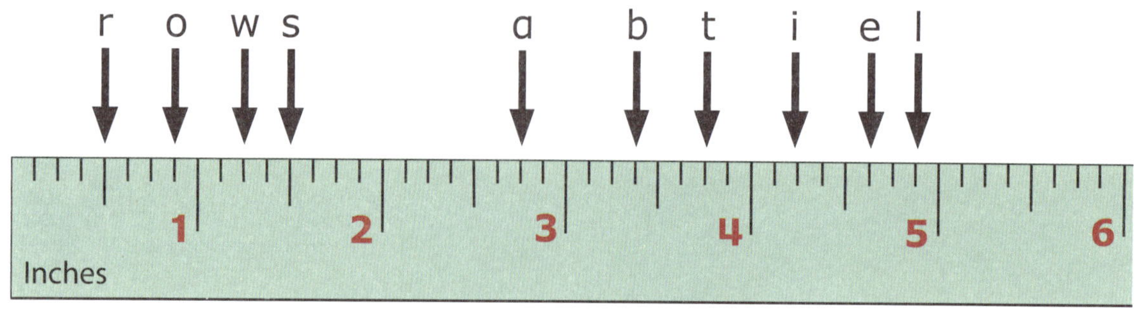

r ______ o ______ w ______ s ______ a ______

b ______ t ______ i ______ e ______ l ______

What gets wetter and wetter the more it dries?

____ ____ ____ ____ ____

$3\frac{3}{4}$ $\frac{7}{8}$ $1\frac{1}{4}$ $4\frac{5}{8}$ $4\frac{7}{8}$

2. Use a ruler to find the length and width of the house in inches.

Length: ________

Width: ________

Customary Units vs. Metric Units

Customary units (feet, pounds, gallons, etc.) used in the United States were once used in the British Empire. In the twentieth century, a variety of measurement units were used throughout the world.

The world recognized a need for a standard measurement system which would aid trade, communication, science, and education. In 1960, an international study by The Committee for Weights and Measurements named the metric system the International System of Units (SI). Only the United States, Liberia, and Myanmar have not adopted SI.

In 1988, the United States government labeled the metric system as the preferred system for trade, science, and industry. Since this was not forcefully imposed as in other countries, the United States only partially adopted it and dual labeling is commonplace.

Since the metric system is a decimal system, it is easy to add, subtract, multiply, divide, and change units in the system. Such operations with customary units can be difficult.

Which item matches the units?

1. 20 ounces/567 grams ________________

2. 1 foot/30.48 centimeters ________________

3. 1 gallon/3.785 liters ________________

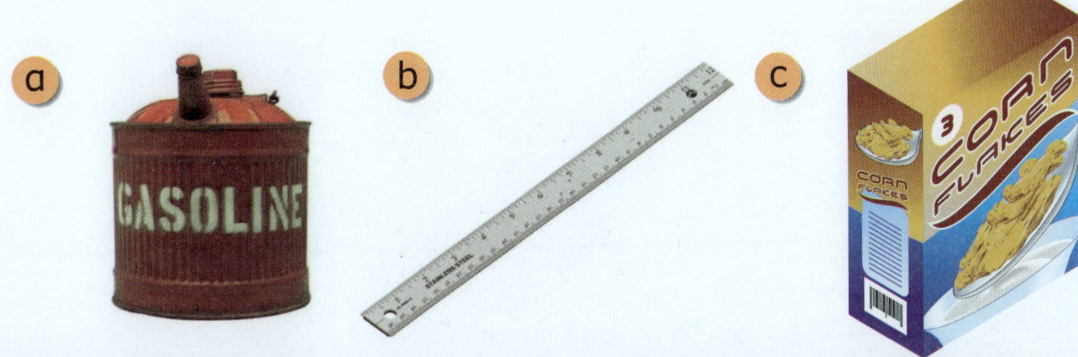

Metric Units

The metric ruler below shows 3 centimeters (cm) and each centimeter is cut into 10 equal parts called millimeters (mm).

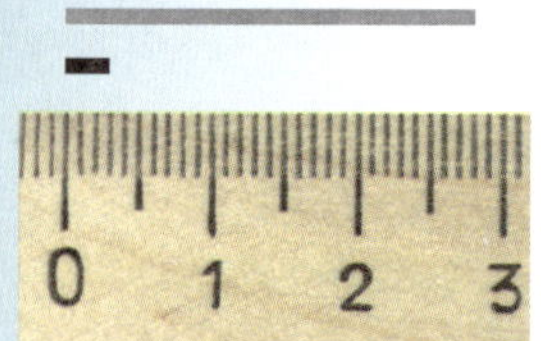

gray line: 2.8 cm or 28 mm
black line: .3 cm or 3 mm

What is the length of each line in centimeters?

1. The rulers below show each centimeter cut into 10 equal parts.

   length of red line: ______

   length of blue line: ______

   length of green line: ______

   length of orange line: ______

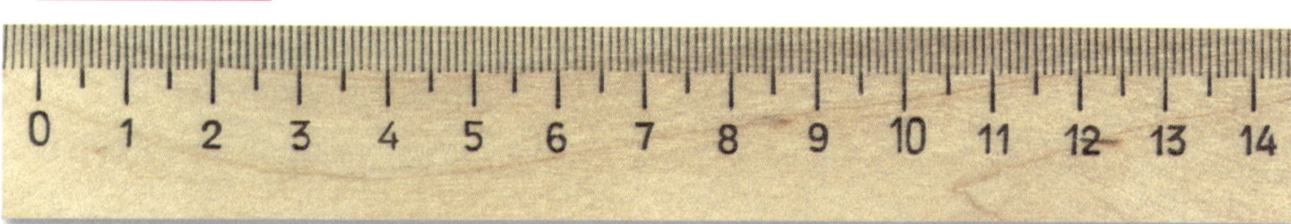

2. length of red line: ______

   length of blue line: ______

   length of green line: ______

   length of orange line: ______

Human fingernails grow at an average rate of .3 centimeters per month.

Metric Units

In the ruler below, each centimeter (cm) is cut into 10 equal parts called millimeters (mm).

1 Use the letters of the measurements to solve the riddle below.

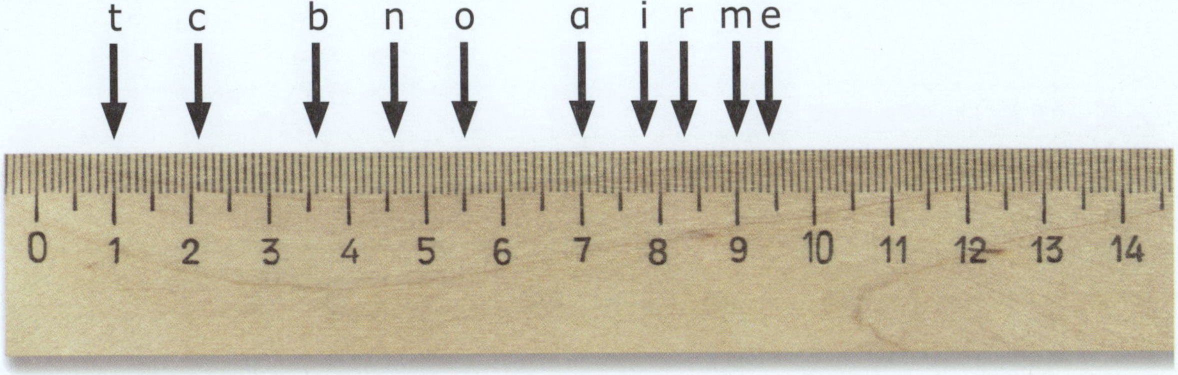

t ____ c ____ b ____ n ____ o ____

a ____ i ____ r ____ m ____ e ____

What gets wetter and wetter the more it rains?

____ ____ ____ ____ ____
5.5 2.1 9.4 7 4.6

2 Use a ruler to find the height and width of the chair in centimeters.

Height: ________

Width: ________

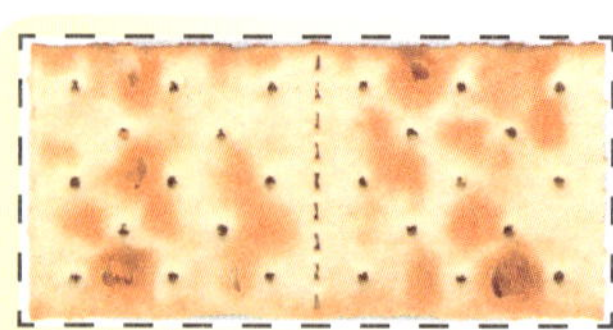

Perimeter is the distance around a polygon. A polygon is a closed figure made with line segments.

1. Find the perimeter of each figure below. Each small square is 1 cm on each side.

2 cm 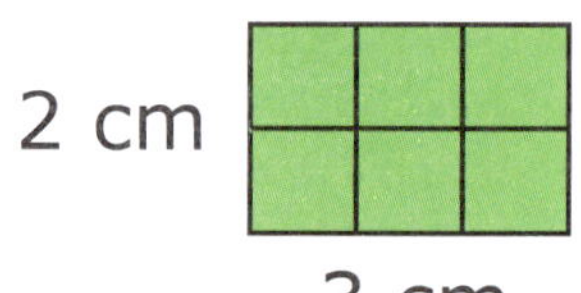 3 cm

perimeter = 2 + 3 + 2 + 3 = 10 cm

2. 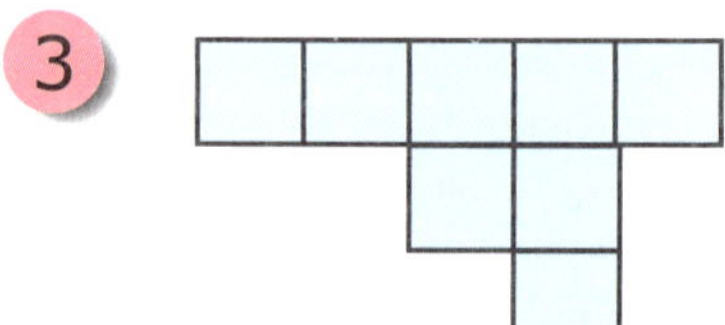 perimeter = _____

3. 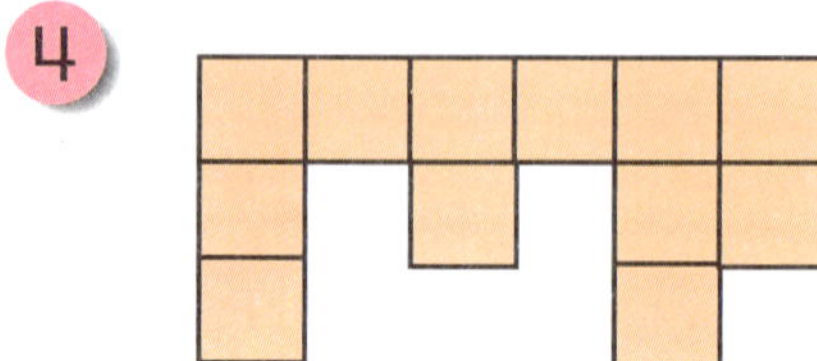 perimeter = _____

4. perimeter = _____

5. What is the perimeter of the stop sign if each side is 9 inches long? _____

6. Using 6 small squares measuring 1 cm on each side, make a figure with a perimeter of 14 cm. Using the six small squares, make a figure with a perimeter of 12 cm.

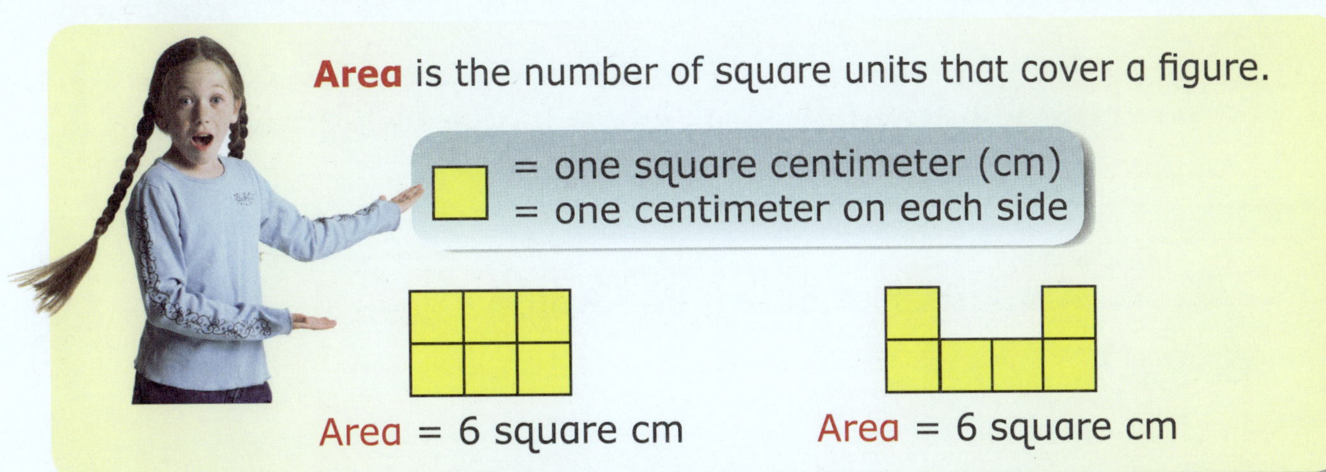

What is the area of the following figures?

1

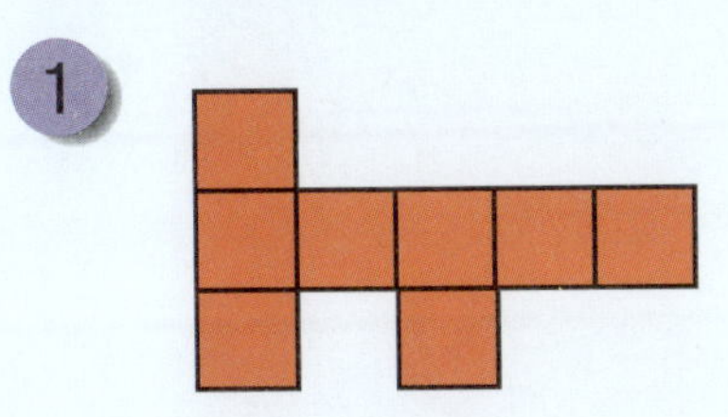

Area = _______

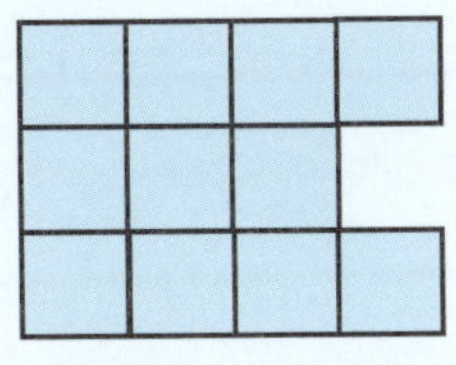

Area = _______

3

Area = _______

For rectangles, the area in square units is equal to the length times the width.

Area = length × width

$A = l \times w$

4. Find the area of a swimming pool with a length of 33 ft and a width of 18 ft.

Area = ______

5. Find the area of a mobile home with a length of 90 ft and a width of 18 ft.

Area = ______

6. Find 3 different dimensions for a rectangle with area of 24 sq ft.

______ by ______ ______ by ______ ______ by ______

In 2010, the average American house had about 2,700 square feet of area.

A **polygon** is a closed figure made with line segments. In a **regular polygon**, all sides are of equal length and all angles are equal too.

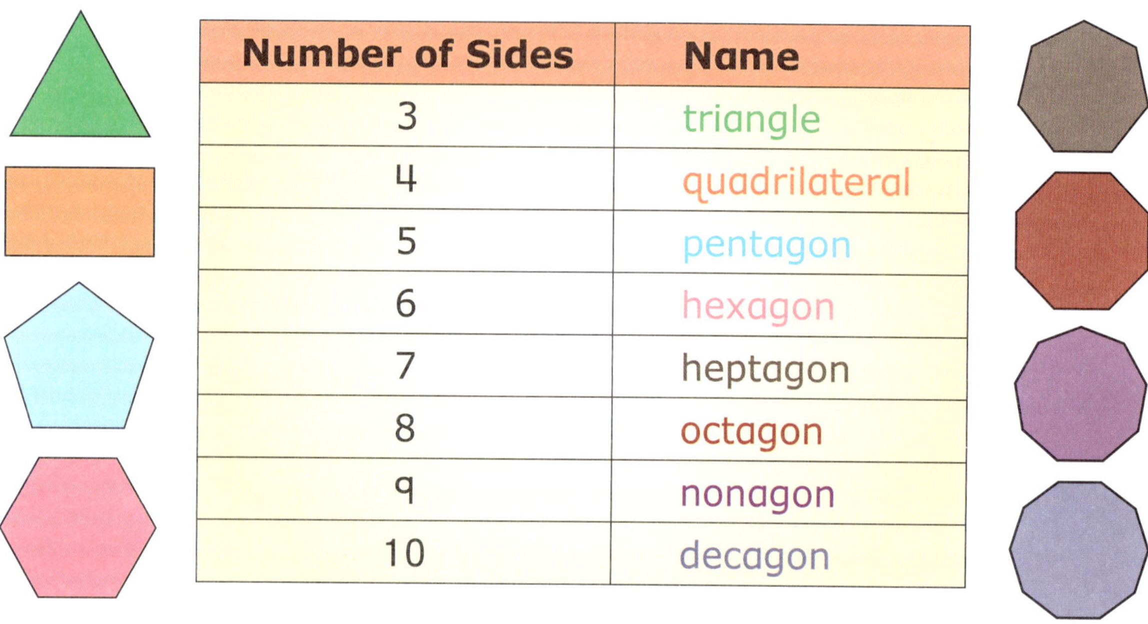

Number of Sides	Name
3	triangle
4	quadrilateral
5	pentagon
6	hexagon
7	heptagon
8	octagon
9	nonagon
10	decagon

Find and circle the eight polygon names listed above. The names can be found in straight lines horizontally, vertically, or diagonally, written forwards or backwards.

<table>
<tr><td>E</td><td>L</td><td>G</td><td>N</td><td>A</td><td>I</td><td>R</td><td>T</td><td>R</td><td>O</td><td>H</td><td>A</td><td>S</td></tr>
<tr><td>O</td><td>N</td><td>T</td><td>A</td><td>G</td><td>R</td><td>O</td><td>A</td><td>B</td><td>S</td><td>E</td><td>T</td><td>U</td></tr>
<tr><td>A</td><td>N</td><td>T</td><td>H</td><td>E</td><td>X</td><td>A</td><td>G</td><td>O</td><td>N</td><td>P</td><td>E</td><td>D</td></tr>
<tr><td>R</td><td>O</td><td>D</td><td>P</td><td>N</td><td>O</td><td>G</td><td>A</td><td>T</td><td>N</td><td>T</td><td>P</td><td>O</td></tr>
<tr><td>R</td><td>G</td><td>N</td><td>O</td><td>G</td><td>A</td><td>T</td><td>C</td><td>O</td><td>R</td><td>A</td><td>C</td><td>T</td></tr>
<tr><td>T</td><td>A</td><td>P</td><td>O</td><td>S</td><td>R</td><td>A</td><td>G</td><td>O</td><td>N</td><td>G</td><td>O</td><td>A</td></tr>
<tr><td>O</td><td>N</td><td>P</td><td>E</td><td>N</td><td>T</td><td>A</td><td>G</td><td>O</td><td>N</td><td>O</td><td>G</td><td>O</td></tr>
<tr><td>T</td><td>O</td><td>T</td><td>R</td><td>I</td><td>C</td><td>O</td><td>N</td><td>A</td><td>W</td><td>N</td><td>T</td><td>A</td></tr>
<tr><td>N</td><td>N</td><td>R</td><td>T</td><td>E</td><td>O</td><td>N</td><td>T</td><td>S</td><td>R</td><td>D</td><td>E</td><td>C</td></tr>
<tr><td>Q</td><td>U</td><td>A</td><td>D</td><td>R</td><td>I</td><td>L</td><td>A</td><td>T</td><td>E</td><td>R</td><td>A</td><td>L</td></tr>
</table>

Tim's Savings

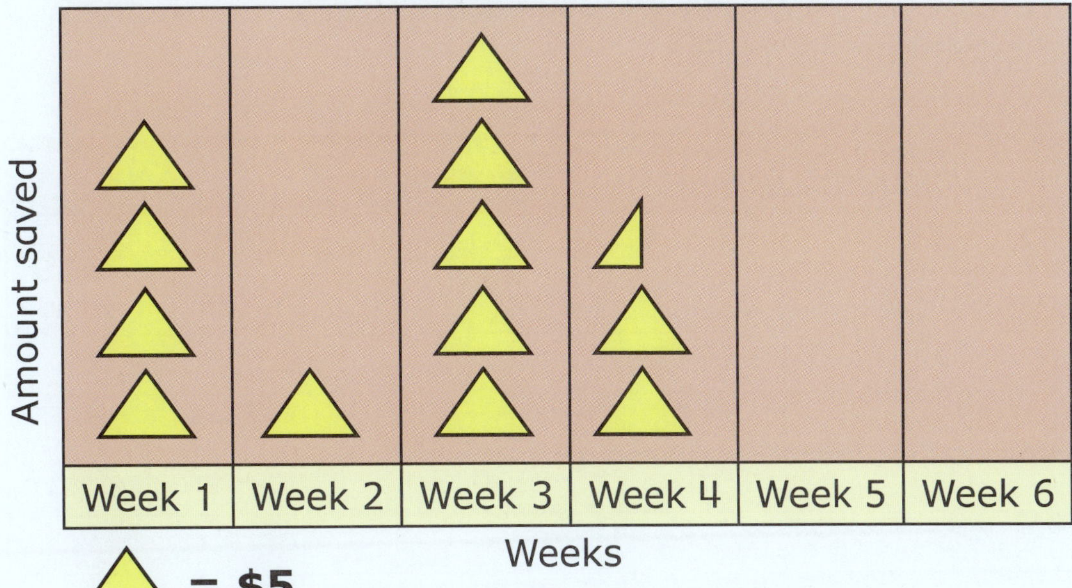

1. How much did Tim save each week?

   week 1 = ______ week 2 = ______

   week 3 = ______ week 4 = ______

2. How much more did he save during week 3 compared to week 2?

   ______

3. How much less did he save in week 2 compared to week 4?

   ______

4. What is the total amount Tim saved during the first four weeks?

   ______

5. Week 5 Tim doubled what he saved in week 4. Complete the graph above for week 5.

6. Week 6 Tim saved half as much as in week 3. Complete the graph above for week 6.

About 1 in 3 students under the age of 18 do not receive an allowance.

Fujita Scale

The **Fujita scale** (F-scale) is a scale for rating tornado intensity. The scale goes from F0 to F5.

Category	Speed	Damage
F0	40-72 mph	slight
F1	73-112 mph	moderate
F2	113-157 mph	significant
F3	158-206 mph	severe
F4	207-260 mph	devastating
F5	261-318 mph	incredible

1) The county of Clay had seven tornados in one year. Their intensity was 120 mph, 218 mph, 156 mph, 191 mph, 101 mph, 78 mph, and 61 mph. Complete the following line graph.

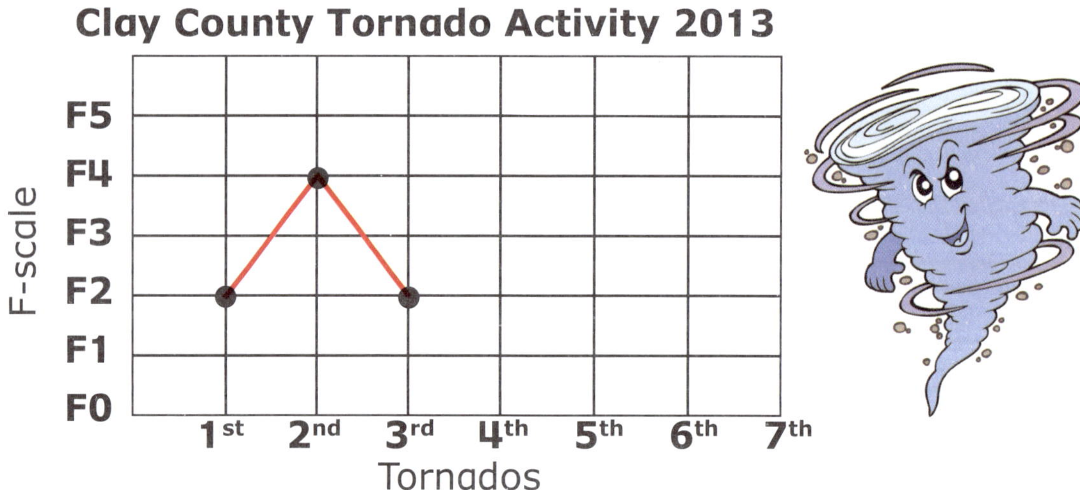

To find the **average** speed of a category F0 tornado, add up the limits of the speed, and divide by two.

The average speed of a F0 = (40 + 72) ÷ 2 = 56 mph.

2) The average speed of a category F2 is ______ mph.

3) The average speed of a category F3 is ______ mph.

What's in Your Pocket?

Find the total money found in each pocket and use the letters to solve the riddle below. Line decimal places up so the same place values are being added together.

$5 = $5.00
$1 = $1.00
quarter = 25¢ = .25
dime = 10¢ = .10
nickel = 5¢ = .05
penny = 1¢ = .01

5.00
3.00
.50
.05
+ .03
$8.58

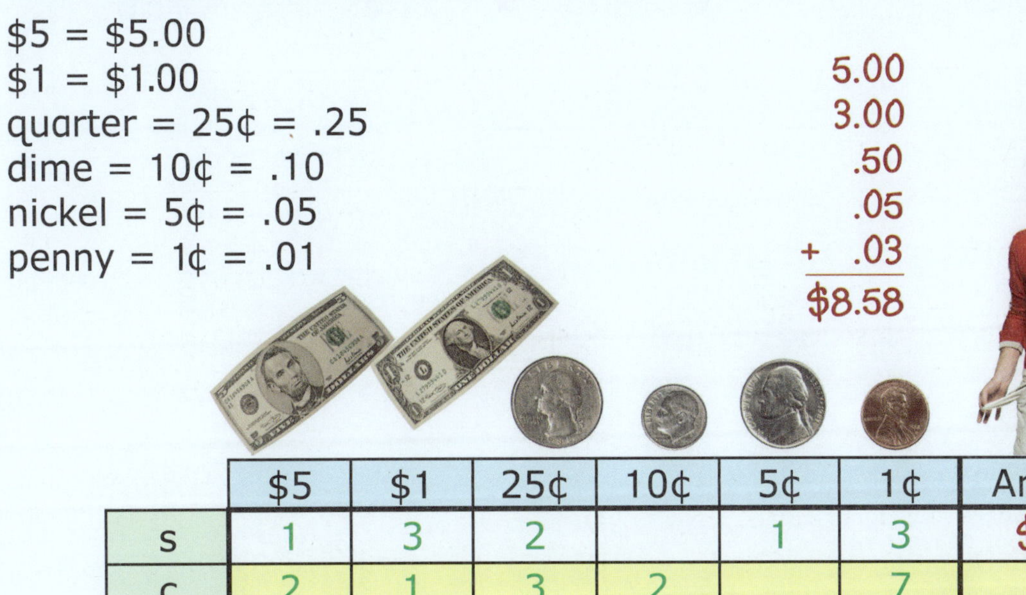

	$5	$1	25¢	10¢	5¢	1¢	Amount
s	1	3	2		1	3	$8.58
c	2	1	3	2		7	
m		8	5	1	3		
e	3		1	5	2	6	
u		7	2	4	6		
n	2		5	3	1	1	
a		4	7	2		8	
s	1	3	1	2	2	3	
o	2	1	4	1	3	1	
r		7	6		8	2	

What do ghosts wear at the beach?

___ ___ ___
$8.58 $8.20 $11.61

___ ___ ___ ___ ___ ___
$8.58 $12.02 $8.92 $15.91 $6.03 $9.50

Order to Go!

Burger	**Cheese Burger**	**Hotdog**	**Fries**	**Drink**
$1.69	$1.98	$1.75	$1.49	$1.25

Find the total of each order before tax is added.

1. cheeseburger, hotdog, and drink = $4.98

$1.98
1.75
+ 1.25
$4.98

2. two burgers, and two drinks = ______

3. hotdog, burger, and two drinks = ______

4. three burgers, three fries, and three drinks = ______

5. one of each = ______

Use the prices to find what items were purchased.

6. The bill for three items was $4.25.

______________ ______________ ______________

7. The bill for three items was $5.42.

______________ ______________ ______________

8. The bill for four items was $5.98.

______________ ______________ ______________ ______________

Exact Change Only

Find the change back from \$5 for a \$1.25 purchase.

\$5 − 1.25 = \$5.00 − 1.25 =

$$\begin{array}{r} \overset{4}{\cancel{\$5}}.\overset{9}{0}\overset{10}{0} \\ -\ 1.25 \\ \hline \$3.75 \end{array}$$

Find the change and match to the answers below.

Be sure to line up the decimals to align with the same place values!

Amount Given	Purchase Price	Change	Match
\$10	\$1.39	\$8.61	D
\$20	\$12.25		
\$5	\$4.09		
\$100	\$59.01		
\$20	89¢		
\$10.50	\$5.29		
\$46.75	\$45.80		
\$20	1¢		
\$10.25	\$10.09		
\$20.50	\$14.30		
\$30	\$21.56		
\$50	\$17.05		

A \$8.44 B \$ .91 C \$19.11 D \$8.61

E \$.95 F \$5.21 G \$19.99 H \$.16

I \$6.20 J \$7.75 K \$40.99 L \$32.95

The average American eats at a restaurant four to five times a week.

Visual Mind Benders®

1 By only touching one glass, how can the top row of glasses match the bottom row?

2 As a farmer looked over his chickens and goats, he counted 10 heads and 28 legs. How many chickens and goats did he have?

3 How can you obtain 1,000 from addends only containing 8s?

A Roll of the Dice!

Find the products and discover a pattern for how the answers relate to a die.

1. 259×429

2. 518×429

3. 777×429

4. $1,036 \times 429$

5. $1,295 \times 429$

6. $1,554 \times 429$

What is the pattern? ______________________________

____

____

____

ZOOM to Mastery!

Solve each problem; then cross out the correct answers below to find the two false answers.

1. $\begin{array}{r} 641 \\ 537 \\ 42 \\ +\ 37 \\ \hline \end{array}$

2. $\begin{array}{r} 512 \\ 285 \\ 29 \\ +\ 132 \\ \hline \end{array}$

3. $\begin{array}{r} 1{,}023 \\ 2{,}016 \\ 1{,}002 \\ +\ 132 \\ \hline \end{array}$

4. $\begin{array}{r} 1{,}000 \\ -\ 706 \\ \hline \end{array}$

5. $\begin{array}{r} 7{,}015 \\ -\ 87 \\ \hline \end{array}$

6. $\begin{array}{r} 41{,}329 \\ -\ 19{,}198 \\ \hline \end{array}$

7. $\begin{array}{r} 250 \\ \times\ 7 \\ \hline \end{array}$

8. $\begin{array}{r} 804 \\ \times\ 96 \\ \hline \end{array}$

9. $\begin{array}{r} 319 \\ \times\ 147 \\ \hline \end{array}$

10. $8\overline{)2{,}312}$

11. $50\overline{)750}$

12. $41\overline{)2{,}542}$

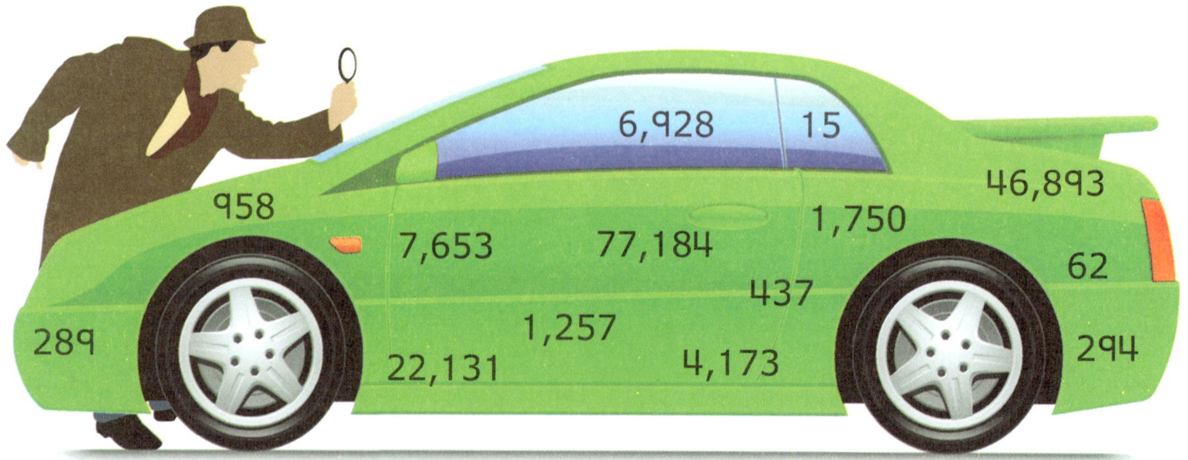

Visual Mind Benders®

1. Turn the triangle upside-down by only moving three coins.

2. Using six equal length sticks, make 8 equilateral triangles.

3. By moving only 3 sticks, make the 5 identical squares into 4 identical squares.

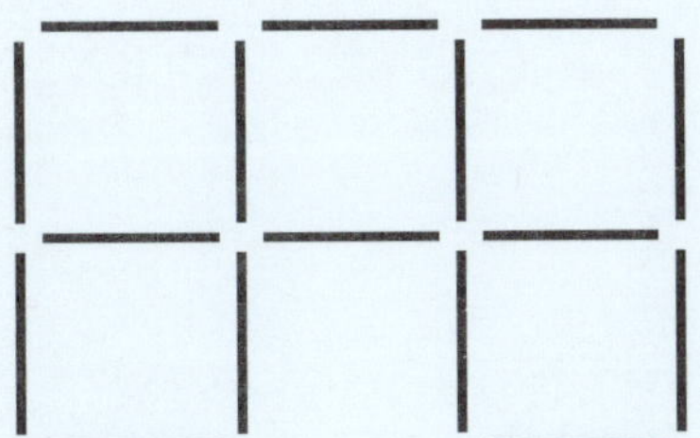

For more activities like this, please see our *Visual Mind Benders®* series.

Steps for **Order of Operations** in solving problems:

Step 1: Do the work inside parentheses.

Step 2: Do multiplication and division from left to right.

Step 3: Do addition and subtraction from left to right.

Example 1

$5 \times 9 - 8 \div 2 =$

Step 1: No parentheses, go to Step 2.

Step 2: $5 \times 9 - 8 \div 2 =$

Step 3: $45 - 4 = 41$

Example 2

$2 \times 9 - (19 - 1) =$

Step 1: $2 \times 9 - (19 - 1) =$

Step 2: $2 \times 9 - 18 =$

Step 3: $18 - 18 = 0$

Solve each problem; then cross out the correct answers on the right to find the two false answers.

1. $100 - (19 + 34) =$ ____
2. $640 \div 8 - 8 \times 5 =$ ____
3. $219 - (60 - 14) =$ ____
4. $75 \div 5 + (100 - 10) =$ ____
5. $(34 - 24) \div 5 \times 2 =$ ____
6. $100 \div 5 + 5 \times 2 + 3 =$ ____

4
47
52
40
105
154
33
173

Place parentheses to make each equation true.

7. $20 - 10 - 10 - 5 = 5$
8. $24 \div 3 + 2 \div 2 \times 2 = 12$

Order of Operations Challenge

When figuring the answer, the following steps must be done in the correct order.

Step 1: Do the work inside parentheses.

Step 2: Do multiplication and division from left to right.

Step 3: Do addition and subtraction from left to right.

Place parentheses to make each equation true. There may be more than one set of parentheses.

1. $8 \div 2 + 6 = 1$ $8 \div (2 + 6) = 1$
2. $4 + 8 \div 8 - 4 = 3$ __________
3. $20 - 12 \div 2 \times 3 = 18$ __________
4. $24 \div 4 + 2 \times 2 = 3$ __________
5. $12 - 6 - 4 - 2 = 8$ __________
6. $4 + 8 - 4 + 2 \times 2 = 16$ __________
7. $24 - 12 \div 2 + 8 \div 2 = 2$ __________
8. $4 \times 2 + 2 \times 2 \div 2 = 16$ __________
9. $100 - 48 + 24 - 12 + 6 = 10$ __________

Measuring Temperature

In metric units, temperature is measured in degrees Celsius (C°).

Water boils at 100° C.

Water freezes at 0° C.

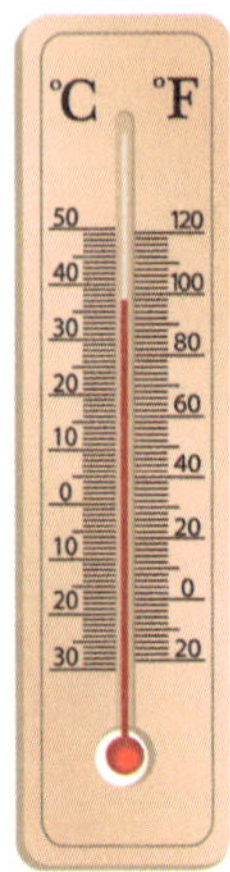

In customary units, temperature is measured in degrees Fahrenheit (F°).

Water boils at 212° F.

Water freezes at 32° F.

1 Find a pattern and complete the table.

Celsius	Fahrenheit
0° C	32° F
5° C	41° F
10° C	50° F
15° C	59° F
20° C	
25° C	
30° C	
35° C	
40° C	
45° C	
50° C	

Celsius	Fahrenheit
55° C	
60° C	
65° C	
70° C	
75° C	
80° C	
85° C	
90° C	
95° C	
100° C	

2 The highest recorded temperature in New Mexico was 122°F on June 27, 1994.

122°F = ______°C

In the study of **statistics**, information is collected, organized, and studied. Mean, median, and mode indicate central tendency.

Mean (or average) = $\frac{\text{total}}{\text{number of numbers}}$

Median = middle number after placement from smallest to largest

Mode = most used number

1. T-shirts for sale cost either \$8, \$20, or \$8.

   mean price = \$12 $\left(\frac{36}{3} = 3\overline{)36}\right)$ 12

   median price = \$8 (8, 8, 20)

   mode price = \$8

2. Joe ran the 100 yard dash in 14, 13, 12, 14, 16, 17, and 19 seconds.

   mean time = _____

   median time = _____

   mode time = _____

3. Five 6th graders measured their smiles at 60, 66, 57, 55, and 57 millimeters.

   mean length = _____

   median length = _____

   mode length = _____

   your smile's length = _____

The world record for the 100 yard dash is 9.07 seconds.

The **mean** is the sum of the data divided by the number of data items.

The **median** is the middle number after the data is placed in order.

The **mode** is the most used data item.

Recorded Temperature Highs for Bay Town

Week	Day	High Temperature
Week 1	Monday	68°F
	Tuesday	80°F
	Wednesday	81°F
	Thursday	81°F
	Friday	73°F
	Saturday	64°F
	Sunday	71°F
Week 2	Monday	79°F
	Tuesday	80°F
	Wednesday	84°F
	Thursday	80°F
	Friday	80°F
	Saturday	79°F
	Sunday	64°F

1. What was the mean temperature for week 1? _____

2. What was the mean temperature for week 2? _____

3. What was the mean temperature for this two week time? _____

4. What was the median temperature for week 1? _____

5. What was the median temperature for week 2? _____

6. What was the mode for week 1? _____

7. What was the mode for week 2? _____

To show the number of **combinations** of things possible, a **tree diagram** can be used. The branches display outcome choices and help organize information.

With a hot dog, you can order either fries, an apple, or a salad. Draw a tree diagram to show possible combinations.

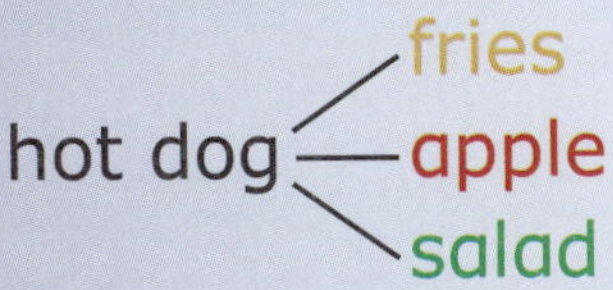

Possible Combinations

hot dog, fries
hot dog, apple
hot dog, salad

If a penny is tossed three times, what are all the possible outcomes.

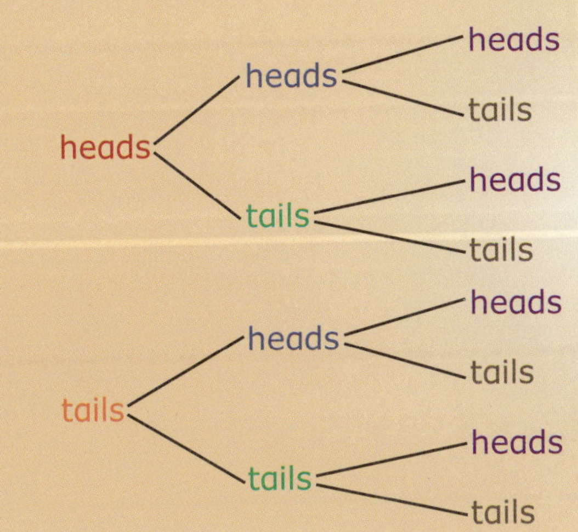

Possible Outcomes

heads, heads, heads
heads, heads, tails
heads, tails, heads
heads, tails, tails
tails, heads, heads
tails, heads, tails
tails, tails, heads,
tails, tails, tails

8 possible outcomes

1. An ice cream stand has four flavors of ice cream (vanilla, chocolate, strawberry, lemon), two different cones (waffle, regular), and two different toppings (nut, candies). Use a separate piece of paper to draw a tree diagram to display all possible combinations.

2. What was the total number of different choices possible in problem #1? ______

In **multiplication**, the order of the factors does not matter (commutative property).

$2 \times 8 \times 5 = 80$
$8 \times 5 \times 2 = 80$
$5 \times 2 \times 8 = 80$

Multiply; then cross out the correct answers below to find the two false answers.

1. $9 \times 4 \times 5 =$ _____
2. $10 \times 7 \times 20 =$ _____
3. $11 \times 2 \times 2 =$ _____
4. $8 \times 30 \times 12 =$ _____
5. $6 \times 34 \times 5 =$ _____
6. $20 \times 20 \times 6 =$ _____
7. $21 \times 9 \times 8 =$ _____
8. $8 \times 2 \times 5 \times 9 =$ _____
9. $5 \times 13 \times 2 \times 5 =$ _____
10. $18 \times 23 \times 3 \times 4 =$ _____

1,512 92 2,400 2,880 4,968 180 44 1,400 1,640 1,020 650 720

11. $10 \times 10 \times 10 \times 10 \times 10 \times 10 =$ _____

12. Compare the number of zeroes in the problem with those in the product.

____

Multiplication can be shown in many different ways. The multiplication sign ×, the word times, the dot •, and when the operation sign is omitted between numbers or variables, they all mean multiply. When no operation is used between numbers, parentheses are added.

$3 \times 4 = 12$
$3 \cdot 4 = 12$
$3(4) = 12$
$(3)4 = 12$

$5 \times 6 \times 7 = 210$
$5 \cdot 6 \cdot 7 = 210$
$5 \cdot 6 \times 7 = 210$
$5(6 \cdot 7) = 210$

Let $n = 4$ and $w = 5$,
$3n = 3 \cdot 4 = 12$
$8nw = 8 \cdot 4 \cdot 5 = 160$

The number before the variable is called the coefficient

Determine the value of the following expressions.

1. $15 \cdot 8 =$
2. $30(12) =$
3. $7 \cdot 6 \cdot 4 =$
4. $(5)(19) =$
5. $5(4 + 6) =$
6. $5 \cdot (9 - 1) =$
7. $10 \cdot 250 =$
8. $(2 + 10)(14 - 2) =$

Let $a = 14$, $n = 10$, and $w = 8$

9. $8n =$
10. $12a =$
11. $anw =$
12. $2w \cdot n =$
13. $7an =$
14. $3w(2a) \cdot n =$

Rules for Even Divisibility

÷ by	evenly (no remainder) if ...
2	the ones place value is even.
3	the sum of the digits is divisible by 3.
4	the last two digits are divisible by 4.
5	the ones place value is 0 or 5.
6	the number is evenly divisible by 2 and 3.
8	the last three digits are divisible by 8.
9	the sum of the digits is divisible by 9.
10	the ones place value is 0.

1. Underline the numbers evenly divisible by **2**.
   1,246   97   90,495   8,888

2. Underline the numbers evenly divisible by **3**.
   13   111   216   30,111

3. Underline the numbers evenly divisible by **4**.
   924   1,000   88   132

4. Underline the numbers evenly divisible by **5**.
   75   810   10,502   904

5. Underline the numbers evenly divisible by **6**.
   33   1,000   120   96

6. Underline the numbers evenly divisible by **8**.
   100   800   5,040   98

7. Underline the numbers evenly divisible by **9**.
   99   209   711   10,800

8. Underline the numbers evenly divisible by **10**.
   20,170   108   90   3,100

A whole number greater than 1 which is only evenly divisible by 1 and itself, is called prime. All other numbers are called composite.

To write a number as a product of primes, also called prime factorization, break down the number into any factors you can and then work those factors down until they are all prime.

60 = 6 × 10
prime factors for 6 are 2 and 3
prime factors for 10 are 2 and 5
60 = 2 × 3 × 2 × 5
60 = 2 × 2 × 3 × 5 (increasing order)

OR

60 = 2 × 30
30 → 5 × 6
6 → 2 × 3
60 = 2 × 2 × 3 × 5

Write the following as products of primes only.

1. 15 = 3 × 5
2. 24 = ___ × ___ × ___ × ___
3. 27 = ___ × ___ × ___
4. 30 = ___ × ___ × ___
5. 18 = ___ × ___ × ___
6. 45 = ___ × ___ × ___
7. 63 = ___ × ___ × ___
8. 28 = ___ × ___ × ___
9. 40 = ___ × ___ × ___ × ___
10. 36 = ___ × ___ × ___ × ___
11. 16 = ___ × ___ × ___ × ___
12. 90 = ___ × ___ × ___ × ___
13. 81 = ___ × ___ × ___ × ___
14. 84 = ___ × ___ × ___ × ___
15. 100 = ___ × ___ × ___ × ___
16. 180 = ___ × ___ × ___ × ___ × ___

An exponent tells how many times a base number is used as a factor.

$$7 \times 7 \times 7 = 7^3$$

(exponent: 3; base: 7)

Fill in the chart, then use the letters to solve the riddle below.

Factored Form	Word Form	Exponent Form	Number Form	
5 × 5	5 squared* (second power)	5^2	25	s
3 × 3 × 3	3 cubed** (third power)	3^3		e
7 × 7	7 squared	7^2		o
2 × 2 × 2 × 2	2 to the fourth power	2^4		m
9 × 9	9 squared	9^2		w
4 × 4 × 4	4 cubed			a
10 × 10				b
5 × 5 × 5				t
6 × 6 × 6 × 6				i
8 × 8				a
2 × 2 × 2 × 2 × 2				p
11 × 11 × 11				r

What do dancers drink for lunch?

____ ____ ____
125 64 32

____ ____ ____ ____ ____
81 64 125 27 1331

* Squared is also called second power.
** Cubed is also called third power.

Multiply Those Exponents!

Use a piece of paper to solve the problems above, then complete the crossword puzzle.

1. 8	2. 1		3.	4.			5.	6.		7.
8.			9.					10.		
11.					12.		13.			
			14.	15.					16.	
17.		18.		19.				20.		
21.							22.			

The area of a rectangle is equal to the length times the width in square units.

Area (A) = length (l) × width (w)

$A = l \times w$

Area indicates how many square units are in a figure.

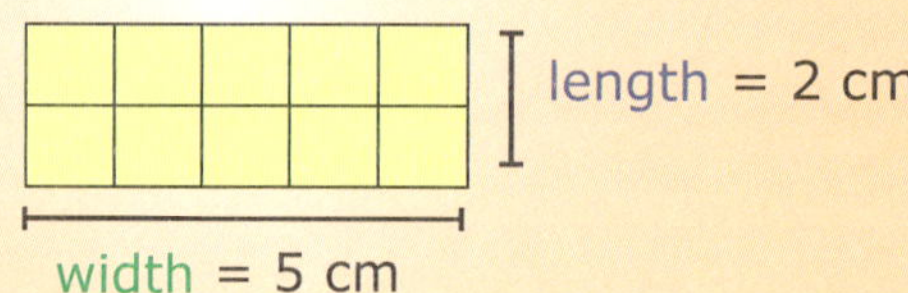

Area = length × width

A = 2 cm × 5 cm

A = 10 sq cm

1) Find the area of each rectangle. Make sure the same units are used for the length and width (12 in. = 1 ft).

Length(l)	Width(w)	Area(A)
20 cm	30 cm	
14 in.	15 in.	
9 m	114 m	
17 ft	20 ft	
25 mm	9 mm	
124 in.	65 in.	
15 in.	1 ft	
6 ft	25 in.	

2) 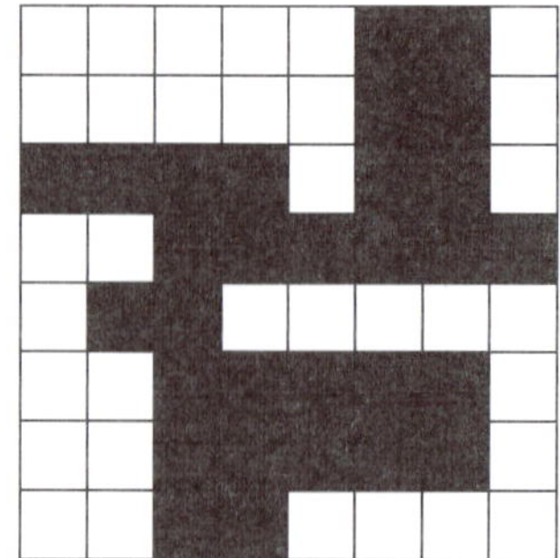

What is the area of the black figure?

Area = ____ square cm

3) What could be the length and width of a rectangle with an area of 82 square cm? l = _____ w = _____

A **parallelogram** is a 4-sided polygon with both pairs of opposite sides parallel.

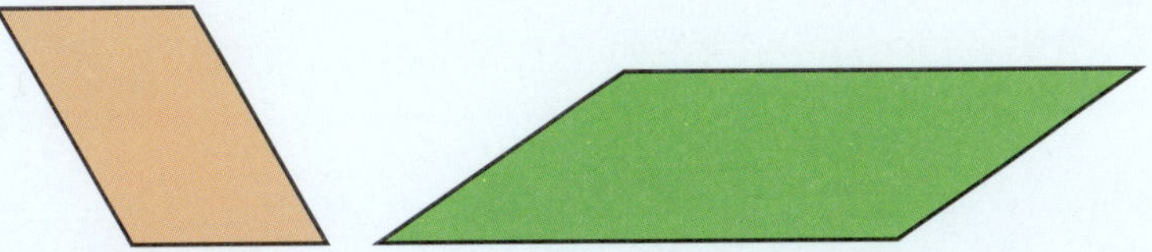

The area (A) of a parallelogram is equal to the base (b) times the height (h). The height is measured perpendicular from the base.

Area (A) = base (b) × height (h)

$A = b \times h$

$A = 4 \times 3$

A = 12 square cm

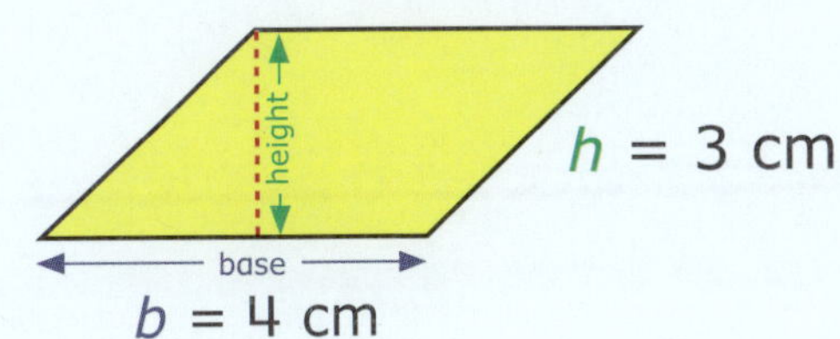

Area indicates how many square units are in a figure.

Notice that any parallelogram can be cut up and moved to be a rectangle.

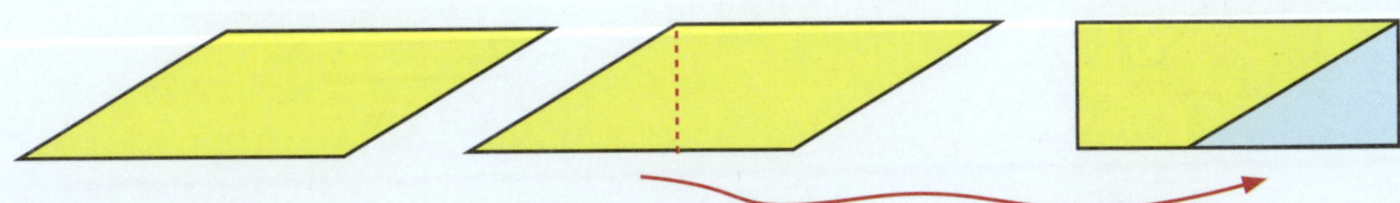

1 Find the area of each parallelogram. Make sure the units are the same for the base and height (12 in.= 1 ft).

Base(b)	Height(h)	Area(A)
45 cm	6 cm	
12 in.	12 in.	
8 m	589 m	
19 ft	30 ft	
107 mm	39 mm	
10 in.	90 in.	
9 in.	2 ft	
4 ft	20 in.	

2 What could be the base and height of a parallelogram with area 85 sq cm? b = _____ h = _____

The area (A) of a triangle is equal to half the base (b) times the height (h). The base is selected and the height is measured perpendicular from the base. The area of a triangle is half the area of a parallelogram.

A triangle's area = $\frac{1}{2}$ × base × height

$A = \frac{1}{2} \times b \times h$

$A = \frac{1}{2} \times (4 \times 3)$

$A = 6$ sq cm

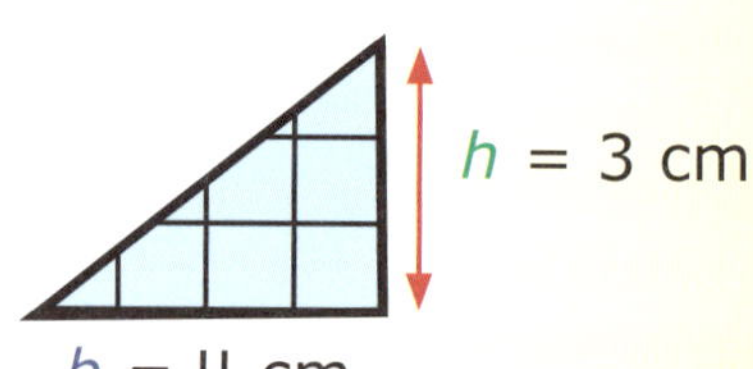

Area indicates how many square units are in a figure.

Find the area of each triangle with units in square centimeters.

1. 16 cm, 15 cm A = ______

2. 50 cm, 48 cm A = ______

3. 42 cm, 19 cm A = ______

4. 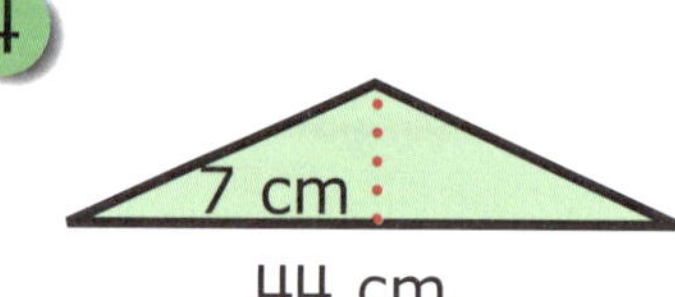

A = ______

5. 30 cm, 40 cm A = ______

6. 9 cm, 110 cm A = ______

7. A triangle has an area of 200 sq ft. If its base is 25 ft, what is its height? ______

Perimeter is the distance around a polygon. The perimeter of a rectangle equals the sum of the four sides or two lengths added to two widths.

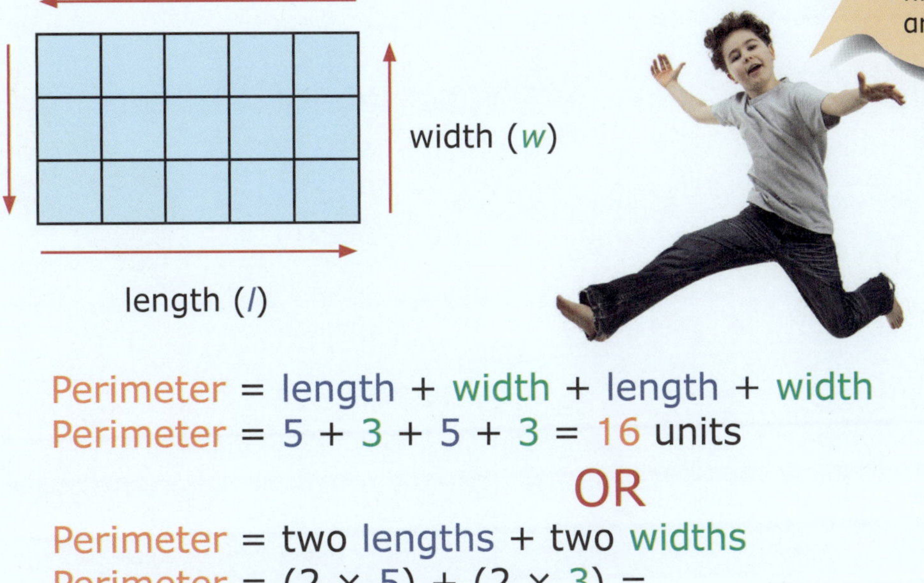

Perimeter = length + width + length + width
Perimeter = 5 + 3 + 5 + 3 = 16 units

OR

Perimeter = two lengths + two widths
Perimeter = $(2 \times 5) + (2 \times 3) =$
$= 10 + 6 = 16$ units

Formula:
$P = (2 \times l) + (2 \times w)$

1. Find the perimeter of the following rectangles. Make sure the units are the same for the length and width.

Length(l)	Width(w)	Perimeter(P)
20 cm	25 cm	
15 in.	15 in.	
9 m	145 m	
18 ft	30 ft	
206 mm	34 mm	
30 in.	50 in.	
10 in.	1 ft	
3 ft	11 in.	

2. An average kid's bedroom is approximately 10 feet by 12 feet.

Perimeter = ______

What is the perimeter of your bedroom? ______

A four sided polygon is called a **quadrilateral**.

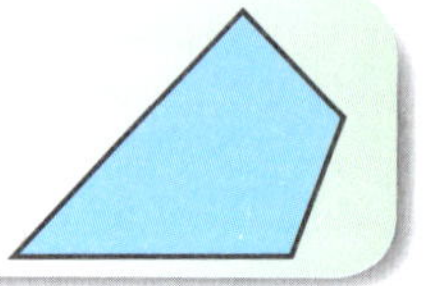

Special Quadrilaterals

A quadrilateral with one pair of parallel sides is called a trapezoid.

A quadrilateral with two pairs of parallel sides is called a parallelogram.

A parallelogram with four right angles is called a rectangle.

A rectangle with four equal sides is called a square.

Answer the follow questions with "true" or "false."

1. All rectangles are parallelograms. ______
2. All squares are parallelograms. ______
3. All quadrilateral are parallelograms. ______
4. All squares are rectangles. ______

Find and circle the five polygon terms defined. The names can be found in straight lines horizontally, vertically, or diagonally, written forwards or backwards.

P	O	R	E	F	O	L	S	Q	P	E	C	T	R	S
R	L	A	R	E	T	A	L	I	R	D	A	U	Q	E
R	E	C	T	R	A	P	E	Z	O	I	D	U	P	A
R	T	P	A	O	S	Q	U	A	R	W	A	T	R	E
P	A	R	A	L	L	E	L	O	G	R	A	M	S	Q
E	R	E	L	G	N	A	T	C	E	R	R	E	C	T

Draw a Rectangle!

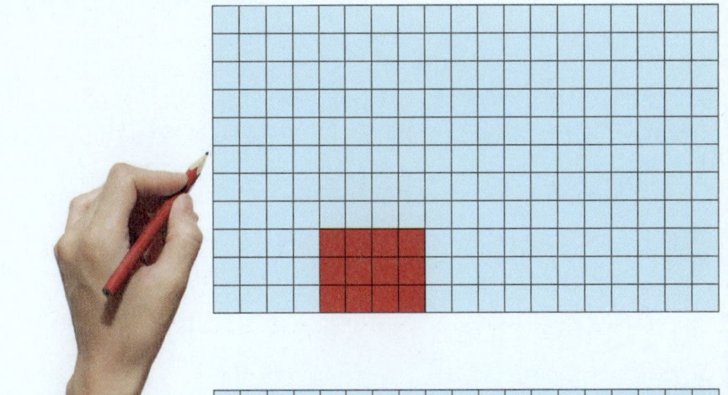

1. Area = 12 square units
   Perimeter = 14 units

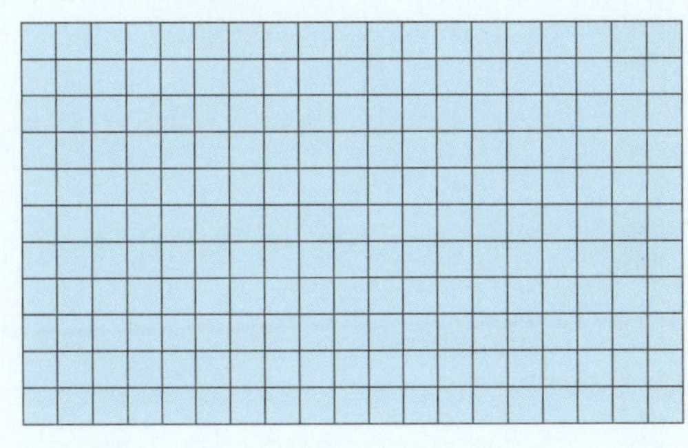

2. Area = 24 square units
   Perimeter = 22 units

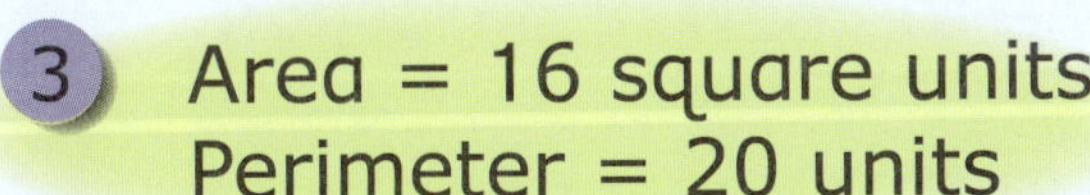

3. Area = 16 square units
   Perimeter = 20 units

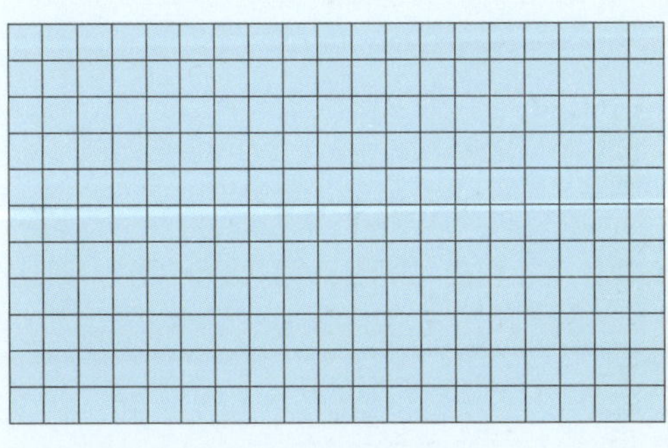

4. Area = 36 square units
   Perimeter = 40 units

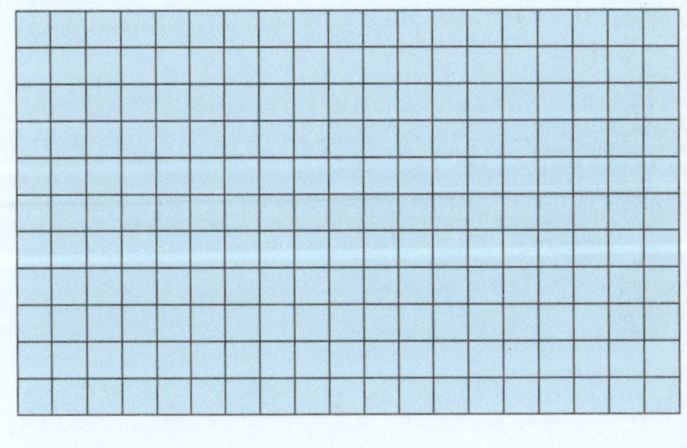

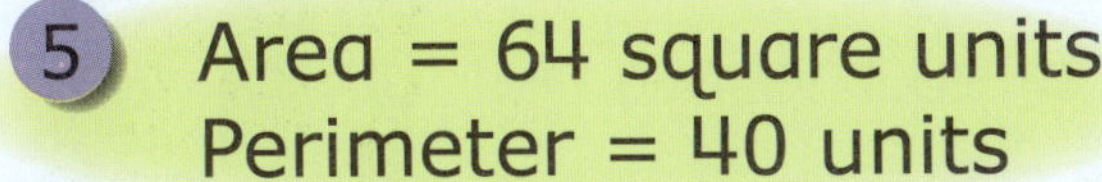

5. Area = 64 square units
   Perimeter = 40 units

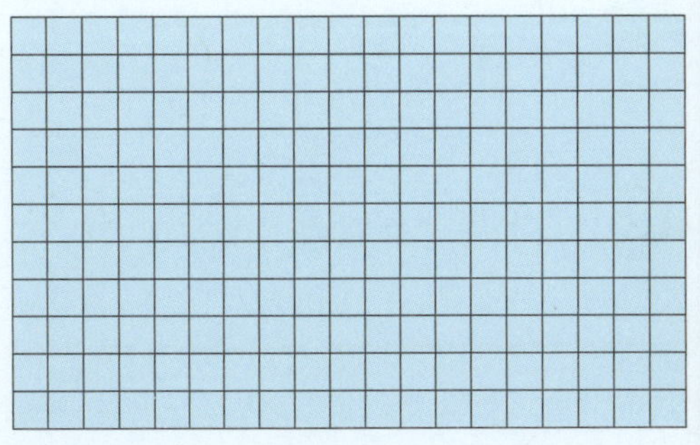

Vocabulary Message

Write the vocabulary word from the choice box that makes each sentence true. The red underlined letters will form the message below.

angle
area
lowest
numerator
perimeter
polygon
prime
product
quadrilateral
quotient
square
sum
triangle
vertex

1. A 3-sided polygon is called a

   __ __ __ __ __ __ __ __.

2. A whole number that is only evenly divisible by itself and 1 is called __ __ __ __ __.

3. A fraction in simplest form is said to be in

   __ __ __ __ __ __ terms.

4. For a rectangle, length times width equals __ __ __ __.

5. The __ __ __ __ __ __ __ __ __ is the top part of a fraction.

6. The answer to an addition problem is the __ __ __.

7. Two sides of an angle meet at the __ __ __ __ __ __.

8. A __ __ __ __ __ __ __ __ __ __ __ __ __ is a 4-sided polygon.

9. The result in a multiplication problem is called the

   __ __ __ __ __ __ __.

10. The distance around a polygon is called the

    __ __ __ __ __ __ __ __ __ .

11. A closed figure made up of line segments is called a

    __ __ __ __ __ __ __.

12. The answer to a division problem is called the

    __ __ __ __ __ __ __ __.

MESSAGE: __ __ __ __ __ __ __ __ __ __ __ __ __

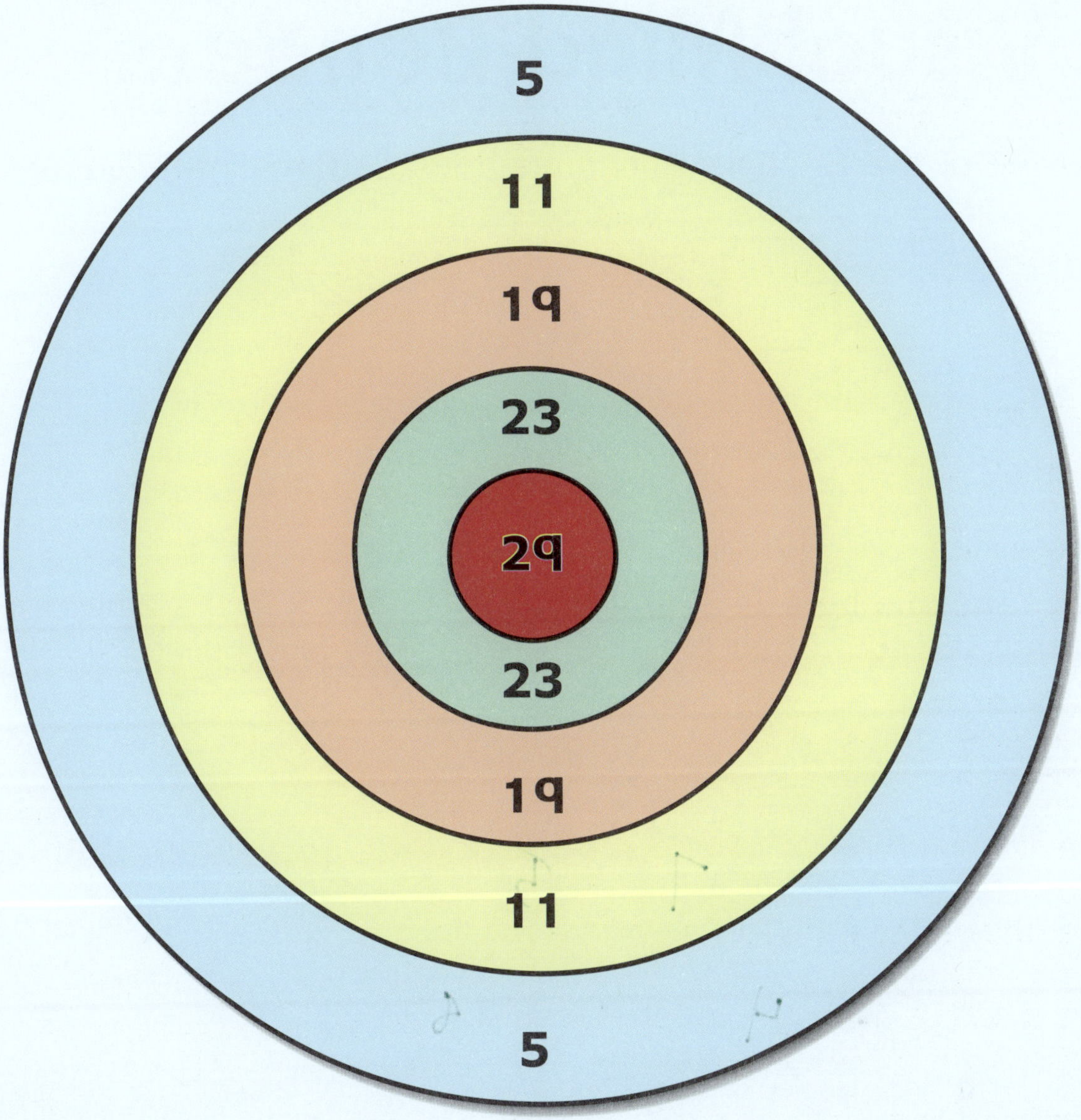

5

11

19

23

29

23

19

11

5

Ali threw all of her four darts at the board. The total of the areas her darts landed on was 100 points.

What four areas did she land on?

____ + ____ + ____ + ____ = 100

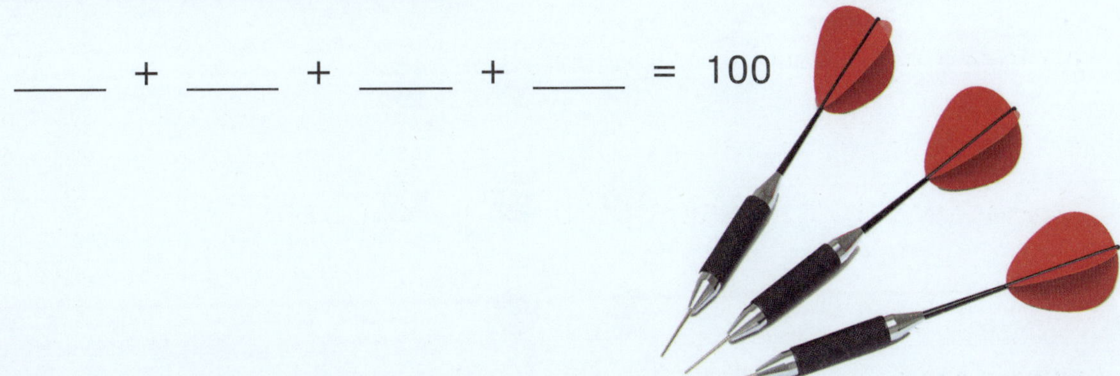

Visual Mind Benders®

1. Move 2 of the 12 sticks to change the 4 squares into 7 squares.

2. Place the numbers 1, 2, 3, 4, 5, 6, 7, 8, and 9 in the nine circles so that the sum of each side of the triangle is equal to 20.

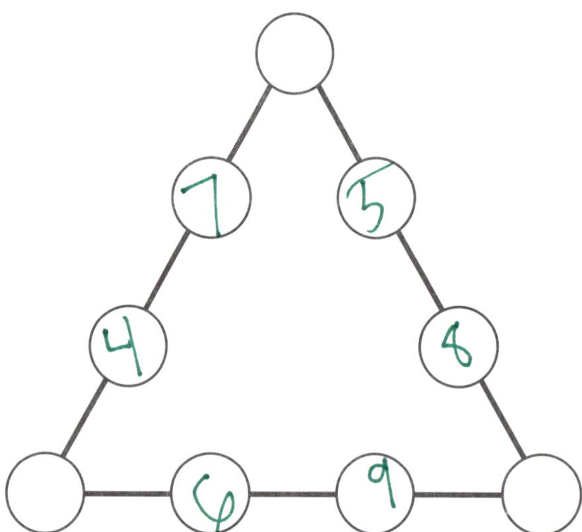

3. Without lifting your pencil, draw 5 lines that cover all the dots.

For more activities like this, please see our *Visual Mind Benders®* series.

Estimation is used when it is difficult to determine the exact number of items.

Sometimes to estimate a large group, a small sample group is selected and counted. After guessing approximately how many of the smaller groups would be in the larger group, multiply the smaller sample group by that number. This should give a good idea of how many are in the larger group.

1. Number of dots in A = ____

2. Multiply number in A by 5 = ____

3. Actual number of dots in the entire rectangle = ____

4. What was the difference between your estimated guess and the actual answer? _____

5. How could you get a good estimation of the number of pieces of cereal in your cereal bowl? ________________________________

____

6. Name something you could estimate using this method.

____

When it is stated that 1,000,000 packages of Jell-O® are sold per day, that is a rounded number used for approximating.

Rules for Rounding	
round to nearest ten	select closest ten*
round to nearest hundred	select closest hundred*
round to nearest thousand	select nearest thousand*

*middle numbers are rounded up

46 rounded to the nearest ten is 50.
179 rounded to the nearest hundred is 200.
2,500 rounded to the nearest thousand is 3,000.

Round each number, then use the letters to solve the riddle on the next page.

1. 21 rounded to the nearest ten is
   - t 20
   - s 30

2. 349 rounded to the nearest hundred is
   - o 300
   - a 400

3. 3,050 rounded to the nearest thousand is
   - a 3,000
   - r 4,000

4. 55 rounded to the nearest ten is
   - t 50
   - l 60

5. 609 rounded to the nearest hundred is
   - u 600
   - i 700

6. 1,500 rounded to the nearest thousand is
   - s 1,000
   - n 2,000

7. 890 rounded to the nearest hundred is
   - r) 800
   - c) 900

8. 999 rounded to the nearest thousand is
   - h) 1,000
   - o) 100

9. 3 rounded to the nearest ten is
   - c) 0
   - n) 10

10. 99 rounded to the nearest hundred is
   - o) 100
   - a) 10

11. 555 rounded to the nearest ten is
   - t) 550
   - u) 560

12. 2,499 rounded to the nearest thousand is
   - n) 2,000
   - s) 3,000

13. 655 rounded to the nearest ten is
   - i) 650
   - t) 660

14. 15,599 rounded to the nearest thousand is
   - a) 15,000
   - e) 16,000

15. 1,999 rounded to the nearest hundred is
   - r) 2,000
   - n) 1,900

Where do math teachers like to go for lunch?

___ ___   ___   ___ ___ ___ ___ ___   ___ ___ ___ ___ ___ ___ ___
1 2   3   4 5 6 7 8   9 10 11 12 13 14 15

Round each number to the nearest ten and do the operation to get a quick estimate of the result.

56 + 70 + 61 = 187
60 + 70 + 60 = 190 Estimated

91 − 17 = 74
90 − 20 = 70 Estimated

39 × 52 = 2,029
40 × 50 = 2,000 Estimated

Estimate each answer; then cross out the correct answers on the right to find the two false answers.

1. 83 + 17 + 31 =	120
2. 92 − 39 =	400
3. 18 × 21 =	80
4. 40 + 39 + 41 =	150
5. 68 − 48 =	900
6. 26 × 34 =	600
7. 99 + 95 + 91 =	130
8. 85 − 7 =	10,000
9. 25 × 15 =	5,300
10. 96 × 99 =	20
11. 49 × 31 =	290
12. 68 × 69 =	50
	4,900
	1,500

13. A bolt of lightning is about 54,000°F and travels at speeds up to 93,000 miles per second. Are these numbers examples of rounding?

❒ yes ❒ no

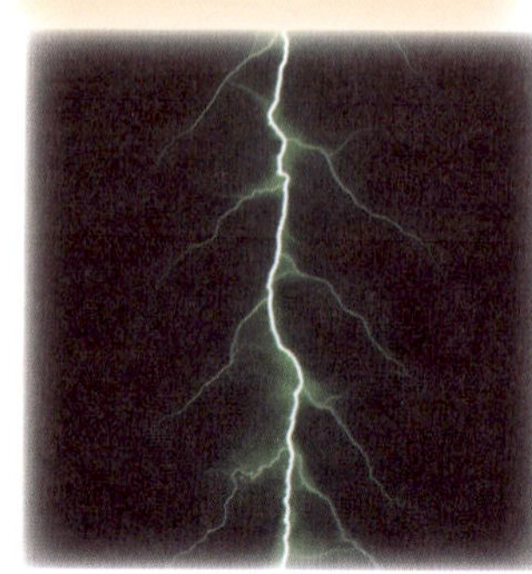

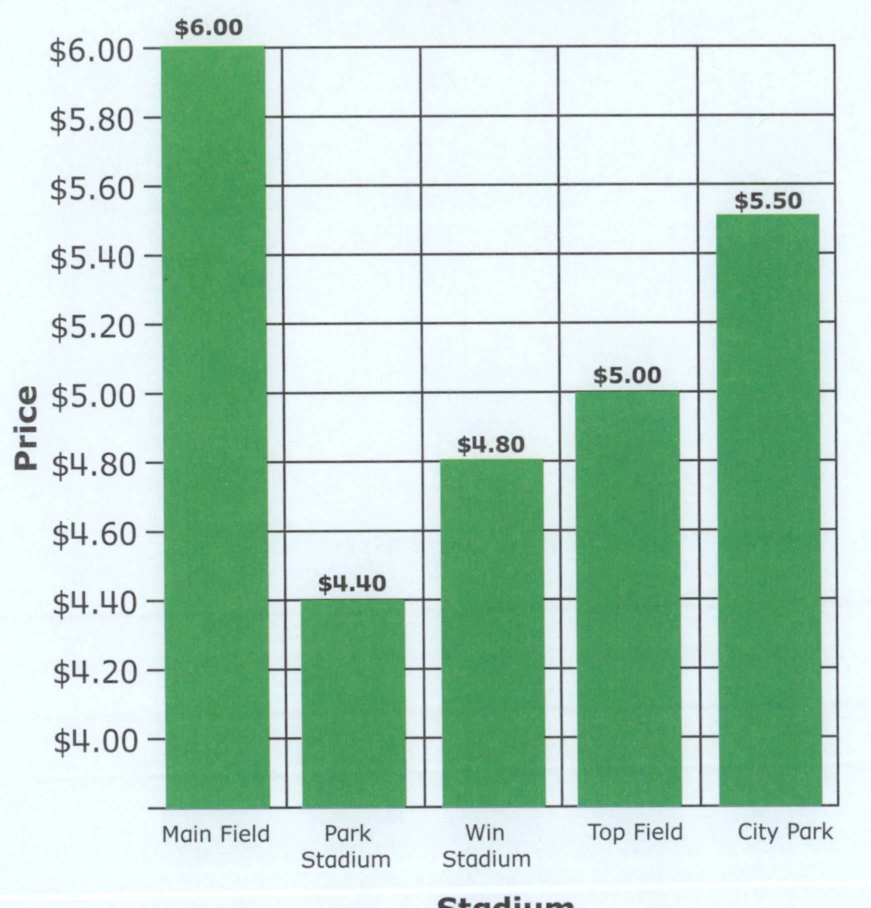

1. Which stadium charges the most? ________________

2. What is the cheapest hot dog price? ________________

3. What is the difference in price of the least and most expensive hot dog? ________________

4. What is the mean (average) price charged for a hot dog at the five stadiums? ________________

5. Why do you think the hot dog prices are different? ________________

Seth kept track of the amount of time in minutes he spent exercising during the past four weeks. Complete the table, bar graph, and the question below.

	Mon.	Tues.	Wed.	Thurs.	Fri.	Sat.	Sun.	Total Minutes for Week
1st week	60	55	40	70	0	35	60	320
2nd week	45	90	25	60	75	60	20	
3rd week	80	90	0	50	60	60	0	
4th week	60	60	75	20	85	60	60	

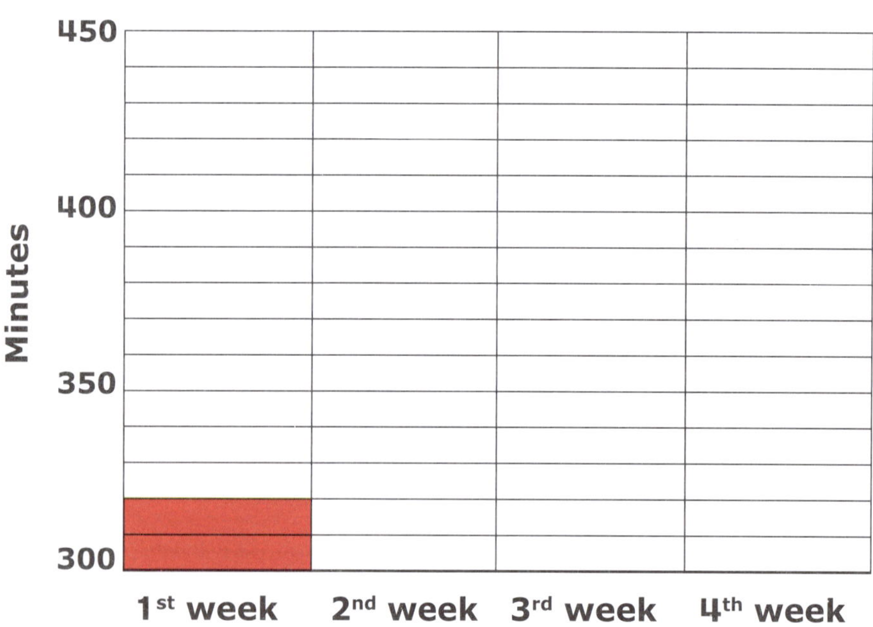

International guidelines recommend an hour a day of moderate activity is suggested for 5- to 18-year-olds. By how many minutes did Seth miss the guidelines for the first week? ______
(1 hour = 60 minutes)

A **Stem-and-Leaf Plot** organizes data from least to greatest. The left column (stems) dislays the tens and the right column (leaves) show the ones of the data.

data: 41, 52, 53, 36, 47, 41, 48

Stems	Leaves
3	6
4	1 1 7 8
5	2 3

shows 52 & 53 → 5

A **Scatter Plot** shows the relationship between two sets of data shown on horizontal and vertical scales. It might show as one variable increases the other decreases, or they both increase over time. Do not connect the dots.

Movie Popcorn

Size	Calories
8 oz	200
16 oz	400
32 oz	800

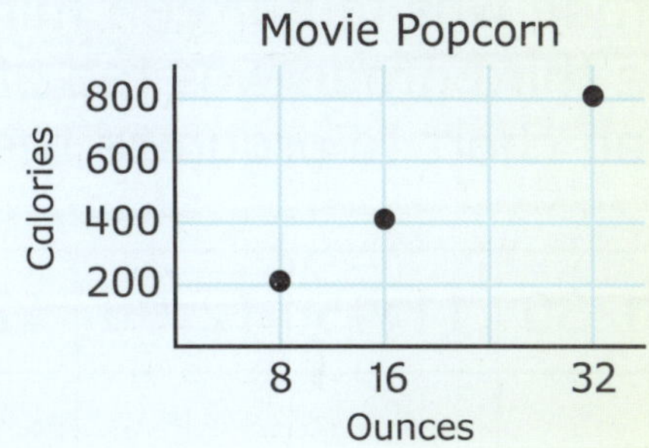

To find the range, subtract the smallest data number from the largest data number. The range of calories is 600.

800 − 200 = 600

1 Make a stem-and-leaf plot using the math test scores of 75, 83, 78, 92, 88, 92, and 89.

2 Make a scatter plot using the information below.

Temperature High Daily	Daily Movie Tickets Sold
90s	100
80s	150
70s	200
60s	250

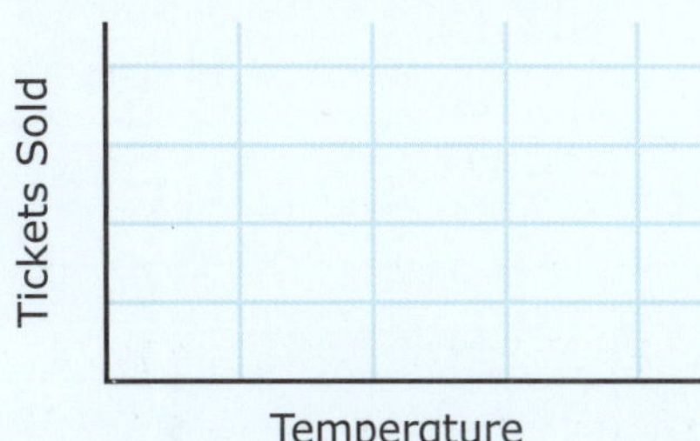

What does the plot show? ______________________

3 Find the range for the data in #1. _____

Lunch Time

Washington Elementary School has grades first through fifth. Unfortunately, it is such a small building that not all grades can eat in the cafeteria at once. The principal decided to work on a plan to schedule different classes at different times. He figured that he would have them come to the cafeteria starting in 15 minute intervals from 11:30 a.m. to 12:30 p.m.

After he finished the schedule, he noticed the second grade was fed before the fifth grade but after the fourth grade. The first grade was fed fifteen minutes after the fourth grade. The third grade was fed after the fifth grade. Use the following chart to organize the schedule.

Grade	11:30	11:45	12:00	12:15	12:30
1st					
2nd					
3rd					
4th					
5th					

At what time did each class go to the cafeteria?

Algebra Questions and Riddle

Find each answer, then use the letters to solve the riddle below.

Jim has $50

	Question	Name		Answer	Letter
1	Jan has $14 more than Jim.	Jan	=	$64	w
2	Lea has twice as much as Jim.	Lea	=	____	o
3	Kali has 4 times as much as Jim, minus $2.	Kali	=	____	r
4	Ava has $19 less than Jim.	Ava	=	____	e
5	Kale has $31 more than $1 less than Jim.	Kale	=	____	t
6	Ann has half as much as Jim.	Ann	=	____	h
7	Bill has $129 more than half of the amount Jim has.	Bill	=	____	n
8	Lee has twice as much as Jim, increased by $117.	Lee	=	____	s
9	Tim has as much as Jim and Kali combined.	Tim	=	____	a
10	Bob has 8 times what Jim has divided by 20.	Bob	=	____	d
11	Cara has the same amount as the sum of Jim, Ava, and Bill.	Cara	=	____	l
12	Dee has the same amount as the difference between Bill's and Ann's amount.	Dee	=	____	u

What is a shark's favorite game?

____	w	____	____	____	____	____		____	____	____
217	64	248	235	235	100	64		80	25	31

____	____	____	____	____	____
235	31	248	20	31	198

The sum of the three angles in a triangle is always 180°. If you fold the three angles together, they form a straight angle of 180°

Given any two angles in a triangle, the third angle can be calculated by taking the sum of the two given angles and subtracting from 180°.

Third Angle = 180° - (sum of two given angles)

Find the missing degrees in each triangle.

1. 90° 60° ______

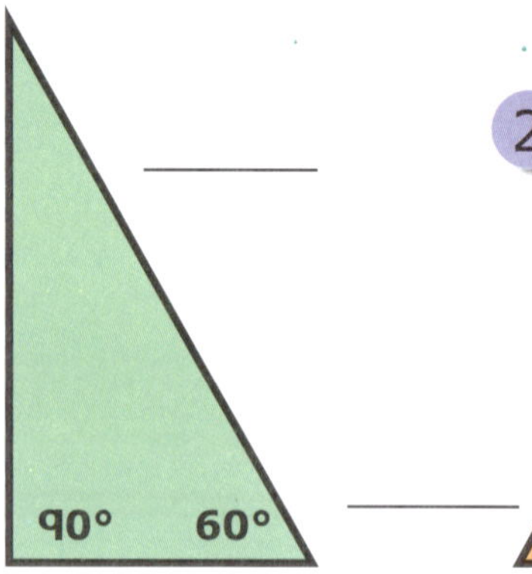

2. 60° 60° ______

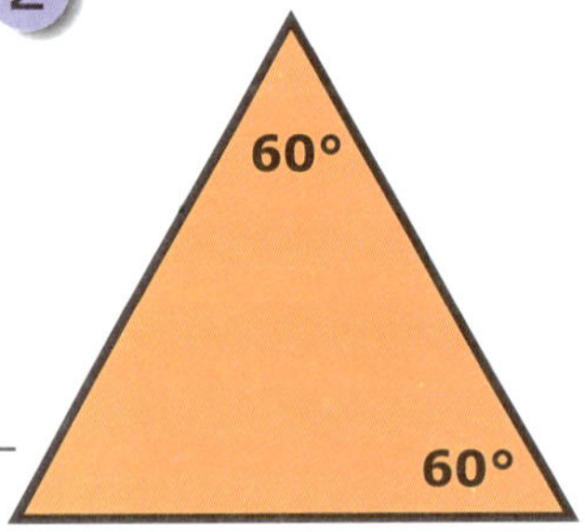

3. 60° 75° ______

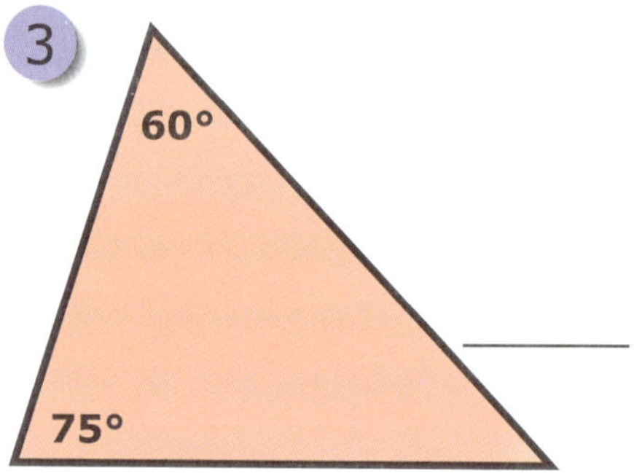

4. 31° 90° ______

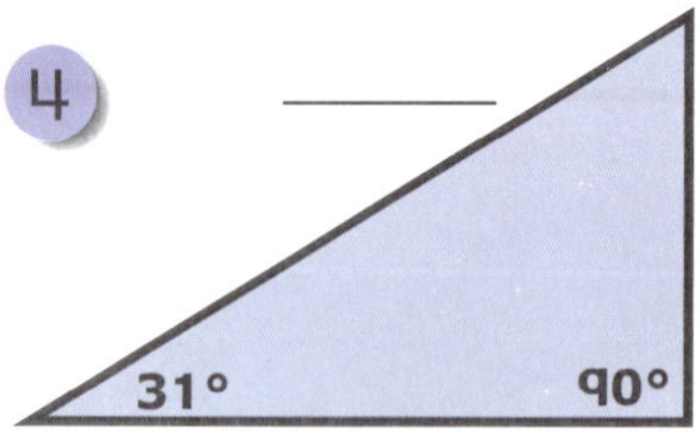

5. 26° 93° ______

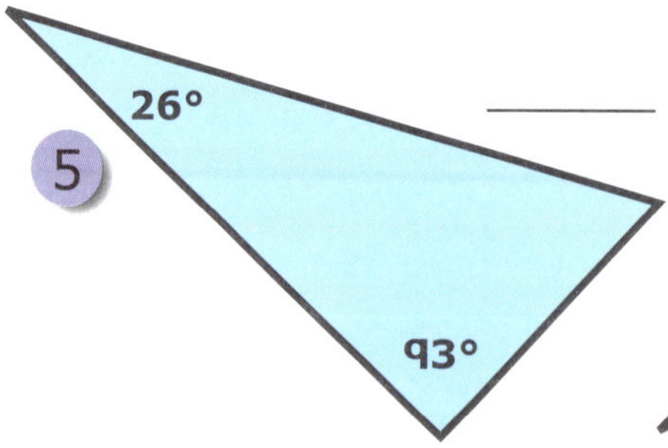

6. 136° 22° ______

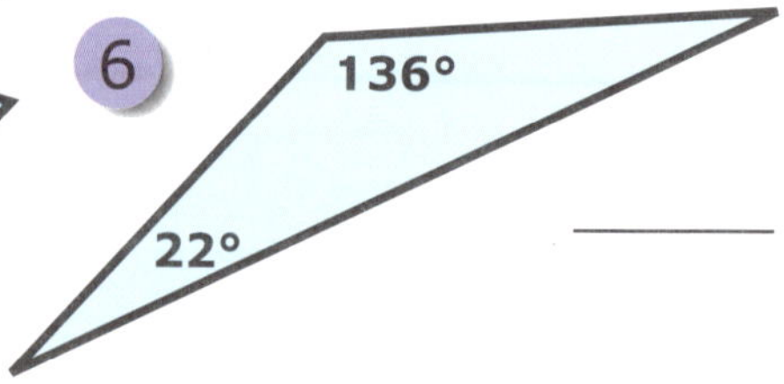

To measure an angle, place the 0° edge of the protractor on the lower ray of the angle with the center of the protractor on the vertex. Then record where the other ray hits the numbers.

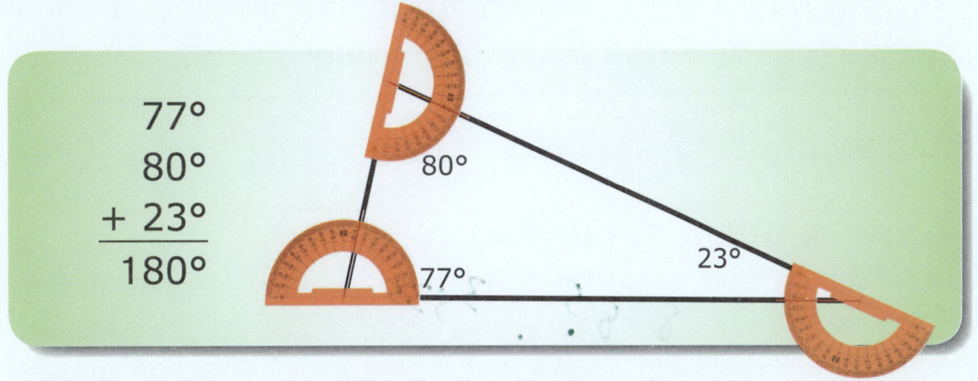

Measure the angles inside each triangle to sum to 180°.

1 ___ + ___ + ___ = 180°

2 ___ + ___ + ___ = 180°

3 Can you draw a triangle where the sum of the angles is not 180°?

____

Critical Thinking Challenge

The following multiplication problem is unique and famous. These are the only two identical numbers to multiply to such an interesting result.

1. Multiply and find the pattern.

$99{,}066^2$ = 99,066 × 99,066 =

2. Arrange the digits in the answer from low to high.

_ _ _ _ _ _ _ _ _ _

3. What is so unique about this multiplication problem?

____

____

____

Equivalent fractions name equal amounts.

Multiplying the numerator and denominator of a fraction by the same number, except zero, makes an equivalent fraction.

$$\frac{1 \times 2}{2 \times 2} = \frac{2}{4}$$

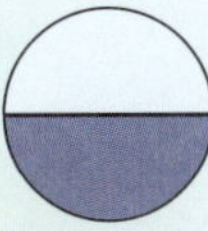 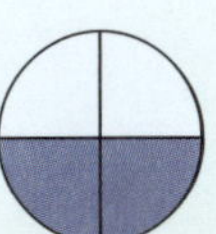

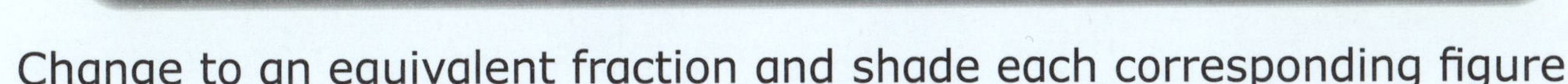

Change to an equivalent fraction and shade each corresponding figure.

1. 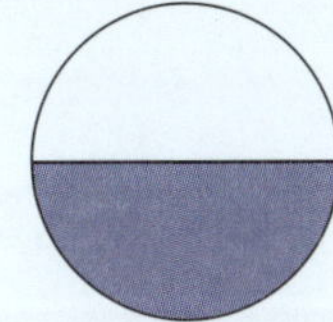 $\frac{1}{2} = \frac{1 \times 4}{2 \times 4} = \frac{}{8}$ 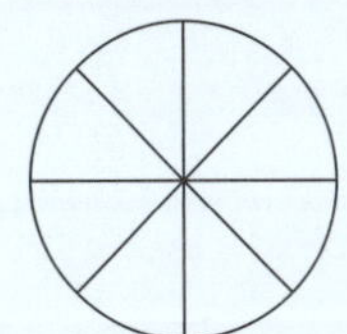

2. 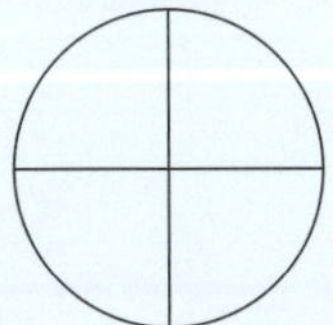 $\frac{3}{4} = \frac{3 \times 2}{4 \times 2} = \frac{}{8}$ 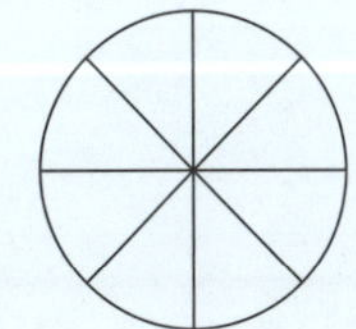

3. 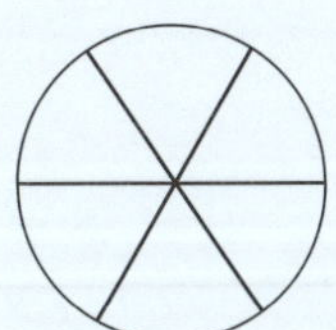 $\frac{1}{6} = \frac{1 \times 2}{6 \times 2} = \frac{}{12}$ 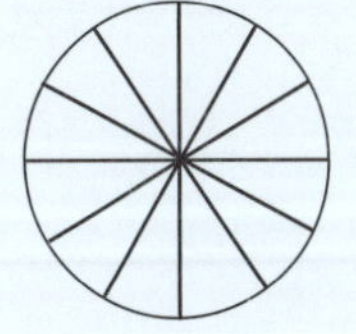

4. $\frac{2}{3} = \frac{2 \times 4}{3 \times 4} = \frac{}{12}$ 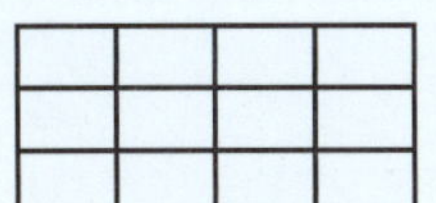

5.  $\frac{3}{5} = \frac{3 \times 2}{5 \times 2} = \frac{}{10}$ 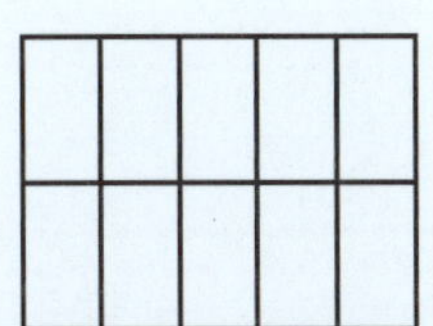

Identify each equivalent fraction; then cross out the correct answers below to find the two false answers.

1. $\frac{3}{4} = \frac{9}{12}$
2. $\frac{2}{3} =$
3. $\frac{1}{2} =$
4. $\frac{5}{6} =$
5. $\frac{1}{4} =$
6. $\frac{2}{5} =$
7. $\frac{1}{3} =$
8. $\frac{1}{6} =$
9. $\frac{1}{9} =$
10. $\frac{7}{8} =$
11. $\frac{1}{10} =$
12. $\frac{3}{20} =$
13. $\frac{7}{18} =$
14. $\frac{4}{9} =$
15. $\frac{4}{5} =$
16. $\frac{11}{12} =$

$\frac{15}{18}$ $\frac{4}{24}$ $\frac{10}{25}$ $\frac{22}{24}$

$\frac{6}{18}$ $\frac{12}{80}$ ~~$\frac{9}{12}$~~ $\frac{16}{20}$

$\frac{4}{6}$ $\frac{2}{8}$ $\frac{5}{8}$ $\frac{3}{27}$ $\frac{6}{12}$

$\frac{21}{24}$ $\frac{14}{24}$ $\frac{21}{54}$ 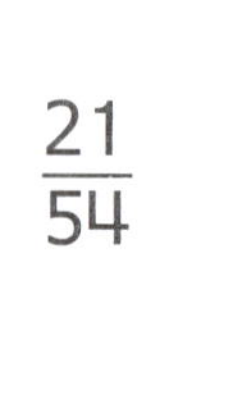 $\frac{2}{20}$ $\frac{16}{36}$

The factors of a number are those numbers that divide into it evenly.

Factors for 16 are 1, 2, 4, 8, 16.

Factors for 7 are 1, 7.

Whole numbers greater than 1 are called prime if the only factors are 1 and itself.

Fill in the missing factors for each number.

1. Factors for 12: 1, 2, 3, 4, _____, _____

2. Factors for 18: 1, 2, 3, _____, _____, _____

3. Factors for 24: 1, 2, _____, _____, _____, _____, _____, _____

4. Factors for 51: _____, _____, _____, _____

5. Factors for 56: _____, _____, _____, _____, _____, _____, _____, _____

Circle the eight prime numbers in the table below.

43	21	101	57	17
20	11	45	1	99
56	72	31	81	29
59	88	91	97	42

Fractions should be written in simplest form which is also called lowest terms.

To find the simplest form of a fraction, divide both the numerator and denominator by their greatest common factor (GCF)*.

To find the simplest form of $\frac{4}{6}$, find the greatest common factor of 4 and 6. The GCF is 2.

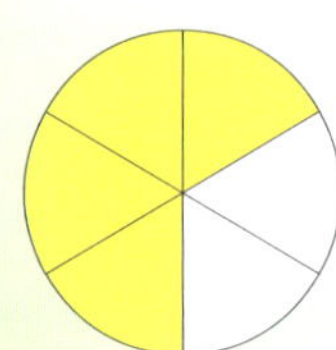

$$\frac{4 \div 2}{6 \div 2} = \frac{2}{3}$$

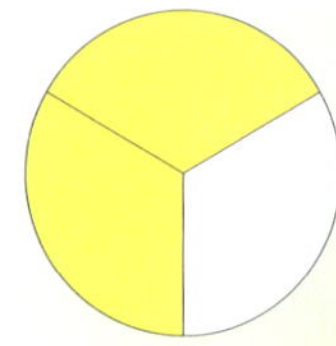

Write each in simplest form.

1. How much cake is left?

$$\frac{\square}{\square} = \frac{\square \div \square}{\square \div \square} = \frac{}{}$$

2. How long is the board?

1 2 3
feet

$$\frac{\square}{\square} = \frac{\square \div \square}{\square \div \square} = \frac{}{}$$

3. How much pizza is left?

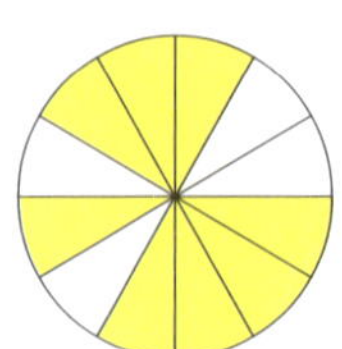

$$\frac{\square}{\square} = \frac{\square \div \square}{\square \div \square} = \frac{}{}$$

* See page 39 to review how to find the greatest common factor of two numbers.

Write each fraction in simplest form, then use the letters to solve the riddle below.

b $\frac{16 \div 4}{20 \div 4} = \frac{4}{5}$

r $\frac{2}{14}$

a $\frac{15}{24}$

s $\frac{12}{16}$

o $\frac{10}{12}$

w $\frac{12}{36}$

h $\frac{5}{45}$

u $\frac{18}{30}$

e $\frac{8}{18}$

x $\frac{72}{81}$

g $\frac{18}{32}$

t $\frac{24}{56}$

What did the baseball umpire say to the sheep?

___ ___ ___ $\frac{4}{9}$ $\frac{1}{3}$ $\frac{4}{9}$

___ ___ ___ $\frac{5}{8}$ $\frac{1}{7}$ $\frac{4}{9}$

___ ___ ___ $\frac{5}{6}$ $\frac{3}{5}$ $\frac{3}{7}$

Slope is a number that tells how slanted a line is. The larger the number, the more the line is slanted. A horizontal line has slope 0.

Slope is written as a ratio comparing the rise of the line (units on y-axis) to the run of the line (units on x-axis). Select two points on the line and starting with the lowest point, figure the rise and run. Slope is written as a fraction in simplest form and never written as a mixed fraction.

$$\text{Slope} = \frac{\text{rise} \uparrow}{\text{run} \rightarrow}$$

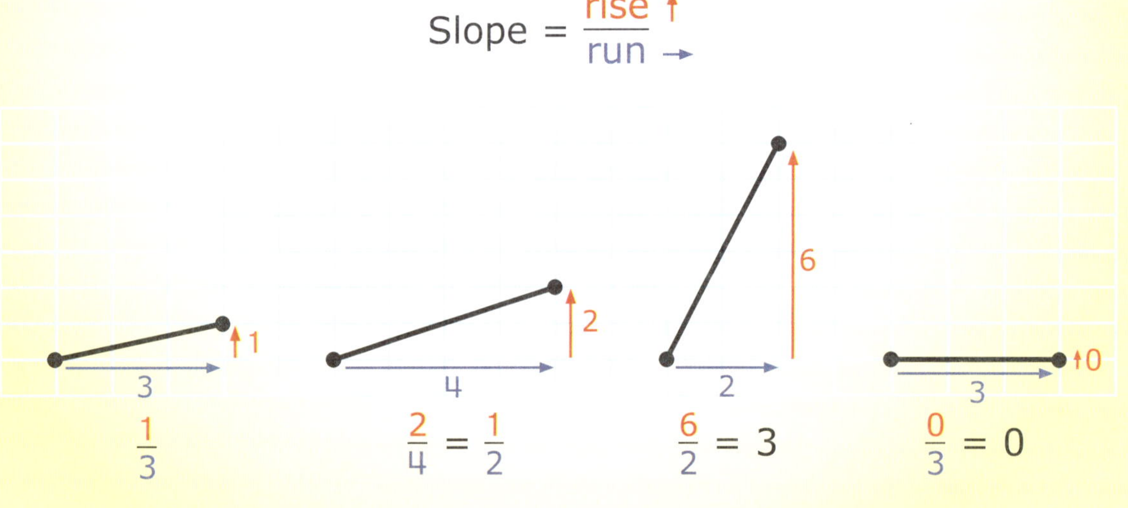

1 What is the slope of the ramp?

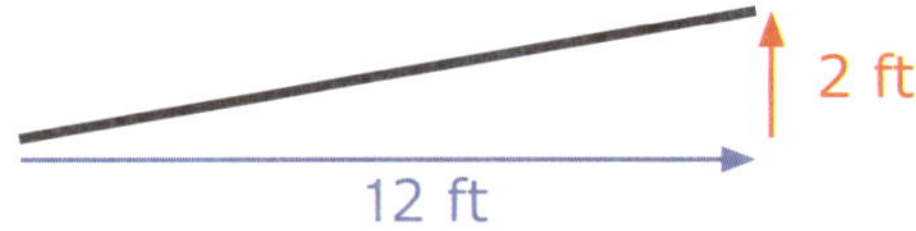

2 What is the slope of the ladder?

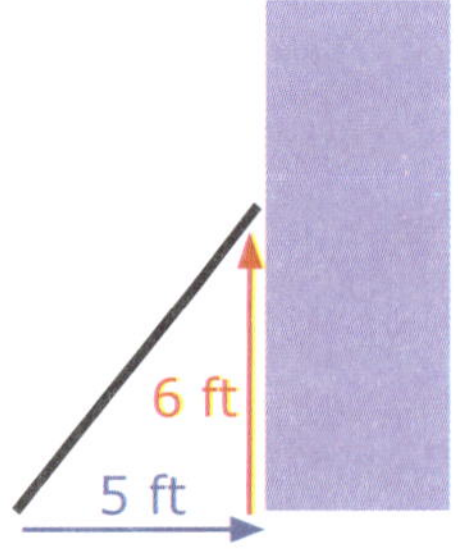

The Americans with Disabilities Act requires a $\frac{1}{12}$ slope for wheelchair ramps for public use.

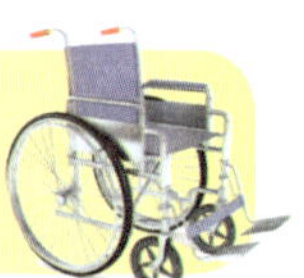

Find the slope of each line.

1. ______

2. ______

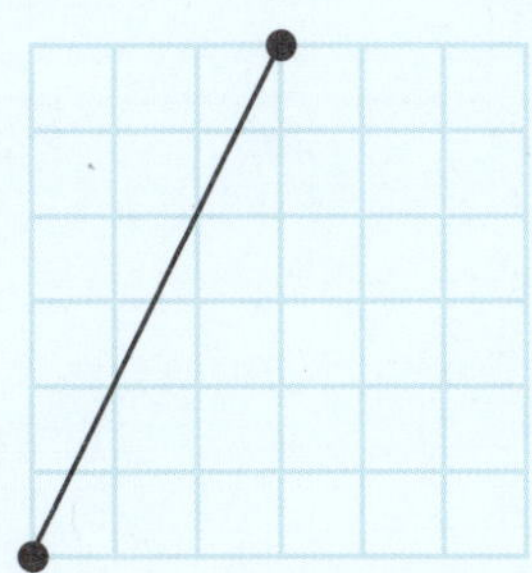

3. ______

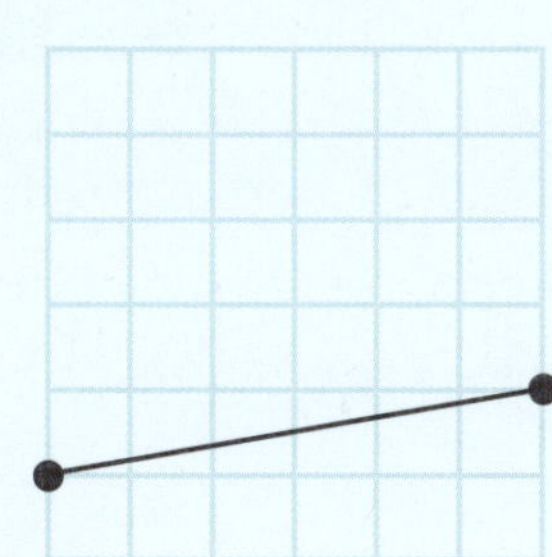

4. ______

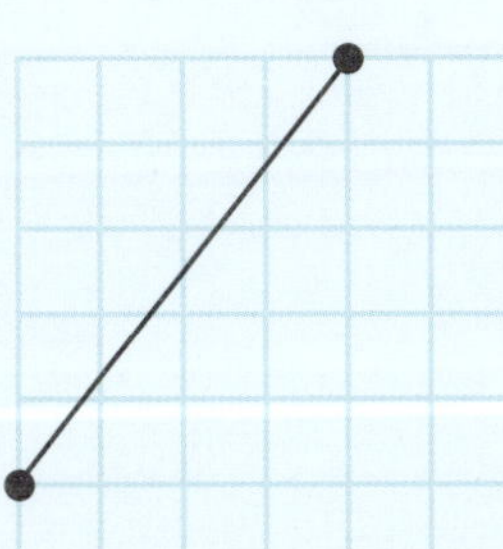

5. ______

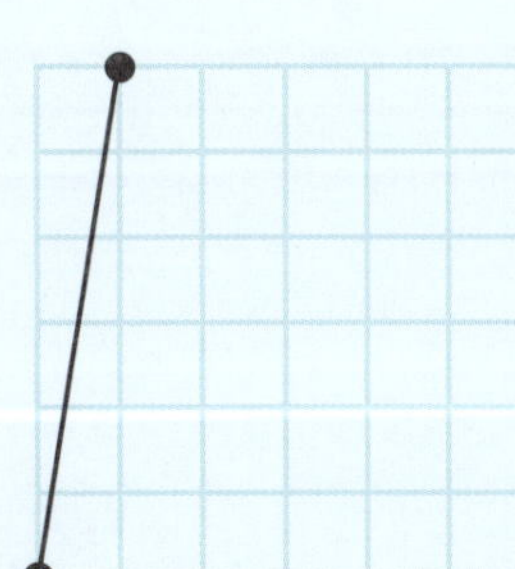

6. ______

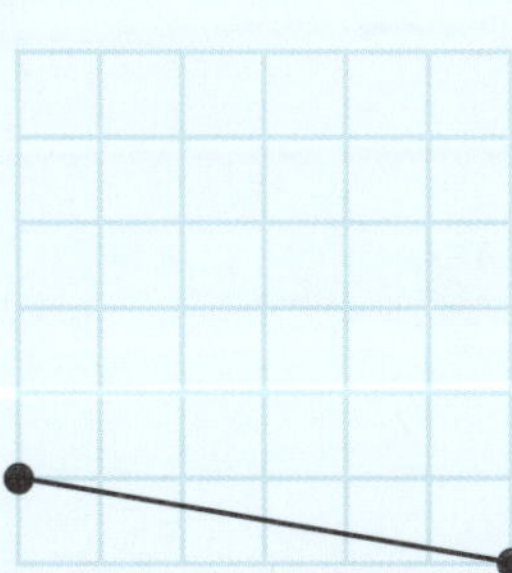

7. ______

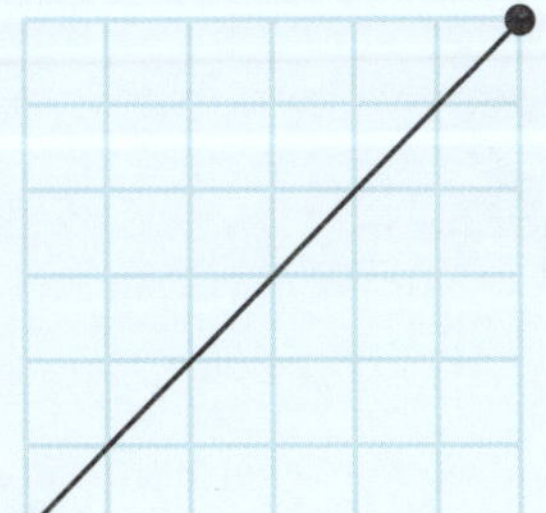

8. ______

9. ______

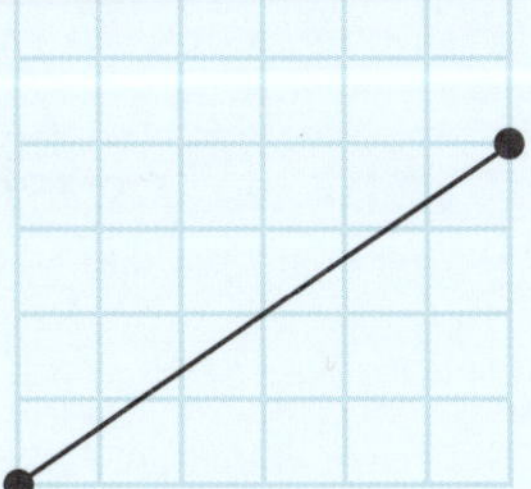

Given equivalent amounts on the first two scales, determine what would be needed on the third scale to show equal amounts.

1

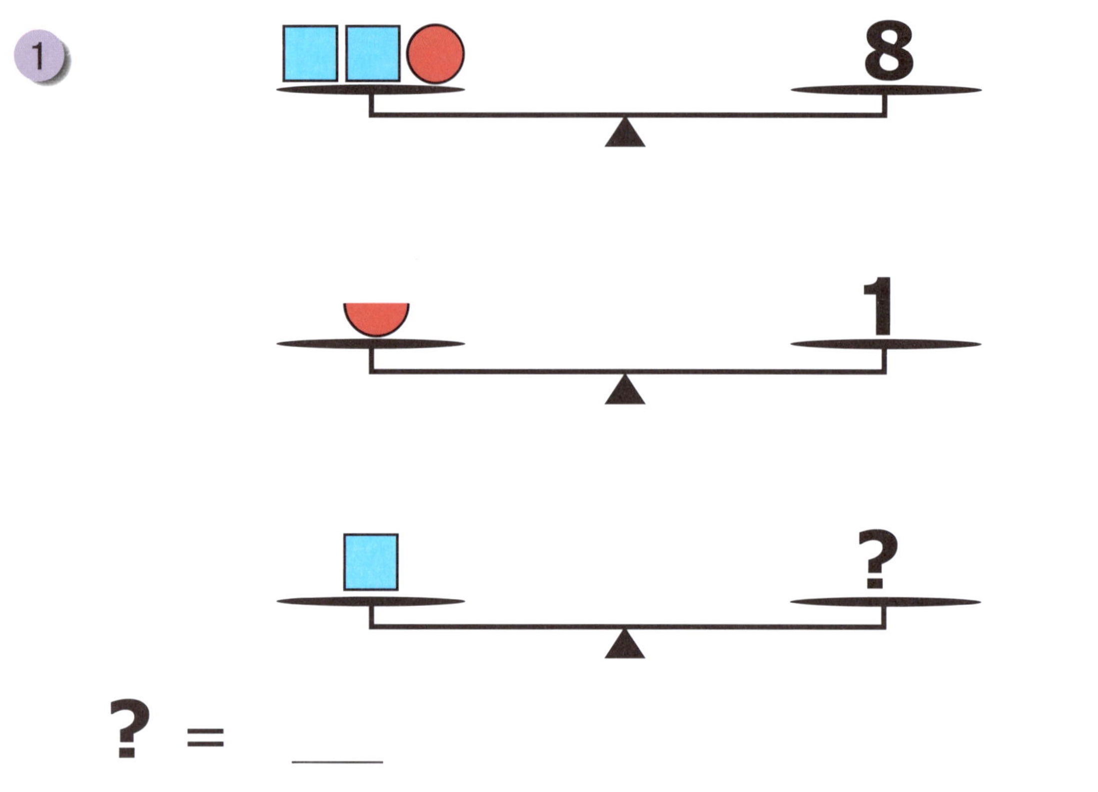

? = ____

2

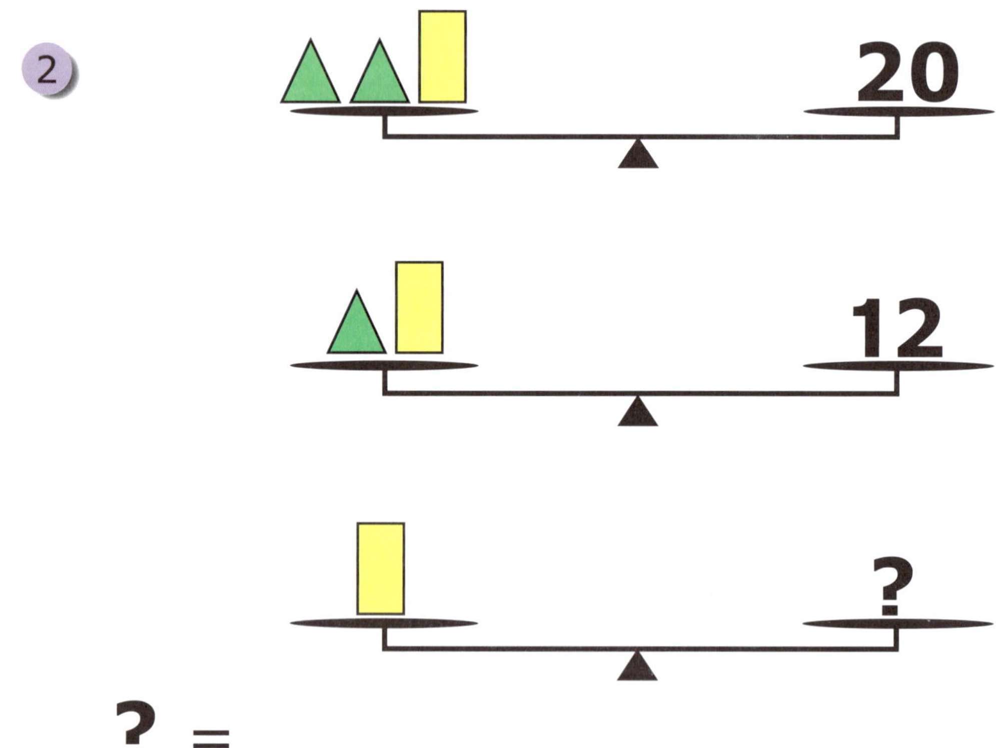

? = ____

For more activities like this, please see our *Balance Math™ and More!* series.

Measurement Vocabulary

range	Celsius	mean	slope	inch	median
millimeter	Fahrenheit	degrees	ordered pair	mode	

Write the correct term from the choice box for each blank.

1. ________________ is the unit used to measure temperature in the metric system.

2. The number that repeats the most in a group of numbers is called the ________________.

3. The measurement of a right angle is 90 ________________.

4. On a rectangular grid, a/an ________________ locates a point.

5. For measuring the length of pencils, a 12 ________________ ruler could be used.

6. ________________ is sometimes called the average.

7. The ________________ is found by subtracting the highest from the lowest number in a group and is used to tell how spread out the numbers are.

8. The number obtained by comparing the rise of a line to its run is called ________________.

9. The exact center of a group of numbers after being placed in order is called the ________________.

10. Water freezes at thirty-two degrees ________________.

11. A/an ________________ is one-tenth of a centimeter.

What do you call 3 feet of trash?
A junkyard.

Tic Tac Total!

Fill in the blanks so that all rows, columns, and two main diagonals add up to the same sum.

5		
9	2	7

8		
13	11	
		14

20		
15		
16	21	

22	29	24
	25	

For more activities like this, please see our *Balance Math™ and More!* series.

The multiple of a number is the product of the number and any other whole number.

Multiples of 2: 2×1, 2×2, 2×3, 2×4, 2×5, ...
2, 4, 6, 8, 10, ...

Multiples of 3: 3, 6, 9, 12, 15, 18, 21, 24, 27, ...

1. Color all squares containing a multiple of 4 for a figure.

35	15	24	22	92
9	50	32	25	12
11	90	40	48	20
51	65	13	27	72
95	22	39	14	60
6	45	9	70	16

2. Color all squares containing a multiple of 9 for a figure.

81	36	45	21	48
72	84	99	30	42
18	90	27	17	35
92	84	63	75	32
28	15	54	24	56
77	48	9	32	68

Different Look, Same Quantity

1 can be written as a fraction with the same numerator and denominator.

$$1 = \frac{2}{2} = \frac{3}{3} = \frac{4}{4} = \frac{5}{5} = \frac{6}{6}$$

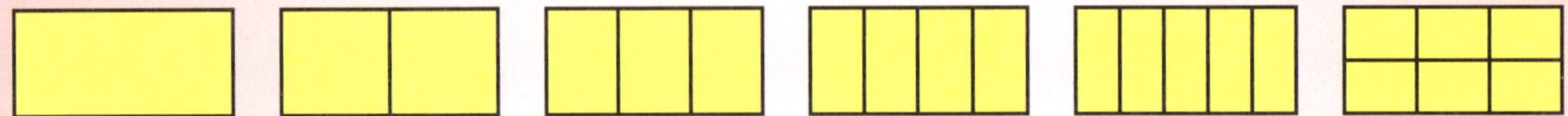

An improper fraction has a numerator greater than its denominator. Improper fractions can be changed to a number that combines a whole number with a fraction called a mixed number.

Change $\frac{7}{4}$ to a mixed number.

$\frac{7}{4}$ equals $4\overline{)7}$ with quotient 1, subtract 4, remainder 3 $= 1\frac{3}{4}$

$$\frac{7}{4} = \qquad = 1\frac{3}{4}$$

Use a piece of paper to write each improper fraction as a mixed number; then use the letters to solve the riddle on the bottom of the next page.

a) $\frac{7}{5}$ = ____

b) $\frac{5}{3}$ = ____

c) $\frac{9}{4}$ = ____

d) $\frac{10}{3}$ = ____

e) $\frac{9}{2}$ = ____

f) $\frac{17}{8}$ = ____

g) $\frac{19}{6}$ = ____

h) $\frac{21}{5}$ = ____

i) $\frac{11}{4}$ = ____

j) $\frac{11}{10}$ = ____ k) $\frac{32}{8}$ = ____ l) $\frac{14}{4}$ = ____

m) $\frac{23}{7}$ = ____ n) $\frac{16}{10}$ = ____ o) $\frac{40}{6}$ = ____

p) $\frac{10}{9}$ = ____ q) $\frac{14}{5}$ = ____ r) $\frac{65}{8}$ = ____

s) $\frac{30}{8}$ = ____ t) $\frac{24}{7}$ = ____ u) $\frac{60}{6}$ = ____

y) Hugh put five one-half cups of blueberries in a bowl. How many cups of blueberries did he put in the bowl? ____

Where do baby monsters stay while their parents go to work?

____ $3\frac{1}{3}$ ____ $1\frac{2}{5}$ ____ $2\frac{1}{2}$ ____ $3\frac{3}{4}$ ____ $2\frac{1}{4}$ ____ $1\frac{2}{5}$ ____ $8\frac{1}{8}$ ____ $4\frac{1}{2}$

____ $2\frac{1}{4}$ ____ $4\frac{1}{2}$ ____ $1\frac{3}{5}$ ____ $3\frac{3}{7}$ ____ $4\frac{1}{2}$ ____ $8\frac{1}{8}$ ____ $3\frac{3}{4}$

To add fractions, start with like fractions (same denominators), then add the numerators. Put the result in simplest form when necessary.

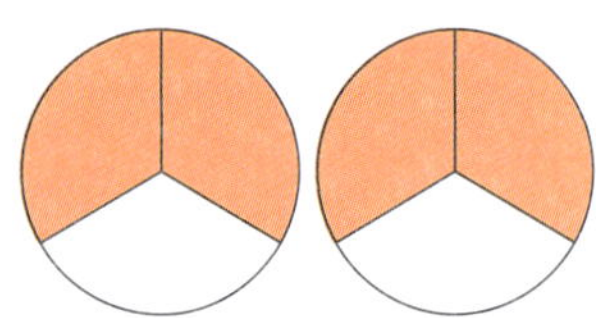

$\frac{2}{3} + \frac{2}{3} = \frac{4}{3} = 1\frac{1}{3}$

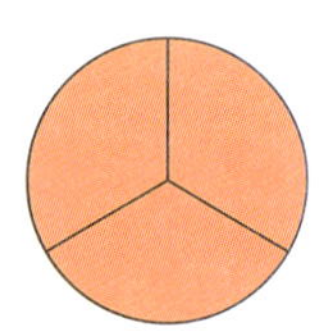
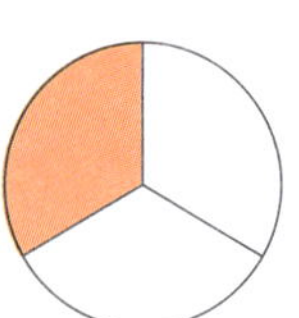

Add; then write the letter of the matching shape on the right.

1. $\frac{1}{3} + \frac{1}{3} =$ _____ _____
2. $\frac{2}{6} + \frac{3}{6} =$ _____ _____
3. $\frac{7}{8} + \frac{2}{8} =$ _____ _____
4. $\frac{3}{4} + \frac{2}{4} =$ _____ _____
5. $\frac{3}{4} + \frac{3}{4} =$ _____ _____
6. $\frac{1}{6} + \frac{5}{6} =$ _____ _____
7. $\frac{1}{4} + \frac{1}{4} =$ _____ _____

a. 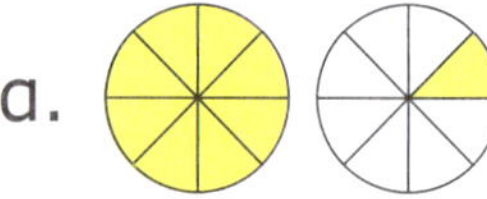

b. 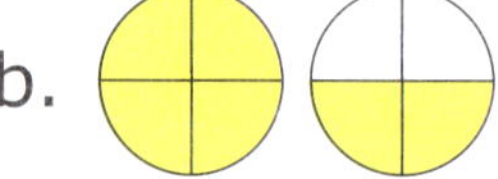

c. 

d.

e. 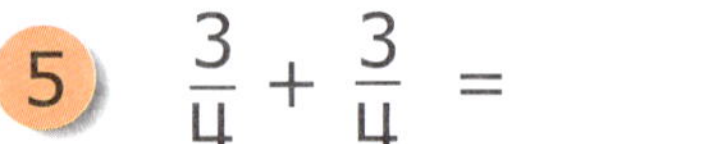 

f. 

g. 

h.

8. Lexie uses $\frac{2}{3}$ cup of sugar to make a batch of cookies.

   If she makes 3 batches of cookies, how much sugar did she use?

   _____ _____

Fast Addition

Mr. Jones decided to give his sixth grade class a problem to do before lunch. He asked them to figure out the sum of the even numbers from 2 through 100. All the students except Sal got out some extra paper to ready themselves for the large addition problem.

Sal said he noticed a pattern and didn't need a lot of paper to figure the problem out. He said all he needed was just enough space on a piece of paper to do one multiplication problem. Mr. Jones had a big smile on his face and asked Sal to give everyone a hint as to how he would do the problem.

Sal wrote the following on the board:

2, 4, 6, 8, 10, 12, 14, ...
100, 98, 96, 94, 92, 90, 88, ...

The other students still did not understand how to find the sum of the even numbers from 2 through 100 quickly. Mr. Jones asked Sal if he could give the class another hint.

Sal made some circles on the board grouping numbers as follows:

2, 4, 6, 8, 10, 12, 14, ...
100, 98, 96, 94, 92, 90, 88, ...

What one multiplication problem can be used to answer the question and why?

Simplest Form

To add mixed fractions with the same denominators, add the whole numbers together and the fractions together. Answers should be in simplest form with no improper fractions.

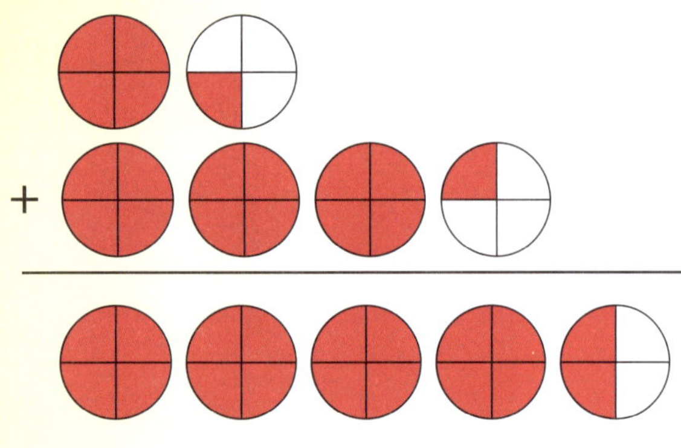

$$\begin{array}{r} 1\frac{1}{4} \\ +\ 3\frac{1}{4} \\ \hline 4\frac{2}{4} \end{array} = 4\frac{1}{2}$$

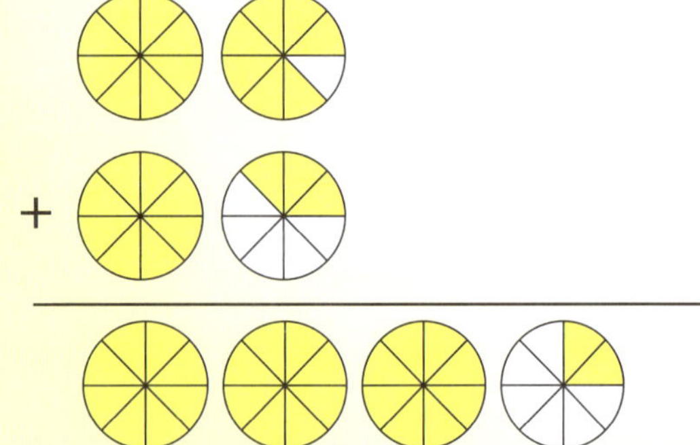

$$\begin{array}{r} 1\frac{7}{8} \\ +\ 1\frac{3}{8} \\ \hline 2\frac{10}{8} \end{array} = 2 + 1\frac{2}{8} = 3\frac{2}{8} = 3\frac{1}{4}$$

Find each sum; then use the letters to solve the riddle on the next page. Put all answers in simplest form.

r) $2\frac{1}{5} + 1\frac{3}{5}$

m) $1\frac{1}{3} + 1\frac{1}{3}$

a) $3\frac{2}{3} + 1\frac{2}{3}$

w) $3\frac{3}{10} + 1\frac{3}{10}$

e) $4\frac{5}{8} + 1\frac{1}{8}$

s) $3\frac{1}{2} + 2\frac{1}{2}$

(o) $1\frac{1}{6} + 1\frac{1}{6}$ = ____

(t) $1\frac{3}{5} + 1\frac{4}{5}$ = ____

(h) $4\frac{3}{4} + \frac{3}{4}$ = ____

(c) $3\frac{5}{6} + 1\frac{5}{6}$ = ____

(x) $2\frac{5}{7} + 1\frac{3}{7}$ = ____

(u) $\frac{7}{8} + 2\frac{5}{8}$ = ____

(b) Glen had a rope $2\frac{1}{8}$ feet long. The rope should have been $1\frac{5}{8}$ feet longer. How long should the rope have been? ____

What did the son of a clock maker say to his father?

____	____	____	____	____
$4\frac{3}{5}$	$5\frac{1}{3}$	$3\frac{2}{5}$	$5\frac{2}{3}$	$5\frac{1}{2}$

____	____
$2\frac{2}{3}$	$5\frac{3}{4}$

Mystery Number

Use the clues below to find which number in the array is the mystery number.

1. is not prime
2. is even
3. is a factor of 180
4. is a multiple of 15
5. is evenly divisible by 4

1	2	3	4	5	6	7	8	9	10
11	12	13	14	15	16	17	18	19	20
21	22	23	24	25	26	27	28	29	30
31	32	33	34	35	36	37	38	39	40
41	42	43	44	45	46	47	48	49	50
51	52	53	54	55	56	57	58	59	60
61	62	63	64	65	66	67	68	69	70
71	72	73	74	75	76	77	78	79	80
81	82	83	84	85	86	87	88	89	90
91	92	93	94	95	96	97	98	99	100

ANSWER: ______

For a group of numbers, the least common multiple (LCM) is the smallest number each can divide into evenly.

Multiples of 3: 3, 6, 9, 12, 15, 18, ...
Multiples of 4: 4, 8, 12, 16, 20, 24, ...

The least common multiple for 3 and 4 is 12.
12 is the smallest number both 3 and 4 divide into evenly.

Multiples of 2: 2, 4, 8, 10, 12, 14, ...
Multiples of 8: 8, 16, 24, 32, ...

LCM for 2 and 8 is 8.

1. Multiples of 6:
Multiples of 9:
LCM is ____.

2. Multiples of 4:
Multiples of 6:
LCM is ____.

3. Multiples of 15:
Multiples of 10:
LCM is ____.

4. Multiples of 6:
Multiples of 8:
LCM is ____.

5. Multiples of 3:
Multiples of 7:
LCM is ____.

6. Multiples of 9:
Multiples of 12:
Multiples of 4:
LCM is ____.

When finding the LCM for denominators, it is called the least common denominator (LCD). Find the LCD by writing the multiples of each denominator until a common number is found. The LCD for $\frac{1}{2}$ and $\frac{1}{3}$ is 6.

$\frac{1}{2} \rightarrow 2, 4, 6$
$\frac{1}{3} \rightarrow 3, 6$

7. Find the least common denominator for $\frac{1}{3}$ and $\frac{1}{8}$.
LCD is ____.

Only add fractions when they are like fractions (same denominators). If the denominators are different, make them like fractions using the lowest common demominator (LCD), and then add the numerators. Put the result in simplest form when necessary.

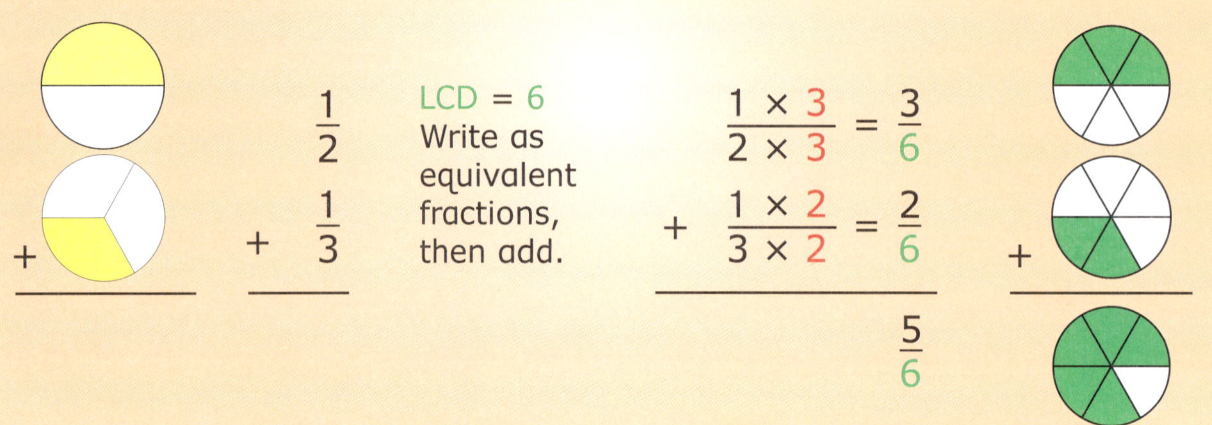

Add; then cross out the correct answers on the next page to find the two false answers.

1. $\frac{1}{2} + \frac{1}{4}$

2. $\frac{1}{6} + \frac{2}{3}$

3. $\frac{1}{3} + \frac{1}{4}$

4. $\frac{1}{6} + \frac{1}{4}$

5. $\frac{2}{5} + \frac{3}{10}$

6. $\frac{1}{6} + \frac{2}{9}$

7. $\frac{1}{2} + \frac{1}{8}$ ______

8. $\frac{1}{3} + \frac{2}{9}$ ______

9. $\frac{2}{7} + \frac{2}{3}$ ______

10. Ryan had a board $\frac{1}{2}$ inch thick, which he placed on another board $\frac{3}{16}$ inch thick. What was the combined thickness of the boards?

______

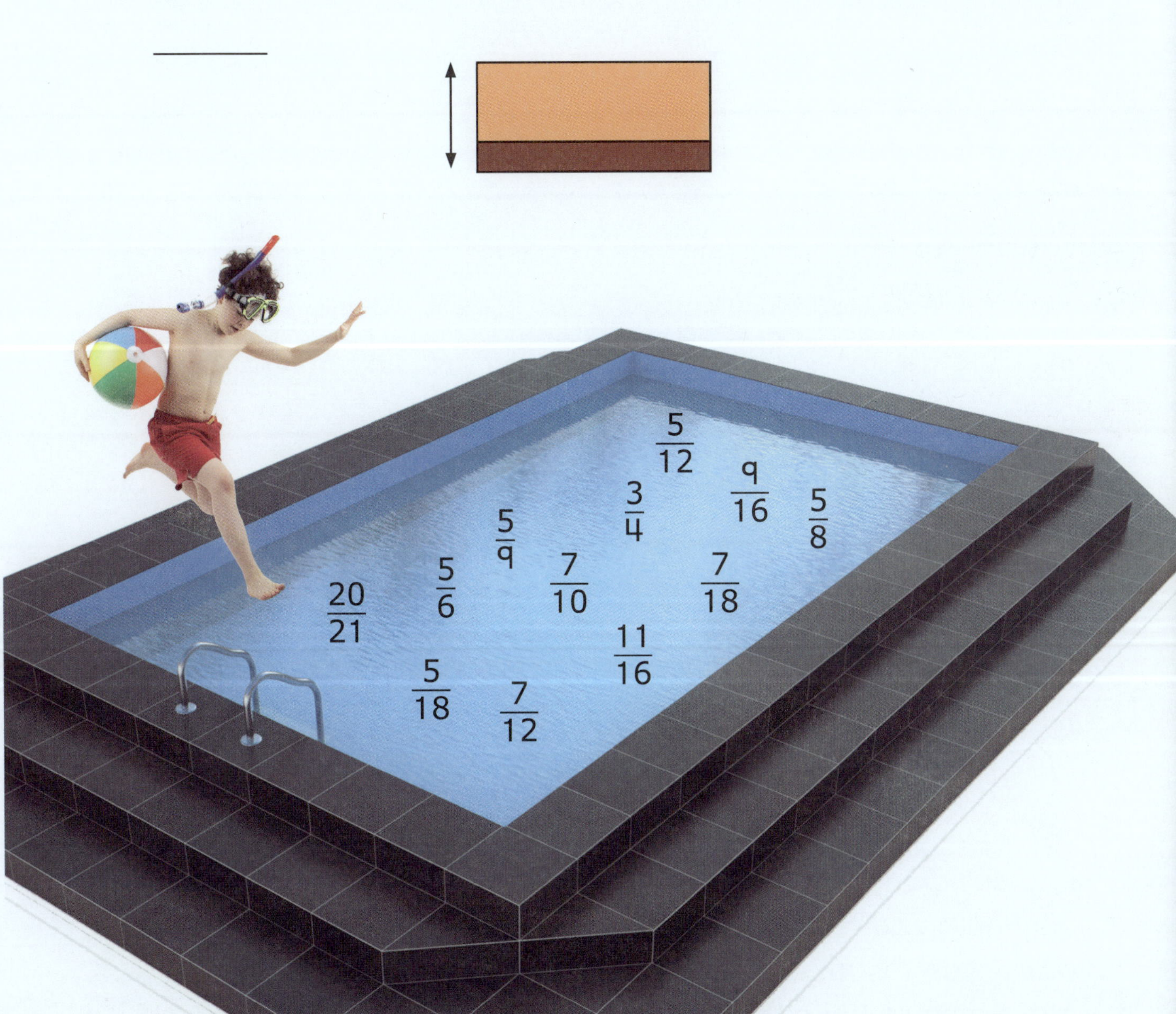

To subtract fractions, start with like fractions (same denominators) then subtract the numerators. Put the result in simplest form when necessary.

$\frac{5}{6} - \frac{1}{6} = \frac{4}{6} = \frac{2}{3}$

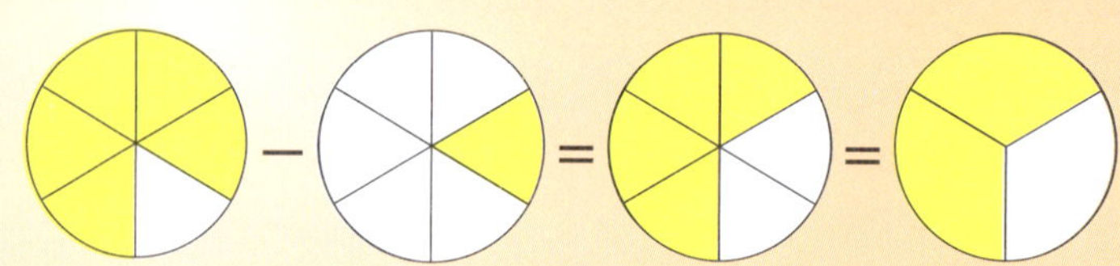

Subtract; then write the letter of the matching figure on the right.

1. $\frac{2}{3} - \frac{1}{3} =$ _____ _____
2. $\frac{7}{8} - \frac{6}{8} =$ _____ _____
3. $\frac{7}{8} - \frac{5}{8} =$ _____ _____
4. $\frac{5}{6} - \frac{1}{6} =$ _____ _____
5. $\frac{7}{8} - \frac{2}{8} =$ _____ _____
6. $\frac{2}{6} - \frac{1}{6} =$ _____ _____
7. $\frac{3}{4}$ hour − $\frac{1}{4}$ hour = _____ _____
8. Rod put $\frac{7}{8}$ cup of butter in a banana bread recipe. If that was $\frac{1}{8}$ cup too much, how much butter should be in the recipe?

_____ _____

a. b. c. d. e. f. g. h.

To subtract fractions, start with like fractions (same denominators) then subtract the numerators. Put the result in simplest form when necessary.

Remember: $1 = \frac{2}{2} = \frac{3}{3} = \frac{4}{4} = \frac{5}{5} = \frac{6}{6}$ and so on.

Whole pizza – 1 piece =

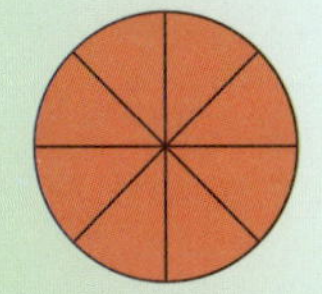 – 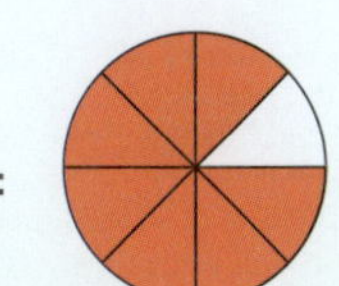 =

$1 - \frac{1}{8} =$

$\frac{8}{8} - \frac{1}{8} = \frac{7}{8}$

Subtract; then cross out the correct answers below to find the two false answers.

1. $1 - \frac{3}{8} =$ ____
2. $1 - \frac{3}{4} =$ ____
3. $1 - \frac{1}{3} =$ ____
4. $1 - \frac{4}{6} =$ ____
5. $1 - \frac{1}{6} =$ ____
6. $1 - \frac{5}{8} =$ ____
7. $1 - \frac{1}{4} =$ ____
8. $1 - \frac{1}{2} =$ ____
9. $1 - \frac{10}{12} =$ ____

Simplest Form

If you saw $1\frac{1}{4}$ feet off a $2\frac{3}{4}$ foot board, how much of the board is left?

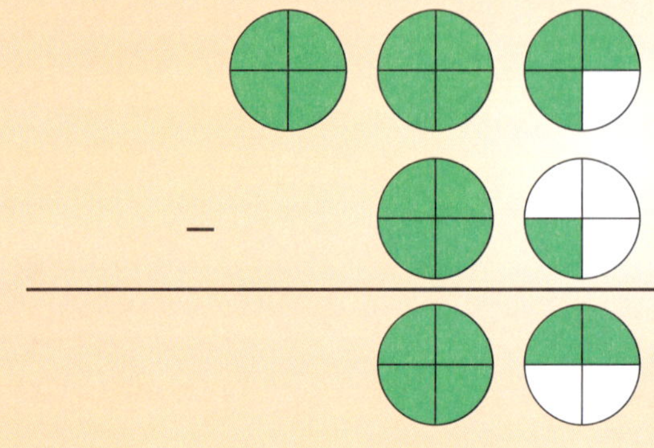

$$\begin{array}{r} 2\frac{3}{4} \\ -\ 1\frac{1}{4} \\ \hline 1\frac{2}{4} = 1\frac{1}{2} \end{array}$$

Find each difference and use the letters to solve the riddle on the next page. Put all answers in simplest form.

s $\begin{array}{r} 4\frac{5}{6} \\ -\ 2\frac{1}{6} \\ \hline \end{array}$

e $\begin{array}{r} 2\frac{2}{4} \\ -\ 1\frac{1}{4} \\ \hline \end{array}$

b $\begin{array}{r} 5\frac{5}{8} \\ -\ 3\frac{3}{8} \\ \hline \end{array}$

m $\begin{array}{r} 7\frac{7}{10} \\ -\ 5\frac{1}{10} \\ \hline \end{array}$

v $\begin{array}{r} 6\frac{7}{8} \\ -\ 4\frac{1}{8} \\ \hline \end{array}$

u $\begin{array}{r} 5\frac{3}{6} \\ -\ 4\frac{1}{6} \\ \hline \end{array}$

g $\begin{array}{r} 9\frac{7}{10} \\ -\ 8\frac{3}{10} \\ \hline \end{array}$

o $\begin{array}{r} 6\frac{11}{12} \\ -\ 4\frac{5}{12} \\ \hline \end{array}$

t $\begin{array}{r} 8\frac{1}{3} \\ -\ 5\frac{1}{3} \\ \hline \end{array}$

r) $\begin{array}{r} 9\frac{14}{15} \\ -\ 7\frac{2}{15} \\ \hline \end{array}$

l) $\begin{array}{r} 3\frac{5}{6} \\ -\ 2\frac{5}{6} \\ \hline \end{array}$

a) $\begin{array}{r} 1 \\ -\ \frac{1}{3} \\ \hline \end{array}$

w) Malia spent $3\frac{3}{4}$ hours baby sitting for a friend. She usually baby sits for $2\frac{1}{4}$ hours. How much longer did she baby sit than normal? ________

What tables should you eat everyday?

___	___	___	___	___	___	___	___	___	___
$2\frac{3}{4}$	$1\frac{1}{4}$	$1\frac{2}{5}$	$1\frac{1}{4}$	3	$\frac{2}{3}$	$2\frac{1}{4}$	1	$1\frac{1}{4}$	$2\frac{2}{3}$

Only subtract like fractions (same denominators). If the denominators are different, change the fractions to like fractions using the LCD before subtracting. Put the result in simplest form when necessary.

$$\begin{array}{r} \frac{7}{8} \\ -\ \frac{3}{4} \\ \hline \end{array}$$

LCD = 8
Write as equivalent fractions, then subtract.

$$\begin{array}{rcl} \frac{7}{8} & = & \frac{7}{8} \\ -\ \frac{3}{4} = \frac{3 \times 2}{4 \times 2} & = & \frac{6}{8} \\ \hline & & \frac{1}{8} \end{array}$$

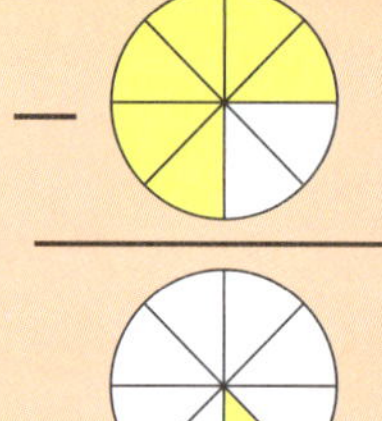

Subtract and use the letters to solve the riddle on the next page.

p $\begin{array}{r} \frac{3}{4} \\ -\ \frac{1}{2} \\ \hline \end{array}$

u $\begin{array}{r} \frac{5}{8} \\ -\ \frac{1}{2} \\ \hline \end{array}$

l $\begin{array}{r} \frac{1}{2} \\ -\ \frac{1}{3} \\ \hline \end{array}$

t $\begin{array}{r} \frac{5}{6} \\ -\ \frac{1}{4} \\ \hline \end{array}$

h $\begin{array}{r} \frac{7}{9} \\ -\ \frac{1}{3} \\ \hline \end{array}$

w $\begin{array}{r} \frac{5}{6} \\ -\ \frac{4}{9} \\ \hline \end{array}$

o $\frac{4}{5} - \frac{2}{3} =$ ____

a $\frac{3}{4} - \frac{2}{3} =$ ____

m $\frac{5}{7} - \frac{1}{2} =$ ____

r $\frac{5}{6} - \frac{1}{12} =$ ____

e $\frac{4}{5} - \frac{3}{4} =$ ____

s $\frac{3}{4} - \frac{2}{9} =$ ____

b What is the difference between $\frac{1}{2}$ hour and one minute ($\frac{1}{2}$ hour − $\frac{1}{60}$ hour)? ____________________

Where do baseball players like to eat their lunches?

___	___	___	___		___	___	___	___	___
$\frac{4}{9}$	$\frac{2}{15}$	$\frac{3}{14}$	$\frac{1}{20}$		$\frac{1}{4}$	$\frac{1}{6}$	$\frac{1}{12}$	$\frac{7}{12}$	$\frac{1}{20}$

Equation Mystery!

Using only the numbers above, fill in the missing digits in the following equations. No number may be used more than once in an equation. Remember order of operations.

1. 5 8 × 4 = 232
2. ___ ___ ÷ ___ = 13
3. ___ ___ × ___ = 360
4. ___ ___ × ___ + ___ = 295
5. ___ × ___ × ___ = 140
6. ___ ___ ÷ ___ = 17
7. ___ ___ ___ ÷ ___ = 52
8. ___ ___ × ___ = 483
9. ___ × ___ ÷ ___ = 10
10. ___ ___ × ___ ___ = 3,120

< is the symbol for less than
> is the symbol for greater than

To compare fractions, start with like fractions (same denominators), then compare the numerators.

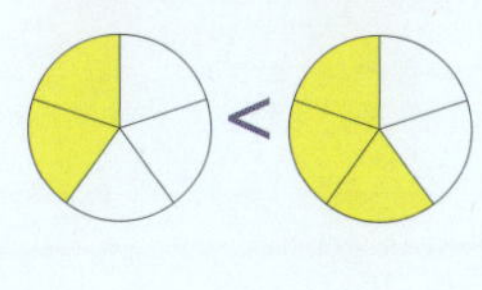

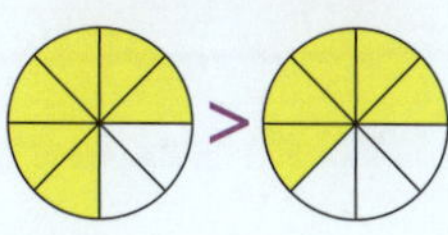

Place <, >, or = between the two amounts.

1. $\frac{7}{8}$ cup of sugar ◯ $\frac{3}{8}$ cup of sugar

2. $\frac{5}{6}$ inch ◯ $\frac{3}{4}$ inch

3. $\frac{2}{3}$ cup of milk ◯ $\frac{5}{8}$ cup of milk

4. $\frac{1}{4}$ hour ◯ $\frac{1}{3}$ hour

5. $\frac{5}{9}$ cm ◯ $\frac{5}{6}$ cm

6. $\frac{4}{11}$ probability ◯ $\frac{1}{3}$ probability

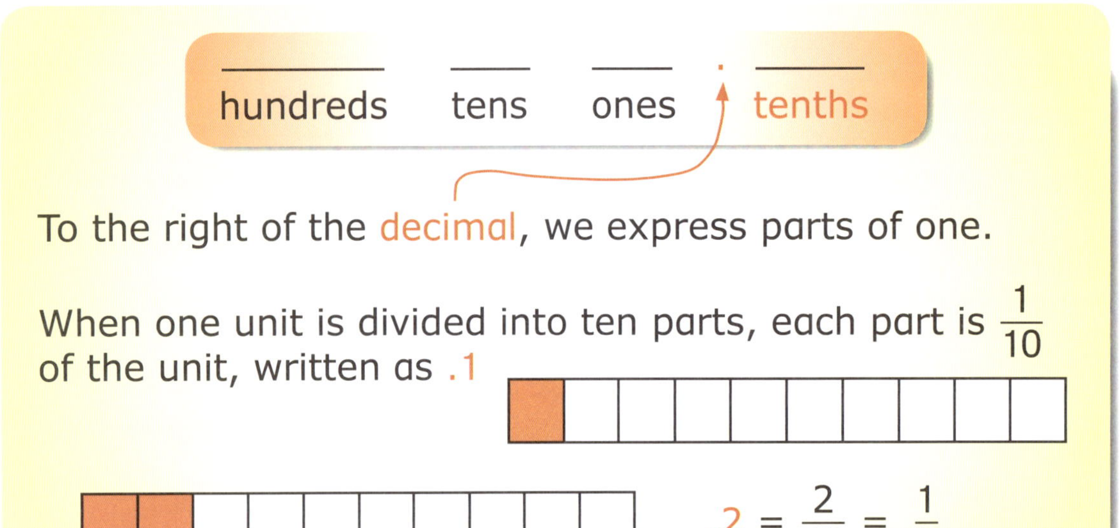

Write the following as decimals and equivalent fractions.

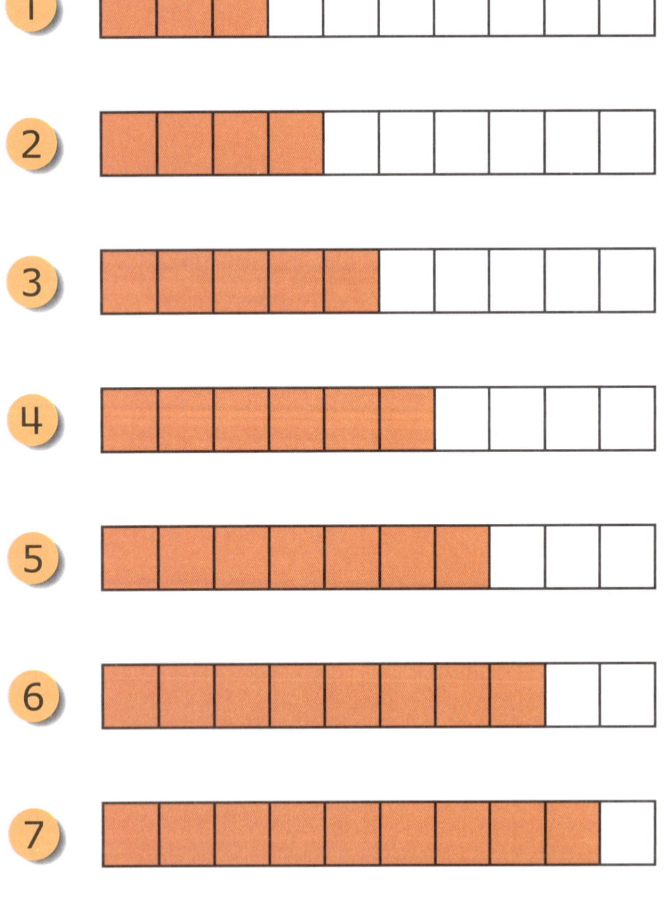

	Decimal	Fraction
1		
2		
3		
4		
5		
6		
7		
8		

___ ___ ___ . ___ ___

hundreds tens ones tenths hundredths

To the right of the decimal, we express parts of one. When one unit is divided into a hundred parts, each part is $\frac{1}{100}$ of the unit, written as .01

$.50 = \frac{50}{100} = \frac{1}{2}$

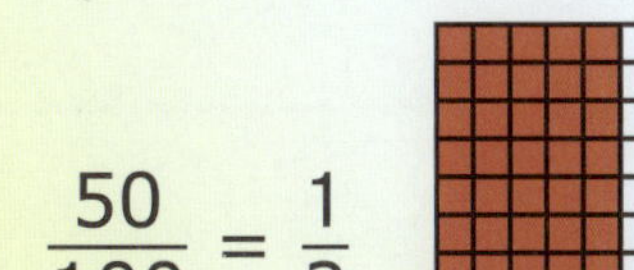

Note: .50 = .5

Write the following as decimals and equivalent fractions.

1

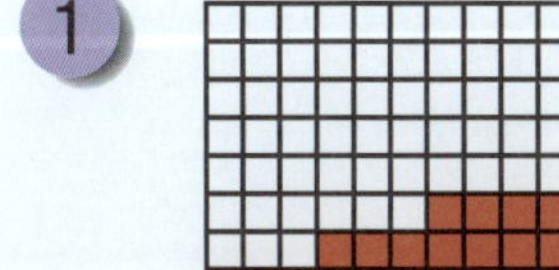

2

3 4

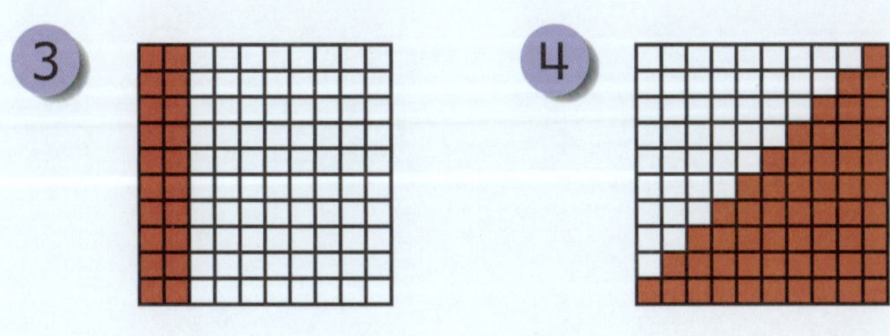

5

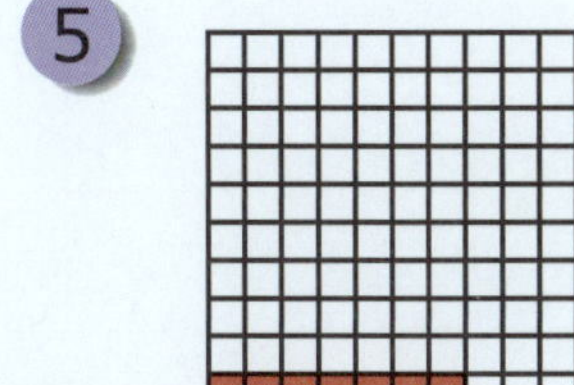

6

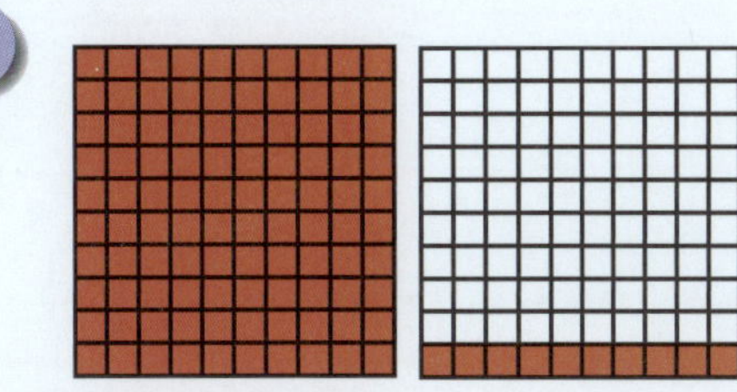

	Decimal	Fraction
1		
2		
3		
4		
5		
6		

Place the numbers in the table below in their correct position on the number line.

1.2	5	.9	9.25	10.5
3.15	9.7	8.3	2.7	11.05
4.5	1.9	7	5.8	3.83

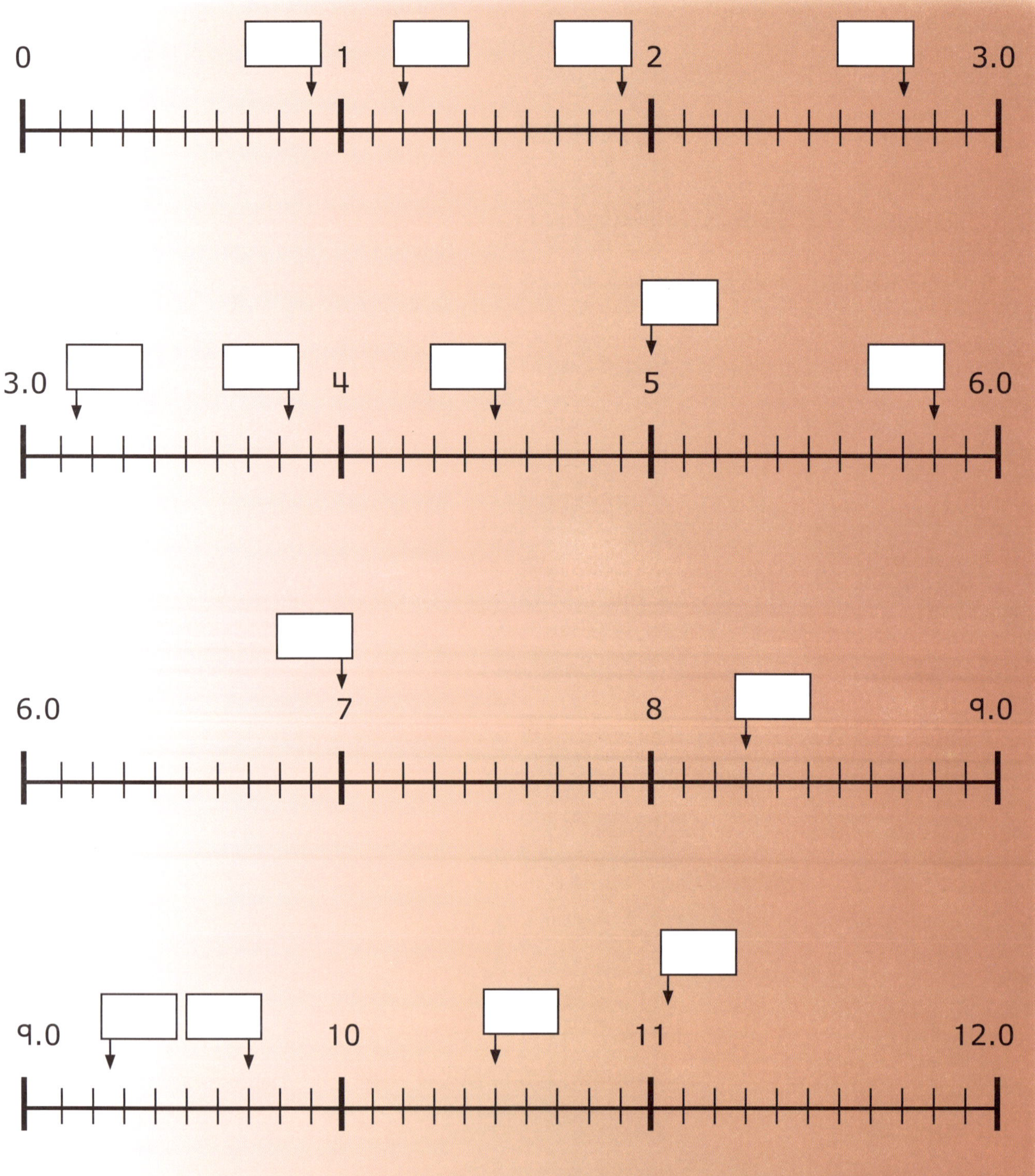

When reading a number with a decimal in it, the decimal is read as and. The decimal separates whole numbers from part of a whole.

• = and

eight and five tenths = 8.5 

two hundred and eight hundredths = 200.08

Write each in number form below.

1. twenty-five and fourteen hundredths
2. one thousand and two tenths
3. sixteen hundredths
4. five hundred one and one hundredth
5. two thousand three
6. three and three hundredths
7. eight thousand seventeen and one tenth
8. one hundred and one hundredth
9. two thousand two hundred and two hundredths
10. sixty and sixty hundredths

1. __ __ . __ __	2. __ __ __ __ . __
3. . __ __	4. __ __ __ . __ __
5. __ __ __ __	6. __ . __ __
7. __ __ __ __ . __	8. __ __ __ . __ __
9. __ __ __ __ . __ __	10. __ __ . __ __

Under the rules of golf, a golf ball weighs no more than 1.62 ounces and has a diameter not less than 1.68 inches.

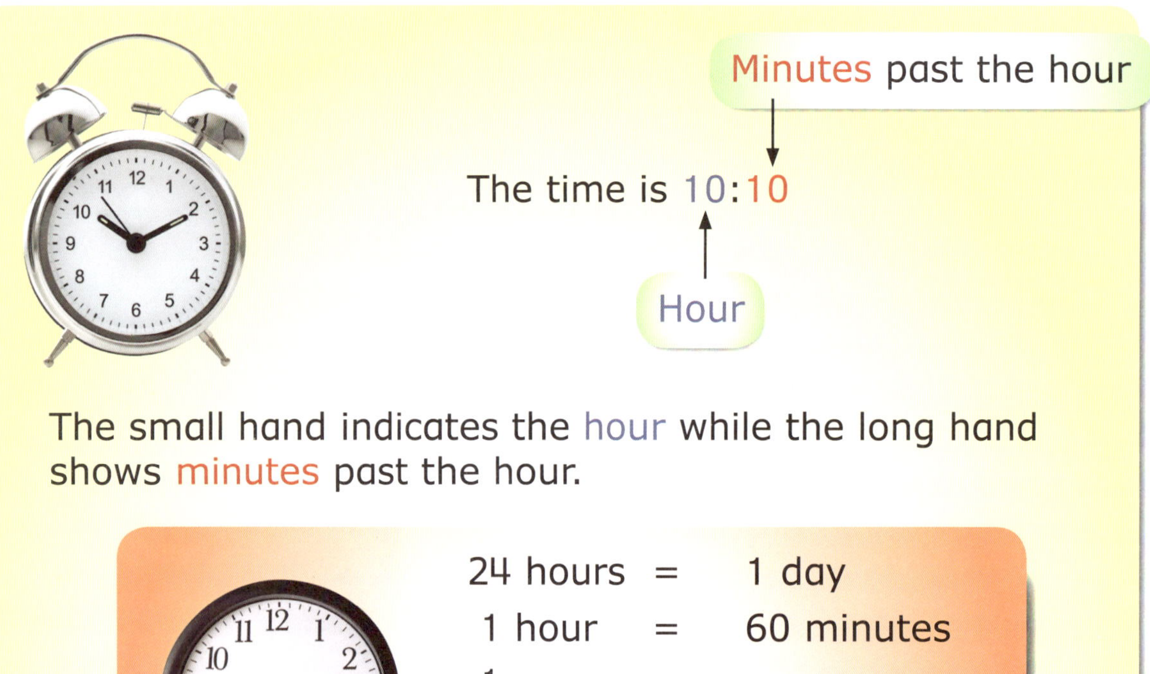

The small hand indicates the hour while the long hand shows minutes past the hour.

9:35

24 hours	=	1 day
1 hour	=	60 minutes
$\frac{1}{2}$ hour	=	30 minutes
$\frac{1}{4}$ hour	=	15 minutes
$\frac{3}{4}$ hour	=	45 minutes

10 minutes later than 1:40 is

$$\begin{array}{r} 1{:}40 \\ +\ 10 \\ \hline 1{:}50 \end{array}$$

$\frac{1}{4}$ hour later than 9:50 is

(Note: 60 minutes = 1 hour)

$$\begin{array}{r} 9{:}50 \\ +\ 15 \\ \hline 10{:}05 \end{array}$$

Determine each time; then use the letters to solve the riddle on the next page.

c) 25 minutes after 11:30 is ______.

h) $\frac{1}{2}$ hour after 4:20 is ______.

i) $\frac{1}{4}$ hour after 1:17 is ______.

e) 55 minutes after 3:10 is ______.

(w) $\frac{3}{4}$ hour after 2:05 is _____.

(a) 35 minutes after 2:17 is _____.

(s) 24 minutes after 9:45 is _____.

(b) 1 hour 10 minutes after 3:00 is _____.

(y) 3 hours 30 minutes after 1:35 is _____.

(r) 2 hours 18 minutes after 2:27 is _____.

(u) $\frac{1}{2}$ hour after 11:45 is _____.

(o) 75 minutes after 11:55 is _____.

What do rabbits do to exercise?

_____	_____	_____	_____	_____	_____	_____	_____	_____
4:50	2:52	4:45	4:05	1:10	4:10	1:32	11:55	10:09

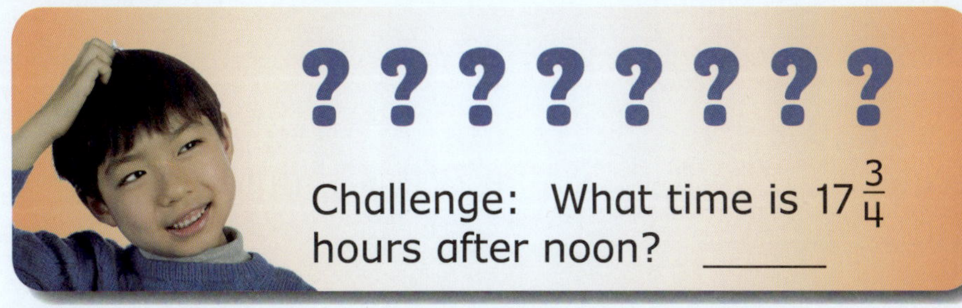

? ? ? ? ? ? ? ?

Challenge: What time is $17\frac{3}{4}$ hours after noon? _____

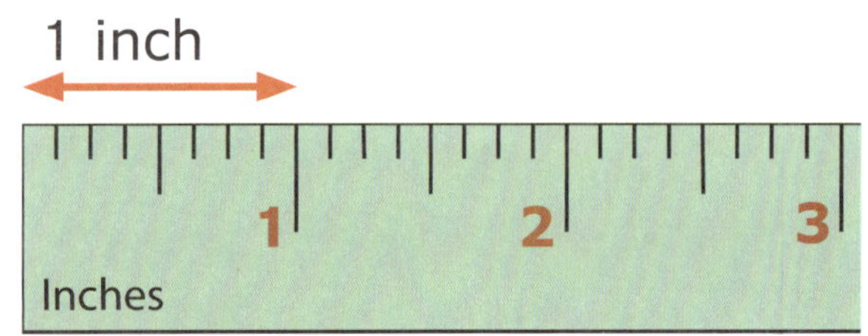

1 foot (ft or ') = 12 inches (in. or ")

2 ft = 2 × 12 = 24 inches or 24"

3 feet 5 inches = 3'5" = 36 + 5 = 41 inches

Write the equivalent quantity for each problem; then cross out the correct answers on the right to find the two false answers.

1) 4 feet = ______

2) 2'9" = ______

3) 10' = ______

4) 5'6" = ______

5) 6 feet = ______

6) 4'11" = ______

33"

66"

53"

72"

84"

59"

48"

120"

7) There are 5,280 ft in a mile. How many inches are in a mile? __________

A stack of a thousand $1 bills is about 4" high!

4"

A **three-dimensional figure** has width, length, and height.

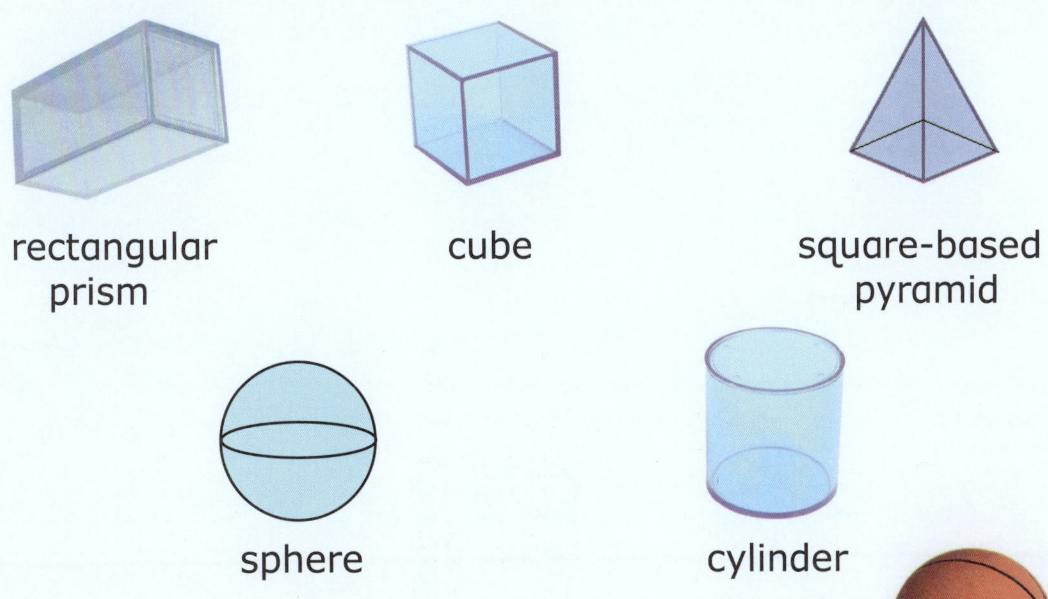

A face is a flat side of a figure.

An edge is where two faces meet.

A vertex is where three or more edges meet.

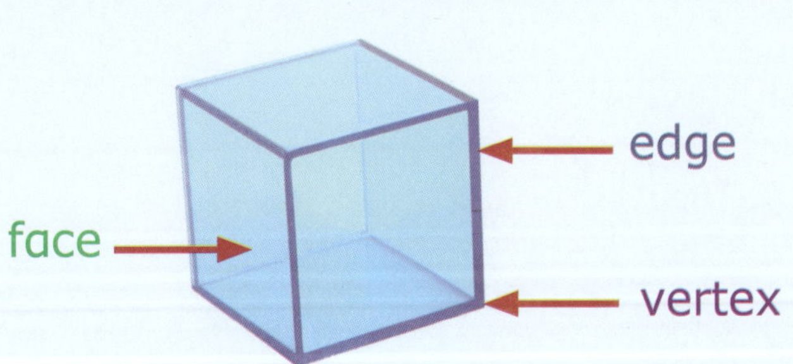

Fill in the chart below with the correct number of faces, edges, and vertices for each shape listed.

Three-Dimensional Figure	Faces	Edges	Vertices
rectangular prism			
cube			
square-based pyramid			

Lines that meet are called intersecting lines. 

Lines in the same plane that are equal distance from each other are called parallel lines. 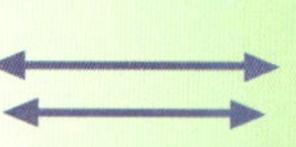

Lines that intersect and form a right angle are called perpendicular lines. 

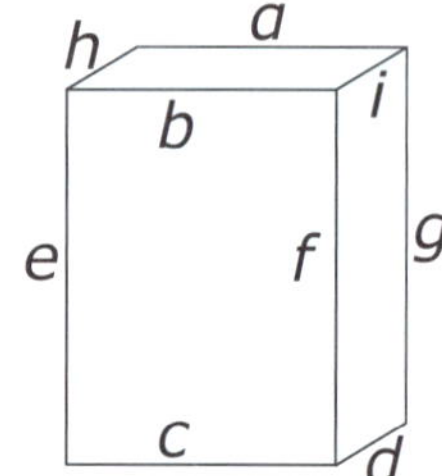

Write *true* or *false* for each statement.

1. Line *a* is parallel to line *b*. ________
2. Line *e* is parallel to line *g*. ________
3. Line *h* is parallel to line *a*. ________
4. Line *c* is perpendicular to line *d*. ________
5. Line *e* is perpendicular to line *h*. ________
6. Line *b* is perpendicular to line c. ________

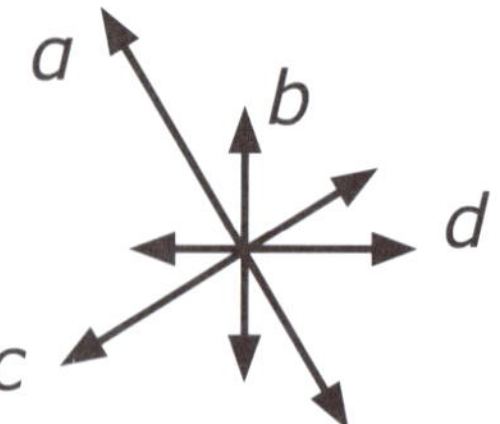

7. What line is perpendicular to line *a*? ________
8. What line is perpendicular to line *b*? ________

1. Place the numbers 1, 2, 3, and 4 in the grid so each column, row, and main diagonal has one of each number.

2			

English	Japanese
1	一
2	二
3	三
4	四

2. Place the numbers 一, 二, 三, and 四 in the grid so each column, row, and main diagonal has one of each number.

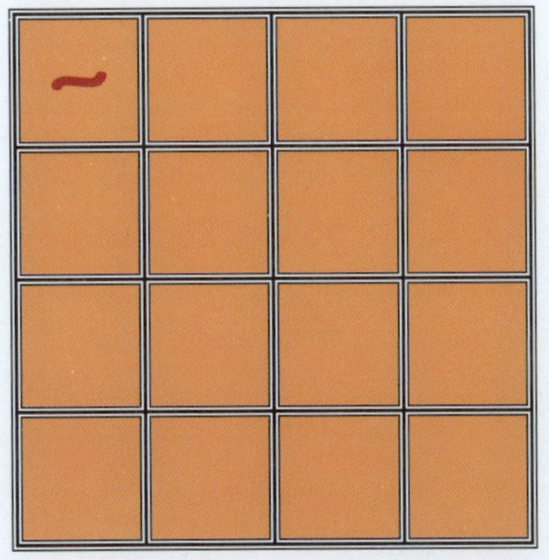

Given equivalent amounts on the first two scales, determine what would be needed on the third scale to show equal amounts.

1

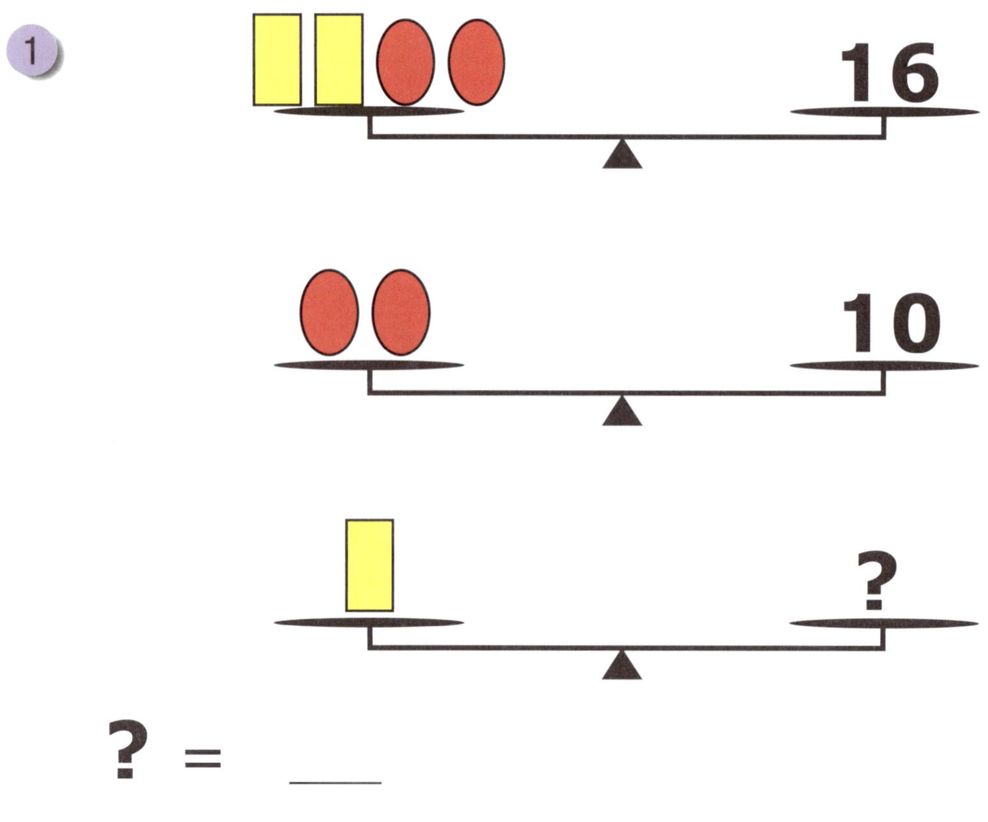

? = ____

2

18

8

?

? = ____

For more activities like this, please see our *Balance Math™ and More!* series.

The probability or chance of something happening can be written as a fraction with the denominator as the total number of choices and the numerator as the number of choices considered.

$$\text{Probability} = \frac{\text{number of choices considered}}{\text{total number of choices}}$$

A penny has two sides called heads and tails.

The chance or probability of a toss of a penny being a head is given by a fraction.

$$\frac{\text{number of choices considered}}{\text{total number of choices}} = \frac{\text{heads}}{\text{heads} + \text{tails}} = \frac{1}{2}$$

The game spinners indicate the number of spaces to move on a game board. Reduce fractions to simplest form.

1. Probability of moving 1 space is ______
2. Probability of moving 2 spaces is ______
3. Probability of moving 3 spaces is ______

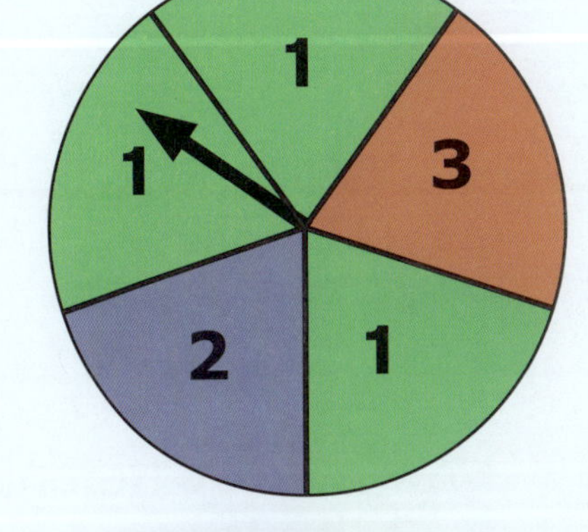

4. Probability of moving 2 spaces is ______
5. Probability of moving 3 spaces is ______
6. Probability of moving 1 space is ______

Using the digits 1 and 2, how many different two-digit numbers can be formed?

1 2 and 2 1

The numbers 12 and 21 can be formed.

1) List the different 3-digit numbers that can be formed using a **1**, **2**, and **3**.

___ ___ ___ ___ ___ ___

2) List the different 4-digit numbers that can be formed using a **1**, **2**, **3**, and **4**.

___ ___ ___ ___
___ ___ ___ ___
___ ___ ___ ___
___ ___ ___ ___
___ ___ ___ ___
___ ___ ___ ___

3) How many different 5-digit numbers can be formed using a **1**, **2**, **3**, **4**, and **5**? _____

4) Can you discover a pattern that would figure out how many different number combinations are possible given a certain number of digits?

Kurt saves $15.25 a week from his $20 mowing job in the summer. He wants to keep an accurate record of his savings. Complete his record.

Date	Amount Added	Total
		$0.00
6/15	$15.25	+$15.25
		$15.25
6/22	$15.25	+$15.25
		$30.50
6/29	$15.25	+$15.25
7/6	$15.25	+$15.25
7/13	$15.25	+$15.25
7/20	$15.25	+$15.25
7/27	$15.25	+$15.25
8/3	$15.25	+$15.25

TOTAL SAVINGS

1. Kurt checked his work by multiplying $15.25 by 8.

$$\begin{array}{r} \$15.25 \\ \times \quad 8 \\ \hline \end{array}$$

2. How much would he have at the end of the summer if he saved $16.75 per week instead of $15.25? ________

Date	Amount
	$1,000.00
1/31	-$65.39
	$934.61
2/28	- $65.39
	$869.22
3/31	- $65.39
4/30	- $65.39
5/31	- $65.39
6/30	- $65.39
7/31	- $65.39
8/31	- $65.39
9/30	- $65.39
10/31	- $65.39
11/30	- $65.39
12/31	- $65.39

Kali's grandmother gave her a new cell phone for her birthday along with $1,000 to pay the monthly phone bills. If Kali pays $65.39 a month for her phone, how much money will she have left at the end of 12 payments?

____

Fill in the form on the left to have a record of how much is left after each month of the year.

Kali checked her work by multiplying $65.39 by 12 and then subtracting the amount from $1,000.00.

$$\begin{array}{r} \$65.39 \\ \times \quad 12 \\ \hline \end{array}$$

$1,000.00 –   = ________

Bananas
$.69 each

Tomatoes
$1.25 each

Apples
$.75 each

Carrots
$.39 each

Red Peppers
$1.17 each

Broccoli
$2/bunch

Potatoes
$.50 each

Onions
$.29/bunch

1. What three items did Michael buy for $2.44?

   __________ __________ __________

2. What three items did Ava buy for $2.31?

   __________ __________ __________

3. What three items did Ethan buy for $3.94?

   __________ __________ __________

4. What four items did Emily buy for $1.93?

   __________ __________ __________ __________

5. What four items did Leon buy for $4.68?

   __________ __________ __________ __________

Expensive Dog Walker

Ralph was going to be out of town for fourteen days and asked Maria to walk and feed his dog everyday. Maria said she would do it for a small fee. She asked to be paid $.01 for the first day, then double that amount on the second day ($.02) and then double that amount for the third day ($.04), etc. Her fee for any day would always be double that of the previous day. Ralph agreed and was gone for 2 weeks.

When Ralph returned, he gave Maria $25. Maria said he owed her lots more money. Ralph handed her $40. Again, Maria said he owed her lots more money. Ralph handed her $50. Maria insisted that he needed to give her more money.

Ralph got out a piece of paper to figure the exact amount that was due Maria. Use the following charts to help figure out Ralph's bill.

Day	Pay
1st Monday	
1st Tuesday	
1st Wednesday	
1st Thursday	
1st Friday	
1st Saturday	
1st Sunday	

Day	Pay
2nd Monday	
2nd Tuesday	
2nd Wednesday	
2nd Thursday	
2nd Friday	
2nd Saturday	
2nd Sunday	

After figuring the bill, they were both surprised. How much does Ralph owe Maria? ________

Given 10 minutes, the three top winners of a national hot dog eating contest ate 65, 58, and 40 hot dogs and buns. They were averaging 6.5, 5.8, and 4 hot dogs per minute. How many hot dogs can the three contestants eat in a minute?

6.5 + 5.8 + 4 = ____

Remember to line up the decimal points to add same place values together. Insert zero placeholders where needed.

```
  1
  6.5
  5.8
+ 4.0
 16.3
```

16.3 hot dogs per minute

Find each sum; then cross out the correct answers on the right to find the two false answers. 1 = 1. = 1.0 = 1.00

1. 8.3 + .61 =
2. 3 + 1.2 + .45 =
3. 4.08 + .2 + .02 =
4. 3.01 + 10 + .1 =
5. .23 + .4 + .56 =
6. 4.2 + .9 + .8 =
7. 3.9 + 2 + .2 =
8. 5 + 2.08 + 1.1 =

13.11
7.64
1.19
6.1
8.91
12.41
5.9
8.18
4.65
4.3

In 2011, Nathan's Hot Dog Eating Contest had over 40,000 spectators in attendance.

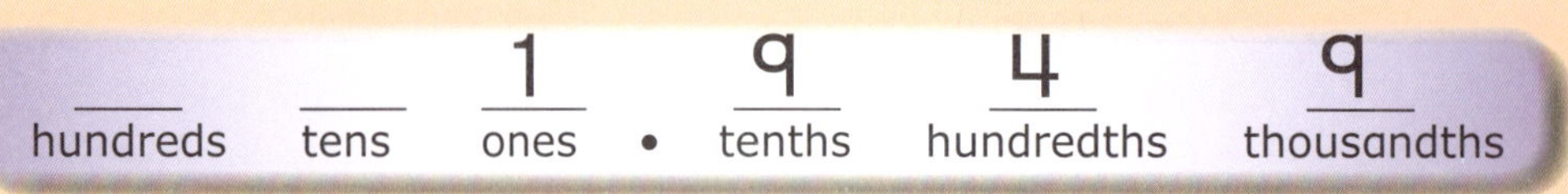

In 2011, 1.949 million people watched Nathan's Hot Dog Eating Contest on television.

To add decimals, line up the decimal points and add same place values together. Insert zeroes for placeholders where needed.

Example:
14 + 1.5 + .653 =

```
    1
  14.000
   1.500
+   .653
  16.153
```

Find each sum; then use the letters to solve the riddle on the next page. Remember, the decimal point is placed to the right of whole numbers.

r
```
   2.34
  12.45
+  5.79
```

w
```
   .001
  2.4
+  .055
```

e
```
  12.34
   1.0
+  5.66
```

c
```
    .12
   7.888
+   .401
```

m
```
  3.4
  2.1
+  .85
```

k
```
   1.094
   3.4
+ 10.74
```

p 5.7 + 12 + 1.02 + .33 = ______

a .608 + 1.202 + 10 + 2.29 = ______

h) 14.4 + 56 + 2.3 + .5 = ______

s) 2.005 + 2.5 + .505 + 5 = ______

u) 10 + 2.062 + .34 + .236 = ______

b) 4.4 + 4.44 + .04 + .004 = ______

n) In 1974, the baseball pitcher Nolan Ryan threw a 100.9 mile per hour pitch. If someone threw a ball 1.1 miles per hour faster, how fast did he throw the ball? Write an equation and solve.

________ + ________ = ________

What is a mouse's favorite dessert?

___	___	___	___	___	___	___	___	___	___
8.409	73.2	19	19	10.01	19	8.409	14.1	15.234	19

To place decimal numbers in order from least to greatest, it is helpful to first write each number with the same number of decimal places before comparing. Decimal places are the number of decimal place values used. The number .057 has **three** decimal places and the number 4.6 has **one** decimal place.

4.6	.057	.48
4.600	.057	.480

.057 is the least
.48 is the second least
4.6 is the greatest

Place the numbers from least to greatest to answer the questions.

1) Who won the 100 yard dash? ________

__ Tim's time was 13.6 seconds.

__ Art's time was 14 seconds.

__ Jim's time was 13.09 seconds.

2) Who threw the fastest ball? ________

__ Ben threw a 86.6 mph pitch.

__ Petro threw a 86.06 mph pitch.

__ Ryan threw a 86.009 mph pitch.

3) Who has the coldest temperature? ________

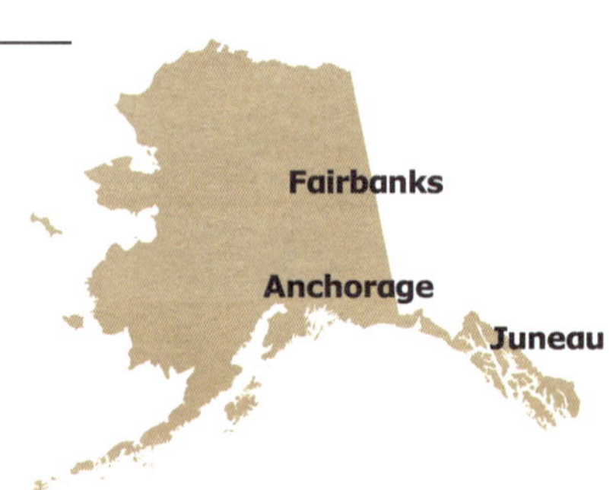

__ Anchorage, Alaska is at 10°F

__ Fairbanks, Alaska is at 9.99°F

__ Juneau, Alaska is at 10.09°F

4) Which is the longest length? ________

__ 35.6 cm

__ 6.9 cm

__ 40 cm

What is the difference between 3 centimeters and 1.4 centimeters? Before subtracting, line up the decimal points and write each number with the same number of decimal places.

$$\begin{array}{r} 3. \\ -\ 1.4 \\ \hline \end{array} \qquad \begin{array}{r} \overset{2}{\cancel{3}}.\overset{1}{0} \\ -\ 1.4 \\ \hline 1.6 \text{ cm} \end{array}$$

Find each difference; then cross out the correct answers below to find the two false answers.

1. $\begin{array}{r} 4.56 \\ -\ 4.12 \\ \hline \end{array}$

2. $\begin{array}{r} 10.67 \\ -\ \ \ 8.3 \\ \hline \end{array}$

3. $\begin{array}{r} 25. \\ -\ 9.05 \\ \hline \end{array}$

4. $\begin{array}{r} 12.34 \\ -\ 8.9 \\ \hline \end{array}$

5. $\begin{array}{r} 21.6 \\ -\ \ 2.31 \\ \hline \end{array}$

6. $\begin{array}{r} 30.03 \\ -\ 7. \\ \hline \end{array}$

7. $\begin{array}{r} 4. \\ -\ 3.001 \\ \hline \end{array}$

8. $\begin{array}{r} 102.1 \\ -\ \ .345 \\ \hline \end{array}$

9. $\begin{array}{r} 2.405 \\ -\ 1.5 \\ \hline \end{array}$

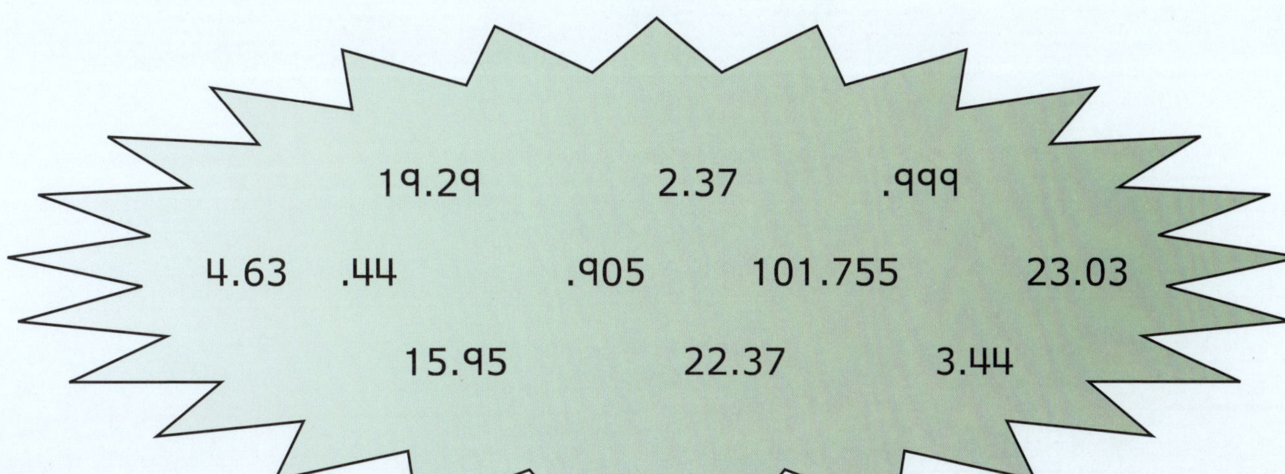

Hail has been reported as half-dollar size and marble size. The size is determined by the distance across the hail. What is the difference in the distance across a half-dollar-sized hail compared to marble-sized hail?

half-dollar-sized

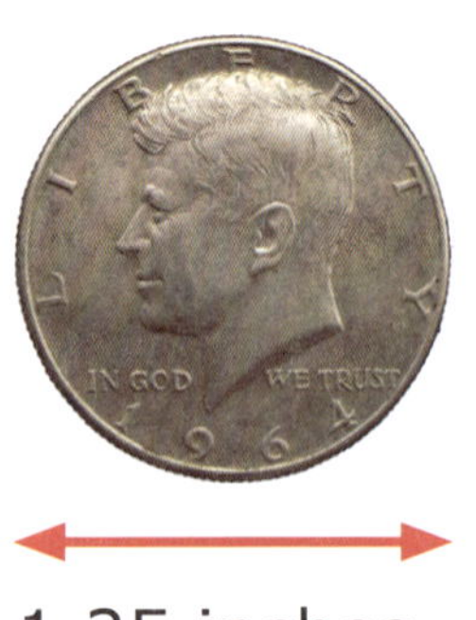

1.25 inches

marble-sized

.5 inches

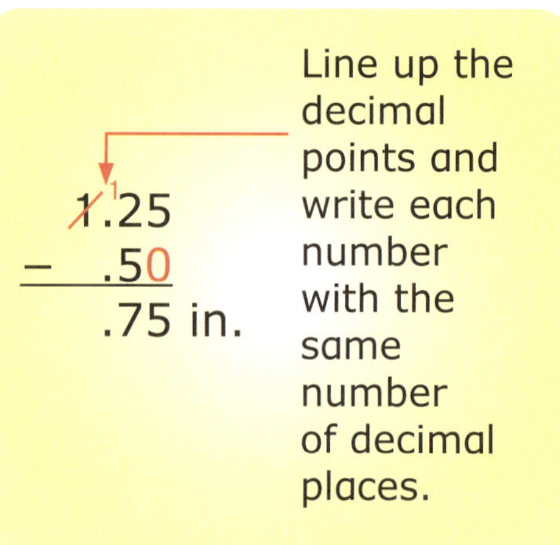

Find the difference; then use the letters to solve the riddle on the next page.

e) 5.28 − 1.49

p) 4.83 − .7

q) 23.47 − 17.28

t) 3.4 − .282

n) 4.392 − 2.6

o) 231.38 − 170.422

h) 50 − .6 =

m) 1.42 − .008 =

c) 1.082 − .13 =

d) .101 − .01 =

w) 10.24 − 9 =

r) 1.2 − .053 =

b) 4.08 − .09 =

a) 105.05 − 1.5 =

y) 1 − .1 =

u) 123.97 − 40.999 =

l) What is the difference in temperature between 101.1° and 98°? Write an equation and solve.

________ − ________ = ________

What bird works at a construction site?

___	___	___		___	___	___	___	___
3.118	49.4	3.79		.952	1.147	103.55	1.792	3.79

Add each problem, then write the answer in the crossword puzzle below. You may need a piece of paper to do your work.

	Across		Down
1	.48 + .4	1	.029 + .81
3	2.3 + .87	2	80 + 1.24
6	10.8 + 15 + .21	3	300 + 44 + .8
10	28.2 + 2.8	4	.006 + .144
11	428 + 29.6	5	75.083 + 2
12	.845 + .049	7	1.8 + 5.01
13	8 + 1.234	8	.082 + .008
14	.005 + .005	9	9 + 5.5
15	.428 + .39	14	.009 + .001
18	.348 + .491	16	.92 + .88
19	4 + 5.86	17	5.2 + 4.6

Two out of every 100 kids ages 5–17 are homeschooled.

$\frac{2}{100}$ or .02

Ethan bought three T-shirts for $5.59 each. What was the cost of the shirts? Addition or multiplication can be used.

$$\begin{array}{r} \overset{1}{\$5}.\overset{2}{5}9 \\ 5.59 \\ +\ 5.59 \\ \hline \$16.77 \end{array} \quad \textbf{or} \quad \begin{array}{r} \overset{1}{\$5}.\overset{2}{5}9 \\ \times \quad 3 \\ \hline \$16.77 \end{array}$$

The number of decimal places in the product is equal to the sum of the number of decimal places in the factors.

Find the cost of the following purchases; then cross out the correct answers below to find the two false answers.

1. 4 pairs of slacks at $21.99 each ________

2. 2 pairs of jeans at $35.79 each ________

3. 2 shirts at $16 each ________

4. 3 pairs of tennis shoes at $31.50 each ________

5. 6 pairs of socks at $3.79 each ________

6. 9 T-shirts at $9.99 each ________

7. a dozen boxes of cookies at $3.40 each ________

8. 5 cases of water at $6.59 a case ________

Enough Money?

1. Emma went shopping at a department store. She bought a dress for $29.98, a pair of shoes for $39, and two belts for $14.99 each. If the sales tax was $7.92, would $100 pay for everything?

   ❑ Yes ❑ No

   Emma's total = ________

2. Dan went to the bookstore. He bought two books on horses at $7.95 each and three comics at $4.95 each. If the sales tax was $2.10, would $32 pay for everything?

   ❑ Yes ❑ No

   Dan's total = ________

3. Chris had lunch at a local café with a friend. He ordered two hamburgers at $2.59 each, two orders of fries at $1.59 each, and two drinks at 99¢ each. If the sales tax was 72¢, would $12 pay for everything?

   ❑ Yes ❑ No

   Chris's total = ________

A piece of currency can be folded forward and back approximately 4,000 times before it will tear.

Subtract each problem, then write the answer in the crossword puzzle below. You may need a piece of paper to work the problems.

Across

1. 1 − .12
3. 10.2 − 1.31
6. 98 − .98
10. 110.1 − 20.1
11. 245.3 − 92.4
12. .4 − .004
13. 5.203 − .9
14. .925 − .505
15. 3.2 − 2.831
18. .526 − .342
19. 10 − .25

Down

1. 1 − .106
2. 95 − 14.65
3. 923.7 − 110.4
4. 2.455 − 1.605
5. 100 − 7.802
7. 9.14 − 1.82
8. .99 − .9
9. 85.2 − 58.8
14. 2 − 1.58
16. 10 − 3.9
17. 10.22 − 1.52

1. .8	2. 8		3.	4.	5.		6.	7.	8.	9.
10.			11.					12.		
13.							14.			
			15.	16.					17.	
				18.				19.		

The smallest bee is about 2.1 millimeters long.

The number line below represents the set of **integers**.

Negative Integers

Positive Integers

To add integers, begin at the first number. When adding a positive number to it, move that many units to the right, if the second number is negative, move that many units to the left.

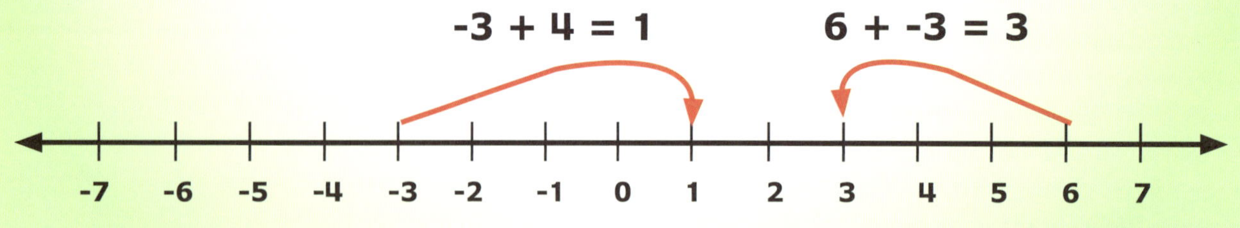

Use a number line to find each sum. Then use the letters to solve the riddle on the next page.

r) 6 + -1 = 5

g) 2 + -6 = -4

o) -1 + -1 = -2

u) 7 + -10 = -3

d) -3 + -4 = -7

t) 6 + -5 = 1

p) 6 + -2 = 4

y) -7 + 7 = 0

i) -2 + 5 = 3

e) -5 + -1 = ___ z) 7 + -5 = ___ s) -5 + 0 = ___

f) -4 + -5 = ___ n) 10 + -4 = ___ b) 1 + -2 = ___

a) 10 + -2 = ___ q) -9 + -3 = ___ v) -1 + 10 = ___

l) 6 + 4 = ___ c) 12 + 0 = ___ h) -5 + -5 = ___

w) -5 + -3 = ___ m) 10 + -3 = ___ z) -5 + -6 = ___

j) 12 + -1 = ___ x) 20 + -6 = ___ k) -5 + -10 = ___

What is the best day of the week to serve hamburgers?

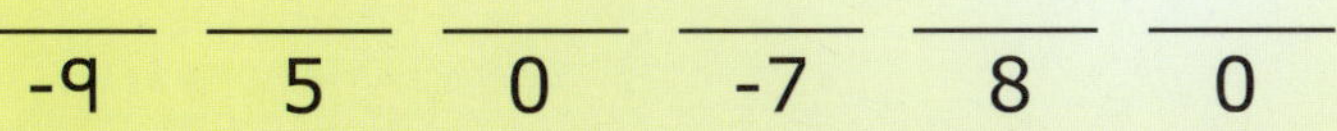

___ ___ ___ ___ ___ ___
-9 5 0 -7 8 0

Negative Integers Positive Integers

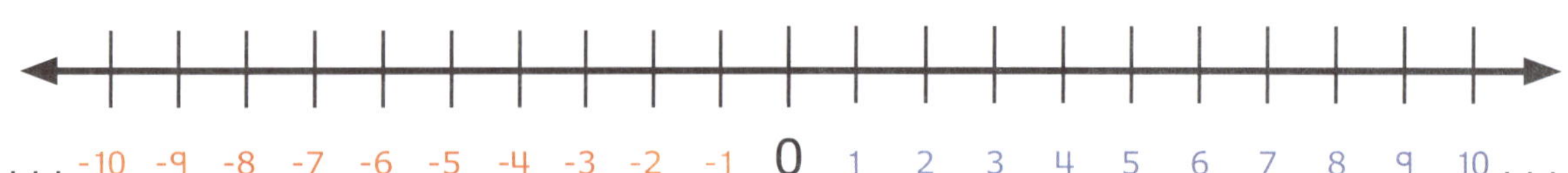

Rules for Adding Integers

same signs: Add and keep the same sign.

4 + 3 = 7 -1 + -2 = -3

different signs: Subtract the numbers as if they were both positive, then use the sign of the number farther from zero.

9 + -10 = -1 -8 + 3 = -5

Find each result; then cross out the correct answers below to find the two false answers.

1. 5 + -2 = _____
2. -4 + -3 = _____
3. 6 + 4 = _____
4. -8 + 7 = _____
5. -2 + -1 = _____
6. 4 + -10 = _____
7. 25 + -14 = _____
8. -10 + -13 = _____
9. -45 + 97 = _____
10. -59 + -23 = _____
11. -26 + 40 = _____
12. -78 + 84 = _____
13. -103 + -247 = _____
14. 149 + -200 = _____
15. -319 + _____ = -483
16. _____ + 87 = -218

10 6 14 -7 -23
11 -3 131 -164 -350
52 3 -1 -144
-82 -305 -6 -51

Negative Integers **Positive Integers**

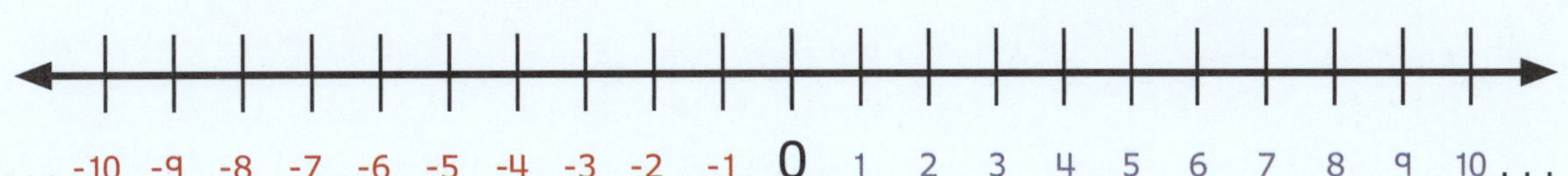

Rules for Subtracting Integers

When subtracting integers, rewrite and use the addition of integers rules. If you are subtracting a negative integer (2 – -3), the two negatives are replaced by a positive sign because the opposite of negative is positive (2 + 3).

	Rewrite	
5 – 2 =	5 + -2 =	3
-4 – 8 =	-4 + -8 =	-12
4 – -1 =	4 + 1 =	5
-3 – -5 =	-3 + 5 =	2

Find each result; then cross out the correct answers below to find the three false answers.

1. 6 – 1 = _____
2. 9 – 12 = _____
3. -1 – 3 = _____
4. -5 – 4 = _____
5. 2 – -7 = _____
6. 8 – -2 = _____
7. 10 – -18 = _____
8. -29 – -11 = _____
9. _____ – -21 = 5
10. 3 – _____ = 17
11. What is the difference in temperature between 88° in San Jose and -11° in Fairbanks? Write an equation and answer.

____

-14	28	10	-4	26	-3	99
5	-40	-9	9	-18	-16	-12

Rules for Multiplying Integers

positive integer × positive integer = positive integer
positive integer × negative integer = negative integer
negative integer × positive integer = negative integer
negative integer × negative integer = positive integer

$5 \times 7 = 35$	$-5 \times 7 = -35$	$-5 \times -7 = 35$
$6 \cdot -8 = -48$	$-4(-2) = 8$	$(-7)3 = -21$

Let $n = -2$, $-9n = -9 \cdot -2 = 18$

Find the product; then cross out the correct answers on the right. There are 19 false answers.

1. $-14 \cdot (-6) =$ ____
2. $3(-12) =$ ____
3. $-25 \times 15 =$ ____
4. $(-1)(-1) =$ ____
5. $-215 \cdot 0 =$ ____
6. $-8 \cdot (-2) \cdot 4 =$ ____
7. $6 \cdot (-4) \cdot 11 =$ ____
8. $-9 \times (-9) =$ ____
9. $-56(5) =$ ____
10. $-102 \times (-1) =$ ____
11. $81 \cdot (-7) =$ ____
12. $(-3)^2 =$ ____

81 -81
-1 1
-102 102
264 -264
567 -567
-36 36
-216 216
9 -9
30 -30
45 -45
84 -84
51 -51
375 -375
0
-280 280
64 -64
144 -144
6 -6

Let $x = 3$ and $n = -2$

13. $17x =$ ____
14. $-15n =$ ____
15. $nx =$ ____
16. $(-12n)(-3n) =$ ____

Rules for Dividing Integers

positive integer ÷ positive integer = positive integer
positive integer ÷ negative integer = negative integer
negative integer ÷ positive integer = negative integer
negative integer ÷ negative integer = positive integer

$20 \div 4 = 5$ $-15 \div 3 = -5$ $-12 \div -4 = 3$

$\frac{24}{-3} = -8$ $6\overline{)-18}$ = -3 $\frac{-16}{-2} = 8$

Find the quotient; then cross out the correct answers below to find the two false answers.

1. $35 \div 7 =$ ____
2. $35 \div (-7) =$ ____
3. $-35 \div (-7) =$ ____
4. $42 \div (-6) =$ ____
5. $-222 \div 6 =$ ____
6. $-420 \div (-10) =$ ____
7. $\frac{-48}{-6} =$ ____
8. $\frac{-30}{-5} =$ ____
9. $\frac{-125}{5} =$ ____
10. $\frac{-250}{2} =$ ____
11. $\frac{114}{-6} =$ ____
12. $\frac{-320}{-80} =$ ____
13. $10\overline{)-200}$
14. $-9\overline{)-216}$
15. $12\overline{)-144}$

Find the missing number.

16. $-40 \div$ ____ $= -5$
17. ____ $\div (-7) = -80$

-37 -8 -20 -7 -125
5 8 560 -12 8
5 -19 -24 -25 6
42 -5 24 4

A **rectangular coordinate system** is used to locate a point on a plane. The grid is made using a horizontal number line (*x*-axis) and a vertical number line (*y*-axis) intersected at a right angle and numbered using an ordered pair of numbers written as (x,y). The first coordinate in an ordered pair, the *x*, can be located on the horizontal axis (*x*-axis) by going right from 0 for positive numbers and left from 0 for negative numbers. The second coordinate in an ordered pair, the *y*, can be located on the vertical axis (*y*-axis) by going up from 0 for positive numbers and down from 0 for negative numbers. The point (0,0) is called the origin.

The star is located at point (4,1) and the triangle is at (-3,-4). The line segment connects point (-5,1) to point (0,1).

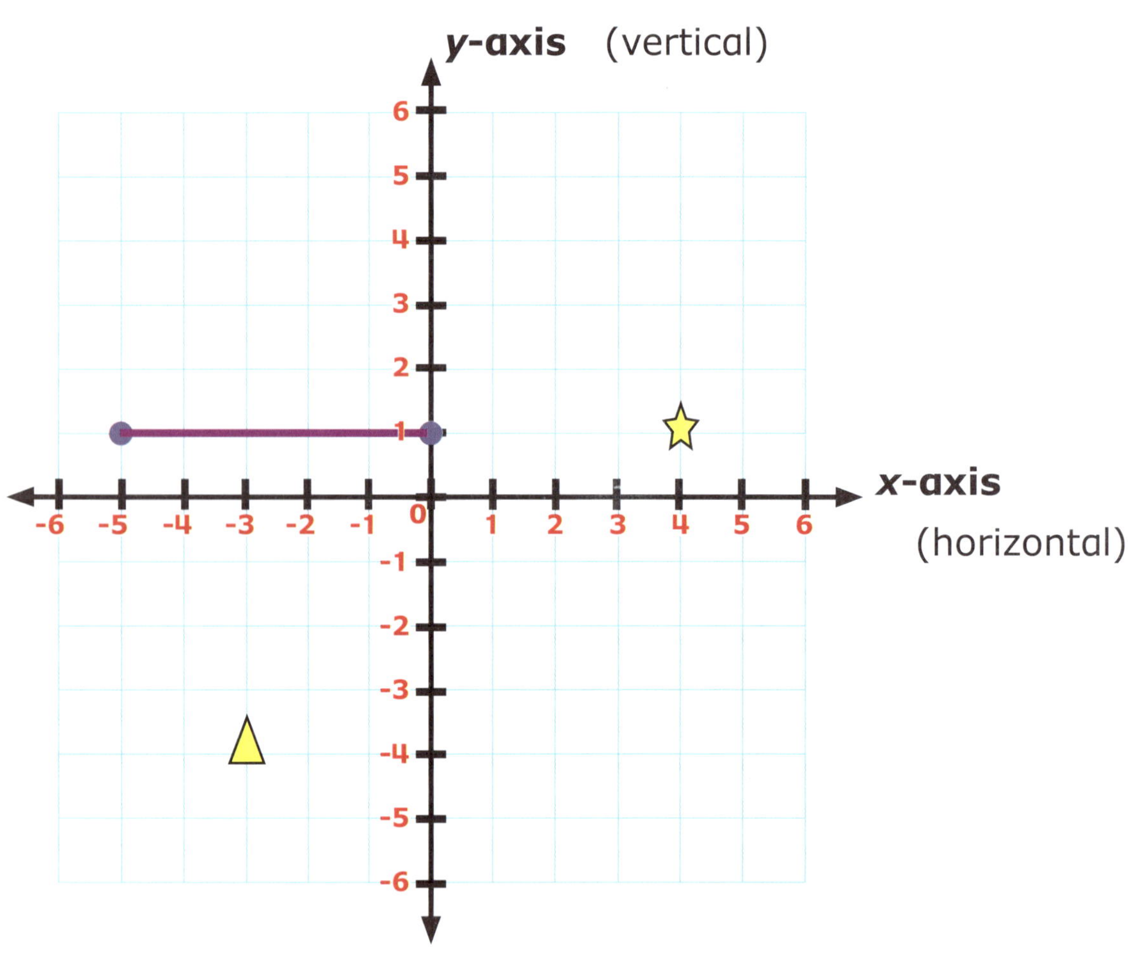

Connect the following points in order. A picture will appear. The red dot is at point (7,1). The black dot is at (2,6).

1. (5,3)
2. (4,3)
3. (2,1)
4. (2,3)
5. (4,4)
6. (4,5)
7. (1,5)
8. (0,6)
9. (1,7)
10. (2,7)
11. (3,8)
12. (5,8)
13. (4,7)
14. (3,7)
15. (6,3)
16. (7,2)
17. (7,0)
18. (6,-1)
19. (2,-1)
20. (3,0)
21. (4,0)
22. (3,1)
23. (3,2)

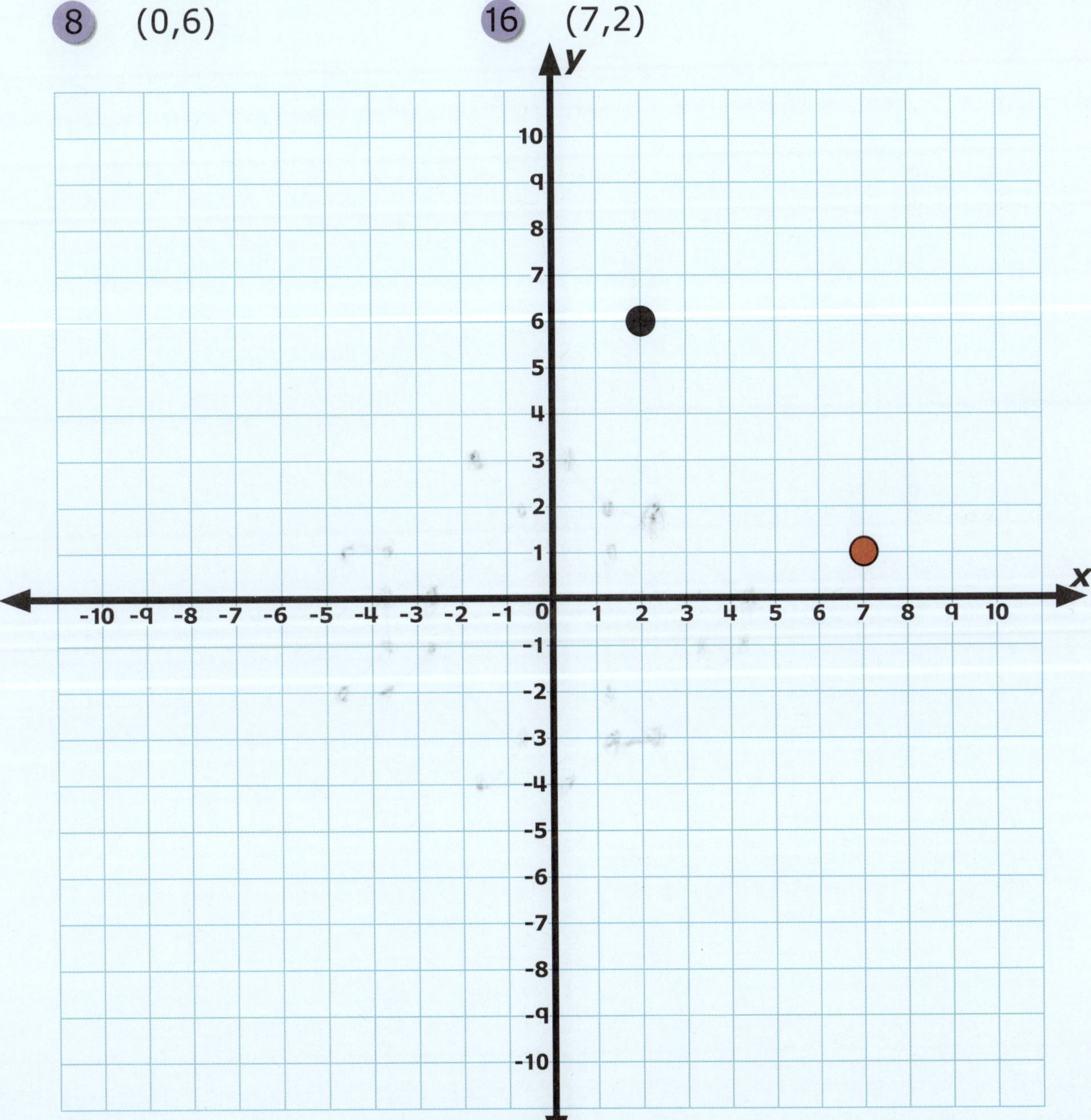

Connect the following points in order. A picture will appear.

1 (-2,2)
2 (-1,1)
3 (-1,-2)
4 (-2,-3)
5 (-4,-1)
6 (-3,-1)
7 (-4,0)
8 (-2,2)
9 (-1,2)
10 (0,3)
11 (2,3)
12 (1,2)
13 (3,0)
14 (4,1)
15 (5,1)
16 (4,0)
17 (4,-1)
18 (5,-2)
19 (4,-2)
20 (3,-1)
21 (1,-3)
22 (2,-4)
23 (0,-4)
24 (-1,-3)
25 (-2,-3)

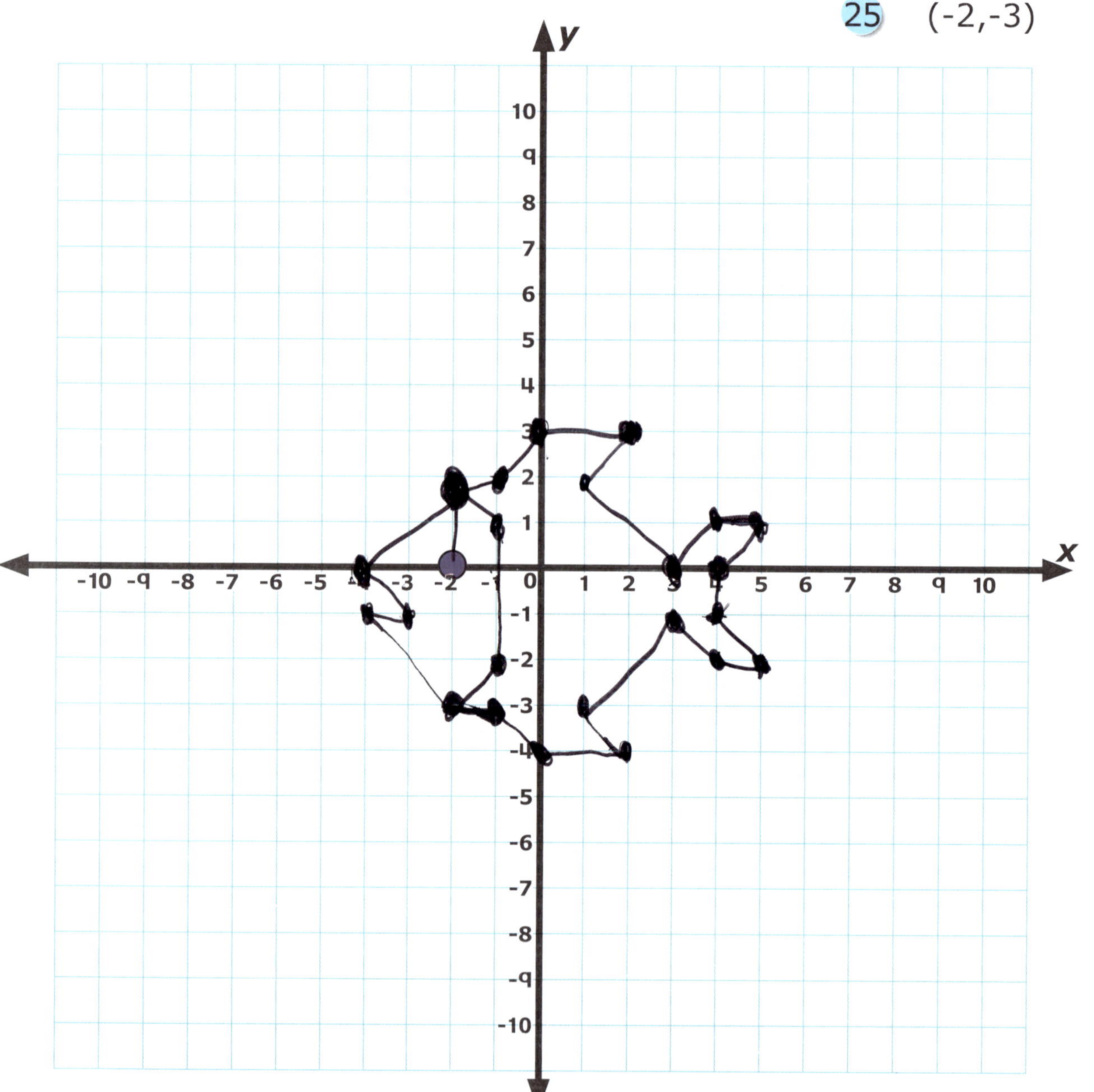

If x is replaced by 2 and y is replaced by 5 in the equation $y = x + 3$, it makes a true equation $5 = 2 + 3$. Substitutions for x and y that make a true equation are called a solution to the equation and may be written as an ordered pair (x,y). The set of all solutions to the equation, when graphed, form a line.*

1 Replace x with the given value and determine what y would have to be to form a true equation.

$y = x + 3$

x	y	(x,y)
0	3	(0,3)
1	4	(1,4)
2	5	(2,5)
4		(4,_)
5		(5,_)

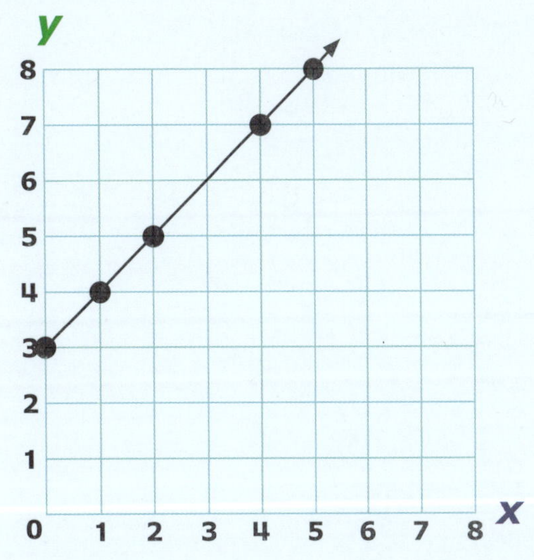

Plot and connect the ordered pairs.

2 Replace x with the given value and determine what y would have to be to form a true equation. Plot and connect the ordered pairs of the solutions.

$y = x - 2$

x	y
8	6
6	
5	
3	
2	

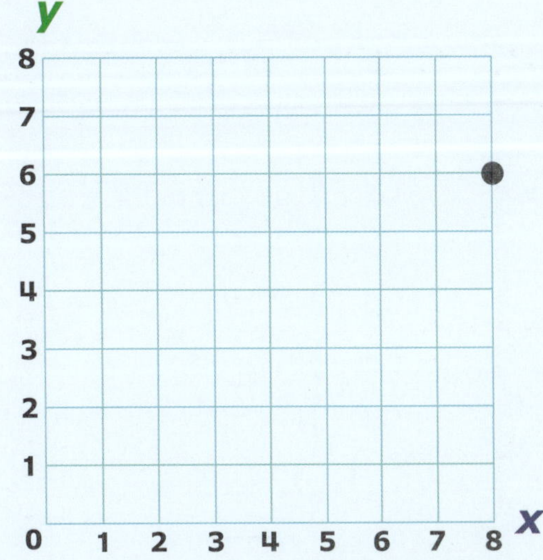

* Equations of the form $y = mx + b$, with m and b as real numbers, are called linear and graph as lines.

The *x*-axis and *y*-axis split the plane into four parts called **quadrants**.

quadrant 2 | quadrant 1
quadrant 3 | quadrant 4

Replace *x* with the given value in the equation and determine what *y* would have to be to form a true equation. Graph and connect the ordered pairs of the solutions.

1) $y = x + 1$

x	y	(x,y)
5	6	(5,6)
3	4	(3,4)
0	1	(0,1)
-2		(-2,_)
-5		(-5,_)

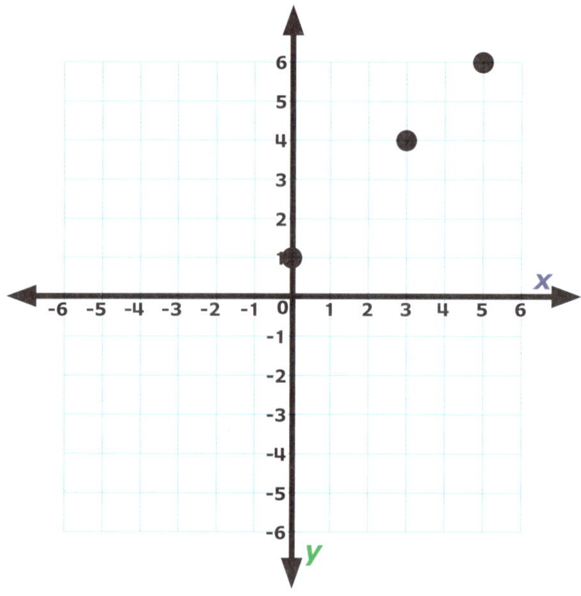

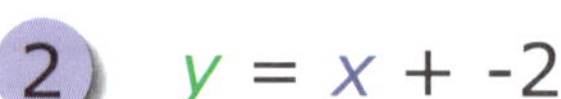

2) $y = x + -2$

x	y	(x,y)
6	4	(6,4)
3		(3,_)
2		(2,_)
0		(0,_)
-4		(-4,_)

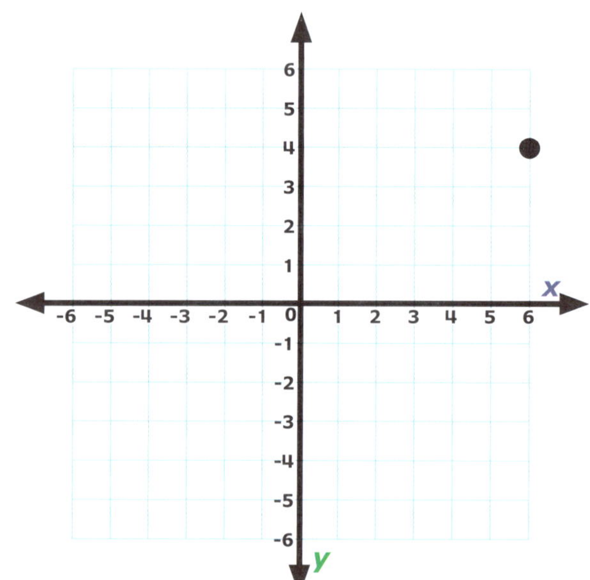

A pattern that relates an in value to an out value is called a **function**.

In x	Out y
0	7
1	8
2	9
3	10
4	11

+ 7

$y =$ x + 7

In x	Out y
8	2
7	1
6	0
5	-1
4	-2

– 6

$y =$ x – 6

In a	Out b
1	5
2	9
3	13
4	17
5	21

times 4 + 1

$b =$ 4a + 1

For each problem, discover a pattern and write the rule for the relationship.

1.

In x	Out y
2	6
3	9
4	12
5	15
6	18

$y =$ ________

2.

In x	Out y
1	-1
2	0
3	1
4	2
5	3

$y =$ ________

3.

In x	Out y
1	1
2	3
3	5
4	7
5	9

$y =$ ________

4.

In a	Out b
0	0
2	1
4	2
6	3
8	4

$b =$ ________

5.

In m	Out n
1	5
2	10
3	15
4	20
5	25

$n =$ ________

6.

In c	Out d
1	-1
2	1
3	3
4	5
5	7

$d =$ ________

Fill in the missing numbers in each problem.

1. $$\begin{array}{r} 16\square \\ +\ 49 \\ \hline 2\square 4 \end{array}$$

2. $$\begin{array}{r} 448 \\ +\ 57 \\ \hline 50\square \end{array}$$

3. $$\begin{array}{r} 69 \\ +\ 29 \\ \hline \square 8 \end{array}$$

4. $$\begin{array}{r} 2\square 6 \\ 38 \\ +\ 6\square \\ \hline 385 \end{array}$$

5. $$\begin{array}{r} 78\square \\ 36 \\ +\ 45 \\ \hline \square 70 \end{array}$$

6. $$\begin{array}{r} 92 \\ \square 5 \\ +\ 68 \\ \hline \square 35 \end{array}$$

7. $$\begin{array}{r} 51 \\ \square 8 \\ 36 \\ +\ 186 \\ \hline 29\square \end{array}$$

8. $$\begin{array}{r} 2\square \\ 49 \\ 58 \\ +\ 6\square 2 \\ \hline 805 \end{array}$$

9. $$\begin{array}{r} 79 \\ 9\square \\ 82 \\ +\ 45 \\ \hline 2\square 7 \end{array}$$

10. $$\begin{array}{r} 23 \\ \square\square \\ 56 \\ +\ \square 42 \\ \hline 357 \end{array}$$

11. $$\begin{array}{r} \square \\ 134 \\ \square 7 \\ +\ 65 \\ \hline \square 20 \end{array}$$

12. $$\begin{array}{r} 123 \\ \square 42 \\ \square 5 \\ +\ 6\square \\ \hline 528 \end{array}$$

Fill in the missing numbers in each problem.

1. $$\begin{array}{r} 57\square \\ -\ 86 \\ \hline \square 87 \end{array}$$

2. $$\begin{array}{r} 404 \\ -\ \square 6 \\ \hline 32\square \end{array}$$

3. $$\begin{array}{r} 161 \\ -\ 85 \\ \hline \square\square \end{array}$$

4. $$\begin{array}{r} 500 \\ -\square 3 \\ \hline 48\square \end{array}$$

5. $$\begin{array}{r} 20\square \\ -\ 146 \\ \hline \square 6 \end{array}$$

6. $$\begin{array}{r} 425 \\ -17\square \\ \hline \square 46 \end{array}$$

7. $$\begin{array}{r} 5{,}800 \\ -\ 3{,}945 \\ \hline \square{,}85\square \end{array}$$

8. $$\begin{array}{r} 2{,}06\square \\ -\ 1{,}\square 90 \\ \hline 7\square 3 \end{array}$$

9. $$\begin{array}{r} \square{,}42\square \\ -\ 1{,}7\square 3 \\ \hline 1{,}\square 45 \end{array}$$

10. $31 + 19 + 25 + \square = 100$

11. $8 + 21 + 37 + 18 + \square = 100$

12. $120 + \square{,}\square\square\square + 1{,}709 = 4{,}281$

13. $\square{,}\square\square\square + 2{,}865 = 5{,}000$

Fill in the missing numbers in each problem.

1.
$$\begin{array}{r} 74 \\ \times\ \square \\ \hline 296 \end{array}$$

2.
$$\begin{array}{r} 164 \\ \times\ \square \\ \hline \square 56 \end{array}$$

3.
$$\begin{array}{r} 7\square 5 \\ \times\ 9 \\ \hline 6{,}705 \end{array}$$

4.
$$\begin{array}{r} 84 \\ \times\ \square \\ \hline 756 \end{array}$$

5.
$$\begin{array}{r} 252 \\ \times\ \square \\ \hline 1{,}\square 12 \end{array}$$

6.
$$\begin{array}{r} 27\square \\ \times\ \square \\ \hline 552 \end{array}$$

7.
$$\begin{array}{r} 23 \\ \times\ 5\square \\ \hline 46 \\ +\,1{,}1\square 0 \\ \hline 1{,}196 \end{array}$$

8.
$$\begin{array}{r} 223 \\ \times\ \square 3 \\ \hline \square 69 \\ +\,8{,}9\square 0 \\ \hline 9{,}589 \end{array}$$

9.
$$\begin{array}{r} 94 \\ \times\ 9\square \\ \hline 376 \\ +\ \square{,}4\square 0 \\ \hline 8{,}836 \end{array}$$

10. $10 \times 10 \times 10 \times \square\square = 70{,}000$

11. $2 \times 3 \times 4 \times 5 \times 6 \times \square = 5{,}040$

12. $4 \times 5 \times 2 \times 3 \times 5 \times \square = 3{,}600$

Fill in the missing numbers in each problem.

1
```
   □□
7)252
  21
   42
   42
```

2
```
   67
□)53□
  48
   56
   56
```

3
```
   □8
9)432
  3□
   72
   72
```

4
```
   □2
□)276
  27
    6
    6
```

5
```
   □□
□)364
  36
    4
    4
```

6
```
   □6
□)608
  □6
   48
   48
```

7
```
     □5
□0)1,75□
   150
    250
    250
```

8
```
     □2
4□)1,76□
   168
     84
     84
```

9
```
     □□
86)3,182
   258
    602
    602
```

10
```
     6□
2□)1,575
   150
     75
     75
```

11
```
     32
□□)2,016
   189
    126
    126
```

12
```
     □5
□6)3,450
   322
    230
    230
```

Mathematical Puzzles

1. Replace **A**, **B**, **C**, **D**, and **E** with the numbers 1, 2, 3, 4, and 5 in such a way as to make the following multiplication true. Each letter will be represented by a different number.

$$\begin{array}{r} A\ B \\ \times \quad C \\ \hline D\ E \end{array}$$

2. Replace the letters **A**, **B**, **C**, **D**, **E**, **F**, **G**, **H**, and **I** with 1, 2, 3, 4, 5, 6, 7, 8, and 9 in such a way as to make the following true. Each letter will be represented by a different number.

$$\begin{array}{r} A\ B \\ \times \quad C \\ \hline D\ E \end{array}$$

$$\begin{array}{r} D\ E \\ +\ F\ G \\ \hline H\ I \end{array}$$

Operations that undo each other are called **inverse operations**.

If 3 is added to 7 and then 3 is subtracted from the answer, we return to 7.

If 30 is divided by 6 and then multiplied by 6, we return to 30.

$3 + 7 = 10$

$10 - 3 = 7$

Subtraction is the inverse (opposite of) addition.
Addition is the inverse (opposite of) subtraction.
Multiplication is the inverse (opposite of) division.
Division is the inverse (opposite of) multiplication.

$30 \div 6 = 5$

$5 \times 6 = 30$

Use inverse operations to solve for the unknown number *n*; then cross out the correct answers on the right to find the two false answers.

1. $n + 29 = 40$ $n =$ _____
2. $n - 32 = 17$ $n =$ _____
3. $n \times 3 = 30$ $n =$ _____
4. $n \div 5 = 22$ $n =$ _____
5. $n + 201 = 742$ $n =$ _____
6. $n - 126 = 83$ $n =$ _____
7. $n \times 6 = 78$ $n =$ _____
8. $n \div 14 = 16$ $n =$ _____
9. $n - 401 = 500$ $n =$ _____
10. $n + 154 = 200$ $n =$ _____

10
541
901
209
11
13
334
224
49
46
892
110

Slide, Flip, and Turn Transformations

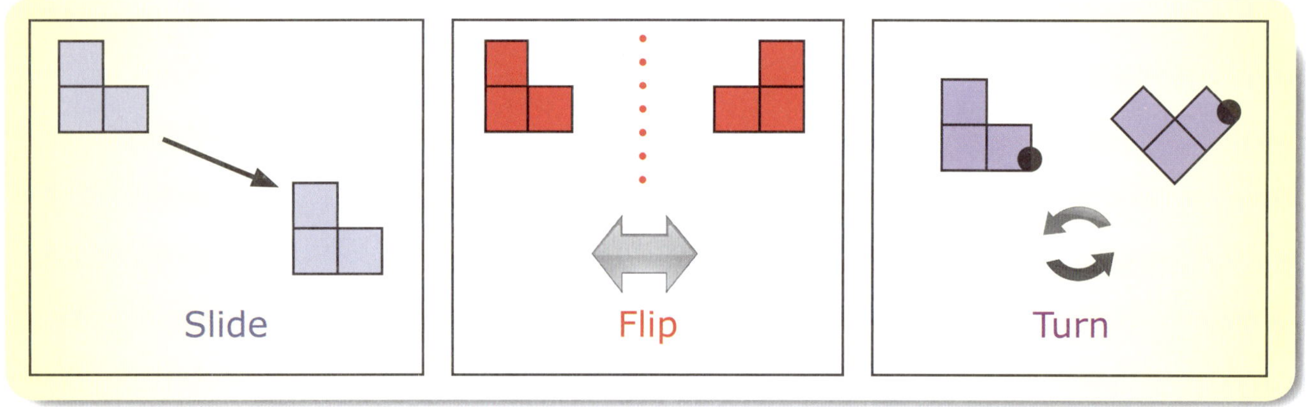

State how each figure was transformed. Write either slide, flip, or turn.

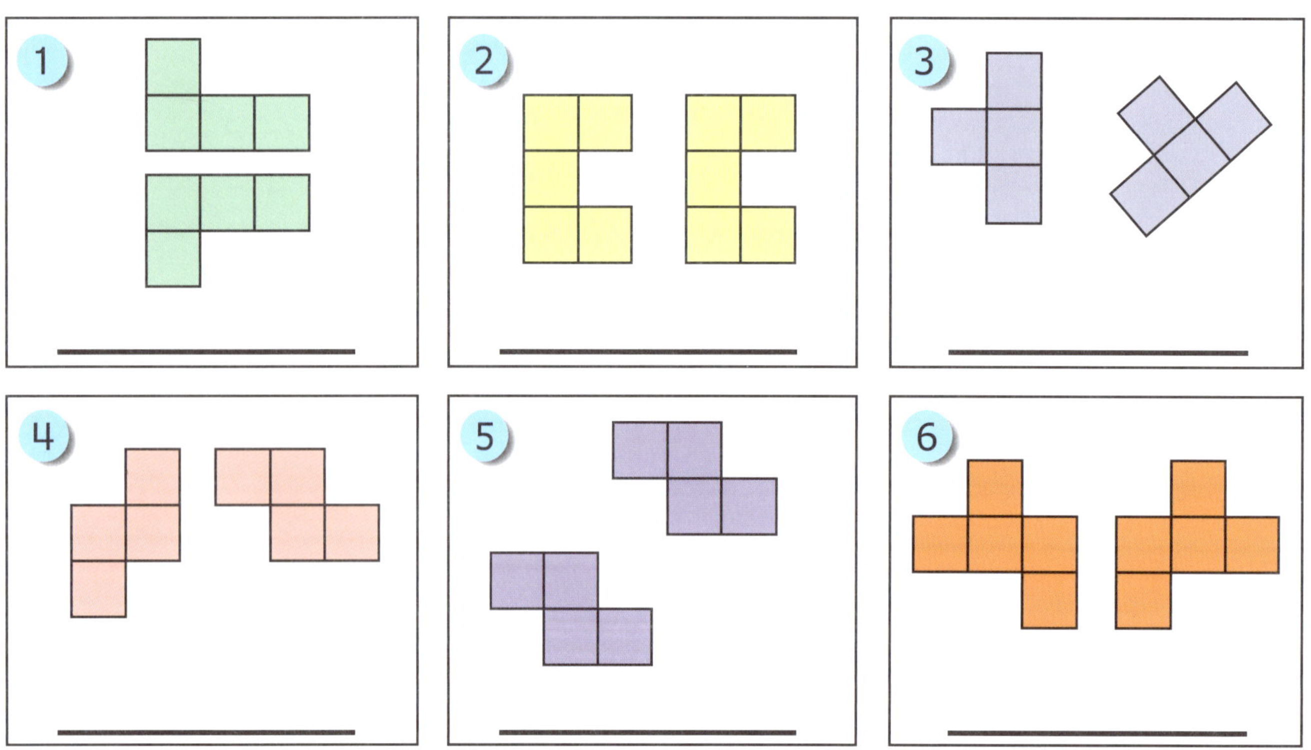

7 Draw a figure and transform it by a slide, flip, and turn.

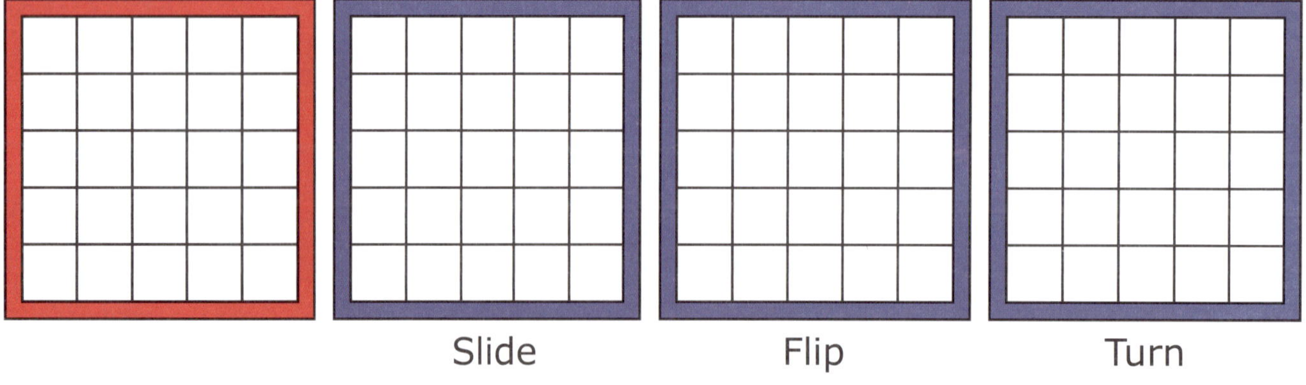

Congruent figures have the same size and shape. A shape has a line of symmetry if folding along the line makes two congruent shapes. A figure may have none, one, two, or more lines of symmetry.

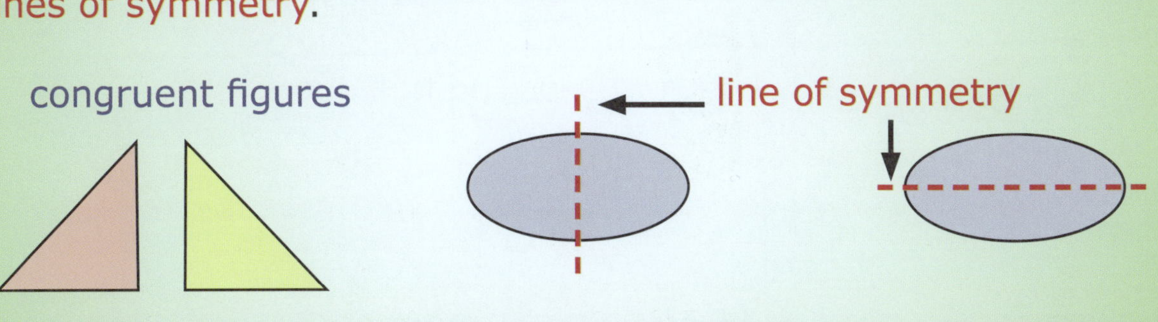

Draw a line of symmetry on each figure if possible.

1

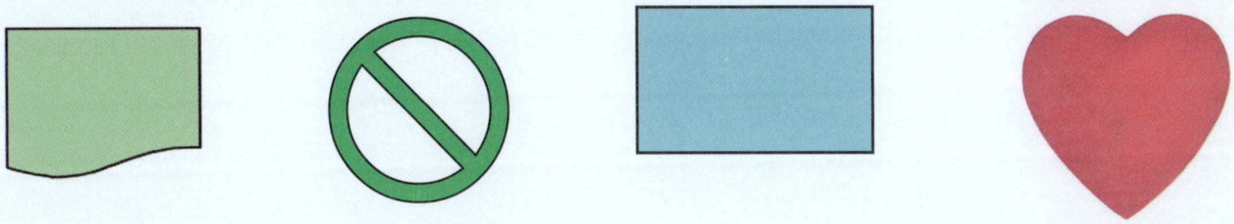

2

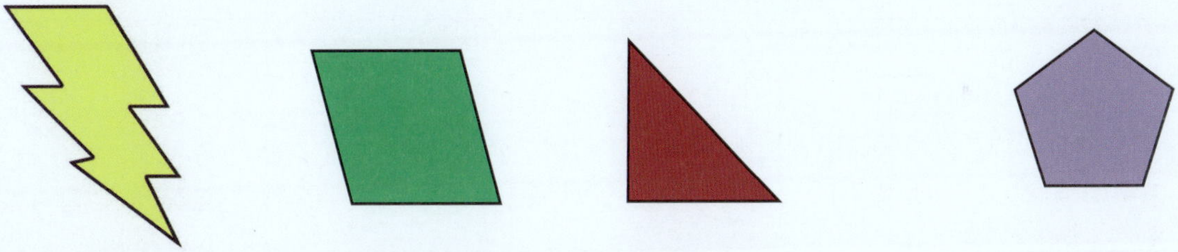

3

Customary units for measuring weight:

1 ounce (oz)

An ounce has about the weight of 1 slice of bread.

1 pound (lb)

A pound has about the weight of a can of vegetables.

16 ounces = 1 pound

Circle the best estimate for the weight of each item.

1. bike
   a. 3 ounces
   b. 30 ounces
   c. 30 pounds

2. shoe
   a. 5 ounces
   b. 15 ounces
   c. 15 pounds

3. key
   a. 1 ounces
   b. 10 ounces
   c. 1 pound

4. apple
   a. 5 ounces
   b. 50 lbs
   c. 5 lbs

5. dog
   a. 15 ounces
   b. 15 lbs
   c. 150 lbs

6. dime
   a. $\frac{1}{4}$ oz
   b. 4 oz
   c. 4 lb

7. A 100 pound student weighs how much in ounces? ________

8. If my cat weighs 80 ounces, how many pounds does my cat weigh? ________

9. What is a grocery item that weighs about one ounce? ________

10. What is a grocery item that weighs about one pound? ________

Metric units for measuring weight:

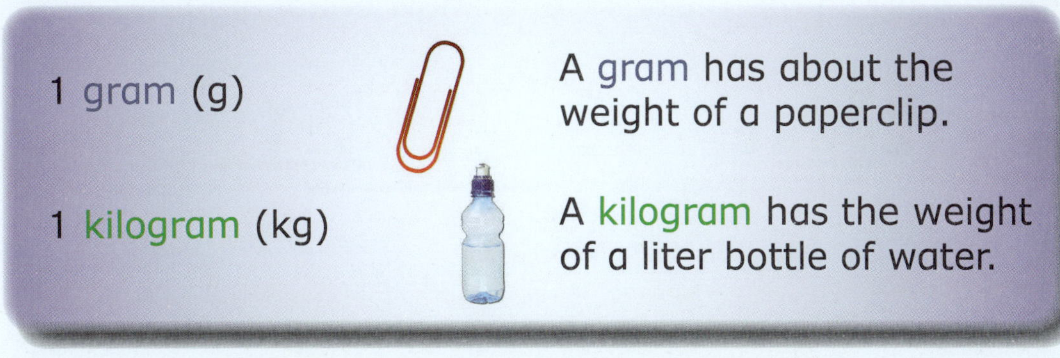

1,000 grams = 1 kilogram

Circle the best estimate for the weight of each item.

1. nickel
   a. 5 grams
   b. 50 grams
   c. 5 kilograms

2. 400 pennies
   a. 1 gram
   b. 100 grams
   c. 1 kilogram

3. bat & ball
   a. 2 grams
   b. 200 grams
   c. 2 kilograms

4. DVD
   a. 1 gram
   b. 100 grams
   c. 1 kilogram

5. button
   a. 1 gram
   b. 10 grams
   c. 1 kilogram

6. book
   a. 20 grams
   b. 200 grams
   c. 2 kilograms

7. If a 6th grader weighs 45 kilograms, how many grams does the 6th grader weigh? __________

8. If a pair of boots weighs 2,000 grams, how many kilograms does the pair of boots weigh? __________

9. What is a grocery item that weighs about a gram? __________

10. What is a grocery item that weighs about a kilogram? __________

Given equivalent amounts on the first two scales, determine what would be needed on the third scale to show equal amounts.

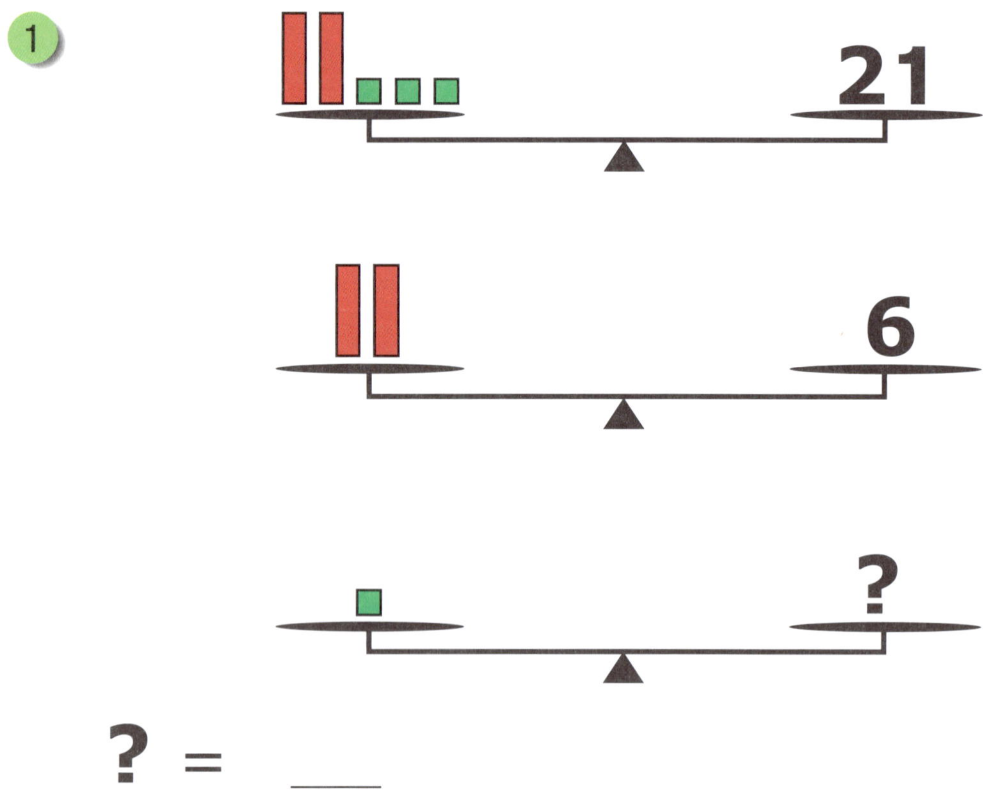

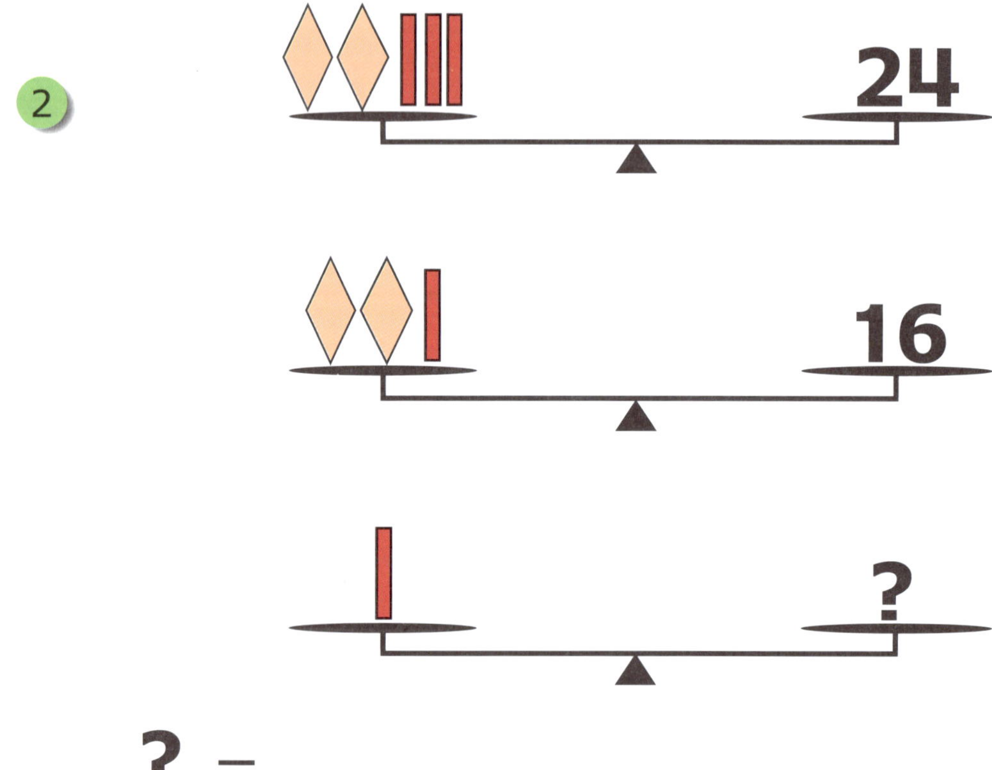

A **hurricane** is a type of tropical cyclone. Hurricanes are classified into five categories based on their wind speed, central pressure, and damage potential.

Category	Sustained Winds (miles per hour)	Damage	Storm Surge*
1	74-95	no real damage to buildings	4-5 feet
2	96-110	some damage to roofs and windows	6-8 feet
3	111-130	some structural damage to small buildings	9-12 feet
4	131-155	more extensive roof and building damage	13-18 feet
5	156 and up	complete roof failure and some building failure	>18 feet

1. A sustained wind speed of 115.8 miles per hour would indicate what category of hurricane? ______

2. What is the difference in sustained wind speed between the minimums for category 3 and category 1? ________

3. What category hurricane produces a $7\frac{1}{2}$ foot storm surge? ______

4. In the past year Cuba had 5 hurricanes with maximum sustained winds of 95 mph, 115 mph, 100 mph, 116 mph, and 132 mph. Complete the bar graph below.

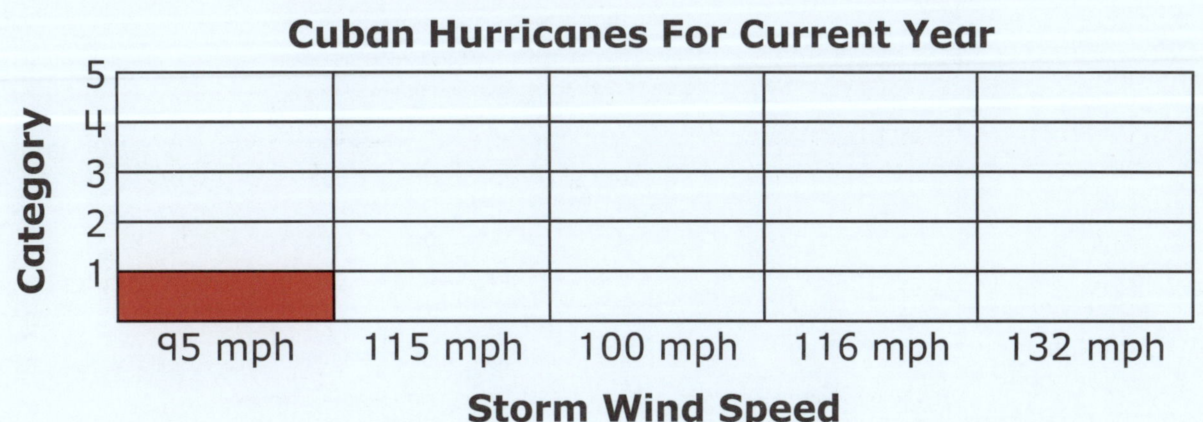

* Surge: waves swelling and rolling on shore

Hail is a form of solid precipitation. It is a ball or irregular lumps of ice. Hail is named by its approximate measurement across the center (diameter). Hail 1 inch or more in diameter is considered severe.

Hail Size (in.)	Name
$\frac{1}{4}$	pea
$\frac{1}{2}$	marble
$\frac{3}{4}$	penny
1	quarter
$1\frac{1}{4}$	half-dollar
$1\frac{1}{2}$	ping-pong ball
$1\frac{3}{4}$	golf ball
2	hen egg

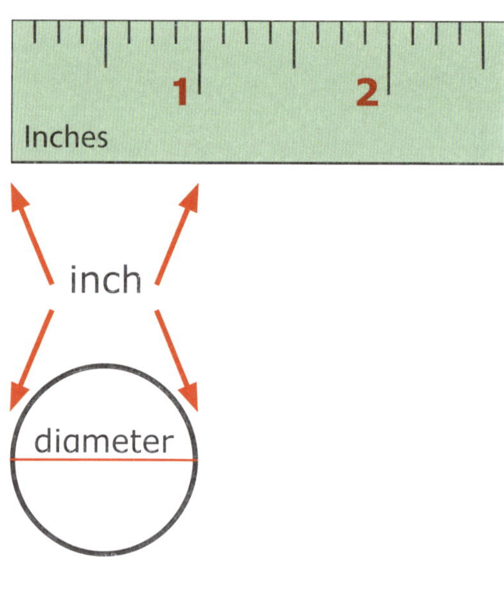

The city of Warren had 8 hail storms last year. Complete the table.

Date	Described	Diameter (in.)
April 4	penny	
May 2	quarter	
May 9	golf ball	
June 11	pea	
June 15	hen egg	
July 18	marble	
August 1	ping-pong ball	
August 28	half-dollar	

1. Measure, then write the diameter of the following hail stones in inches and state how they would be described.

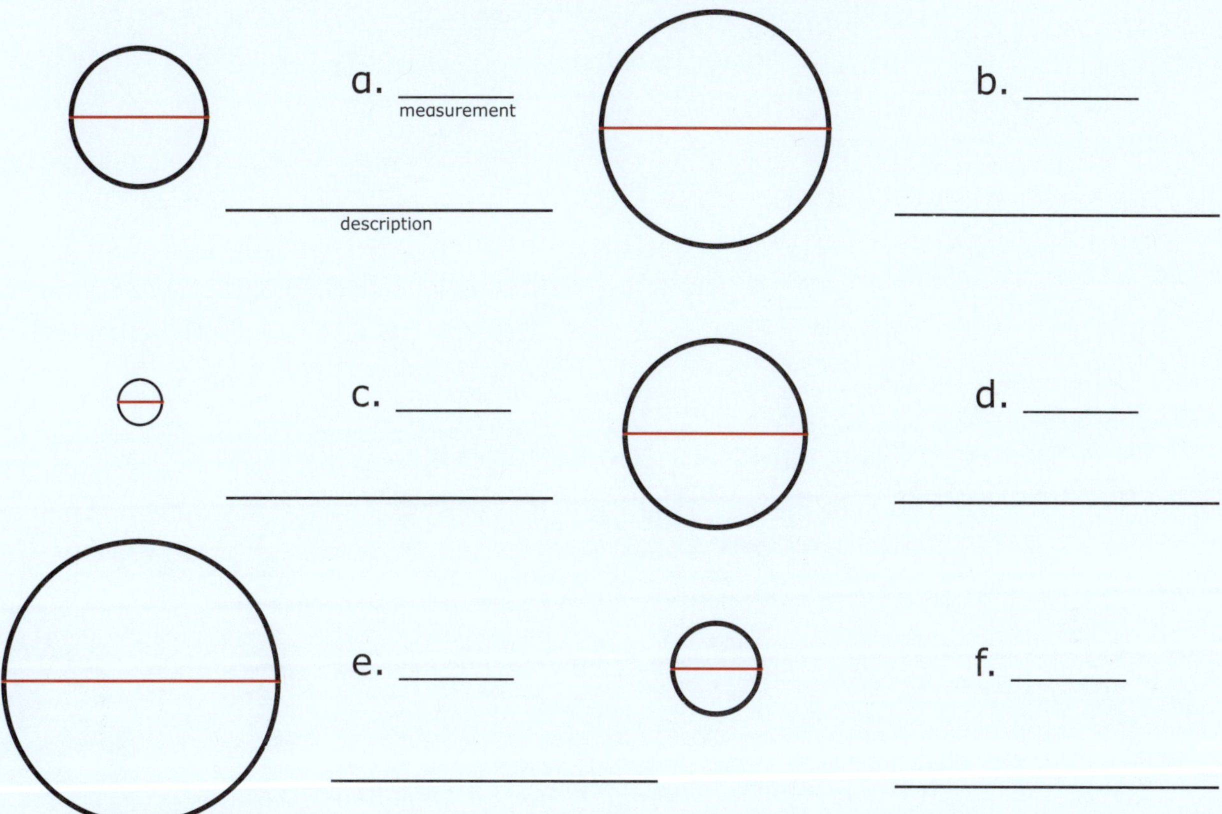

2. Use a ruler to draw a penny-sized hail stone and a golf ball-sized hail stone.

Juan said it takes him 20 minutes to walk home from school. Jim said it takes him just half as long as Juan to walk home from school. Joe lives the longest distance from school and it takes him 40 minutes to walk home. However, Joe always takes the bus to school and home.

The sixth grade teacher, Miss Green, told everyone that she loved to walk as many places as she could. She told the class that exercise was important for health and an average 120 pound person, which is her weight, burns up about 200 calories in an hour's walk.

60 minutes = 1 hour
7 days = 1 week

Find each answer.

1 In a 5-day school week, how many minutes does Juan use walking to and from school?

____

2 In a 5-day school week, how many minutes does Jim use walking to and from school?

____

3 What is the difference in minutes that it would take Jim and Joe to walk home?

____

4 If Joe had to walk home from school for three 5-day school weeks, how long would it take him in minutes? In hours?

_______________ _______________

5. How many calories can Miss Green burn walking for 2 hours?

____

6. How many calories can Miss Green burn walking an hour?

____

7. How many calories will Miss Green burn walking 45 minutes?

____

8. To lose 1 pound, Miss Green has to burn 3,500 calories. If she wanted to lose 2 pounds, how many hours would she have to walk?

____

9. If Miss Green eats a large serving of fries with 500 calories, how many minutes would it take for her to burn that many calories? In hours?

__________ __________

10. An 11-year-old consumes approximately 2,000 calories in a day. How many calories is that in a week?

____

When copying a shape, to keep it from being distorted, a constant **scale** must be maintained. In the first grid, each unit is $\frac{1}{2}$ centimeter, while in the second grid each unit is 1 centimeter. Copy the shape to the second grid to double its size without any distortion. Start at the red arrow and place lines in corresponding positions.

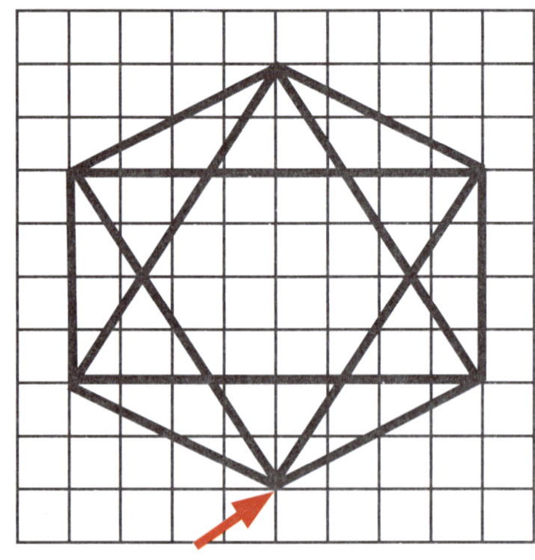

1 unit = $\frac{1}{2}$ centimeter

1 unit = 1 cm

Challenge: What is the area inside the second figure? ________

To copy a figure without distorting it, a constant **scale** must be applied. In the first grid, 1 unit = 1 centimeter, while in the second grid 1 unit = $\frac{1}{2}$ centimeter. Copy the figure to the second grid to reduce its size to one-half without any distortion. Start at the red arrow and place lines in corresponding positions.

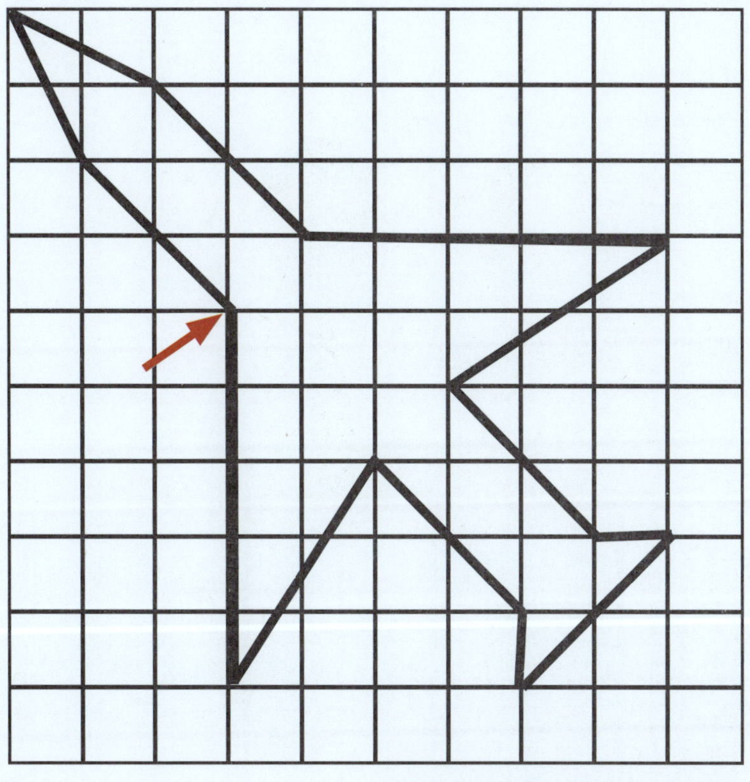

1 unit = 1 cm

1 unit = $\frac{1}{2}$ cm

Figures that are the same shape but not necessarily the same size are called **similar**.

Draw a picture on the first grid. Make an enlargement of the drawing on the second grid. Since each unit is twice as large, the picture will be twice as large. A line on the small grid should be located on the same corresponding position on the large grid.

A **ratio** is used to compare things. If every two hours you send five text messages, as a ratio or comparison, that relationship can be written three different ways.

2 to 5 2:5 $\frac{2}{5}$

→ Ratios are always written in simplest form.

$\frac{1}{2}$ not $\frac{2}{4}$

→ Ratios should always compare the same units.

17 minutes compared to 1 hour should be written

$\frac{17 \text{ minutes}}{60 \text{ minutes}}$ not $\frac{17 \text{ minutes}}{1 \text{ hour}}$

Write each problem as a fractional ratio; then cross out the correct answers below to kfind the two false answers.

1. Erica spent 20¢ on a candy bar and 60¢ on a pen. What is the ratio of money spent on the candy bar to money spent on the pen? ______

2. Ali called Kali six times today and Kali called Ali eight times today. What is the ratio of Ali's calls to Kali's? ______

3. Leon spent 50¢ on an apple and \$2 on a hot dog. What was the ratio of money spent on an apple compared to money spent on a hot dog? ______

One sandwich costs \$3 and three sandwiches cost \$9.

$\frac{\text{one sandwiches}}{\$3} = \frac{\text{three sandwiches}}{\$9}$ $\frac{1}{3} = \frac{3}{9}$

Two equal ratios make a **proportion**. Sandwiches and money may be different, but the relationship is the same and they change at the same rate.

Fill out the charts with proportion relationships.

1

miles	55					
hours	1	2	3	4	5	6

2

dollars	\$3.50					
gallons	1	2	3	4	5	6

3

dollars			\$15.45			
tickets	1	2	3	4	5	6

4

pounds	1	2	3	4	5	6
dollars				\$1.20		

Two equal ratios form a **proportion**.

On a road map, 2 inches equals 30 miles and 3 inches equals 45 miles.

$$\frac{\text{2 inches}}{\text{30 miles}} = \frac{\text{3 inches}}{\text{45 miles}}$$

The numerator of the first fraction and the denominator of the second fraction are the extremes of the proportion. The denominator of the first fraction and the numerator of the second fraction are called the means of the proportion.

$$\frac{\text{2 inches (extreme)}}{\text{30 miles (mean)}} = \frac{\text{3 inches (mean)}}{\text{45 miles (extreme)}}$$

If the proportion is true, the product of the extremes equals the product of the means.

TRUE

$$\frac{2}{30} = \frac{3}{45}$$

$$2 \times 45 = 30 \times 3$$

$$90 = 90$$

Mark each proportion true or false.

1. $\frac{2}{8} = \frac{3}{12}$ ________

2. $\frac{1}{2} = \frac{5}{10}$ ________

3. $\frac{5}{9} = \frac{11}{23}$ ________

4. $\frac{6}{8} = \frac{15}{20}$ ________

5. $\frac{8}{12} = \frac{14}{21}$ ________

6. $\frac{12}{20} = \frac{15}{25}$ ________

7. $\frac{4}{18} = \frac{6}{27}$ ________

8. $\frac{14}{30} = \frac{18}{26}$ ________

Shade in the areas with true proportions in green and false proportions in yellow to see a pattern. In true proportions, the product of the extremes equals the product of the means.

$$\frac{\text{extreme}}{\text{mean}} = \frac{\text{mean}}{\text{extreme}}$$

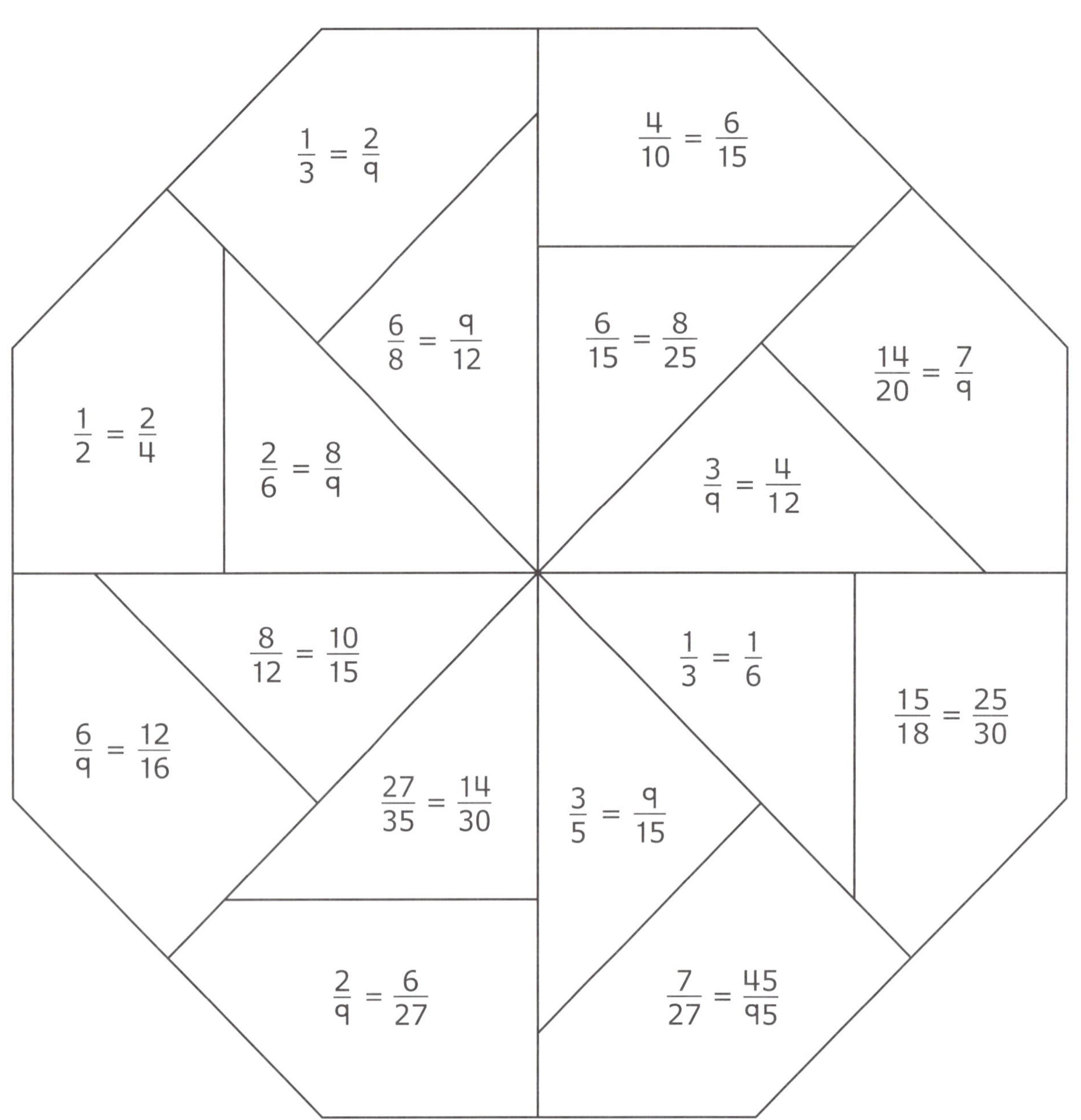

On a road map, 2 inches equals 15 miles. What distance would 5 inches equal? ______

$$\frac{2}{15} = \frac{5}{?}$$

Four of each of the five numbers in each row have something in common. Circle the number that is unlike the others, then unscramble the letters of the answers to write the message below.

1	s = 28	a = 36	r = 18	t = 45	n = 81
2	o = $\frac{1}{2}$	r = $\frac{8}{16}$	a = $\frac{4}{8}$	t = $\frac{3}{4}$	i = $\frac{12}{24}$
3	s = 1	n = .1	c = 1.	d = 1.0	a = 1.00
4	a = 125	r = 310	n = 75	e = 32	n = 140
5	e = 216	a = 137	n = 510	r = 114	i = 32
6	r = 118	t = 83	a = 75	b = 217	d = 31
7	e = 33	r = 110	p = 14	s = 88	t = 22
8	m = 7	r = 35	t = 11	n = 49	o = 63

Find the word the scrambled letters of the answers form.

____ ____ ____ ____ ____ ____ ____ ____

A proportion is two equal ratios. If four cans of tuna cost $10, what would six cans of tuna cost? To solve a proportion, first make two equal ratios comparing cans to money.

$$\frac{4 \text{ cans}}{\$10} = \frac{6 \text{ cans}}{\$n}$$

$$4 \times n = 10 \times 6$$

Write an equation showing the product of the extremes equals the product of the means.

$$4 \times n = 60$$

$$\frac{4 \times n}{4} = \frac{60}{4}$$

To solve for the unknown number *n*, use the inverse operation of multiplication by dividing both sides of the equation by 4.

$$\frac{\not{4} \times n}{\not{4}} = \frac{60}{4}$$

$$n = \$15$$

NOTE: $4 \times n$ can be written as $4n$.
$1 \times n$ can be written as n.

Solve each proportion; then use the letters to solve the riddle on the next page.

h $\frac{5}{6} = \frac{15}{n}$

a $\frac{2}{5} = \frac{6}{n}$

r $\frac{4}{6} = \frac{14}{n}$

t $\frac{9}{12} = \frac{6}{n}$

s $\frac{3}{7} = \frac{6}{n}$

i $\frac{8}{10} = \frac{16}{n}$

n $\frac{2}{15} = \frac{8}{n}$

c $\frac{10}{15} = \frac{16}{n}$

w $\frac{6}{16} = \frac{15}{n}$

d If the cost of eight tickets is $50, what is the cost of 12 tickets? Make a proportion and solve.

e If Jim can walk 5,000 ft in 10 minutes, how long would it take him to walk 12,500 ft? Make a proportion and solve.

f Joe measured his house and made a scale drawing. The scale of the drawing was 1 in. = 4 ft. If the actual width of his house was 48 ft, how wide was the house in the drawing? Make a proportion and solve.

What would you find on a haunted beach?

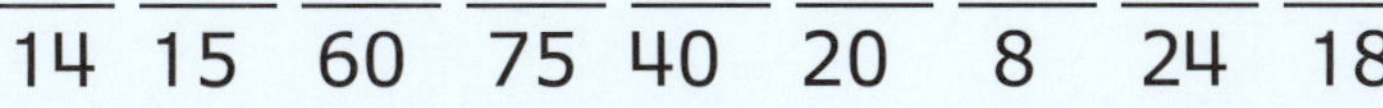

___ ___ ___ ___ ___ ___ ___ ___ ___
14 15 60 75 40 20 8 24 18

A mile is equal to 5,280 feet.

A **rate** is a fixed ratio between two things.

Two bananas costing 25¢ is a fixed ratio.

$$\frac{2}{25} = 2 \text{ to } 25 = 2 : 25$$

If two bananas cost 25¢, how much do six bananas cost? This can be solved as a proportion problem, letting n be that cost.

$$\frac{2}{25} = \frac{6}{n}$$

(product of means = product of extremes) → $2 \cdot n = 25 \cdot 6$

$2n = 150$ ← divide each side by 2

$n = 75¢$

If in 3 hours Jim drives 120 miles, how far can he drive in 5 hours?

$$\frac{3}{120} = \frac{5}{n}$$

$3 \cdot n = 120 \cdot 5$ ← cross multiply

$3n = 600$ ← divide each side by 3

$n = 200$ miles

Solve each problem.

1. If Rea made $81 working part-time in 3 days, how long will it take her to earn $135 part-time? What is her daily rate?

2. Mai walks 5,280 feet (1 mile) in 12 minutes. How long will it take her to walk 8,800 feet? What is her rate per minute?

3. Elly can read 25 pages in 90 minutes. How long will it take her to read 15 pages? What is her rate per page?

To figure the number of possible **combinations**, a **tree diagram** can be used. Each entire branch indicates a possible outcome.

Given two pizzas (one sausage and one vegetable), if you were going to eat three slices, what are all the possible combinations of your choices?

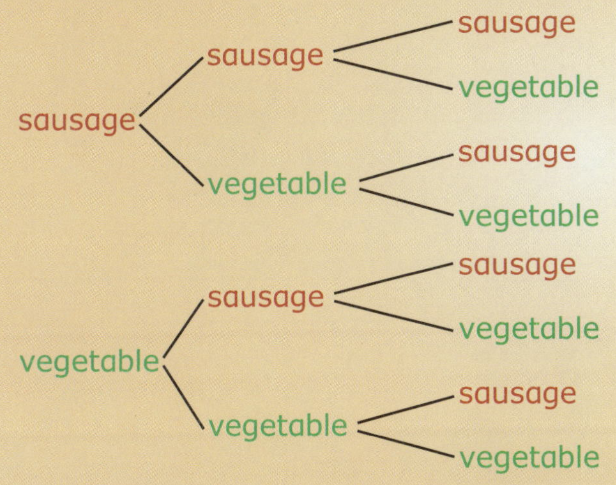

Possible Combinations

sausage, sausage, sausage
sausage, sausage, vegetable
sausage, vegetable, sausage
sausage, vegetable, vegetable
vegetable, sausage, sausage
vegetable, sausage, vegetable
vegetable, vegetable, sausage
vegetable, vegetable, vegetable

8 possible outcomes

1. A spinner has areas marked with a 1, 2, or 3. If the spinner is used three times, what are all the possible combinations of outcomes? Use a separate sheet of paper to draw a tree diagram.

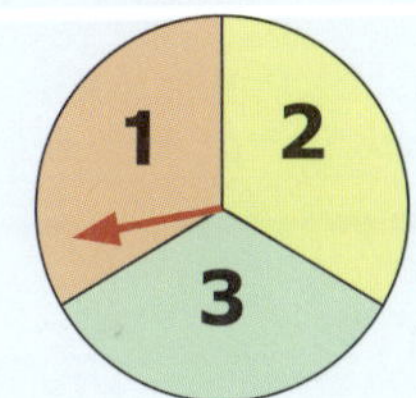

2. What was the total number of different outcomes possible in problem #1? ______

Probability tells the likelihood that an event will happen. The larger the number the larger the chance of the occurrence.

$$\text{Probability} = \frac{\text{number of favorable outcomes}}{\text{number of possible outcomes}}$$

probability of landing on blue = $\frac{1}{4}$

probability of landing on red = $\frac{2}{4} = \frac{1}{2}$

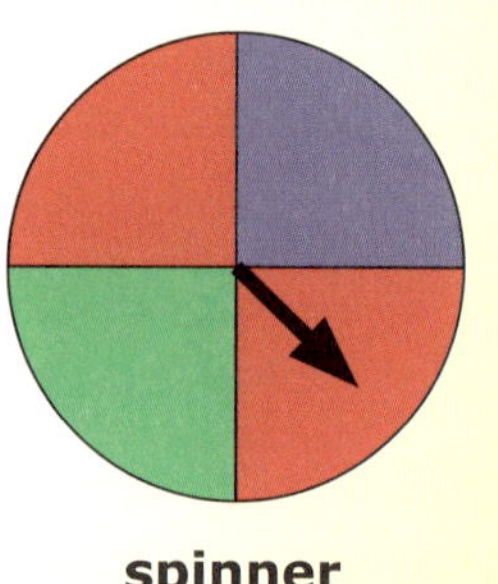
spinner

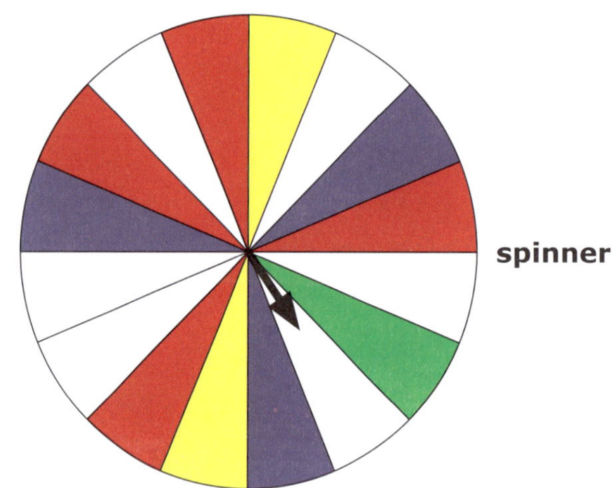
spinner

Find the probability of the arrow landing on a color, then write the letter of the answer on the line provided.

1. probability of landing on green _____ a. $\frac{1}{8}$
2. probability of landing on yellow _____ b. $\frac{1}{4}$
3. probability of landing on blue _____ c. $\frac{3}{8}$
4. probability of landing on red _____ d. $\frac{1}{16}$
5. probability of landing on white _____ e. 0
6. probability of landing on purple _____ f. $\frac{3}{16}$

$$\text{Probability} = \frac{\text{number of favorable outcomes}}{\text{number of possible outcomes}}$$

Always express the probability in simplest form.

1. What is the probability of tossing a penny and it landing with heads up?

______

2. What is the probability of rolling a die and the number 4 is rolled?

______

3. What is the probability of rolling a die and the number comes up either 5 or 6?

______

4. What is the probability of selecting an ace off the top of a 52-card shuffled deck?

______

5. What is the probability of selecting a two, three, or four of diamonds off the top of a 52-card shuffled deck?

______

6. Jake usually makes three baskets out of every four free throw tries. If he takes 100 shots, how many baskets should he expect to make?

______

Color the marbles, showing the probability of drawing a certain color marble out of a bag as described on the chart. It is helpful to change the probabilities to equivalent fractions with the same common denominators before beginning. In the first problem, the common denominator is 6.

1

Color	Probability
red	$\frac{1}{6}$
blue	$\frac{1}{3}$
yellow	$\frac{1}{2}$

2

Color	Probability
red	$\frac{1}{12}$
green	$\frac{1}{6}$
blue	$\frac{1}{4}$
yellow	$\frac{1}{3}$
purple	$\frac{1}{6}$

Percent (%) means per hundred. If 40% of the new vehicles bought are trucks, that means 40 out of every 100 newly purchased vehicles are trucks.

$$40 \text{ trucks out of } 100 \text{ vehicles} = \frac{40}{100} = .40 = 40\%$$

QUICK RULES:

1. To change a percent to a decimal number, move the decimal point two places to the left and drop the percent sign.
   40% = .40

2. To change a decimal number to a percent, move the decimal point two places to the right and add the percent sign.
   .40 = 40%

Choose the correct answer in each row and use the letter of the answer to write the message below.

45% =	y .45	t 4.5	r 45
.15 =	r 1.5%	m .15%	o 15%
.09 =	a 90%	u 9%	t .9%
60% =	a .6	c .06	o 600
5% =	s .5	m 50	r .05
.72 =	t 7.2%	s .72%	e 72%
.3 =	n 3%	a 30%	b 300%
2% =	m .02	y 20	r 200
25% =	s 2.5	n 25	a .25
.81 =	t 81%	u .81%	o 8.1%
1% =	b .1	h .01	d 10
.111 =	e 1.11%	a 111%	w 11.1%
34.5% =	o 34.5	h .345	n 3.45
.005 =	i .5%	s 5%	a 50%
100% =	n .10	t .1	z 1

___ ___ ___ ___ ___ ___ ___ ___ ___ ___ ___

___ ___ ___ ___!

Percent (%) means "out of 100 equal parts" or "per hundred."
100% is the entire amount.

The shaded area in the grid can be written as:

$\frac{3}{100}$ = .03 = 3% = three hundredths

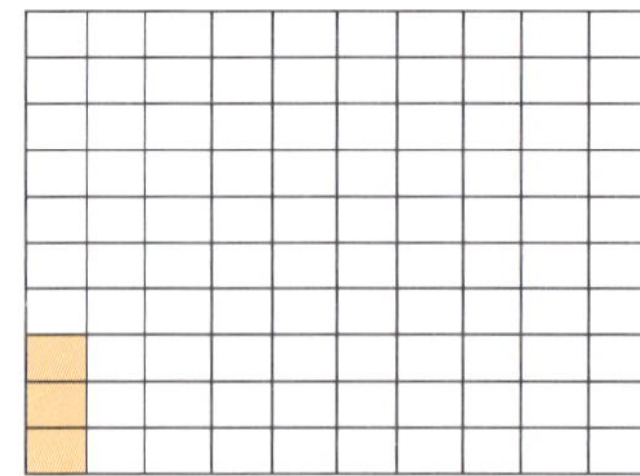

The shaded area in the grid can be written as:

$\frac{10}{100}$ = .10 = 10% = 10 hundredths

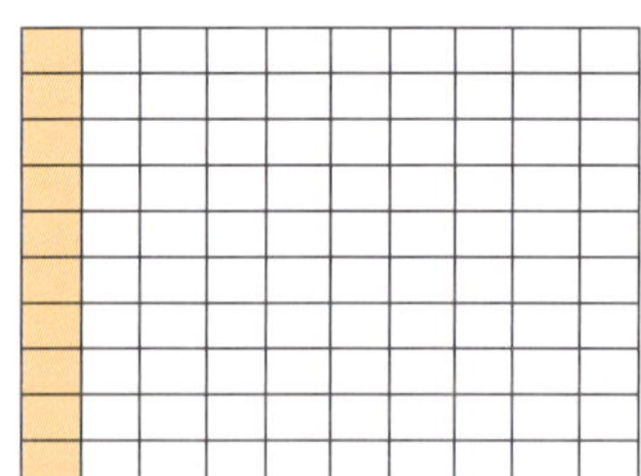

Fill in the missing blanks. Write fractions in simplest form.

Decimal	Fraction	Percent
.27		
	$\frac{89}{100}$	
		7%
	$\frac{25}{100}$	
.5 (.50)		
		75%

Write as a percent and shade that amount.

$.06 = \frac{6}{100} = 6\%$

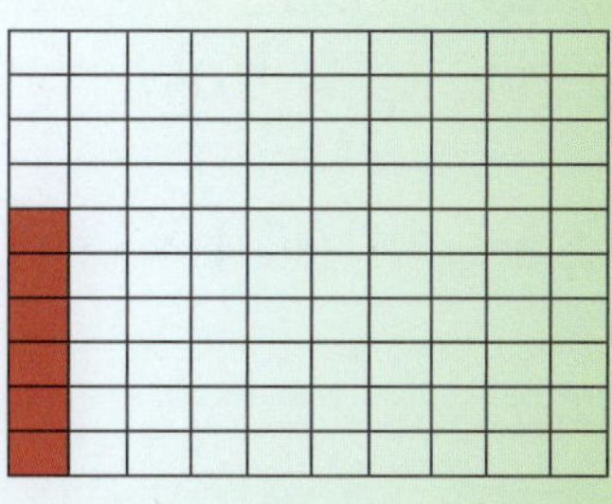

Multiply the numerator and denominator by the same number to get an equivalent fraction with a denominator of 100.

$\frac{1}{2}$

$\frac{1 \times 50}{2 \times 50} = \frac{50}{100} = 50\%$

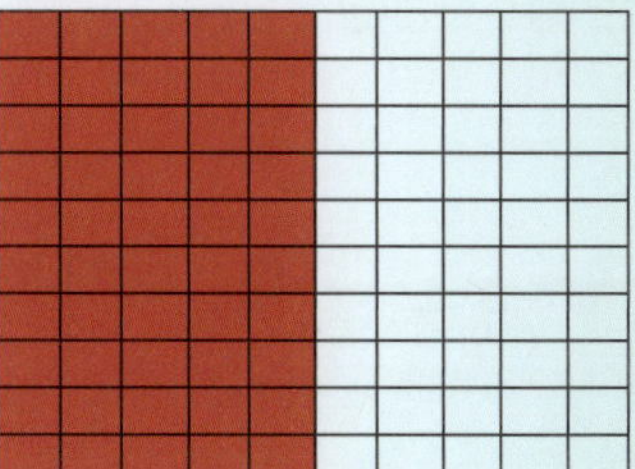

Complete each activity to show the fraction, decimal amount, percent, and complete the graph to match.

1. $\frac{13}{100}$ .13 ____%

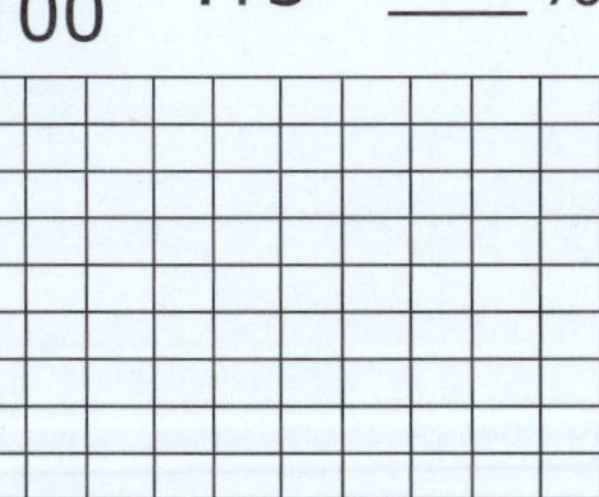

2. ____ .09 ____%

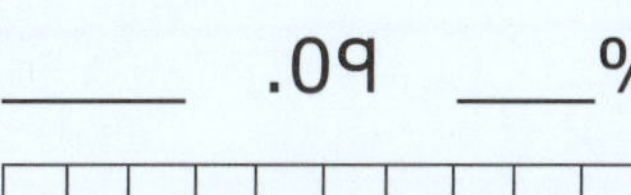

3. ____ .____ 99%

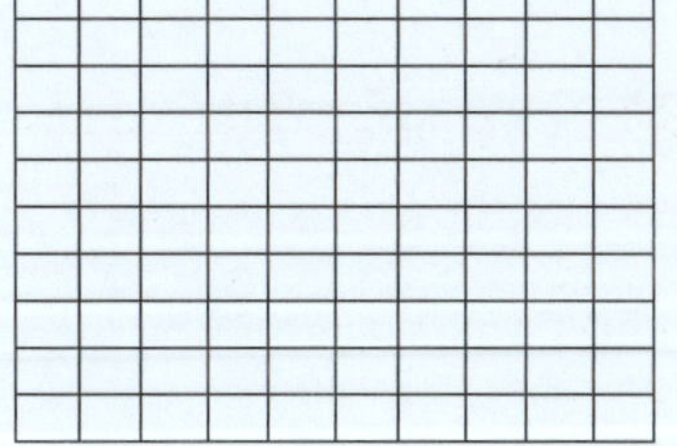

4. $\frac{17}{100}$.____ ____%

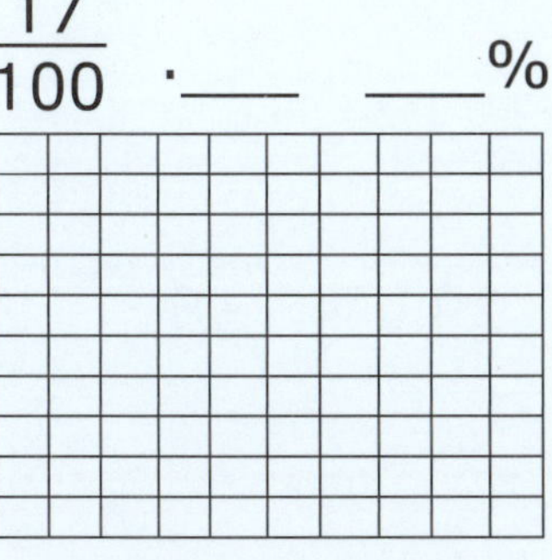

5. $\frac{3}{4}$.____ ____%

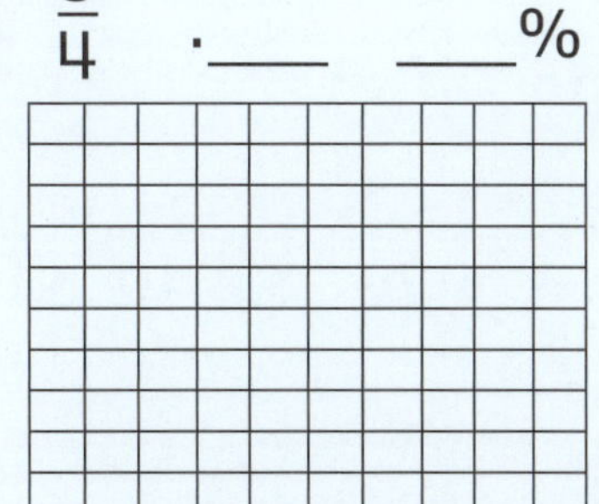

6. ____ .____ ____%

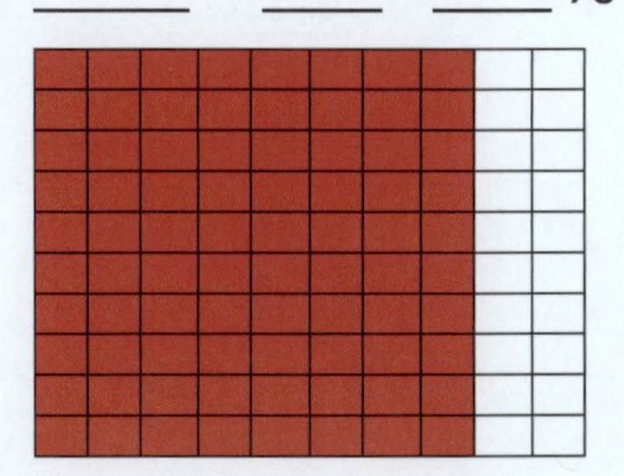

The department store had a 25% discount day. If George wanted to buy some jeans for $24, how much of a discount would he get?

25% of $24 = .25 × 24 = $6.00 off

To find a percent of a number, change the percent to a decimal number and multiply. The word of in mathematics indicates multiplication.

Find the amount of each discount; then use the letters to solve the riddle below.

e 75% of $16 = ___	h 20% of $30 = ___	r 15% of $14 = ___
s 18% of $35 = ___	t 60% of $48 = ___	n 6% of $120 = ___
u 10% of $36 = ___	w 50% of $7 = ___	c 35% of $84 = ___
i 40% of $32 = ___	a 8% of $240 = ___	g 100% of $42 = ___

What happens when corn catches a cold?

___ ___ ___ ___ ___ ___
$12.80 $28.80 $42 $12 $28.80 $6.30

___ ___ ___ ___ ___ ___ ___ ___ ___
$19.20 $7.20 $12 $19.20 $2.10 $19.20 $29.40 $6 $12

Juan bought a $50 pair of shoes at a 25% discount. How much were the shoes discounted?

25% of $50 = .25 × 50 = $12.50 discounted*

Solve and place the answers in the grid below.

1. Emily paid 35% less than the price of $25. How much was her discount? ________

2. Jim had to pay 8% tax on his $69 video game. How much tax did Jim pay on his video game? ________

3. If Lexie has a 40% off coupon, how much will she get off of a $64 coat? ________

4. Dan noticed a 25% off sign at the toy store. How much would a $219 bike be discounted? ________

5. If the tax on a $176 item was 9%, how much would the tax be? ________

6. If Bob bought a $29 shirt at a 15% discount, how much would the shirt cost before tax is added? ________

* To find a percent of a number, change the percent to a decimal number and multiply.

Isabella had eight coins in her purse. Every coin was either a penny, nickel, or dime. She told her friend that she had more dimes than nickels and more nickels than pennies. There are two different amounts of money she could have.

What are they? Write the answers in the tables below.

1

number of dimes	number of nickels	number of pennies	total amount

2

number of dimes	number of nickels	number of pennies	total amount

The Lincoln penny was designed in 1909 in honor of Abe Lincoln's 100th birthday.

A penny stays in circulation for about 30 years.

About 42% of all change is in pennies.

Use a pencil to divide the grid into four equal parts, each with the same size and shape, with each part holding the same number of pennies.

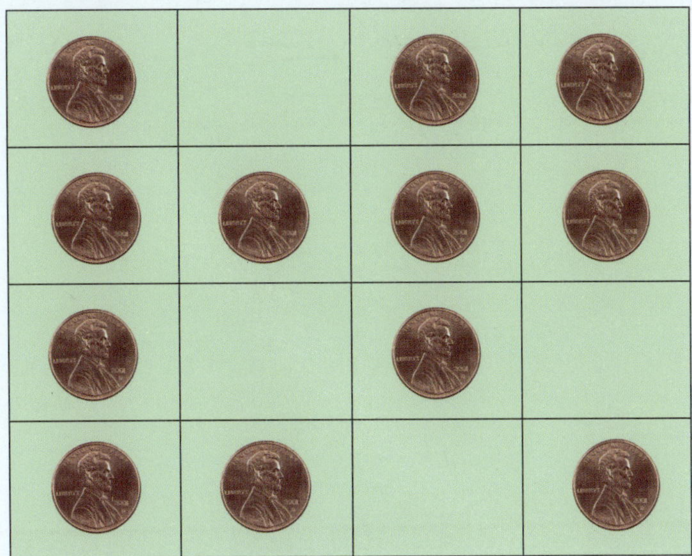

Shapes that are equal in size and shape are called **congruent.**

Super Challenge

Use four colors to divide the chessboard into 4 congruent shapes with one penny in each. You cannot move the pennies.

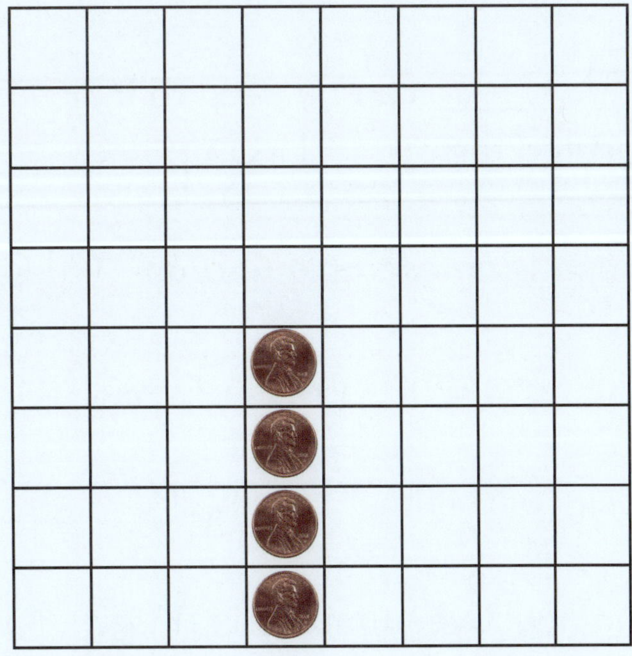

negative integers ratio
rate diameter origin proportion
probability quadrants exponent

Write the correct term from the choice box for each blank.

1) The rectangular coordinate system is cut into four quadrants.

2) A/an ratio can be used to compare two quantities.

3) The chance of an event happening is probability.

4) The distance across a circle through the center is called the diameter.

5) The number line is marked with integers.

6) A/an exponent can be used to indicate the number of identically repeated factors. 4x4

7) The price per unit is an example of a/an rate.

8) Two equal ratios form a/an proportion.

9) The ordered pair (0,0) is the origin.

10) The sum of two negative numbers is negative.

-3 + -3 =

-(-3)

Write the letter of the illustration that matches the vocabulary.

1) b product
2) f prime number
3) c difference
4) h denominator
5) a factor
6) m hexagon
7) k divisor
8) i obtuse angle
9) g numerator
10) l proportion
11) d pentagon
12) e acute angle
13) j quotient
14) n right angle
15) o composite number

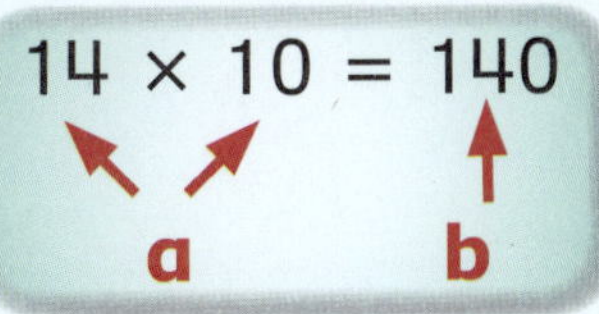

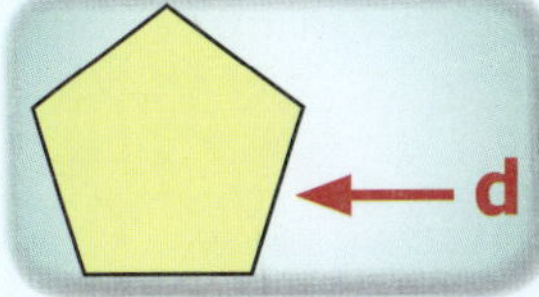

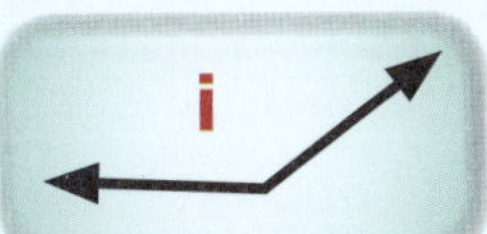

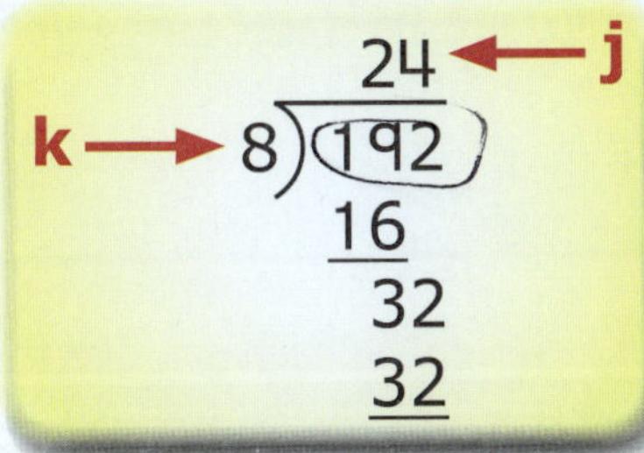

$\frac{3}{9} = \frac{2}{6}$ **l**

m

n

30 **o**

Solve each math analogy.

1. $<$ is to $>$ **AS** $\leq$ is to _____.

2. **Sum** is to **difference** **AS** **product** is to __________________.

3. **Triangle** is to **hexagon** **AS** **pentagon** is to ______________.

4. **30°** is to **acute angle** **AS** **90°** is to ______________________.

5. **Numerator** is to **denominator** **AS** **dividend** is to ____________________.

6. **.15** is to $\frac{15}{100}$ **AS** **39%** is to _____.

7. **1,000** is to **thousand** **AS** **1,000,000** is to _______________.

8. **5** is to **prime** **AS** **8** is to ____________________.

For more activities like this, please see our *Math Analogies* series.

The mean is the sum of the data divided by the number of data items. It is a measure of central tendency.

The median is the middle number after the data is placed in order.

The mode is the most used data item.

The following table shows the number of texts sent by the students surveyed in the last month.

Student	Text Messages Sent Last Month
Trent	221
Alva	214
Ryan	84
Liz	214
Alvin	560
Theo	36
Sara	105
Jana	254

1. What was the total number of text messages sent by the eight students in the last month? ________

2. Find the mean of text messages sent last month from the eight students. ________

3. Find the median of text messages sent last month from the eight students. ________

4. Find the mode of text messages sent last month from the eight students. ________

5. Without Alvin, what is the mean for the remaining seven students to the nearest whole number? ________

6. Why do you think the mean for the seven students compared to the mean for the eight students differs so much?

____

____

Place Values

Group Names

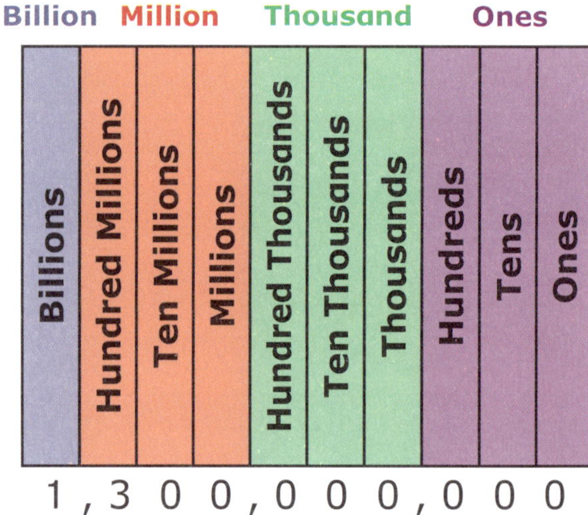

China has more people than any other country in the world. There are over one billion, three hundred million people living in China. When writing large numbers, separate them into groups of three using commas and starting from the right. When reading, we begin at the left and read each group of digits separately, saying the name of the group as reached. "And" is not used between group names.

The population of California given in the 2010 census was 37 million, two hundred fifty-three thousand, nine hundred fifty-six.

California population: 37,253,956 people

The population of Wyoming given in the 2010 census was five hundred sixty-three thousand, six hundred twenty-six.

Wyoming population: 563,626 people

Write the following in number form.

1. five billion, twenty thousand, fourteen ________________

2. four hundred million, three hundred thousand, two ________________

3) two billion, two million, two thousand, two ________

4) seven hundred thirty million, six hundred one thousand, four hundred one ________

5) eight billion, thirty million, eleven thousand, nine ________

6) forty-two thousand, three hundred eight ________

7) one billion, one million, one thousand, one ________

8) four hundred seven million, two hundred nine thousand, thirty-nine ________

9) eight billion, fifty million, fifty thousand, eight ________

10) two hundred three million, six hundred twenty-two thousand, four hundred thirty ________

11) It takes about 6,998,681 soda cans to fill an Olympic-sized swimming pool. Write this number in word form.

____

____

12) The latest official world population mid-year 2011 was 6,928,198,253 people. Write the population in word form.

____

____

13) If you earned $50,000 per year, it would take you 20,000 years to earn one billion dollars. Write one billion dollars in number form.

____

On the road to addition mastery, sum each problem; then cross out the correct answers below to find the three false answers.

Before beginning an addition problem, line up the same place values.

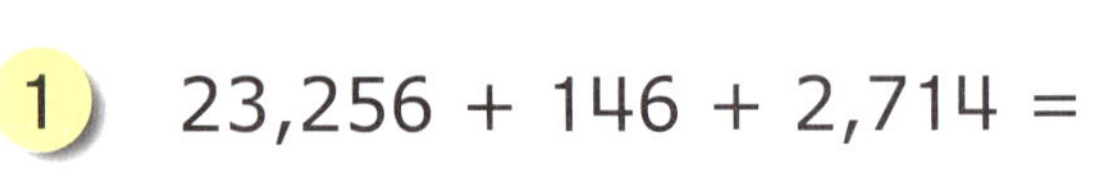

1) 23,256 + 146 + 2,714 =

```
  1 1 1
  23,256
     146
+  2,714
  26,116
```

2)
```
  103,453
7,240,117
+  25,523
```

3)
```
     193
  56,004
+  1,546
```

4)
```
      89
  34,502
+  6,704
```

5)
```
    6,429
  203,471
+  86,272
```

6)
```
2,390,218
   16,803
+ 307,117
```

7)
```
   56,198
    4,209
+ 652,714
```

8) 34,102 + 234 + 6,305 = ____________

9) 13 + 348 + 2,562 + 734,903 = ____________

737,826	396,172	~~26,116~~	296,172
41,641	2,714,138	7,369,093	727,826
57,743	41,295	713,121	40,641

On the road to subtraction mastery, subtract each problem; then cross out the correct answers below to find the three false answers.

Before beginning a subtraction problem, line up the same place values and regroup when necessary.

1. 15,006 − 920 =

```
  4 9 1
  15,006
-    920
  ------
  14,086
```

2. 104,672 − 45,123

3. 19,003 − 3,916

4. 496,219 − 98,724

5. 28,450 − 16,274

6. 701,277 − 135,681

7. 1,200,234 − 807,307

8. 823,000 − 5,000 = ___________

9. 205,194 − 88,889 = ___________

10. 1,000,000 − 998,505 = ___________

On the road to multiplication mastery, multiply the problems; then cross out the correct answers below to find the false answer.

When multiplying, remember the order of the factors does not change the product. This is the commutative property of multiplication.

1) 243 × 36 =

$$\begin{array}{r} 36 \\ \times\ 243 \\ \hline 108 \\ 1{,}440 \\ 7{,}200 \\ \hline 8{,}748 \end{array} \qquad \begin{array}{r} 243 \\ \times\ 36 \\ \hline 1{,}458 \\ 7{,}290 \\ \hline 8{,}748 \end{array}$$

2) $\begin{array}{r} 58 \\ \times\ 43 \\ \hline \end{array}$

3) $\begin{array}{r} 79 \\ \times\ 29 \\ \hline \end{array}$

4) $\begin{array}{r} 64 \\ \times\ 64 \\ \hline \end{array}$

5) $\begin{array}{r} 403 \\ \times\ 25 \\ \hline \end{array}$

6) $\begin{array}{r} 129 \\ \times\ 36 \\ \hline \end{array}$

7) $\begin{array}{r} 572 \\ \times\ 80 \\ \hline \end{array}$

8) 564 × 128 = ____________

10,075 | 2,494 | 73,192 | ~~8,748~~ | 45,760 | 72,192 | 2,291 | 4,644 | 4,096

On the track to division mastery, divide each problem; then cross out the correct answers below to find the two false answers.

1. $5{,}256 \div 8 =$

$$\begin{array}{r} 6 \\ 8\overline{)5{,}256} \\ -48 \leftarrow 8 \times 6 \\ 45 \end{array}$$

$$\begin{array}{r} 657 \\ 8\overline{)5{,}256} \\ -48 \\ 45 \\ -40 \leftarrow 8 \times 5 \\ 56 \\ -56 \leftarrow 8 \times 7 \end{array}$$

2. $5\overline{)825}$

3. $6\overline{)1{,}524}$

4. $7\overline{)5{,}075}$

5. $4\overline{)9{,}732}$

6. $9\overline{)1{,}566}$

7. $8\overline{)4{,}656}$

8. $7{,}215 \div 3 =$ ____________

On the road to division mastery, find each quotient; then cross out the correct answers below to find the two false answers.

1) $585 \div 45 =$

$$\begin{array}{r} 1 \\ 45\overline{)585} \\ -45\downarrow \\ \hline 135 \end{array} \leftarrow 45 \times 1$$

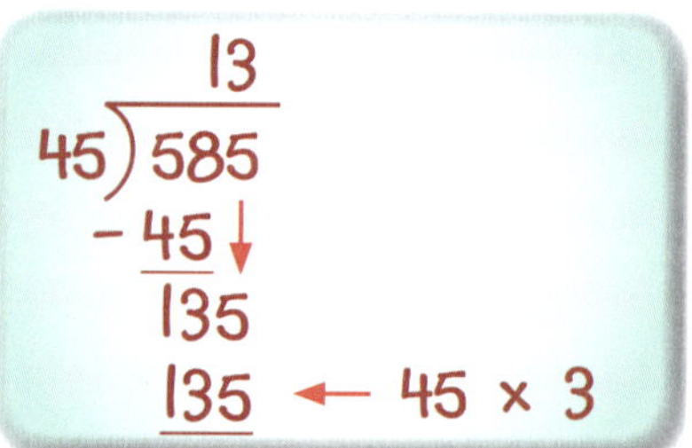

2) $50\overline{)1,550}$

3) $23\overline{)1,196}$

4) $61\overline{)4,514}$

5) $92\overline{)5,796}$

6) $74\overline{)2,590}$

7) $82\overline{)5,494}$

8) $5,986 \div 73 =$ ____________

Notice the pattern of odd numbers. What is the sum of the seventh row? ______

Always do the following steps when solving a problem. If the steps are not done in the correct order, an incorrect answer may occur.

Steps for **Order of Operations** when parentheses, exponents, addition, subtraction, multiplication and division may be involved:

Step 1: Work inside parentheses.
Step 2: Figure exponents.
Step 3: Do multiplication and division from left to right.
Step 4: Do addition and subtraction from left to right.

Exponents are used to multiply several like factors.

$$5^2 - (9 + 2) =$$
$$5^2 - 11 =$$
$$25 - 11 = 14$$

$$8 \div 2^3 + 2 \times 3 =$$
$$8 \div 8 + 2 \times 3 =$$
$$1 + 6 = 7$$

Work each problem; then use the letters to solve the riddle on the next page.

t) $9^2 - (9 + 36) =$ ______________

o) $54 \div 6 \times 9 =$ ______________

m) $(8 - 2)^2 - 8 \cdot 3 + 4 =$ ______________

b) $12 - 8 + 2 \times 2 + 2 =$ ______________

l) $4^3 - (5 + 2)^2 + 5^2 + 14 =$ ______________

p) $8(1.5)^2 - (144 \div 8 - 11) =$ ______________

y) $8 \times 4^2 - 8^2 - 2 \times 13 =$ __________

w) $4 \times 6 \div 6 \times 6 \div 2 =$ __________

i) $(14 + 3^2) - 2 \times 4 =$ __________

u) $2^2(126 \div 9) - 5 \times 10 - 1 =$ __________

s) $(1.95 + .05)(4.7 - 2.7) =$ __________

n) $(3 \times 2)^2 + 7 - 10 \div 5 =$ __________

What did the duck say to the waiter about how he would pay for the meal?

___ ___ ___   ___ ___   ___ ___   ___ ___   ___ ___ ___ ___

11 5 36   15 36   81 41   16 38   10 15 54 54

Challenge: Place parentheses to make the equation true.

1) $16 - 8 \div 4 \times 2 = 1$

2) $24 - 18 - 12 \div 2 + 1 = 13$

Find each missing number.

1. _____ + 14 = 50
2. _____ + 17 = 56
3. _____ + 39 = 83
4. _____ + 28 = 71
5. _____ + 101 = 456
6. _____ + 101 = 200
7. _____ + 90 = 463
8. _____ + 194 = 387
9. _____ + 37 = 401
10. _____ + 47 = 111
11. _____ + 89 = 93
12. 89 + _____ = 93
13. 74 + _____ = 205
14. 102 + _____ = 300
15. _____ + 75 = 150
16. _____ + 68 = 411
17. _____ + 43 = 341
18. _____ + 55 = 930
19. _____ + 81 = 119
20. 197 + _____ = 214

21 ____ + 107 = 200

22 ____ + 210 = 500

23 44 + ____ = 107

24 65 + ____ = 215

25 ____ + 560 = 1000

26 ____ + 275 = 500

27 ____ + 305 = 400

28 ____ + 1,390 = 2,100

29 ____ + 1,064 = 2,111

30 ____ + 18 = 4,109

31 Julia has exercised for 21 minutes. She had decided to exercise for a total of 90 minutes. How many more minutes will she be exercising? Write an equation and solve.

____ + ____ = ____ ____

32 Joe is saving to buy a $125 telescope. So far Joe has saved $34. How much more does Joe need to save to buy the telescope? Write an equation and solve.

____ + ____ = ____ ____

Finding the unknown (n) quantity in equations of the form $n + 18 = 24$ should be done by the following steps.

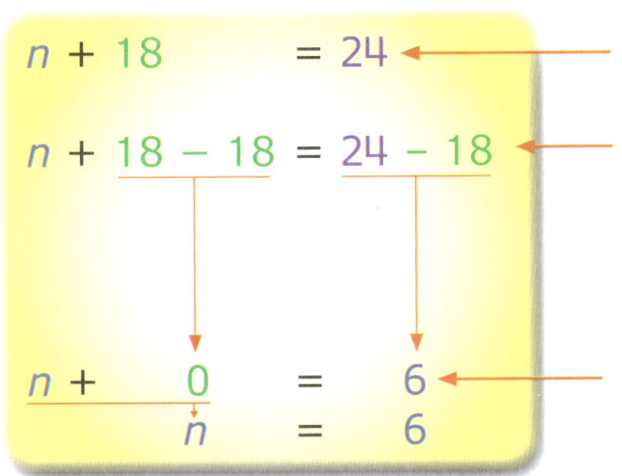

1. Solve for n.
2. Subtract 18 from both sides. If the same amount is not subtracted from both sides, the equation will no longer be true.
3. Check to see if $n = 6$ makes the equation true. $6 + 18 = 24$

Use the steps above to solve the following equations for n.

1. $n + 47 = 50$

2. $n + 13 = 21$

3. $n + 15 = 43$

4. $n + 25 = 119$

5. $n + 74 = 89$

6. $n + 56 = 102$

7. $n + 36 = 71$

8. $n + 9 = 60$

9) $n + 28 = 52$

10) $n + 19 = 40$

11) $50 + n = 119$

12) $n + \frac{1}{2} = \frac{5}{6}$

13) $n + \$2.45 = \$5.50$

14) $n + \$6 = \$10.45$

15) Hal received $16 from his mother and now has $40. How much money did Hal have originally? Write an equation and solve.

16) Jan needs $25 more dollars to buy a $54 coat. How much money does she have now? Write an equation and solve.

Find each missing number.

1. 45 – _____ = 1
2. 60 – _____ = 11
3. 21 – _____ = 12
4. 21 – _____ = 14
5. 17 – _____ = 8
6. 87 – _____ = 68
7. 98 – _____ = 45
8. 101 – _____ = 6
9. 52 – _____ = 30
10. 73 – _____ = 28
11. 49 – _____ = 34
12. 76 – _____ = 29
13. 90 – _____ = 37
14. 80 – _____ = 11
15. 88 – _____ = 49
16. 100 – _____ = 15
17. 200 – _____ = 25
18. 225 – _____ = 199
19. 505 – _____ = 75
20. 108 – _____ = 9

21) 200 – _____ = 75

22) 140 – _____ = 37

23) 500 – _____ = 401

24) 309 – _____ = 14

25) 1,000 – _____ = 50

26) 680 – _____ = 610

27) 2,500 – _____ = 700

28) 1,000 – _____ = 101

29) 2,000 – _____ = 1,050

30) 1,001 – _____ = 10

31) Jimmy has saved $42. He owes his brother $25. How much money can Jimmy spend and still have enough left over to pay his brother the money he is owed? Write an equation and solve.

______ – ______ = ______ ______

32) Joanie has decided to write a paperback novel. She was told that an average page would contain 440 words. If Joanie has 156 words written, how many more should she write to complete the first page? Write an equation and solve.

______ – ______ = ______ ______

Finding the unknown (n) quantity in equations of the form $n - 12 = 9$ should be done by the following steps.

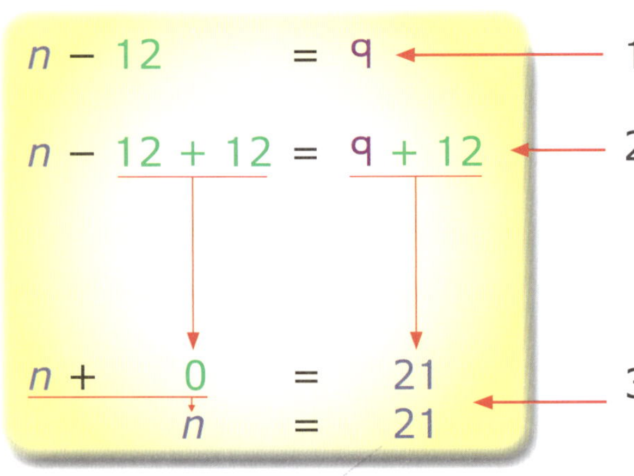

1. Solve for n.
2. Add 12 to both sides. If the same amount is not added to both sides, the equation will no longer be true.
3. Check to see if $n = 21$ makes the equation true. $21 - 12 = 9$

Use the steps above to solve the following equations for *n.*

1) $n - 8 = 11$

2) $n - 11 = 6$

3) $n - 35 = 26$

4) $n - 19 = 50$

5) $n - 49 = 27$

6) $n - 108 = 14$

7) $n - 57 = 25$

8) $n - 24 = 58$

9) $n - 9 = 9$

10) $n - 129 = 75$

11) $n - 1.2 = .43$

12) $n - \frac{1}{2} = \frac{1}{3}$

13) $n - \$1.03 = \$1.59$

14) $n - \$8 = \$19.01$

15) George needs enough money to buy a movie ticket for $6 and still have $8 for his share of a pizza. How much money does George need? Write an equation and solve.

16) Sarah spent $9.99 and still had $12.45 left. How much money did she start with? Write an equation and solve.

Find each missing number.

1) $7 \times$ _____ $= 42$

2) $8 \times$ _____ $= 64$

3) $6 \times$ _____ $= 54$

4) $9 \times$ _____ $= 81$

5) $5 \times$ _____ $= 75$

6) $3 \times$ _____ $= 72$

7) $4 \times$ _____ $= 84$

8) $2 \times$ _____ $= 58$

9) $8 \times$ _____ $= 400$

10) $6 \times$ _____ $= 180$

11) $9 \times$ _____ $= 3{,}600$

12) $10 \times$ _____ $= 200$

13) $8 \times$ _____ $= 120$

14) $5 \times$ _____ $= 240$

15) $7 \times$ _____ $= 315$

16) $4 \times$ _____ $= 300$

17) _____ $\times 8 = 216$

18) _____ $\times 3 = 450$

19) _____ $\times 10 = 1{,}000$

20) $50 \times$ _____ $= 2{,}000$

21. 20 × _____ = 700

22. 30 × _____ = 750

23. _____ × 40 = 800

24. 25 × _____ = 400

25. 11 × _____ = 220

26. 55 × _____ = 1,100

27. 21 × _____ = 252

28. 63 × _____ = 1,890

29. _____ × 200 = 10,000

30. 70 × _____ = 910

31. The total amount spent on buying 8 child movie tickets was $56. How much did each ticket cost? Write an equation and solve.

_____ × _____ = _____ _____

32. Susie drove to her aunt's house averaging 55 miles per hour. If her aunt's house was 165 miles away, how long did it take to drive there? Write an equation and solve.

_____ × _____ = _____ _____

Finding the unknown (n) quantity in equations of the form $2 \times n = 18$ should be done by the following steps.

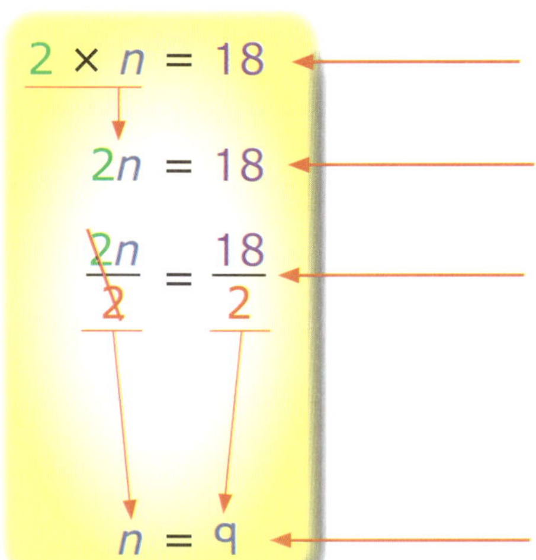

1. Solve for n.
2. $2 \times n$ can be written as $2n$.
3. Undo x by 2 with the inverse operation of ÷ by 2.

   Do the same to each side of the equation or it will not remain true.
4. Check to see if $n = 9$ makes the equation true. $2 \times 9 = 18$

Use the steps above to solve the following equations for *n*.

1) $7n = 28$

2) $9n = 81$

3) $4n = 88$

4) $5 \times n = 35$

5) $10n = 90$

6) $8n = 104$

7) $7n = 273$

8) $9n = 468$

9) $6n = 294$

10) $6 \times n = 282$

11) $5n = 485$

12) $1{,}000 = 10n$

13) $3n = \$1.50$

14) $5n = \$8.25$

15) If three concert tickets cost $78, what is the price of one ticket? Write an equation and solve.

16) Hugh bought eight candy bars for $10.80. How much did each candy bar cost? Write an equation and solve.

Find each missing number.

1. ____ ÷ 5 = 9
2. ____ ÷ 6 = 4
3. ____ ÷ 9 = 3
4. ____ ÷ 2 = 20
5. ____ ÷ 8 = 7
6. ____ ÷ 3 = 30
7. ____ ÷ 4 = 50
8. ____ ÷ 5 = 11
9. ____ ÷ 6 = 12
10. ____ ÷ 4 = 15
11. ____ ÷ 9 = 15
12. ____ ÷ 7 = 90
13. ____ ÷ 6 = 62
14. ____ ÷ 3 = 1,800
15. ____ ÷ 20 = 10
16. ____ ÷ 50 = 15
17. ____ ÷ 7 = 35
18. ____ ÷ 9 = 48
19. ____ ÷ 40 = 10
20. ____ ÷ 25 = 52

21) ____ ÷ 11 = 7

22) ____ ÷ 24 = 8

23) ____ ÷ 43 = 6

24) ____ ÷ 29 = 5

25) ____ ÷ 30 = 9

26) ____ ÷ 95 = 6

27) ____ ÷ 75 = 4

28) ____ ÷ 98 = 60

29) ____ ÷ 40 = 40

30) ____ ÷ 18 = 180

31) How many game tokens are needed to be able to give 12 tokens each to 8 children? Write an equation and solve.

____ ÷ ____ = ____ ____

32) What was the total amount collected if each of the 23 students in the class each collected $4? Write an equation and solve.

____ ÷ ____ = ____ ____

Finding the unknown (n) quantity in equations of the form $n \div 4 = 7$ should be done by the following steps.

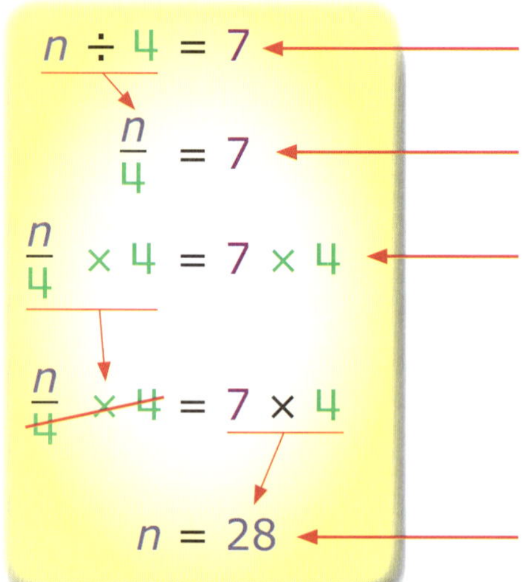

1. Solve for n.
2. $n \div 4$ can be written as $\frac{n}{4}$.
3. Undo $\div$ by 4 with the inverse operation of $\times$ by 4.

   Do the same to each side of the equation or it will not remain true.
4. Check to see if $n = 28$ makes the equation true. $28 \div 4 = 7$

Use the steps above to solve the following equations for n.

1) $\frac{n}{3} = 10$

2) $\frac{n}{9} = 8$

3) $\frac{n}{8} = 45$

4) $\frac{n}{6} = 46$

5) $\frac{n}{4} = 203$

6) $\frac{n}{7} = 59$

7) $\frac{n}{12} = 8$

8) $\frac{n}{20} = 30$

9) $\frac{n}{9} = 26$

10) $\frac{n}{12} = 12$

11) $\frac{n}{3} = \$1.45$

12) $25 = \frac{n}{5}$

13) $\frac{n}{25} = 15$

14) $\frac{n}{9} = 0$

15) John and his three friends each put $3.35 in to buy a basketball. How much did the basketball cost? Write an equation and solve.

16) How much money would Maria need if she wanted to buy six students a $5.50 meal? Write an equation and solve.

Right angles measure 90°.

Acute angles measure < 90°.

Obtuse angles measure between 90° and 180°.

Straight angles measure 180°.

The sum of the three inside angles in a triangle always adds to 180°.

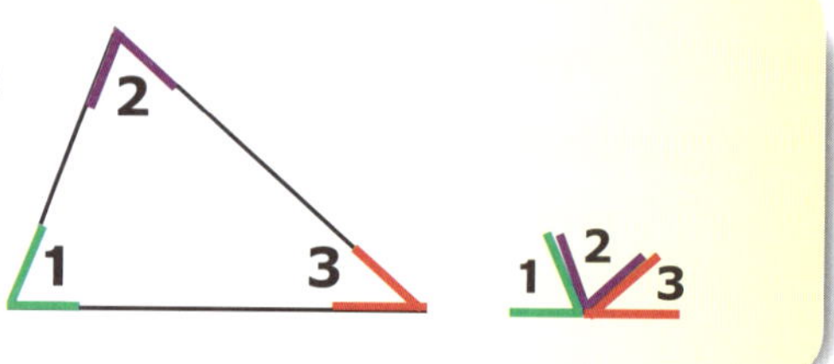

1. Draw a triangle, cut out the angles (see above) and show that together the angles form a straight angle.

2. Draw a triangle with a right angle. Cut out the angles and show that together the angles form a straight angle which measures 180°.

3.

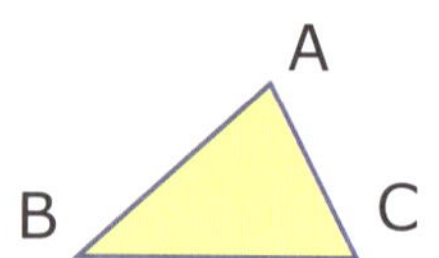

$\angle A = 55^\circ$

$\angle B = 46^\circ$

$\angle C =$ ____

4.

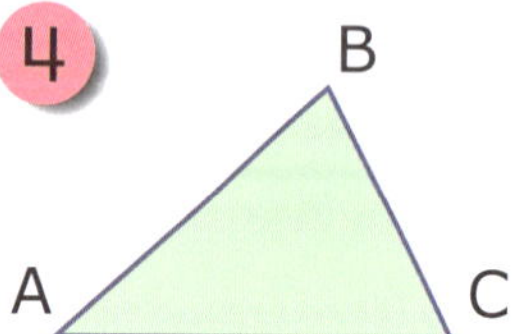

$\angle A =$ ____

$\angle B = 73^\circ$

$\angle C = 39^\circ$

5.

C B A

$\angle A = 45^\circ$

$\angle B = 90^\circ$

$\angle C =$ ____

6.

B C A

$\angle A = 28^\circ$

$\angle B =$ ____

$\angle C = 35^\circ$

Vertical angles are the angles opposite each other when two lines cross. Their measurements are equal.

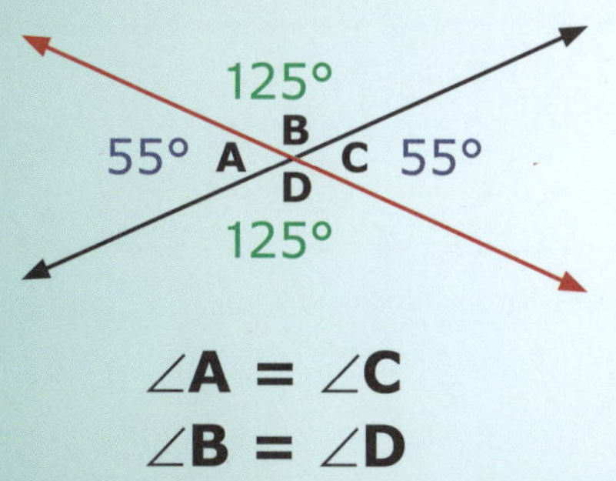

∠A = ∠C
∠B = ∠D

Straight angles measure 180°.

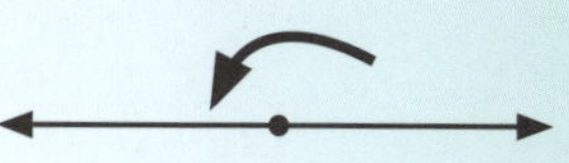

Around a point is 360°.

Figure the degrees in the angles; then cross out the correct answers below to find the two false answers.

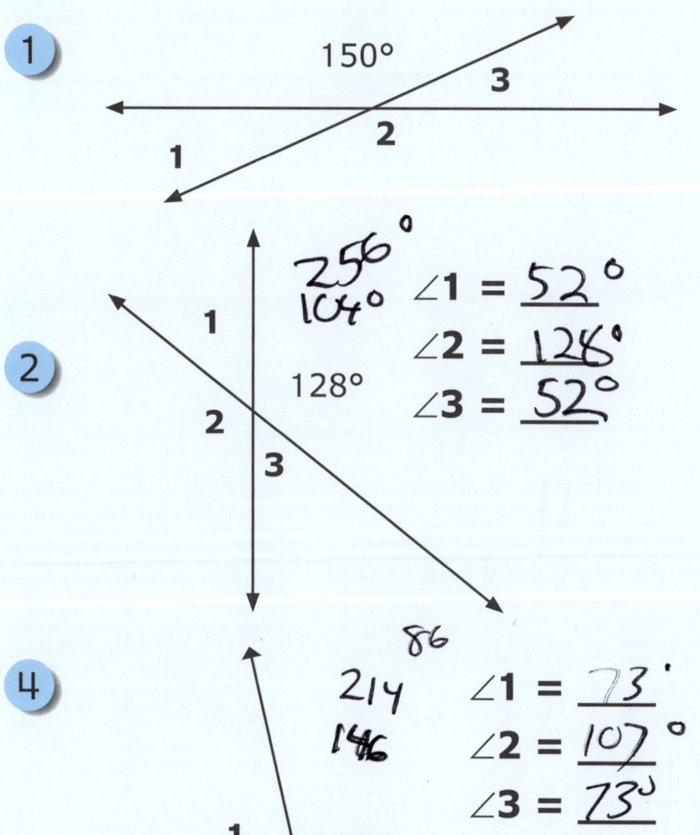

1. ∠1 = 30°
   ∠2 = 150°
   ∠3 = 30°

2. ∠1 = 52°
   ∠2 = 128°
   ∠3 = 52°

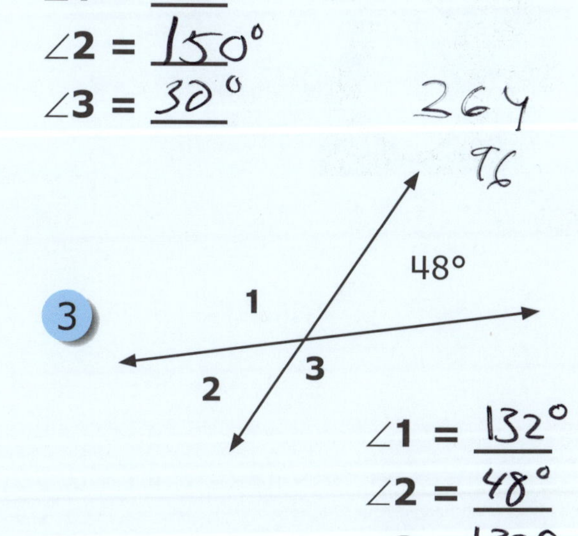

3. ∠1 = 132°
   ∠2 = 48°
   ∠3 = 132°

4. ∠1 = 73°
   ∠2 = 107°
   ∠3 = 73°

1 How many triangles do you see? 5

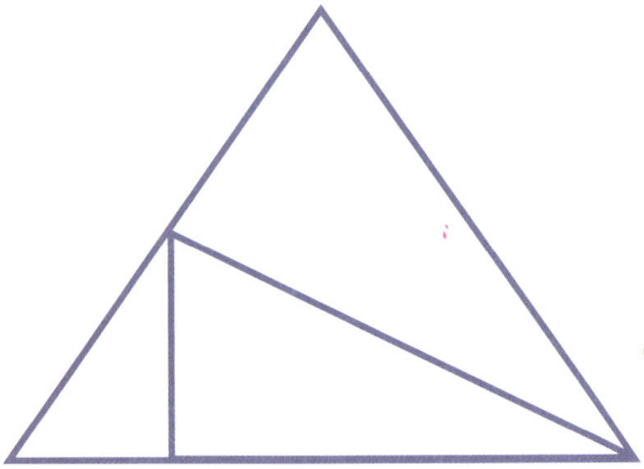

There are five triangles!

2 How many triangles do you see? 11

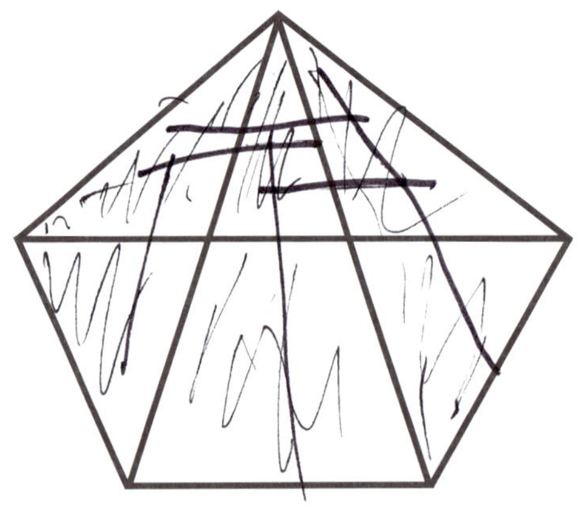

A right angle measures 90°. 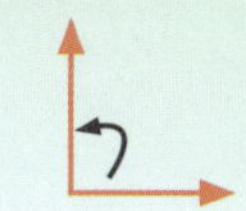

A straight angle measures 180°. 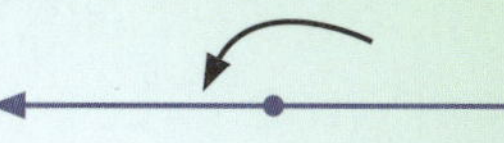

The sum of the inside angles in a triangle is 180°.

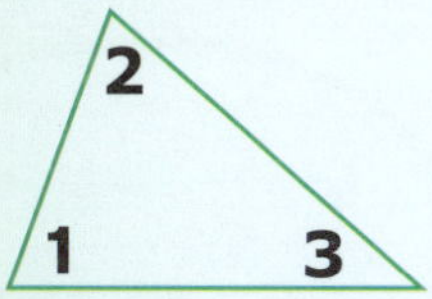

$\angle 1 + \angle 2 + \angle 3 = 180°$

The sum of the inside angles in a 4-sided polygon is 360°.

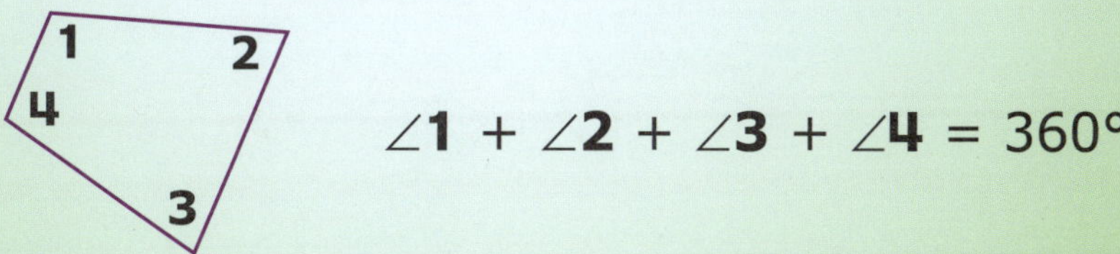

$\angle 1 + \angle 2 + \angle 3 + \angle 4 = 360°$

Find the measurement of the noted angle; then circle the two false answers.

1. ? 70° ______

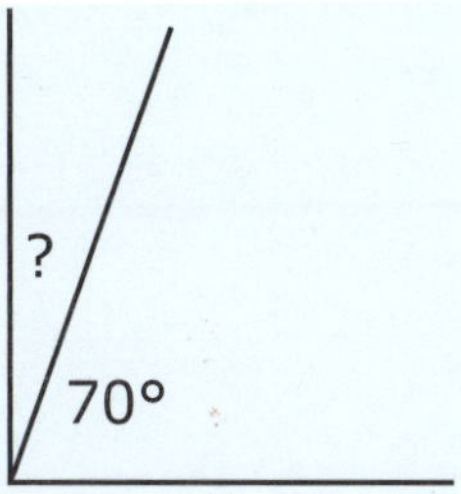

2. ? 120° ______

3. 60° 55° ? ______

4. 70° ? 60° ______

5. 15° 58° ? 52° ______

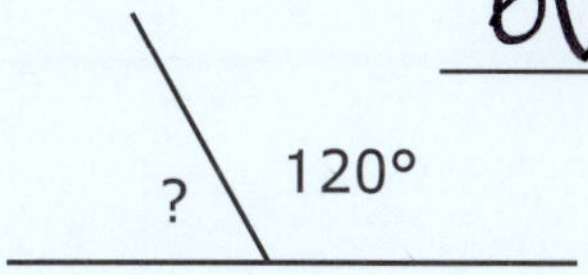

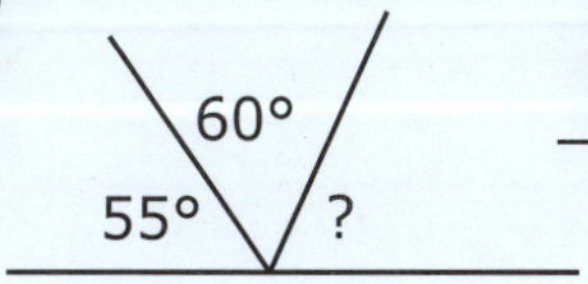

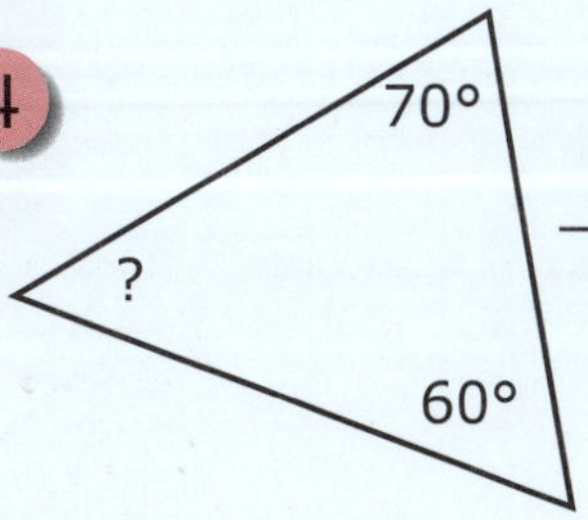

6. ? 80° 100° 110° ______

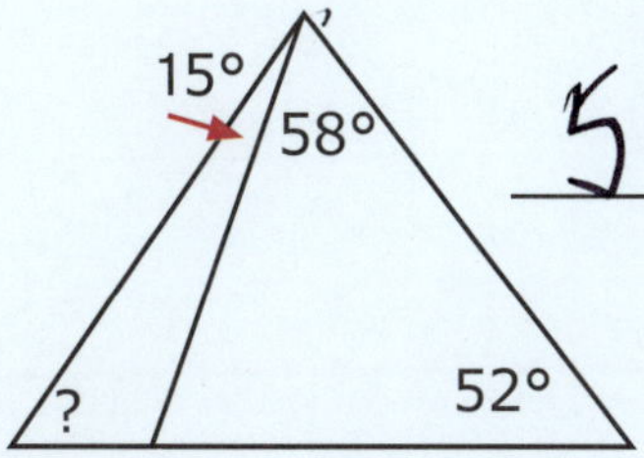

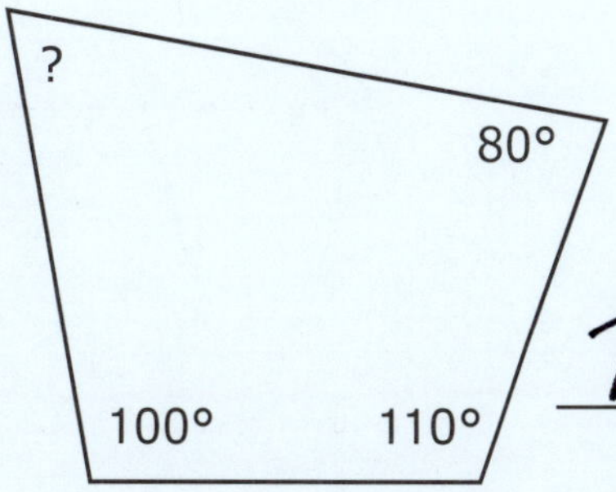

55°
70°
65°
45°
20°
75°
50°
60°

Each time the ball bounces it goes half the distance forward that it went on the last bounce.

Write the missing distances and calculate how far the ball has moved from the beginning point after 5 bounces.

1 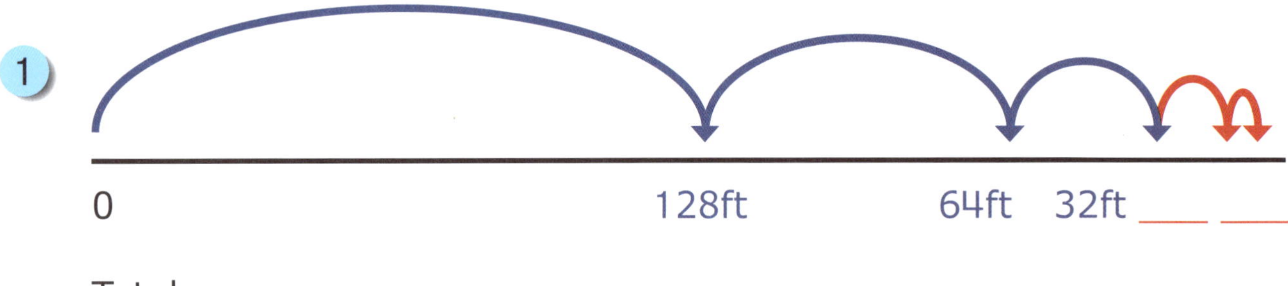

Total = ________

2 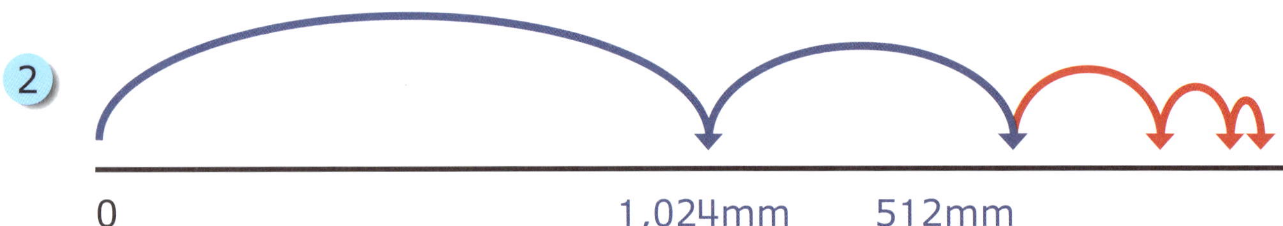

Total = ________

3 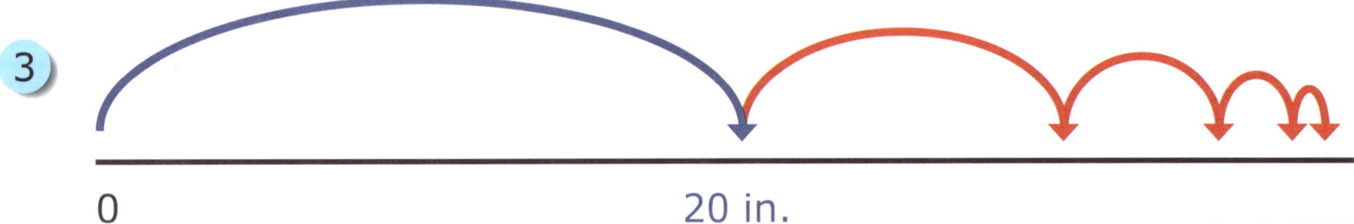

Total = ________

The distance from zero to a number is called the absolute value of the number. Since distance is always positive, the absolute value of a number is always positive. The symbol for absolute value is two vertical lines (| |).

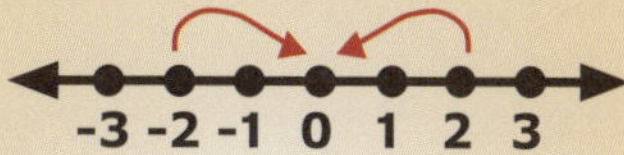

The absolute value of 2 is 2. $|2| = 2$
The absolute value of -2 is 2. $|-2| = 2$

Always complete any operations inside the absolute value sign first. $|-3 + 2| = |(-3 + 2)| = |-1| = 1$

The use of ×, •, or no operation sign between numerical values indicates multiplication. $2 \times 5 = 2 \cdot 5 = 2(5) = 10$

Solve each problem.

1) $|18| =$

2) $|-11| =$

3) $|0| =$

4) $|-\frac{3}{8}| =$

5) $|4.75| =$

6) $|-1| =$

7) $4 \cdot |-5| =$

8) $4|5| =$

9) $|15| \cdot |25| =$

10) $|15| \cdot |-25| =$

11) $-|-23| =$

12) $80|-10| =$

13) $|95 - 18| =$

14) $|-20 + 10| =$

15) $12 \cdot |-12| =$

16) $|-48| \cdot |0| =$

17) $|23| + |-23| + |8| - |-8| =$

Draw a straight line through the square, making the highest score possible.

Example:

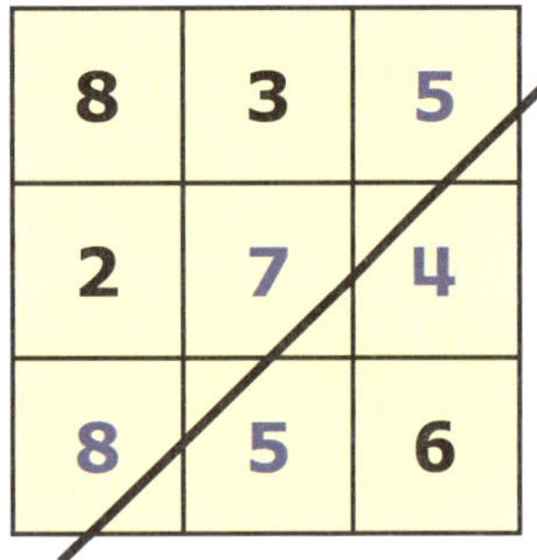

$5 + 4 + 7 + 5 + 8 = 29$

5	4	9
9	6	2
3	8	7

To put fractions in simplest form, divide the numerator and denominator by their greatest common factor (GCF). The GCF for 6 and 9 is 3.

$$\frac{6 \div 3}{9 \div 3} = \frac{2}{3}$$

Write each problem in simplest form; then solve the riddle below.

s $\frac{8}{10}$ =   b $\frac{9}{12}$ =   d $\frac{2}{6}$ =   j $\frac{5}{20}$ =

n $\frac{4}{20}$ =   l $\frac{6}{9}$ =   r $\frac{6}{16}$ =   o $\frac{4}{8}$ =

w $\frac{6}{10}$ =   m $\frac{20}{32}$ =   u $\frac{2}{20}$ =   t $\frac{6}{15}$ =

a $\frac{10}{12}$ =   z $\frac{2}{16}$ =   c $\frac{14}{49}$ =   e $\frac{45}{81}$ =

What part of a cowboy is the saddest?

___ ___ ___ ___   ___ ___ ___ ___ ___

$\frac{3}{4}$ $\frac{2}{3}$ $\frac{1}{10}$ $\frac{5}{9}$ $\frac{1}{4}$ $\frac{5}{9}$ $\frac{5}{6}$ $\frac{1}{5}$ $\frac{4}{5}$

Slope is a number that tells how slanted a line is. A line with slope 0 is horizontal, like a flat driveway. Slope is a ratio comparing rise to run. It is written as a fraction in lowest terms.

$$\text{Slope} = \frac{\text{rise} \uparrow}{\text{run} \rightarrow}$$

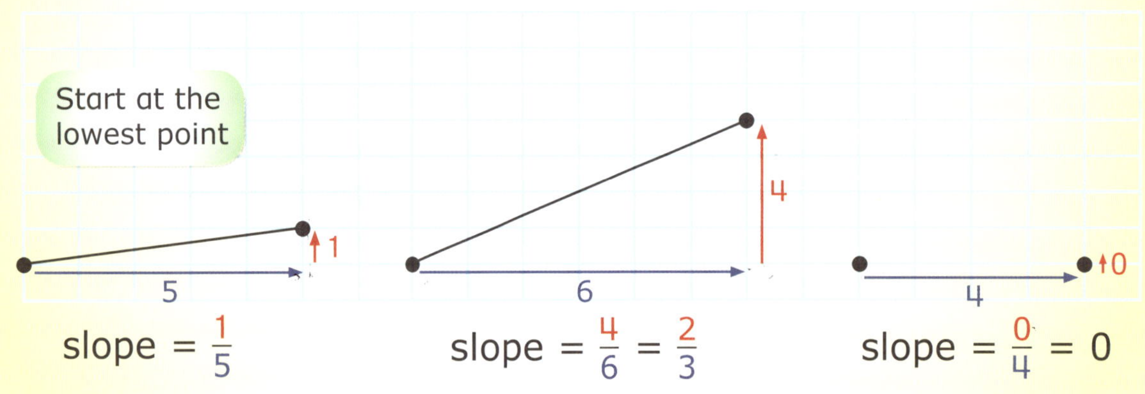

Find the slope of each line.

1 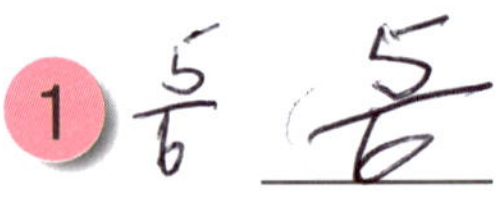 

2 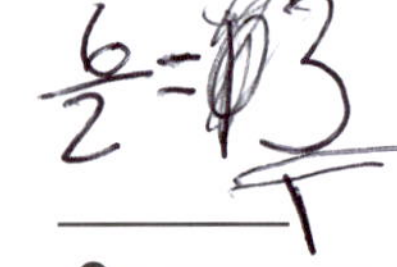 

3 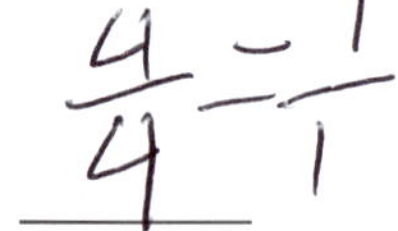

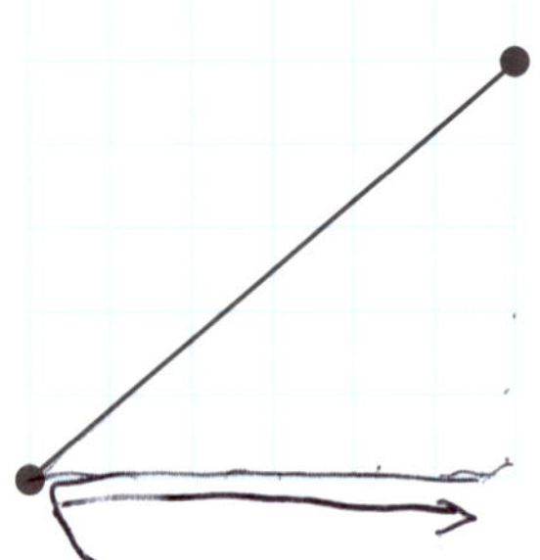

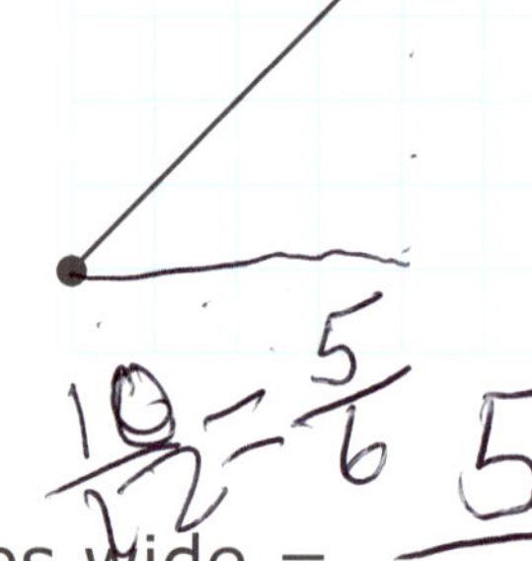

4 Slope of a step 10 inches high and 12 inches wide = ______

5 Slope of a string connecting the top of the tent to the stake in the ground. ______

48 in.

16 in.

6 Slope of the roof = ______

15 ft

20 ft

Find the slope of each line.

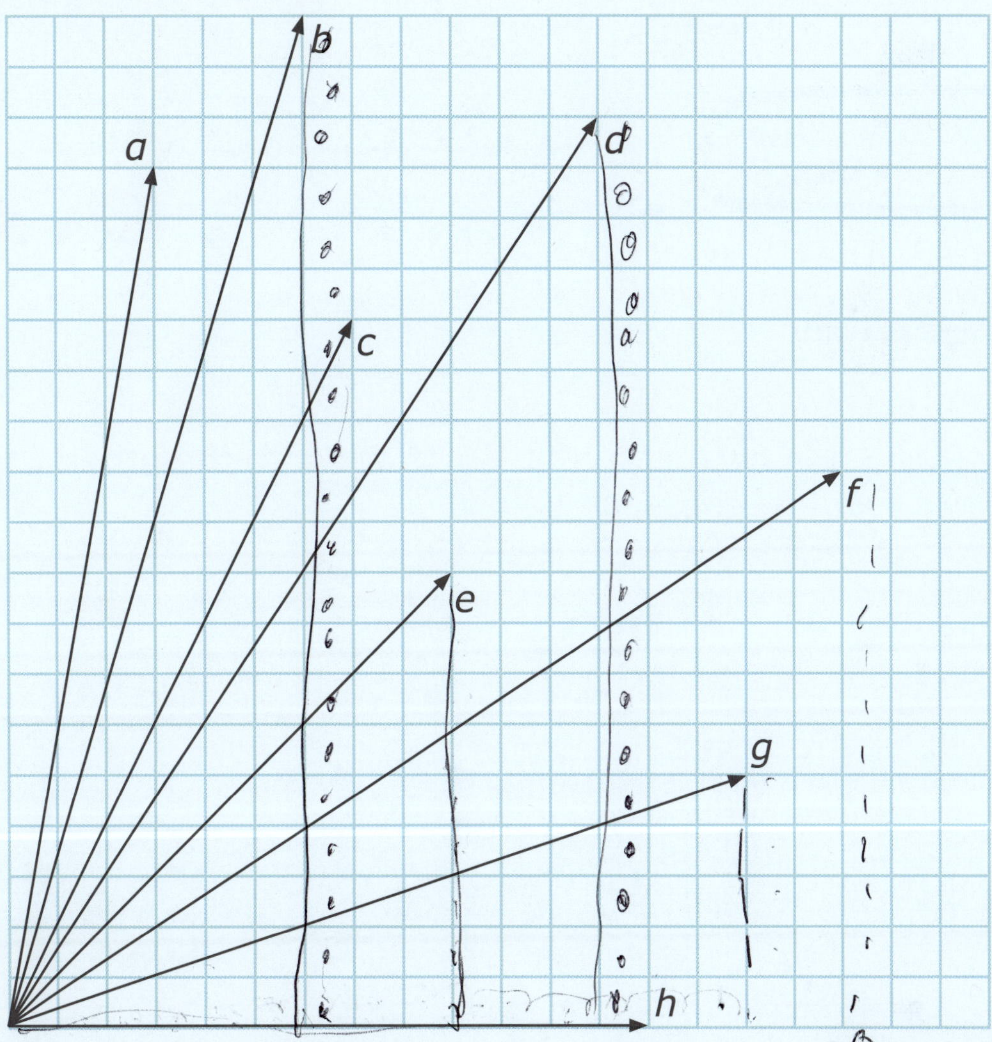

1. line *a* = ______

2. line *b* = ______

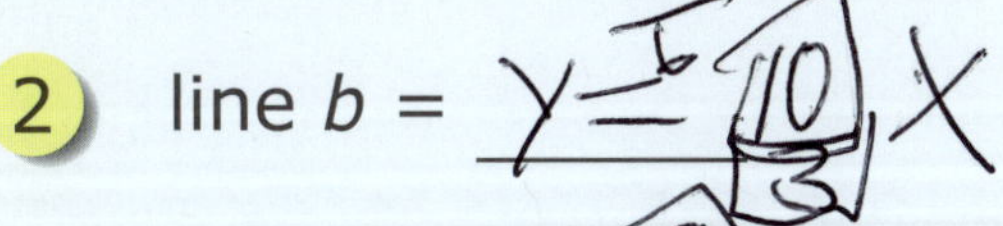

3. line *c* = ______

4. line *d* = ______

5. line *e* = ______

6. line *f* = ______

7. line *g* = ______

8. line *h* = ______

Multiplying the numerator and denominator of a fraction by the same whole number greater than zero, makes an equivalent fraction.

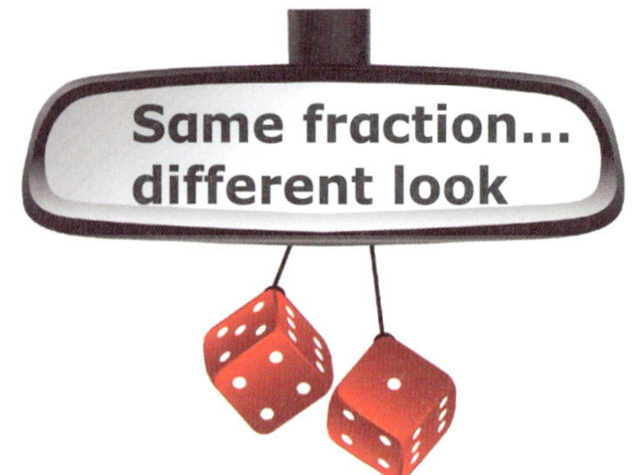

$$\frac{2 \times 2}{3 \times 2} = \frac{4}{6}$$

$$\frac{1 \times 3}{2 \times 3} = \frac{3}{6}$$

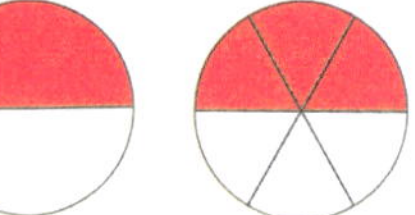

Circle the fraction in each row that is not equal to the others; then use the letters to read the message below.

1	r $\frac{2}{8}$	s $\frac{1}{4}$	g $\frac{4}{6}$	t $\frac{3}{12}$
2	o $\frac{1}{3}$	a $\frac{2}{12}$	t $\frac{1}{6}$	u $\frac{5}{30}$
3	r $\frac{10}{15}$	n $\frac{2}{3}$	i $\frac{8}{12}$	o $\frac{6}{8}$
4	d $\frac{12}{18}$	r $\frac{18}{24}$	a $\frac{3}{4}$	s $\frac{27}{36}$
5	a $\frac{10}{20}$	b $\frac{3}{6}$	t $\frac{9}{18}$	j $\frac{10}{14}$
6	r $\frac{6}{16}$	o $\frac{15}{32}$	u $\frac{9}{24}$	n $\frac{15}{40}$
7	t $\frac{8}{12}$	d $\frac{12}{18}$	b $\frac{32}{45}$	s $\frac{18}{27}$

____ ____ ____ ____   ____ ____ ____!

1

$\frac{1}{2}$ $\frac{1}{2}$

$\frac{1}{6}$ $\frac{1}{3}$ $\frac{1}{2}$

$\frac{1}{4}$ $\frac{1}{4}$ $\frac{1}{2}$

$\frac{1}{3}$ $\frac{1}{3}$ $\frac{1}{3}$

$\frac{1}{6}$ $\frac{1}{6}$ $\frac{1}{6}$ $\frac{1}{2}$

$\frac{1}{6}$ $\frac{1}{6}$ $\frac{1}{3}$ $\frac{1}{3}$

$\frac{1}{6}$ $\frac{1}{4}$ $\frac{1}{4}$ $\frac{1}{3}$

$\frac{1}{4}$ $\frac{1}{4}$ $\frac{1}{4}$ $\frac{1}{4}$

$\frac{1}{6}$ $\frac{1}{6}$ $\frac{1}{6}$ $\frac{1}{6}$ $\frac{1}{3}$

$\frac{1}{6}$ $\frac{1}{6}$ $\frac{1}{6}$ $\frac{1}{4}$ $\frac{1}{4}$

$\frac{1}{6}$ $\frac{1}{6}$ $\frac{1}{6}$ $\frac{1}{6}$ $\frac{1}{6}$ $\frac{1}{6}$

Use the chart of equivalent fractions above to answer the following questions in simplest form.

1. $\frac{1}{4} + \frac{1}{4} =$

2. $\frac{1}{6} + \frac{1}{6} + \frac{1}{6} =$

3. $\frac{1}{2} + \frac{1}{2} =$

4. $\frac{1}{6} + \frac{1}{3} =$

5. $\frac{1}{3} + \frac{1}{3} + \frac{1}{3} =$

6. $\frac{1}{6} + \frac{1}{6} =$

Check if the equation is true or false.

7. $\frac{1}{3} + \frac{1}{3} + \frac{1}{6} + \frac{1}{6} = 1$ ❐ True ❐ False

8. $\frac{1}{4} + \frac{1}{4} + \frac{1}{2} = 1$ ❐ True ❐ False

9. $\frac{1}{2} + \frac{1}{3} + \frac{1}{6} = 1$ ❐ True ❐ False

Fractions can only be added when they are like fractions (same denominators). A fraction in which the numerator is larger than or equal to the denominator is called an improper fraction. Improper fractions can be rewritten as mixed fractions.

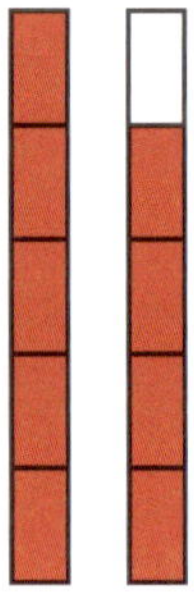

$$\frac{9}{5} = \frac{5}{5} + \frac{4}{5} = 1\frac{4}{5}$$

improper fraction ↑ (9/5)   mixed fraction ↑ (1 4/5)

Change an improper fraction into a mixed fraction.

$$\frac{4}{3} = \frac{3}{3} + \frac{1}{3} = 1\frac{1}{3}$$

OR

$$\frac{4}{3} = 4 \div 3 = 3\overline{)4} = 1\frac{1}{3}$$

(quotient 1; 4 − 3 = 1)

$$\frac{10}{4} = \frac{4}{4} + \frac{4}{4} + \frac{2}{4}$$

$$1 + 1 + \frac{2}{4} = 2\frac{2}{4}$$

$$2\frac{1}{2}$$

OR

$$\frac{10}{4} = 10 \div 4$$

$$4\overline{)10} = 2\frac{2}{4} = 2\frac{1}{2}$$

(quotient 2; 10 − 8 = 2)

Write each problem as a mixed fraction; then use the letters to solve the riddle on the next page.

m $\frac{11}{6} =$

s $\frac{10}{8} =$

o $\frac{1}{4} + \frac{1}{4} + \frac{1}{4} + \frac{1}{4} + \frac{1}{4} + \frac{1}{4} =$

b [two circles divided into sixths: first fully shaded, second with 4 of 6 shaded] =

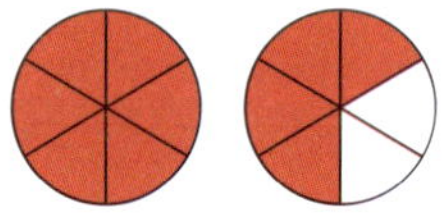

r $\frac{24}{20} =$

a $\frac{33}{8} =$

u 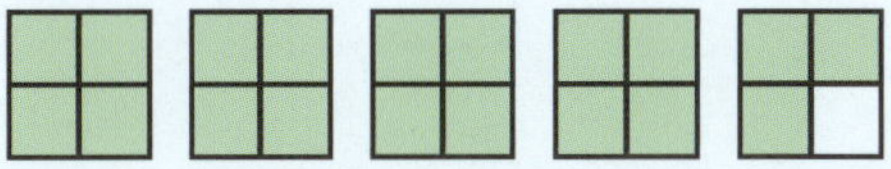 =

n $\frac{26}{6} =$

x $\frac{1}{5} + \frac{1}{5} + \frac{1}{5} + \frac{1}{5} + \frac{1}{5} =$

j $\frac{11}{3} =$

i $\frac{48}{9} =$

g $\frac{21}{4} =$

v $\frac{12}{10} =$

w $\frac{38}{4} =$

c $\frac{17}{6} =$

d $\frac{54}{8} =$

z $\frac{1}{2} + \frac{1}{2} + \frac{1}{2} + \frac{1}{2} + \frac{1}{2} + \frac{1}{2} + \frac{1}{2} + \frac{1}{2} + \frac{1}{2} =$

t If Jim had 7 half-dollars, how many dollars would he have? ______

p Jan tripled the recipe which needed $\frac{3}{4}$ of a cup of milk. How many cups of milk did she need? ______

What kind of suit does a kangaroo like?

___ $4\frac{1}{8}$ ___ $3\frac{2}{3}$ ___ $4\frac{3}{4}$ ___ $1\frac{5}{6}$ ___ $2\frac{1}{4}$ ___ $1\frac{1}{4}$ ___ $4\frac{3}{4}$ ___ $5\frac{1}{3}$ ___ $3\frac{1}{2}$

Kangaroos cannot walk backwards.

Fractions with the same denominators are called like fractions. Only add like fractions. Put the result in simplest form when necessary.

RULE: $\frac{a}{b} + \frac{c}{b} = \frac{a+c}{b}$

$\frac{2}{5} + \frac{1}{5} = \frac{3}{5}$

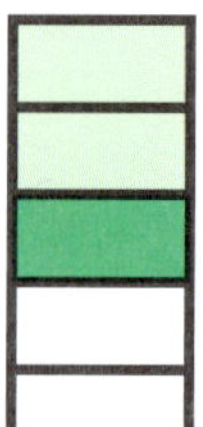

$\frac{5}{8} + \frac{5}{8} = \frac{10}{8} = 1\frac{2}{8} = 1\frac{1}{4}$

$$\begin{array}{r} 1\frac{4}{5} \\ +\ 7\frac{3}{5} \\ \hline 8\frac{7}{5} = 8 + 1\frac{2}{5} = 9\frac{2}{5} \end{array}$$

Add each problem; then cross out the correct answers on the next page to find the two false answers.

1. $\frac{3}{8} + \frac{2}{8} =$

2. $\frac{5}{8} + \frac{1}{8} =$

3. $\frac{7}{8} + \frac{3}{8} =$

4. $\frac{4}{9} + \frac{7}{9} =$

5. $\frac{3}{5} + \frac{4}{5} =$

6. $\frac{3}{8} + \frac{4}{8} =$

7. $$\begin{array}{r} 2\frac{1}{9} \\ +\ 1\frac{7}{9} \\ \hline \end{array}$$

8. $$\begin{array}{r} 1\frac{3}{8} \\ +\ 2\frac{7}{8} \\ \hline \end{array}$$

9. $$\begin{array}{r} 2\frac{5}{12} \\ +\ 3\frac{2}{12} \\ \hline \end{array}$$

10. $\frac{1}{6} + \frac{1}{6} =$

11. $\frac{1}{10} + \frac{6}{10} =$

12) $\frac{5}{7} + \frac{1}{7} =$

13) $\frac{1}{15} + \frac{11}{15} =$

14) $3\frac{1}{5} + 2\frac{1}{5}$

15) $5\frac{1}{12} + \frac{5}{12}$

16) $1\frac{5}{12} + 2\frac{8}{12}$

17) To make 12 brownies, $1\frac{3}{4}$ cups of flour is used. How much flour is needed for 24 brownies?

____

$\frac{6}{7}$ $\frac{3}{4}$ $\frac{7}{8}$ $1\frac{2}{5}$ $\frac{4}{5}$

$\frac{5}{8}$ $\frac{7}{10}$ $\frac{3}{8}$

$4\frac{1}{12}$ $1\frac{1}{4}$ $5\frac{7}{12}$

$3\frac{1}{2}$ $3\frac{8}{9}$ $\frac{1}{3}$

$4\frac{1}{2}$

$4\frac{1}{4}$ $5\frac{1}{2}$

$1\frac{2}{9}$ $5\frac{2}{5}$

1) Given equivalent amounts on the first scale, circle the answer that would be needed on the second scale to show equal amounts.

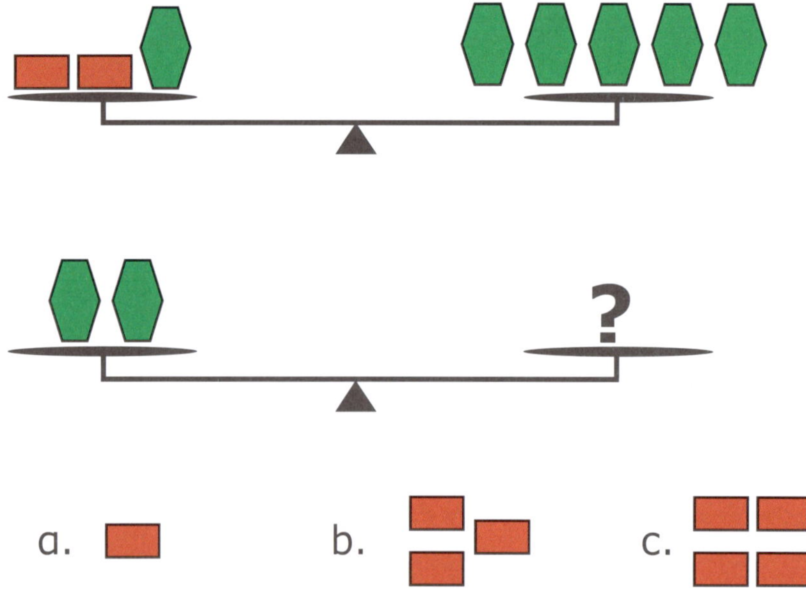

2) Given equivalent amounts on the first two scales, circle the answer that would be needed on the third scale to show equal amounts.

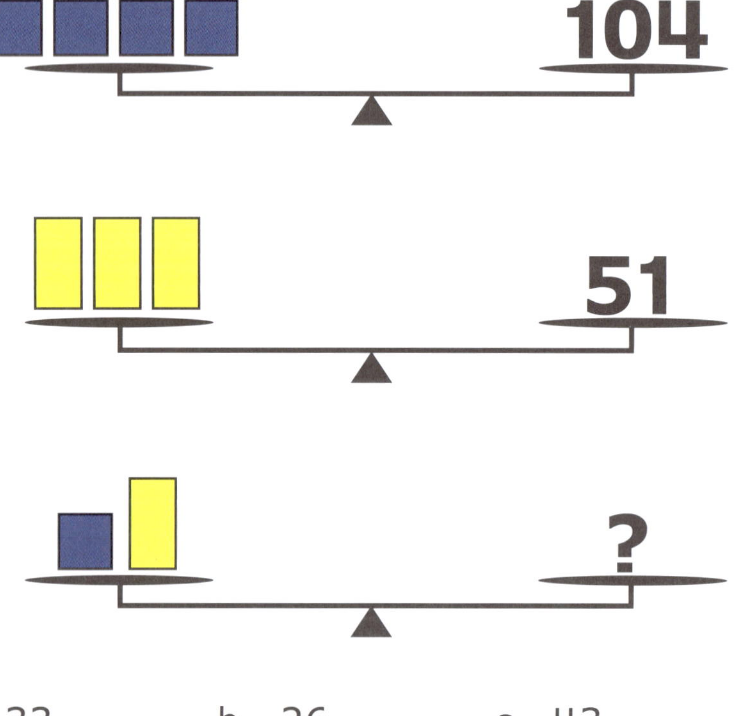

a. 33 b. 26 c. 43 d. 17

For more activities like this, please see our *Balance Benders*™ series.

The least common multiple (LCM) for a set of numbers is the smallest number each can divide into evenly. One way to find the least common multiple is to write multiples of the numbers until there is a match.

multiples of 3: 3, 6, 9, 12, 15, 18, 21, 24,...
multiples of 4: 4, 8, 12, 16, 20, 24, 28,...

The least common multiple (LCM) of 3 and 4 is 12.

Write the LCM for each set of numbers; then cross out the correct answers on the right to find the two false answers.

1	3 and 7	_____	20
2	6 and 8	_____	24
3	4 and 9	_____	18
4	10 and 25	_____	50
5	6 and 9	_____	21
6	3 and 6	_____	22
7	4 and 5	_____	36
8	2, 3, and 4	_____	6
			12
			8

The least common multiple for a set of denominators is called the least common denominator (LCD).

9 Find the LCD for $\frac{1}{2}$ and $\frac{4}{5}$. _____

Fractions with the same denominators are called like fractions. When adding fractions, change every fraction into an equivalent fraction using the least common denominator (LCD).

$$\frac{1}{4} + \frac{2}{3} = \quad \frac{1}{4} = \frac{1 \times 3}{4 \times 3} = \frac{3}{12}$$

$$+\ \frac{2}{3} = \frac{2 \times 4}{3 \times 4} = \frac{8}{12}$$

$$\frac{11}{12}$$

LCD for 3 and 4 is 12.

$$\frac{5}{6} + \frac{1}{2} = \quad \frac{5}{6} = \frac{5 \times 1}{6 \times 1} = \frac{5}{6}$$

$$+\ \frac{1}{2} = \frac{1 \times 3}{2 \times 3} = \frac{3}{6}$$

$$\frac{8}{6} = 1\frac{2}{6} = 1\frac{1}{3}$$

LCD for 2 and 6 is 6.

Add the fractions; then use the letters to solve the riddle on the next page.

a $\frac{5}{6} + \frac{1}{2}$ = ____

g $\frac{1}{8} + \frac{3}{4}$ = ____

e $\frac{2}{3} + \frac{1}{2}$ = ____

h $\frac{1}{6} + \frac{1}{3}$ = ____

b $\frac{1}{4} + \frac{1}{3}$ = ____

t $\frac{5}{9} + \frac{5}{6}$ = ____

m $\frac{3}{5} + \frac{1}{3}$ ____

i $\frac{3}{8} + \frac{5}{6}$ ____

l $\frac{2}{3} + \frac{1}{7}$ ____

o $\frac{5}{6} + \frac{2}{3}$ ____

s $\frac{3}{5} + \frac{2}{15}$ ____

z $\frac{2}{9} + \frac{3}{8}$ ____

n If a board one-eighth inch thick is placed on top of a board one-half inch thick, what is the total thickness of the two boards?

____

p The stock was priced at \$20 a share. If it increases by one-half dollar and then one-fourth dollar, how much over \$20 is the stock price now? ____

How does a lumberjack start his computer?

____ ____   ____ ____ ____ ____   ____ ____

$\frac{1}{2}$ $1\frac{1}{6}$ $\frac{17}{21}$ $1\frac{1}{2}$ $\frac{7}{8}$ $\frac{11}{15}$ $1\frac{1}{2}$ $\frac{5}{8}$

1 Given equivalent amounts on the first scale, circle the figure that would be needed on the second scale to show equal amounts.

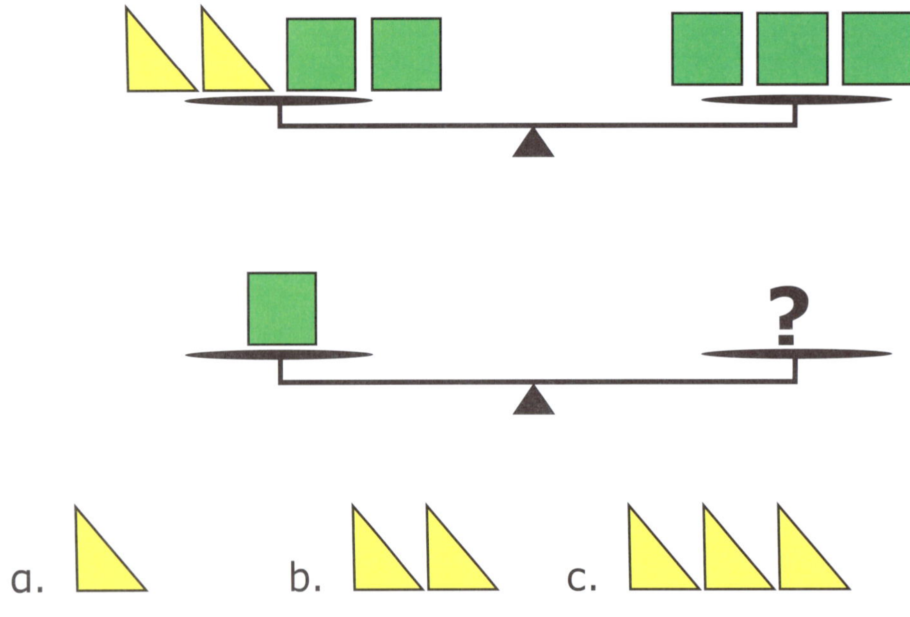

a. b. c.

2 Given equivalent amounts on the first two scales, circle the figure that would be needed on the third scale to show equal amounts.

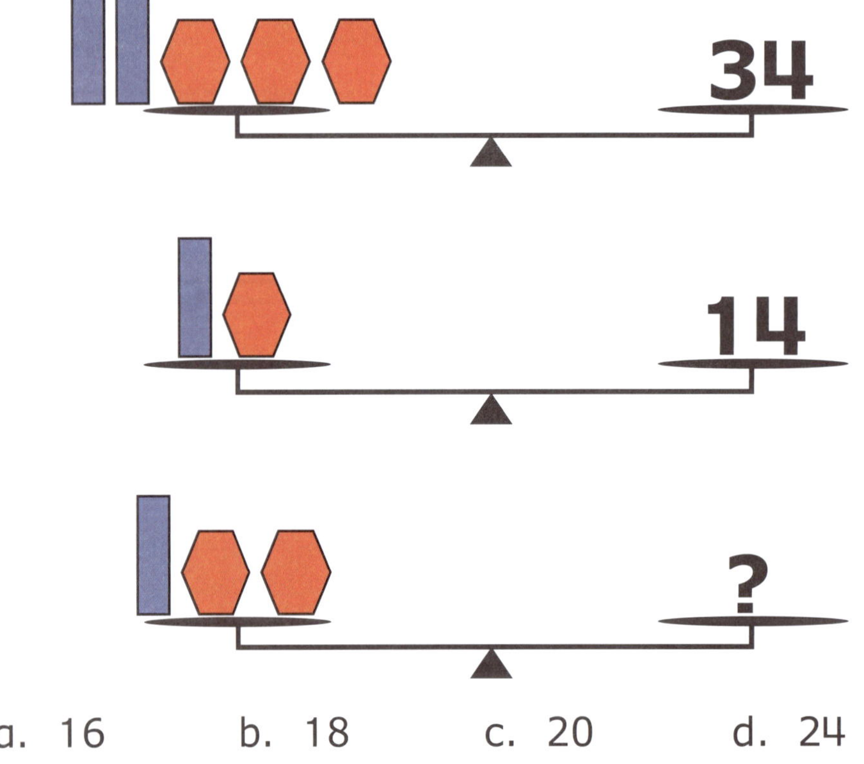

a. 16 b. 18 c. 20 d. 24

Find the least common denominator (LCD) and rewrite the fractions into like fractions before adding.

$$\begin{array}{rl} 1\frac{3}{4} & = 1\frac{3}{4} \\ +\ 2\frac{1}{2} & = 2\frac{2}{4} \\ \hline & 3\frac{5}{4} = 3 + 1\frac{1}{4} = 4\frac{1}{4} \end{array}$$

Find each sum; then cross out the correct answers below to find the two false answers.

1. $1\frac{1}{2} + 1\frac{1}{4}$

2. $2\frac{1}{4} + 1\frac{3}{8}$

3. $2\frac{2}{5} + \frac{1}{2}$

4. $1\frac{1}{6} + 2\frac{2}{3}$

5. $4\frac{5}{6} + \frac{1}{4}$

6. $2\frac{3}{4} + 1\frac{5}{8}$

7. $2\frac{5}{9} + 2\frac{2}{5}$

8. $1\frac{5}{6} + 3\frac{3}{4}$

$3\frac{5}{6}$ $3\frac{1}{4}$ $5\frac{7}{12}$ $3\frac{5}{8}$ $4\frac{3}{8}$

$2\frac{3}{4}$ $4\frac{43}{45}$ $1\frac{2}{3}$ $5\frac{1}{12}$ $2\frac{9}{10}$

To subtract fractions, start with like fractions, then subtract the numerators. Put the result in simplest form when necessary.

RULE: $\frac{a}{b} - \frac{c}{b} = \frac{a-c}{b}$

$\frac{2}{3} - \frac{1}{3} = \frac{2-1}{3} = \frac{1}{3}$

$\frac{5}{8} - \frac{1}{2} = \frac{5}{8} - \frac{4}{8} = \frac{5-4}{8} = \frac{1}{8}$

Subtract each problem and color in the correct target.

1. $\frac{4}{5} - \frac{1}{5} =$ a. $\frac{3}{5}$ b. $\frac{4}{5}$ c. $\frac{2}{5}$

2. $\frac{5}{6} - \frac{4}{6} =$ a. $\frac{1}{3}$ b. $\frac{1}{2}$ c. $\frac{1}{6}$

3. $\frac{7}{8} - \frac{3}{8} =$ a. $\frac{1}{4}$ b. $\frac{1}{2}$ c. $\frac{1}{3}$

4. $\frac{8}{9} - \frac{2}{9} =$ a. $\frac{1}{3}$ b. $\frac{5}{9}$ c. $\frac{2}{3}$

5. $\frac{11}{12} - \frac{7}{12} =$ a. $\frac{1}{3}$ b. $\frac{1}{2}$ c. $\frac{1}{4}$

6. $\frac{1}{2} - \frac{1}{4} =$ a. $\frac{1}{3}$ b. $\frac{1}{2}$ c. $\frac{1}{4}$

7. $\frac{7}{8} - \frac{1}{2} =$ a. $\frac{3}{8}$ b. $\frac{1}{4}$ c. $\frac{2}{3}$

8. $\frac{1}{2} - \frac{1}{3} =$ a. $\frac{1}{3}$ b. $\frac{1}{2}$ c. $\frac{1}{6}$

9. $\frac{5}{6} - \frac{2}{3} =$ a. $\frac{1}{3}$ b. $\frac{1}{2}$ c. $\frac{1}{6}$

10. $\frac{3}{4} - \frac{1}{3} =$ a. $\frac{2}{3}$ b. $\frac{5}{12}$ c. $\frac{5}{6}$

11. $\frac{5}{6} - \frac{3}{4} =$ a. $\frac{1}{3}$ b. $\frac{1}{4}$ c. $\frac{1}{12}$

12. $\frac{4}{5} - \frac{2}{3} =$ a. $\frac{3}{5}$ b. $\frac{2}{15}$ c. $\frac{4}{15}$

13. $\frac{7}{8} - \frac{5}{6} =$ a. $\frac{1}{24}$ b. $\frac{1}{12}$ c. $\frac{1}{8}$

Find the least common denominator (LCD) and rewrite the fractions into like fractions before subtracting. Regroup when necessary and always write the answer in simplest form. The number 1 may be rewritten as:

$$\frac{2}{2}, \frac{3}{3}, \frac{4}{4}, \frac{5}{5}, \frac{6}{6}, \ldots$$

$$3\frac{3}{4} - 2\frac{1}{2} = 3\frac{3}{4} - 2\frac{1}{2} =$$

$$3\frac{3}{4} - 2\frac{2}{4} = 1\frac{1}{4}$$

$$8\frac{1}{6} - 2\frac{1}{3} = 8\frac{1}{6} - 2\frac{1}{3} =$$

$$8\frac{1}{6} - 2\frac{2}{6}$$

$$7 + \frac{6}{6} + \frac{1}{6} - 2\frac{2}{6}$$

$$7\frac{7}{6} - 2\frac{2}{6} = 5\frac{5}{6}$$

$$7\frac{1}{4} - 3\frac{2}{3} = 7\frac{1}{4} - 3\frac{2}{3} =$$

$$7\frac{3}{12} - 3\frac{8}{12}$$

$$6 + \frac{12}{12} + \frac{3}{12} - 3\frac{8}{12}$$

$$6\frac{15}{12} - 3\frac{8}{12} = 3\frac{7}{12}$$

Subtract each problem; then circle the three false answers below.

1. $3\frac{3}{4} - 2\frac{1}{2}$
2. $5\frac{7}{8} - 1\frac{1}{4}$
3. $4\frac{3}{4} - 1\frac{2}{3}$
4. $6\frac{2}{3} - 2\frac{2}{9}$
5. $4\frac{1}{2} - 1\frac{2}{3}$
6. $5\frac{1}{2} - 1\frac{3}{4}$
7. $3\frac{3}{4} - 1\frac{7}{8}$
8. $5\frac{2}{3} - 4\frac{6}{7}$
9. $5\frac{1}{2} - 2\frac{1}{4}$
10. $4\frac{5}{6} - 2\frac{2}{3}$
11. $3\frac{1}{8} - 1\frac{1}{2}$
12. $6\frac{3}{4} - 2\frac{5}{6}$

Vocabulary Match!

Write the letter that matches the vocabulary.

1. denominator _____

2. numerator _____

3. equivalent fractions _____
4. mixed fractions _____
5. improper fractions _____
6. simplest form _____
7. least common multiple _____
8. greatest common factor _____
9. like fractions _____
10. unlike fractions _____

$\frac{1}{3}$ & $\frac{2}{3}$ = ← e

$\frac{11}{9}$ ← b

$5\frac{1}{8}$ ← j

$\frac{5}{10} = \frac{1}{2}$ ← d

$\frac{2}{3}$ & $\frac{4}{6}$ = ← a

$\frac{5}{6}$ (numerator ← f, denominator ← g)

$\frac{2}{9}$ & $\frac{5}{6}$ = ← h

For 12 & 18 the answer is 36. ← c

For 12 & 18 the answer is 6. ← i

Solve the following baker problems as a fractions review.

1. Tim is making some cupcakes. If Tim buys a bag of flour with 4 cups of flour in it and he uses $2\frac{1}{2}$ cups of flour, how much flour is left?

2. June put $1\frac{3}{4}$ cups of milk in the batter and then another $1\frac{1}{2}$ cups of milk. What was the total amount of milk used?

3. Maria had muffins in the oven baking for $\frac{1}{4}$ hour and realized they needed to bake $\frac{1}{4}$ hour more. How long did the muffins bake?

4. Ted needed $2\frac{1}{3}$ cups of sugar for a recipe but only had $1\frac{1}{2}$ cups of sugar. How much more sugar does he need to buy to make the recipe?

5. If Tam has poured in $1\frac{1}{4}$, $1\frac{1}{2}$, and $\frac{1}{2}$ cups of water into the bowl, how much is in the bowl?

A **circle** is a two-dimensional figure formed by a set of points equal distance from a center point. The radius (r) of a circle is the line segment connecting a point on the circle to the center. The diameter (d) of a circle is the line segment connecting two points on the circle that passes through the center point. The diameter is always twice the length of the radius.

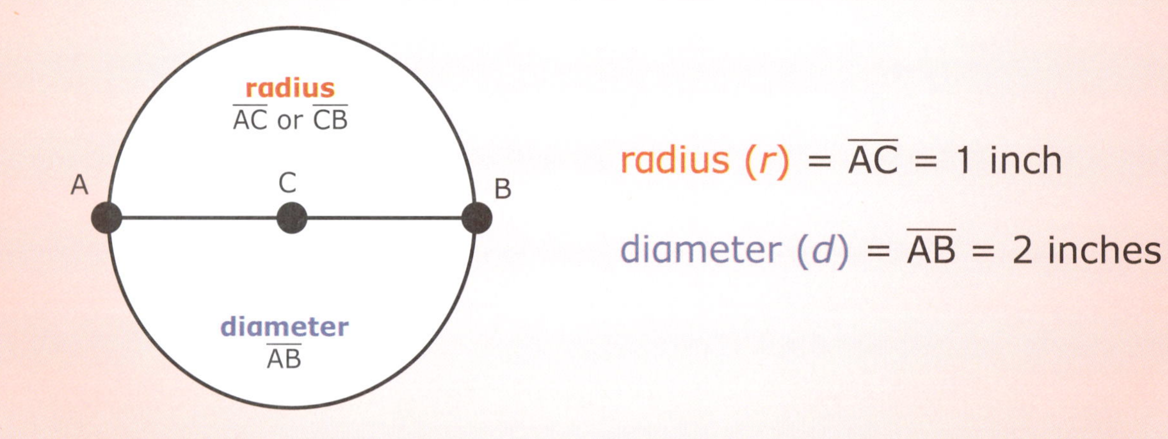

Find either the length of the radius or diameter in the circles below.

1

radius = 32 in.
diameter = ______

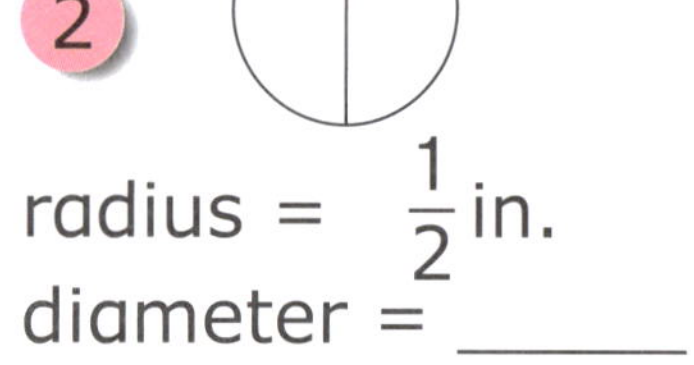

2

radius = $\frac{1}{2}$ in.
diameter = ______

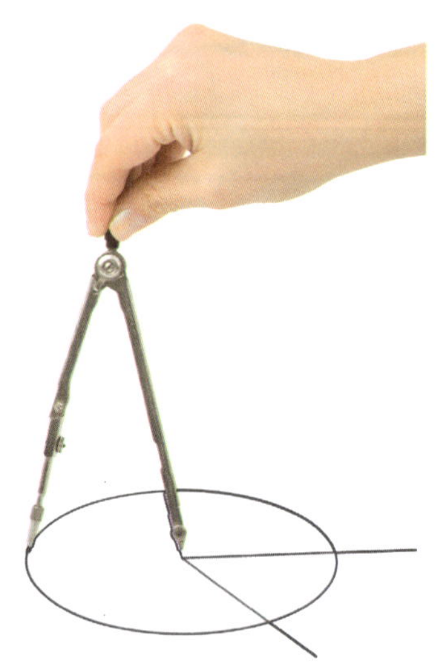

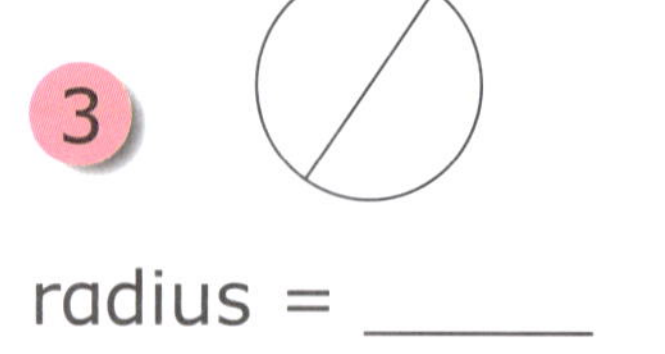

3

radius = ______
diameter = 132 ft

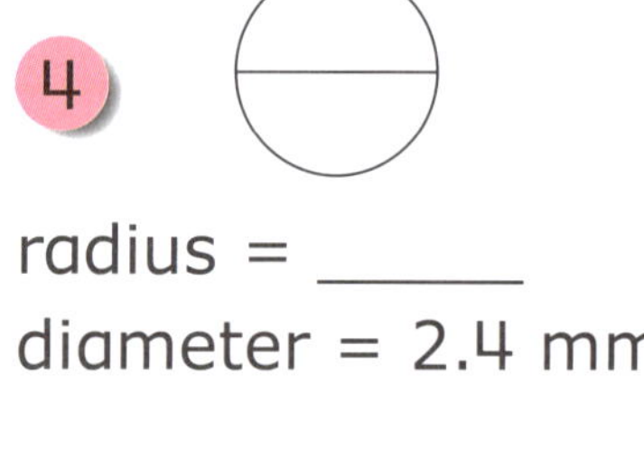

4

radius = ______
diameter = 2.4 mm

5. radius = 236 m
diameter = ______

6. radius = 4.8 mm
diameter = ______

7. radius = ______
diameter = 72 in.

8. radius = ______
diameter = 45 yards

Measure to the nearest millimeter.

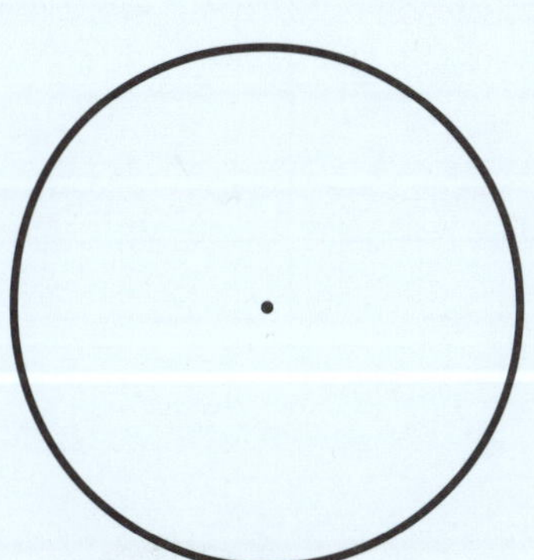

9. radius = ______
diameter = ______

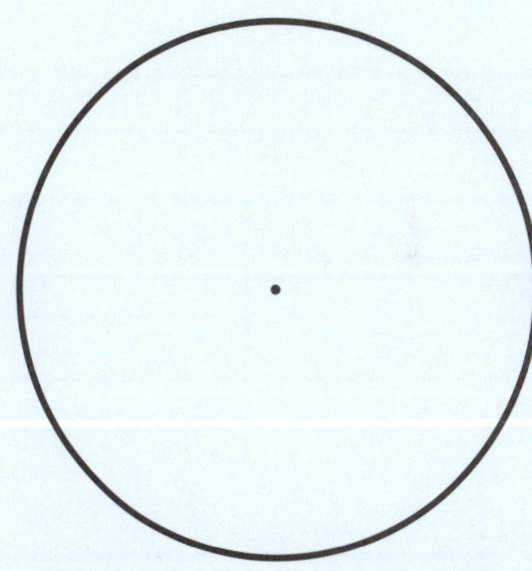

10. radius ______
diameter = ______

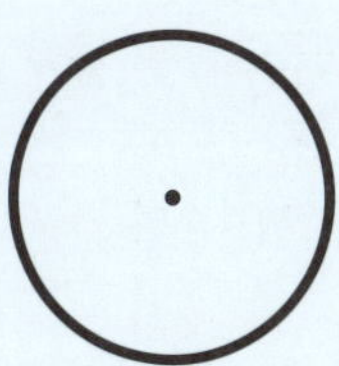

11. radius = ______
diameter ______

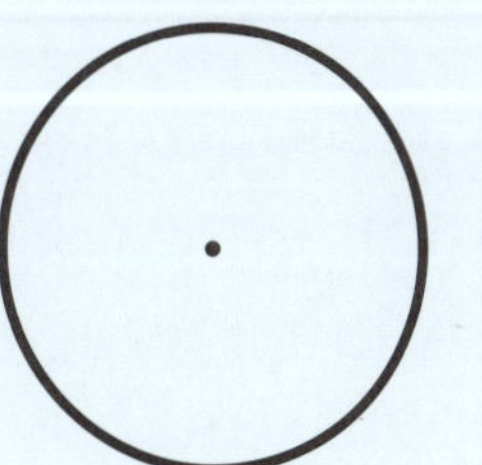

12. radius = ______
diameter ______

The distance around a circle is called the circumference (C) of the circle.

After seeing how much string is needed to go around an object, place the string on a metric ruler to determine the distance around the circle.

Complete the chart using string and a metric ruler. Use a calculator for column four.

Object	Circumference (C)	Diameter (d)	$C \div d$
soda can			
glass			
clock			
tire			

Column four should be a little more than 3 times as long as the diameter. The circumference of a circle is a constant ratio represented by the Greek letter π, called pi. Pi is approximately 3.14.

RULE: The circumference of a circle is equal to π times its diameter (d).

$C = \pi \times d$ or simply $C = \pi d$

Find the circumference (C) of each circle with the given diameter (d) and use the letters to solve the riddle below.

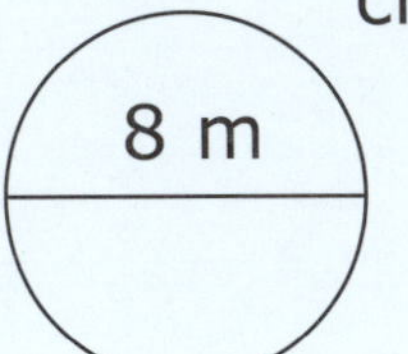

circumference (C) = π (3.14) times diameter (d)

$C = \pi d$

$C = 3.14 \times 8$

$C = 25.12$ m

b 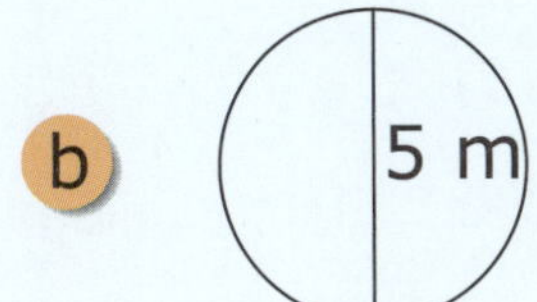

i 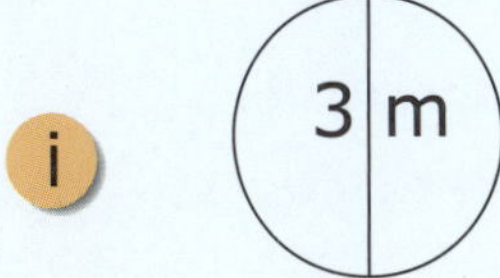

t 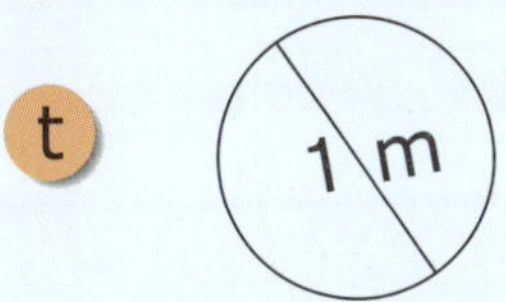

g 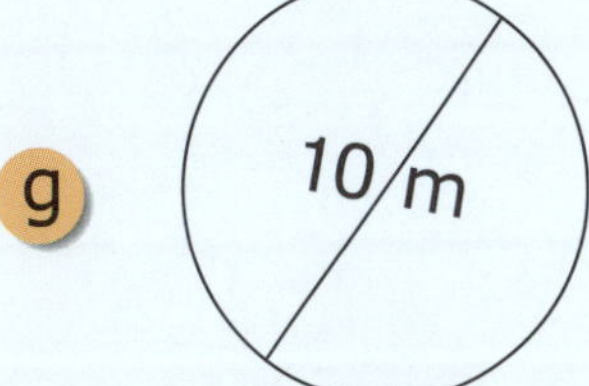

n 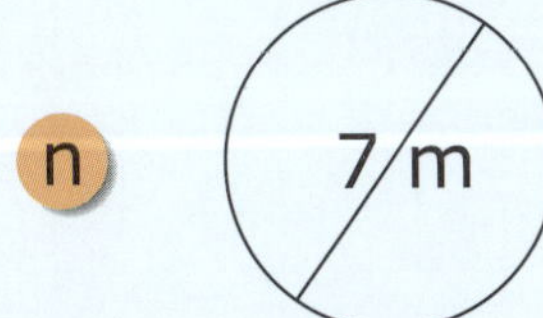

a 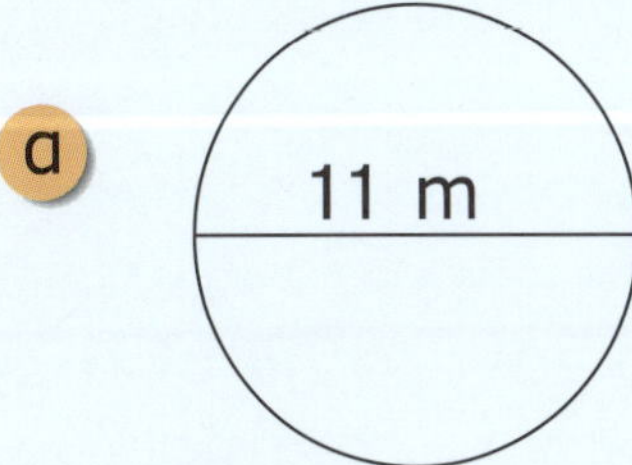

If the radius is given, multiply it by 2 to have the length of the diameter.

s 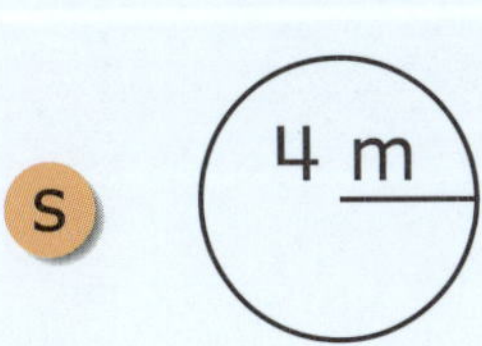

u 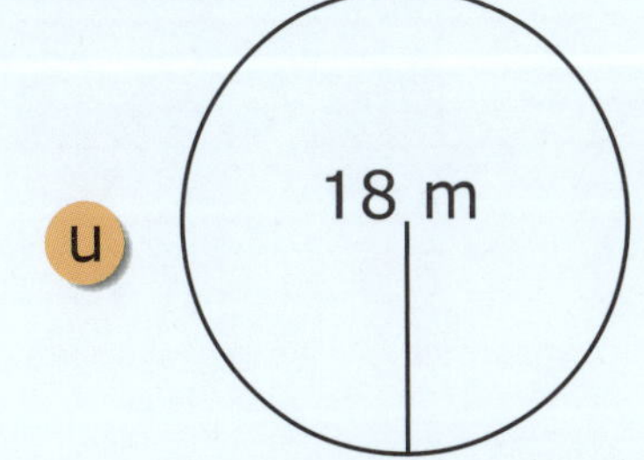

What kind of ant is 10 feet tall?

_____ 31.4   _____ 9.42   _____ 34.54   _____ 21.98   _____ 3.14

π (pi) is the symbol for the ratio of the circumference (C) of a circle to its diameter (d). The ratio $\frac{C}{d}$ is written as π. It is customary to approximate pi as 3.14. With the use of computers, pi has been approximated to over a trillion decimal places. Pi is an **irrational number** which means its decimal places continue forever with no repeating pattern.

pi = 3.1415926535897932384626433832795028841971
69399375105820974944592307816406286208998
62803482534211706798214808651...

Pi is used to find the area of a circle, the volume of a sphere, the distance around a circle, and many other measurements.

Use the colors below to fill in the chart on the next page to illustrate the lack of pattern to the placement of decimal place digits. Color the "0" marked areas with red, the "1" marked areas with orange, etc.

Red	Orange	Yellow	Green	Blue	Indigo	Violet	Black	Gray	White
0	1	2	3	4	5	6	7	8	9

π = 3.14159265358979
32384626433832
795028841
9716939937
5105820974
9445923...

3.

1	4	1	5	9	2	6	5	3	5
8	9	7	9	3	2	3	8	4	6
2	6	4	3	3	8	3	2	7	9
5	0	2	8	8	4	1	9	7	1
6	9	3	9	9	3	7	5	1	0
5	8	2	0	9	7	4	9	4	4
5	9	2	3	0	7	8	1	6	4
0	6	2	8	6	2	0	8	9	9
8	6	2	8	0	3	4	8	2	5
3	4	2	1	1	7	0	6	7	9
8	2	1	4	8	0	8	6	5	1

■ ■ ■

In metric units, temperature is measured in degrees Celsius (C°) with water boiling at 100°C and freezing at 0°C. In customary units, temperature is measured in degrees Fahrenheit (F°) with water boiling at 212°F and freezing at 32°F.

Complete the temperature chart below to discover the pattern.

Water boils at 100°C or 212°F. →

38°C is sick with an elevated temperature. →

Room temperature is about 20°C or 68°F. →

Water freezes at 0°C or 32°F. →

Celsius	Fahrenheit
100°	212°
95°	203°
	194°
	185°
75°	
	149°
	140°
55°	
40°	104°
35°	95°
	86°
	77°
15°	
10°	50°
5°	41°
0°	32°

Factoid: A lightning bolt is about 54,000°F.

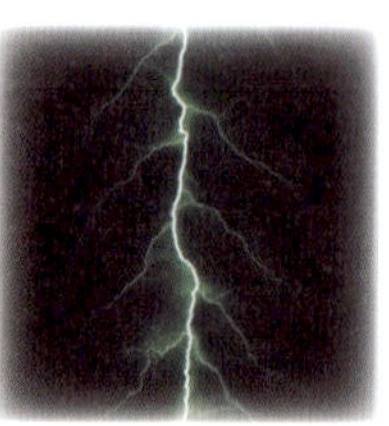

Use the thermometer on the previous page to answer the questions below.

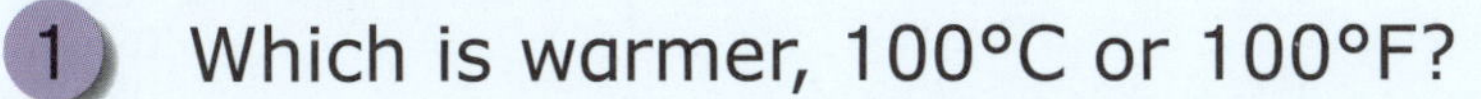

1. Which is warmer, 100°C or 100°F? __________

2. Which is colder, 0°C or 0°F? __________

3. Would it be snowing at 30°C or 30°F? __________

4. If a child had an elevated temperature with the flu, would it be 37.5°C or 37.5°F? __________

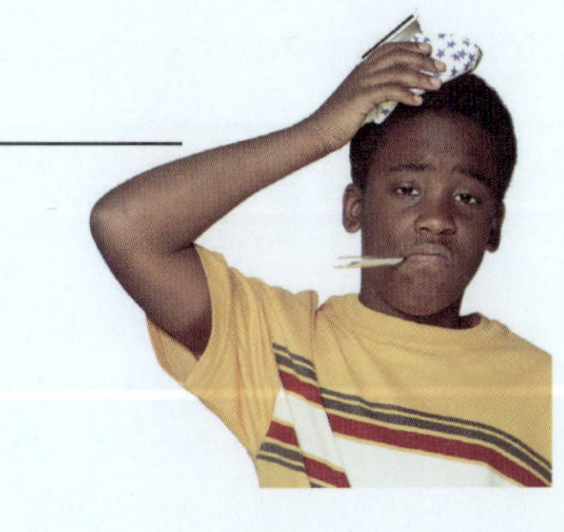

5. In the metric temperature system, what is the degree difference between water freezing and boiling? __________

6. In the customary temperature system, what is the degree difference between water freezing and boiling? __________

7. At which temperature, 60°C or 60°F, would you need a sweater? __________

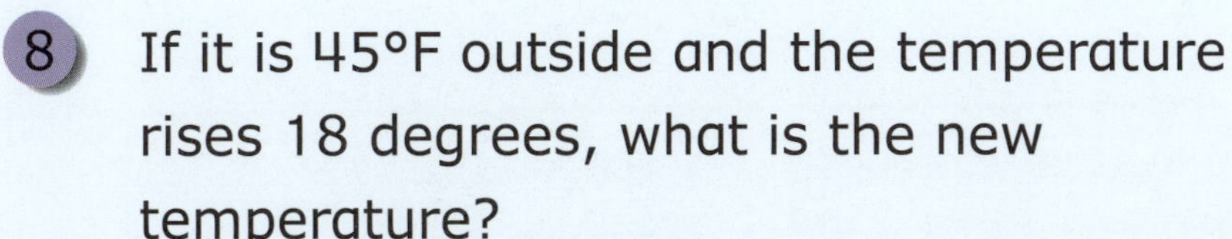

8. If it is 45°F outside and the temperature rises 18 degrees, what is the new temperature? __________

Capacity is the amount a container can hold. In the customary system, ounces, cups, pints, and gallons are units of capacity.

1 oz 1 oz 1 oz 1 oz 1 oz 1 oz 1 oz 1 oz	=	cup	8 ounces (oz) = 1 cup (c)
cup cup	=	pint	2 cups (c) = 1 pint (pt)
pint pint	=	quart	2 pints (pt) = 1 quart (qt)
quart quart quart quart	=	gallon	4 quarts (qt) = 1 gallon (gal)

If 1 cup holds 8 ounces of fluid, make the following equations true.

1. cup + cup = ______ ounces.

2. pint + pint = ______ ounces.

3. cup + pint + quart = ______ ounces.

4. cup + cup + cup + cup = ______ pints.

5. quart + quart = ______ pints.

6. cup + cup + pint = ______ ounces.

7. pint + pint + pint + pint = ______ quarts.

8. cup + cup + cup + pint = ______ ounces.

9. cup + cup + pint + quart + quart = ______ quarts.

Capacity is the amount a container can hold. In the metric system, milliliters (mL) and liters (L) are units of capacity.

1,000 milliliters = 1 liter

An eye dropper holds about one milliliter (mL).

A large container of milk or soda holds about one liter (L).

Circle the best estimate.

1. A large water bottle holds about:
   a. 200 mL b. 800 mL c. 2 L

2. A gulp of water is about:
   a. 30 mL b. 300 mL c. 3 L

3. A car gas tank holds about:
   a. 1 L b. 8 L c. 80 L

4. A cup of coffee holds about:
   a. 3 mL b. 350 mL c. 8 L

Make each equation true.

5. 2 L = _______ mL

6. 3,000 mL = _______ L

7. 1,000 mL = _______ L

8. 19 L = _______ mL

9. 45,000 mL = _______ L

10. 8,100 mL = _______ L

A **protractor** measures angles in degrees (°).

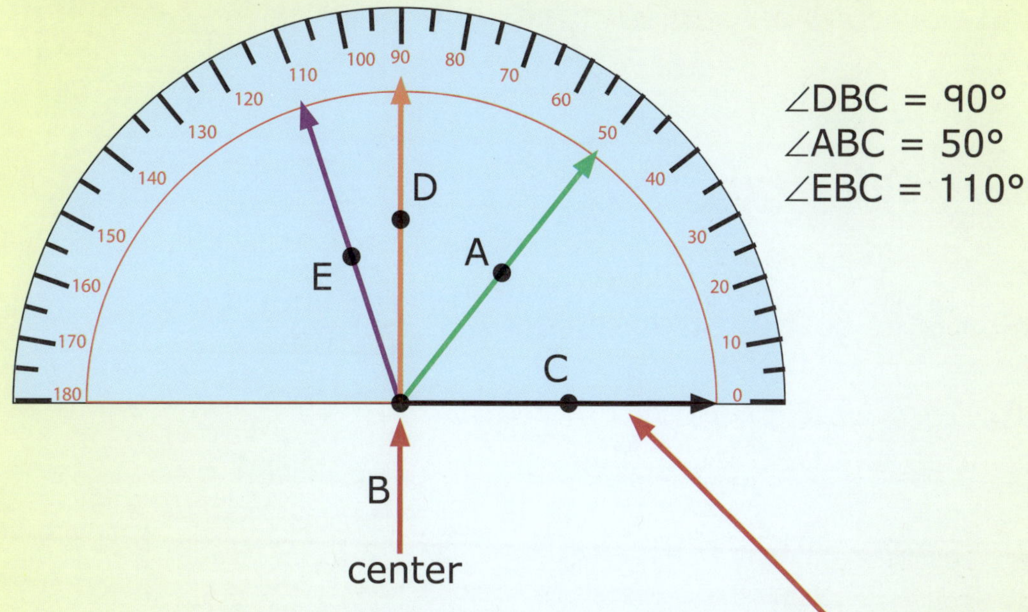

∠DBC = 90°
∠ABC = 50°
∠EBC = 110°

To measure an angle, place one side on the 0° edge starting at the center and record where the other side hits the numbers.

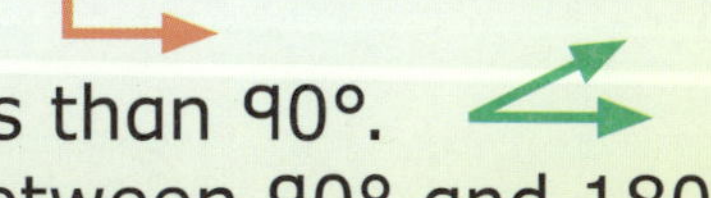

A right angle measures 90°.
An acute angle measures less than 90°.
An obtuse angle measures between 90° and 180°.

How many of each type of angle is inside the kite?

1) _____ right angles

2) _____ acute angles

3) _____ obtuse angles

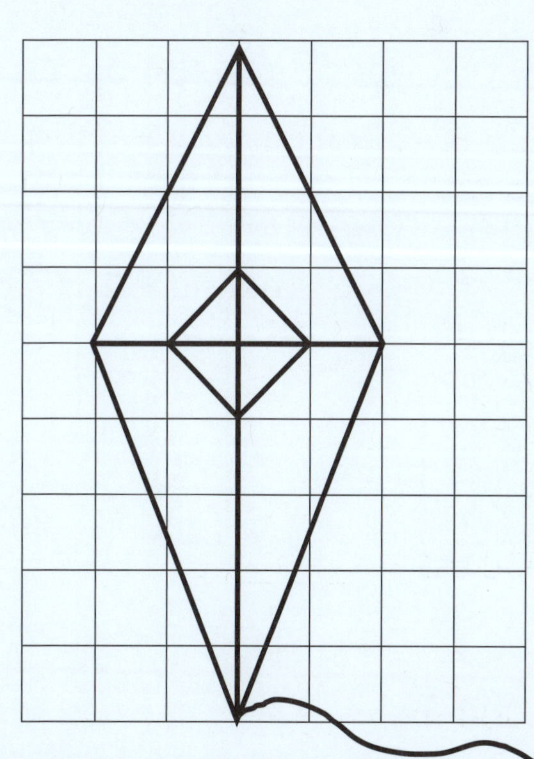

A **polygon** is a closed figure made up of line segments. Four-sided polygons are called quadrilaterals.

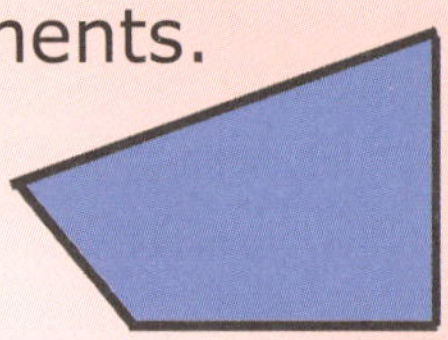

SPECIAL QUADRILATERALS

A quadrilateral with one pair of parallel sides is called a trapezoid.

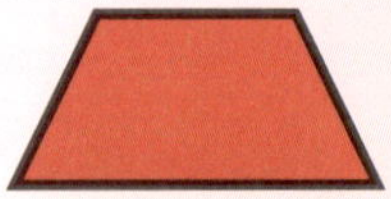

A quadrilateral with two pairs of parallel sides is called a parallelogram.

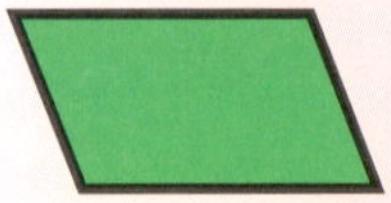

A parallelogram with 4 right angles is called a rectangle.

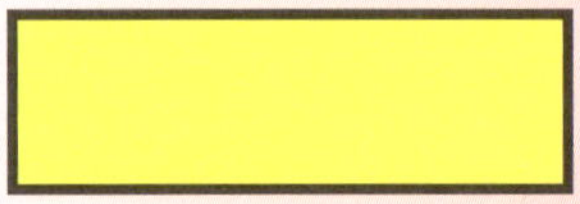

A rectangle with 4 equal sides is called a square.

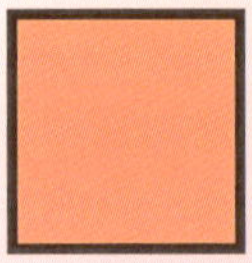

How many rectangles are in the picture?

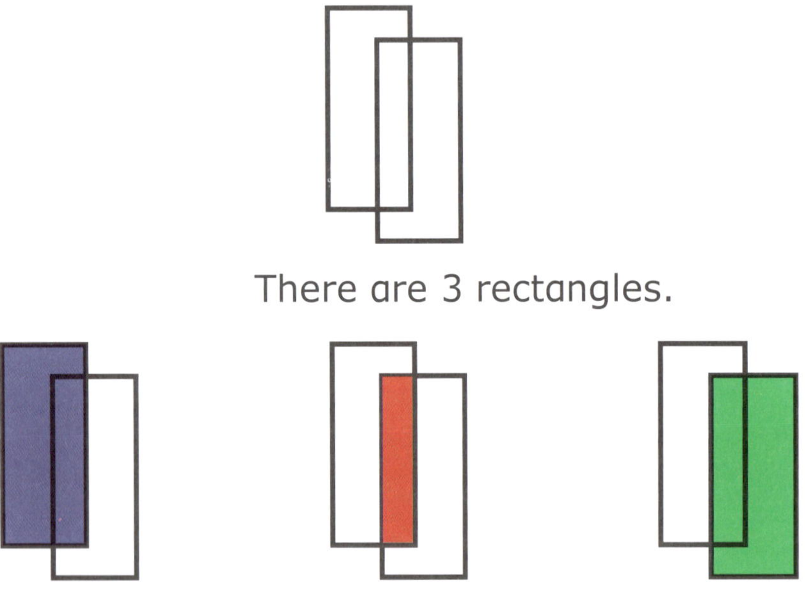

1. How many rectangles do you see in the picture? ____

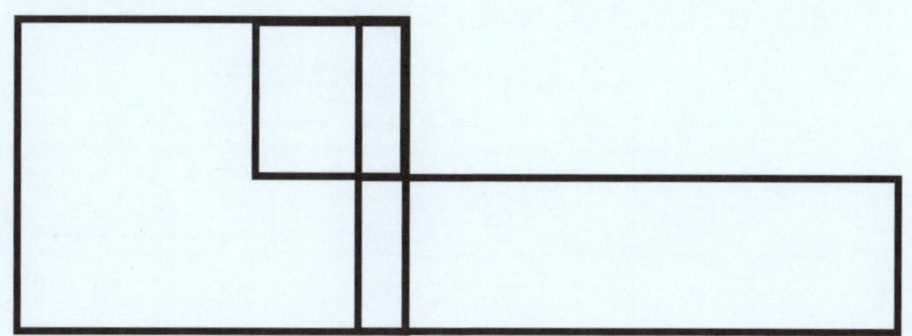

2. How many squares do you see in the picture? ____

3. How many parallelograms do you see in the picture? ____

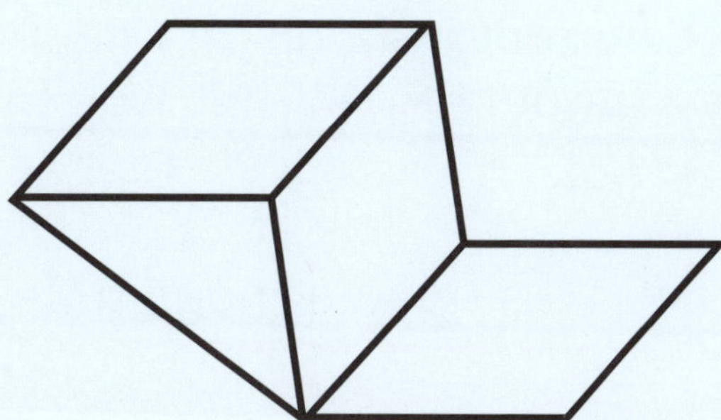

4. How many trapezoids do you see in the picture? ____

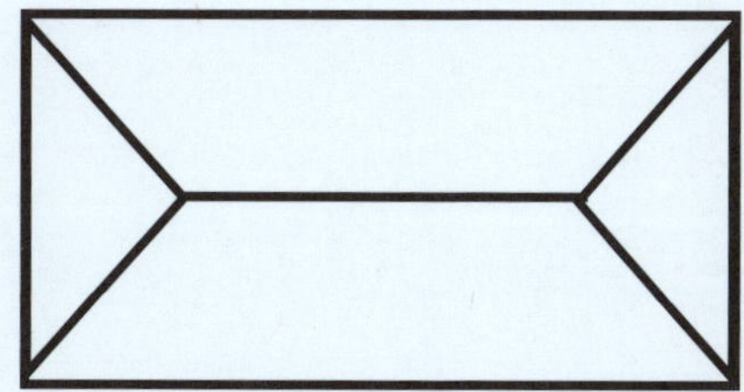

Scientists classify earthquakes by **energy strength**.

Categories of Strength or Magnitude of Earthquakes

Magnitude	Effect	Estimated Number Each Year
2.5 to 5.4	Light	30,000
5.5 to 6.0	Moderate	500
6.1 to 6.9	Strong	100
7.0 to 7.9	Major	20
8.0 or greater	Great	1 every 5 to 10 years

1. What is the effect of a 5.7 magnitude earthquake? ____________

2. If an earthquake produced light damage, what would its magnitude be? ____________

3. The largest earthquake in California history centered at Fort Tejon in 1857 with magnitude 7.9. What was the effect of this earthquake? ____________

4. About how many earthquakes have a magnitude of between 6.1 and 6.9 per year? ____________

5. About how many earthquakes are there per year? ____________

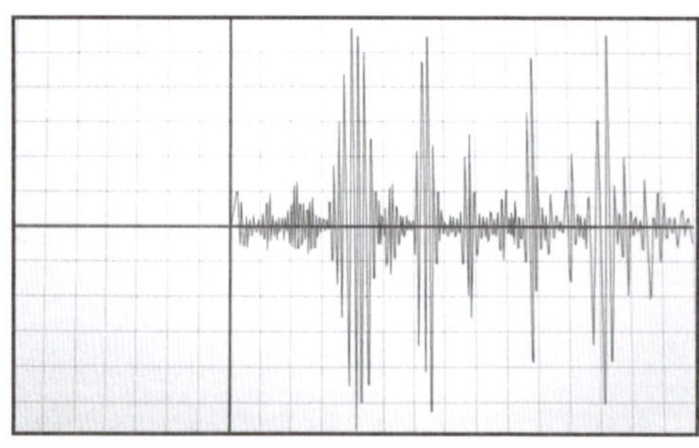

Fortunately, most of the earthquakes that occur each year are of magnitude less than 2.5 which is too small to be felt by most people.

Food Figures

1. For a team snack after baseball practice, Rob needs 22 granola bars. If the granola bars come 6 to a package, how many packages will he need to buy and how many candy bars will be left over?
   Number of packages = ____ left over = ____

2. Madi is making trail mix for a camp out. Cereal costs 50¢ a cup, nuts are $1 a cup, and dried fruit costs $1.25 a cup. What would it cost to make the following basic trail mix? ____

   Trail Mix Recipe
   4 cups of cereal
   2 cups of dried fruit
   2 cups of nuts

3. A small package of drink boxes cost $3 and has 6 drink boxes in it. A large package of drink boxes cost $4 and has 10 drink boxes in it. What is the least amount that can be spent to purchase 42 drink boxes? ____

A **factor** of a whole number divides into it evenly.

2 is a factor of 14	(14 ÷ 2 = 7)
2 is not a factor of 15	(15 ÷ 2 = 7 remainder 1)
4 is a factor of 48	(48 ÷ 4 = 12)
4 is not a factor of 22	(22 ÷ 4 = 5 remainder 2)

Circle the colored path(s) that contain only numbers where either 4 or 6 are factors?

Blue Yellow Green Red

36	24	4	100	32	60	56	64	28
40	52	88	45	27	39	48	72	90
66	80	18	42	84	96	60	81	45
52	20	80	36	42	76	72	24	16
					32	56	63	20
					24	90	24	124
					40	44	104	92
					56	12	49	27
					80	28	244	30
					35	32	18	6
					12	88	20	18
					64	4	150	40
					6	36	58	48

Hooked on Math

Solve each problem; then cross out the correct answers below to find the two false answers.

1.
```
   456
    34
 3,671
+  305
```

2.
```
  3,457
 20,183
    204
+ 2,005
```

3.
```
   239
 1,248
    23
+   58
```

4.
```
    19
 5,692
 1,462
+  307
```

5.
```
  942
- 271
```

6.
```
 103,482
- 29,453
```

7.
```
 45,900
- 6,709
```

8.
```
  3,127
- 1,099
```

9.
```
 3,651
×    6
```

10.
```
  34
× 27
```

11.
```
 123
×  46
```

12.
```
  208
× 135
```

13. $5\overline{)95}$

14. $4\overline{)2,588}$

15. $60\overline{)4,980}$

16. $23\overline{)552}$

5,658	1,568	2,028	4,466
781	7,480	918	74,029
21,906	19	75,350	39,191
671	647	24	28,080
	83	25,849	

An equivalent fraction can be formed by multiplying the numerator and denominator of a fraction by the same non-zero number.

$\frac{1}{2} =$ 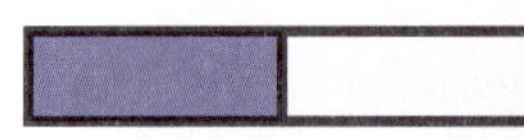

$\frac{1 \cdot 2}{2 \cdot 2} = \frac{2}{4}$ 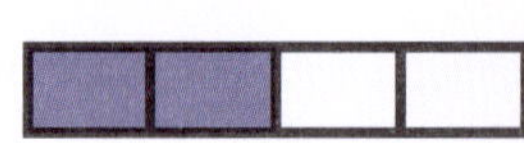

1) Shade each figure to show $\frac{2}{3}$.

2) Shade each figure to show $\frac{3}{4}$.

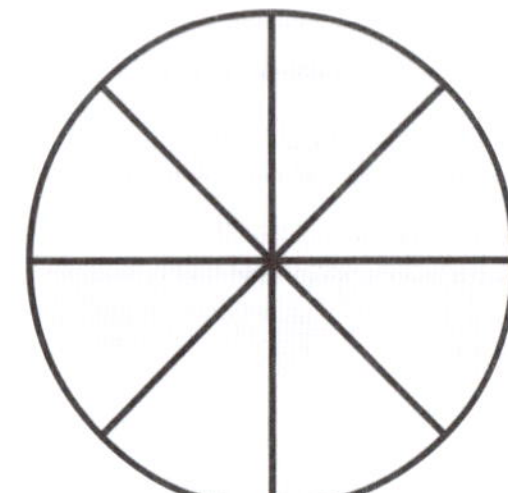

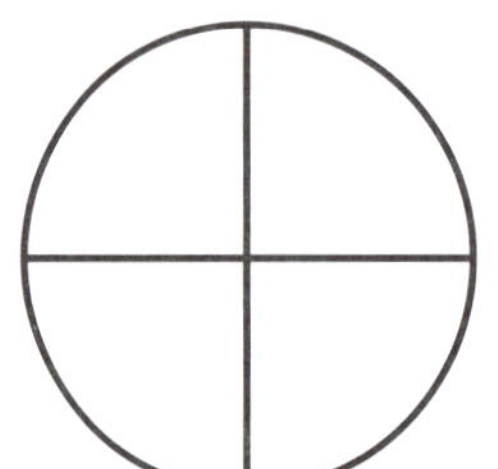

3) Shade each figure to show $\frac{4}{5}$.

Rules for Adding and Subtracting Fractions

$\frac{a}{b} + \frac{c}{b} = \frac{a + c}{b}$ $\frac{a}{b} - \frac{c}{b} = \frac{a - c}{b}$

To add or subtract fractions, the fractions must have the same denominators before adding or subtracting the numerators. Always put answers in simplest terms.

$\frac{5}{7} + \frac{1}{7} = \frac{6}{7}$

$\frac{2}{3} - \frac{1}{4} =$

$\frac{8}{12} - \frac{3}{12} = \frac{5}{12}$

Find each answer; then use the letters to solve the riddle below.

r $\frac{4}{5} - \frac{1}{5} =$

n $\frac{5}{8} + \frac{1}{8} =$

e $\frac{5}{6} - \frac{1}{6} =$

t $\frac{1}{4} + \frac{1}{4} =$

i $\frac{3}{8} + \frac{1}{4} =$

s $\frac{5}{6} - \frac{2}{3} =$

b $\frac{2}{3} + \frac{1}{5} =$

a $\frac{1}{4} + \frac{1}{6} =$

What is a drummer's favorite vegetable?

____ ____ ____ ____ ____

$\frac{13}{15}$ $\frac{2}{3}$ $\frac{2}{3}$ $\frac{1}{2}$ $\frac{1}{6}$

Bob has to give Jonnie $\frac{1}{2}$ of his six quarters. How many is that?

To find $\frac{1}{2}$ of a quantity, divide by 2.

To find $\frac{1}{3}$ of a quantity, divide by 3.

To find $\frac{1}{4}$ of a quantity, divide by 4.

To find $\frac{1}{5}$ of a quantity, divide by 5.

...

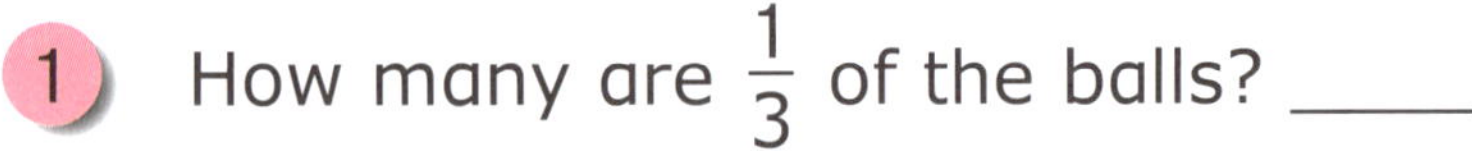

2. How many are $\frac{1}{4}$ of the pennies? _____

3. How many are $\frac{1}{5}$ of the candy pieces? _____

4. How many are $\frac{1}{6}$ of the dollars? _____

5. How much is $\frac{1}{4}$ of $56? ________

6. How much is $\frac{1}{8}$ of $256? ________

7. How much is $\frac{1}{3}$ of $111? ________

8. How much is $\frac{1}{2}$ of $112? ________

9. How much is $\frac{1}{6}$ of $384? ________

10. How much is $\frac{1}{10}$ of $300? ________

11. How much is $\frac{1}{5}$ of $611? ________

12. Ali had to divide the $42 ticket price total among three people. How much should each pay? ________

13. $64 is spent on 8 student admissions to a park. How much is the ticket price for each student? ________

14. In a 36 cookie recipe, 4 cups of flour is needed. If only 18 cookies are made, how much flour should be used? ________

15. What is one-fourth of one million dollars? ________

When multiplying fractions, multiply the numerators together and the denominators together. The word of indicates multiplication.

Find $\frac{1}{2}$ of $\frac{3}{4}$ $\frac{1}{2} \times \frac{3}{4} = \frac{3}{8}$

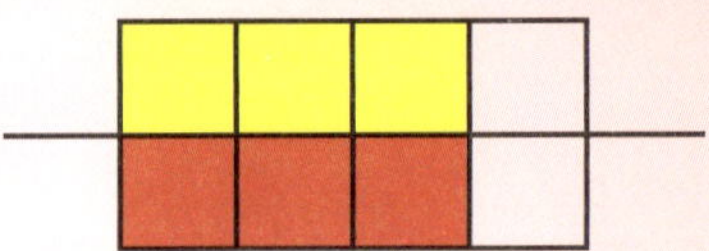

Find $\frac{1}{2}$ of \$8 $\frac{1}{2} \times \frac{8}{1} = \frac{8}{2} = \$4$

An alternate way to multiply fractions is to divide any common factors out of a numerator and denominator before multiplying.

$$\frac{1}{\cancel{2}_1} \times \frac{\cancel{8}^4}{1} = \frac{4}{1} = \$4$$

Find each product. Simplify if needed.

1. $\frac{1}{2} \times \frac{1}{3} =$ _____
2. $\frac{1}{4} \times \frac{3}{4} =$ _____
3. $\frac{1}{3}$ of $\frac{1}{3} =$ _____
4. $\frac{3}{4}$ of 4 = _____
5. $\frac{2}{3} \times \frac{2}{5} =$ _____
6. $\frac{2}{3} \times 6 =$ _____
7. $\frac{1}{4} \times 12 =$ _____
8. $\frac{3}{5} \times \frac{5}{5} =$ _____
9. $\frac{2}{5}$ of 15 = _____

10. $\frac{2}{3} \times \frac{1}{4} =$ _____

11. $\frac{1}{3} \times \frac{3}{5} =$ _____

12. $\frac{3}{8} \times \frac{2}{9} =$ _____

13. If a recipe needs $\frac{1}{2}$ cup of flour and you are only making half the recipe, how much flour do you need? _____

14. Four out of the six students were present at a party. The other two students were going to be 45 minutes late. If there were 24 cookies on the table, how many would be left for the late students if everyone would get the same number of cookies?

_____

Multiplication of Fractions Rule: $\frac{a}{b} \cdot \frac{c}{d} = \frac{a \cdot c}{b \cdot d}$

Before multiplying with fractions, change any mixed number or whole number into an improper fraction.

$\frac{2}{3}$ of $12 = \frac{2}{3} \times \frac{12}{1} = \frac{24}{3} = 8$ or $\frac{2}{\cancel{3}_1} \times \frac{\cancel{12}^4}{1} = \frac{8}{1} = 8$

$2\frac{2}{3} \times 1\frac{1}{4} =$

$\frac{8}{3} \times \frac{5}{4}$

$\frac{\cancel{8}^2}{3} \times \frac{5}{\cancel{4}_1} = \frac{10}{3} = 3\frac{1}{3}$

Find each product; then use the letters to solve the riddle on the next page.

y $\frac{1}{2} \times \frac{1}{3} =$

d $\frac{3}{4} \times 12 =$

i $\frac{2}{3} \times \frac{2}{3} =$

o $15 \times \frac{2}{3} =$

c $\frac{1}{3} \times 1\frac{1}{2} =$

t $\frac{3}{8} \times 1\frac{1}{7} =$

w $2\frac{3}{4} \times \frac{3}{11} =$

a $\frac{1}{2} \times 1\frac{1}{4} =$

u $\frac{1}{2} \times 2\frac{1}{2} =$

g $\frac{2}{3} \times \frac{5}{9} =$

r $1\frac{2}{3} \times 2 =$

b $\frac{5}{8} \times 3 =$

h $\frac{5}{6} \times \frac{3}{8} =$

z $2 \times \frac{1}{2} =$

l $1\frac{1}{3} \times 2\frac{1}{4} =$

x $4\frac{2}{3} \times 2\frac{4}{7} =$

e Moe's share of the $24 was one-third. What was Moe's share? _____

m If it takes $2\frac{1}{2}$ yards of material to make a dress, how many yards would be needed to make three dresses? ____

What kind of bear loves to play in the rain?

___	___	___	___	___	___	___	___
$\frac{5}{8}$	9	$3\frac{1}{3}$	$\frac{4}{9}$	1	1	3	$\frac{1}{6}$

___	___	___	___
$1\frac{7}{8}$	8	$\frac{5}{8}$	$3\frac{1}{3}$

The **reciprocal** of a fraction is formed when a fraction or improper fraction is inverted.

original fraction = $\frac{a}{b}$	reciprocal = $\frac{b}{a}$
original fraction = $\frac{2}{3}$	reciprocal = $\frac{3}{2}$
original fraction = 4 or $\frac{4}{1}$	reciprocal = $\frac{1}{4}$
original fraction = $3\frac{4}{5}$ or $\frac{19}{5}$	reciprocal = $\frac{5}{19}$

Find each reciprocal; then use the letters to solve the riddle below.

r $\frac{5}{6}$	n $\frac{3}{4}$	e $\frac{1}{2}$
h $1\frac{2}{3}$	m 3	p 5
u $1\frac{1}{2}$	t $2\frac{2}{5}$	o $\frac{2}{3}$
l $1\frac{1}{4}$	s $\frac{19}{20}$	x $3\frac{1}{3}$
w 6	a 1	f $4\frac{1}{2}$

What insect has the least courage?

____ ____ ____   ____ ____ ____ ____

$\frac{5}{12}$ $\frac{3}{5}$ 2 $\frac{2}{9}$ $\frac{4}{5}$ 2 1

To divide fractions, write as either a proper or improper fraction, then multiply by the reciprocal of the divisor.

If a $2\frac{1}{2}$ inch board is cut into four equal parts, how long would each of the parts be? $2\frac{1}{2} \div 4 = ?$

$$2\frac{1}{2} \div 4 = \frac{5}{2} \div \frac{4}{1} = \frac{5}{2} \times \frac{1}{4} = \frac{5}{8} \text{ inch}$$

multiply by the reciprocal of the divisor

Rule for division of fractions:

$$\frac{a}{b} \div \frac{c}{d} = \frac{a}{b} \cdot \frac{d}{c} = \frac{a \cdot d}{b \cdot c}$$

Find each quotient; then cross out the correct answers below to find the two false answers.

1. $\frac{3}{4} \div \frac{1}{4} =$ ________
2. $\frac{7}{8} \div 7 =$ ________
3. $\frac{3}{7} \div \frac{1}{2} =$ ________
4. $5 \div \frac{1}{4} =$ ________
5. $1\frac{1}{2} \div \frac{3}{4} =$ ________
6. $2\frac{1}{2} \div \frac{1}{4} =$ ________
7. $\frac{5}{8} \div 2 =$ ________
8. $7\frac{1}{2} \div 1\frac{1}{2} =$ ________

20	$\frac{1}{8}$	$\frac{5}{16}$	5	4	3	10	$\frac{1}{4}$	$\frac{6}{7}$	2

Rules for Multiplication and Division of Fractions

Multiplication

$$\frac{a}{b} \cdot \frac{c}{d} = \frac{a \cdot c}{b \cdot d}$$

$$3\tfrac{1}{2} \times \frac{1}{7} = \frac{\cancel{7}^{1}}{2} \times \frac{1}{\cancel{7}_{1}} = \frac{1}{2}$$

Division

$$\frac{a}{b} \div \frac{c}{d} = \frac{a}{b} \cdot \frac{d}{c} = \frac{a \cdot d}{b \cdot c}$$

$$3\tfrac{1}{2} \div \frac{1}{2} = \frac{7}{\cancel{2}_{1}} \times \frac{\cancel{2}^{1}}{1} =$$

$$\frac{7}{1} \times \frac{1}{1} = \frac{7}{1} = 7$$

1) Kenley was told she needed to save $\frac{1}{4}$ of her baby-sitting money and could spend $\frac{3}{4}$ of it. If she made $20 baby-sitting during the weekend, how much money does she have to spend? ______

2) Kali has 3 cups of milk. If she needs $\frac{3}{4}$ cup of milk in a recipe for cookies, how many batches can she make with the milk she has? ______

3) To make a table, Leon needs four legs. If he has a 10 foot board to cut into 4 equal parts, how long will each part be? ______

4) Rod makes $\$10\frac{1}{2}$ per hour at his job. If he works five hours, how much would he make? ______

The United States Mint coin diameters are listed in the table below. Diameter (*d*) is the distance across a circle through the center of the circle.

Coin	Diameter
penny	.75 in.
nickel	.835 in.
dime	.705 in.
quarter	.955 in.
half-dollar	1.205 in.
dollar	1.043 in.

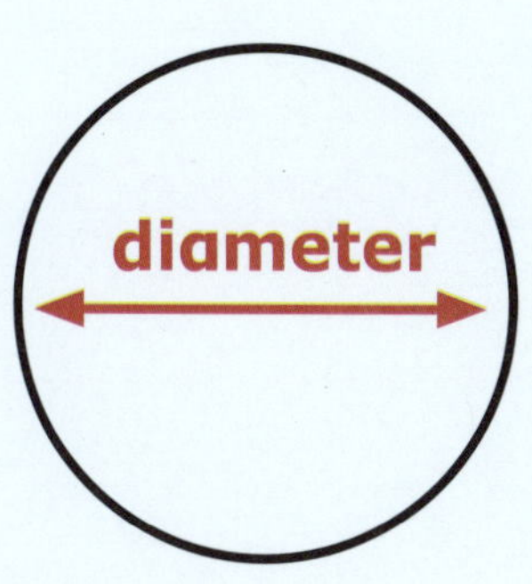

Write the letter of the size that matches the coin.

1. penny = _____
2. nickel = _____
3. dime = _____
4. quarter = _____
5. fifty cent piece = _____
6. dollar = _____

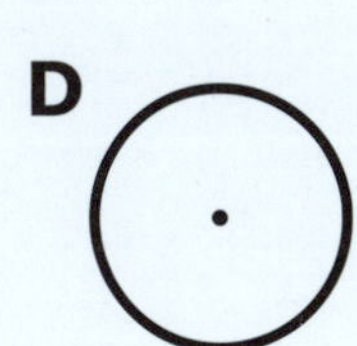

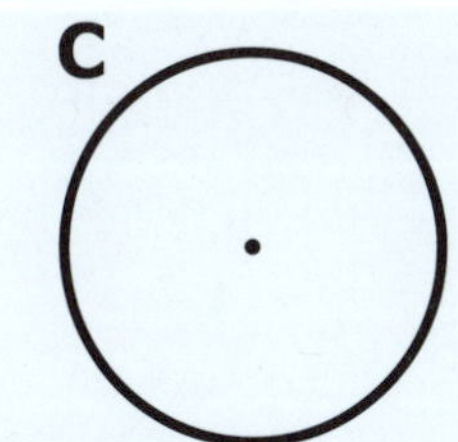

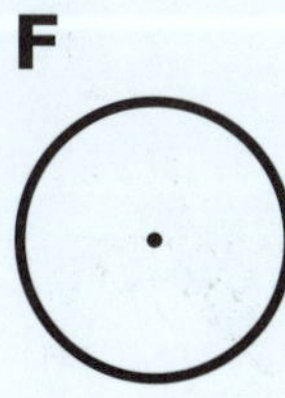

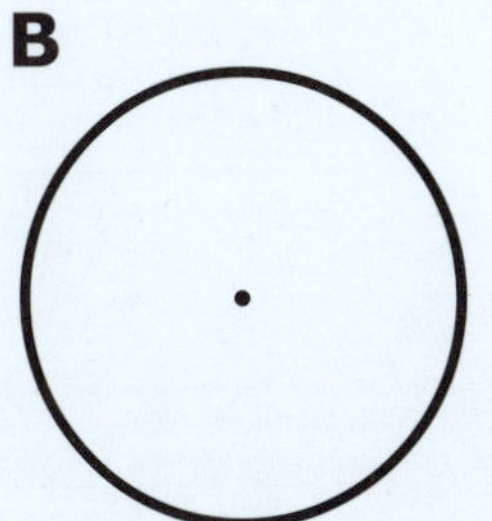

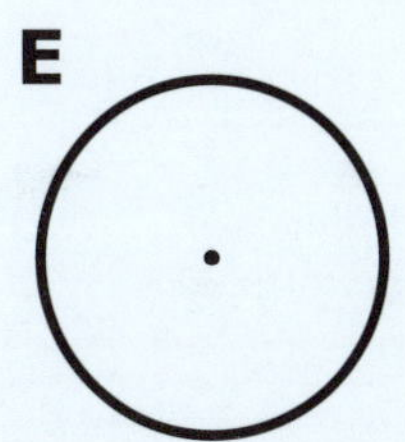

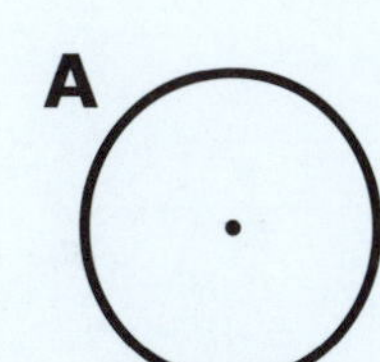

Play a game of bowling to review adding and subtracting decimals. Before working a problem, line up the decimal points to add or subtract same place values together. Fill empty place values with zeroes.

$$5.23 + 12.4 + 2 = \begin{array}{r} 5.23 \\ 12.40 \\ +\ 2.00 \\ \hline 19.63 \end{array}$$

$$3 - 1.29 = \begin{array}{r} \overset{2}{\cancel{3}}.\overset{9}{\cancel{0}}\overset{1}{0} \\ -\ 1.29 \\ \hline 1.71 \end{array}$$

Solve each problem; then cross out the correct answers below to find the two false answers.

1. 6.46 + 1.72 =
2. 5.23 − 1.25 =
3. 3 + 4.2 + 5 =
4. 2.7 − .01 =
5. 5.07 + .33 =
6. 3.4 − .38 =
7. 4.9 + 52.82 =
8. .217 − .03 =
9. .25 + 1.85 + .9 =
10. 7 − .29 =

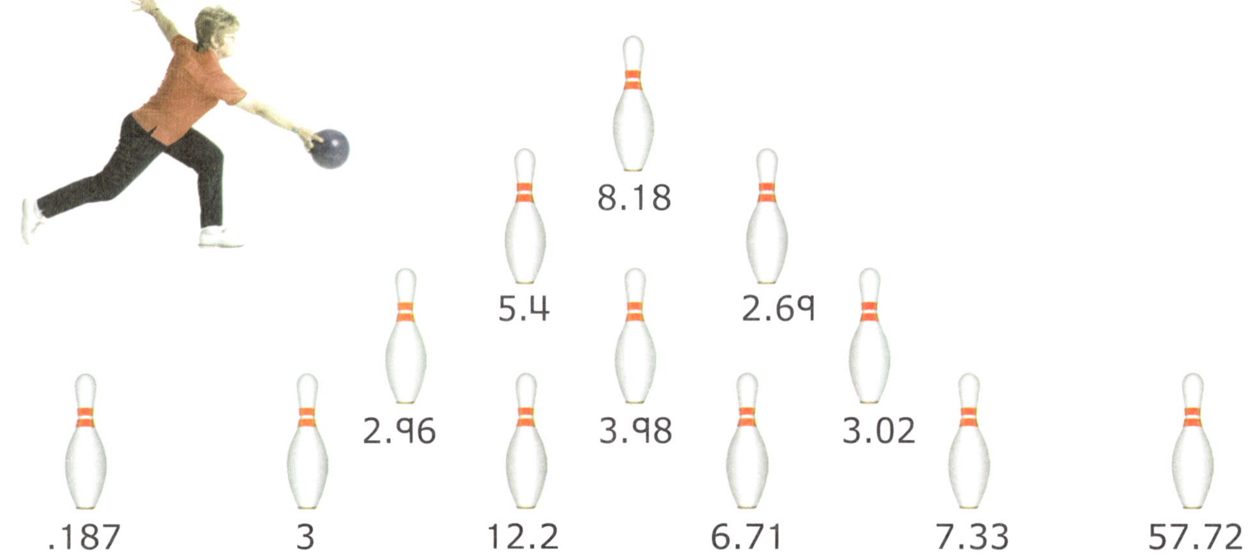

Buying in Bulk

How much is 12 rolls of toilet paper at $1.25 per roll?

```
  $1.25   ← total of two decimal places in factors
×    12
    250
   125
 $15.00   ← total of two decimal places in the product
```

The total number of decimal places in the factors **equal** the total number of decimal places in the product.

Find each total cost, then fill in the grid.

1. 3 belts at $15.17 each = _______
2. 8 shirts at $18.02 each = _______
3. 9 jackets at $34.59 each = _______
4. a dozen donuts at 99¢ each = _______
5. 20 notebooks at $5.99 each = _______
6. 25 candy bars at 65¢ each = _______
7. 6 tickets at $75.30 each = _______
8. pay for 15 hours at $27.54 each hour = _______
9. 13 pairs of socks at $2.97 per pair = _______

1		4	5	.	5	1
2				.	1	
3			1	.		
4		1		.		
5	1			.		
6		1		.		
7			1	.		
8				.	1	
9				.		1

What is $\frac{1}{10}$ of 20? $\frac{1}{\cancel{10}_1} \times \frac{\cancel{20}^2}{1} = \frac{2}{1} = 2$

What is .1 of 20? $.1 \times 20 = 2.0 = 2$

(.1: total of one decimal place in the factors; 2.0: total of one decimal place in the product)

Decimal places are the number of place values to the right of the decimal.

3 has no decimal places
14.7 has 1 decimal place
2.86 has 2 decimal places
.001 has 3 decimal places

RULE:
To multiply with decimals, multiply as with whole numbers and put the total number of decimal places in the factors in the product. If there is a total of three decimal places in the factors, there must be three decimal places in the product. Zeroes can be added to the product to achieve the correct number of decimal places.

$.2 \times 3.46 =$

$$\begin{array}{r} 346 \\ \times\ \ 2 \\ \hline 692 \end{array} \qquad \begin{array}{r} 3.46 \\ \times\ \ .2 \\ \hline .692 \end{array}$$

$.11 \times .32 =$

$$\begin{array}{r} 32 \\ \times\ 11 \\ \hline 32 \\ 320 \\ \hline 352 \end{array} \qquad \begin{array}{r} .32 \\ \times\ .11 \\ \hline .0352 \end{array}$$

Place the decimal in each product.

1.
$$\begin{array}{r} 3.6 \\ \times\ 4 \\ \hline 144 \end{array}$$

2.
$$\begin{array}{r} .36 \\ \times\ 4 \\ \hline 144 \end{array}$$

3.
$$\begin{array}{r} 36 \\ \times\ .4 \\ \hline 144 \end{array}$$

4.
$$\begin{array}{r} .36 \\ \times\ .04 \\ \hline 144 \end{array}$$

5.
$$\begin{array}{r} 7.3 \\ \times\ 8 \\ \hline 584 \end{array}$$

6.
$$\begin{array}{r} .73 \\ \times\ 8 \\ \hline 584 \end{array}$$

7.
$$\begin{array}{r} .73 \\ \times\ .08 \\ \hline 584 \end{array}$$

8.
$$\begin{array}{r} 7.3 \\ \times\ .8 \\ \hline 584 \end{array}$$

9.
$$\begin{array}{r} 8.2 \\ \times\ 2.4 \\ \hline 328 \\ 1640 \\ \hline 1968 \end{array}$$

10.
$$\begin{array}{r} 1.5 \\ \times\ .68 \\ \hline 120 \\ 900 \\ \hline 1020 \end{array}$$

11.
$$\begin{array}{r} 14 \\ \times\ 5.3 \\ \hline 42 \\ 700 \\ \hline 742 \end{array}$$

12.
$$\begin{array}{r} 1.1 \\ \times\ .88 \\ \hline 88 \\ 880 \\ \hline 968 \end{array}$$

13.
$$\begin{array}{r} 5.6 \\ \times\ 2.3 \\ \hline 168 \\ 1120 \\ \hline 1288 \end{array}$$

14.
$$\begin{array}{r} 20.9 \\ \times\ .73 \\ \hline 627 \\ 14630 \\ \hline 15257 \end{array}$$

15.
$$\begin{array}{r} .920 \\ \times\ .023 \\ \hline 2760 \\ 18400 \\ \hline 21160 \end{array}$$

16.
$$\begin{array}{r} .133 \\ \times\ .02 \\ \hline 266 \end{array}$$

Find each product; then use the letters to solve the riddle on the next page. The number of decimal places in the factors should equal the number of places in the product.

One decimal place in the factors.

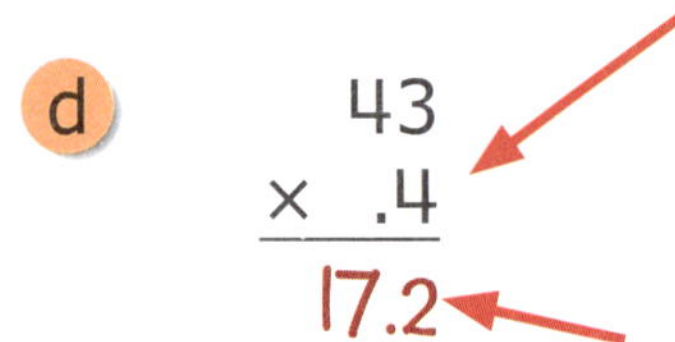

d) $43 \times .4 = 17.2$

One decimal place in the product.

o) $4.3 \times .04$

r) $.43 \times 4$

h) 1.29×6

g) $.129 \times .06$

e) $129 \times .006$

a) $78 \times .23$

l) 78×2.3

w) $.078 \times 23$

v) 4.06×91

p) 406×9.1

i) $406 \times .091$

k) $.056 \times 1.1 =$

m) $.3 \times .3 =$

s) 2.4 × 54

x) .07 × 264 =

q) .03 × .03

c) 2.45 × 7.3 =

b) Jami entered a pumpkin weighing contest. Her pumpkin weighed 9.95 kilograms. The winner's pumpkin weighed 1.5 times hers. What is the weight of the winning pumpkin?

z) The length of a pencil is 15.8 centimeters. What is the length of four pencils placed end-to-end?

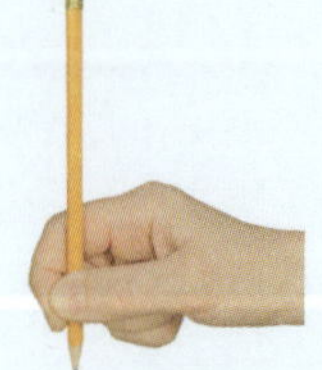

n) If a motor boat is traveling at a speed of 13.5 miles an hour for 1.25 hours, how far has the boat traveled?

What game is loved by baby cows?

___	___	___	___ -	___ -	___	___	___
3,694.6	.774	.774	.0616	17.94	.09	.172	.172

To divide a decimal by a whole number, divide as usual and place the decimal in the quotient directly above the decimal in the dividend.

$\$1.54 \div 2 = ?$

$2\overline{)1.54}$

$$\begin{array}{r} 77 \\ 2\overline{)154} \\ \underline{14} \\ 14 \\ \underline{14} \end{array}$$

$$\begin{array}{r} .77 \\ 2\overline{)1.54} \end{array}$$

check

$$\begin{array}{r} .77 \\ \times \quad 2 \\ \hline \$1.54 \end{array}$$

Insert zero placeholders where needed.

$.0012 \div 3 = ?$

$3\overline{).0012}$

$$\begin{array}{r} .0004 \\ 3\overline{).0012} \\ \underline{12} \end{array}$$

check

$$\begin{array}{r} .0004 \\ \times \quad 3 \\ \hline .0012 \end{array}$$

Divide and check each problem.

1. $6\overline{).462}$
2. $8\overline{)51.2}$
3. $9\overline{).1755}$
4. $4\overline{)7.32}$
5. $9\overline{)284.4}$
6. $3\overline{).0171}$
7. $7\overline{)9.282}$
8. $8\overline{)10.24}$
9. $70\overline{).140}$
10. $30\overline{)15.60}$
11. $23\overline{)32.2}$
12. $11\overline{).1331}$

To divide a decimal by a whole number, divide as usual and place the decimal in the quotient directly above the decimal in the dividend.

Examples:

$$\begin{array}{r} .47 \\ 3\overline{)1.41} \\ \underline{1\,2} \\ 21 \\ \underline{21} \end{array} \qquad \begin{array}{r} .002 \\ 6\overline{).012} \\ \underline{12} \end{array} \qquad .4 \div 5 = \begin{array}{r} .08 \\ 5\overline{).40} \\ \underline{40} \end{array}$$

Insert zero placeholders where needed.

Insert zero placeholders where needed.

Divide; then cross out the correct answers below to find the two false answers.

1) $8\overline{)27.04}$

2) $7\overline{).0602}$

3) $4\overline{)348}$

4) $5\overline{)2.40}$

5) $3\overline{).0015}$

6) $5\overline{)5.60}$

7) $4\overline{)9.36}$

8) $6\overline{)1.23}$

9) $2\overline{)30.1}$

10) $21\overline{)6.3}$

11) $53\overline{)2.226}$

12) $6\overline{)3.0}$

.7 15.05 .205

.042 2.34

.0086

12.32 .3

When dividing by a decimal number, multiply the divisor by a power of 10 necessary to make it a whole number. Multiply the dividend by the same power of 10 so that the relationship between the divisor and dividend stays the same.

- Multiplying by 10 moves decimal point one place to the right in both the divisor and dividend.
- Multiplying by 100 moves decimal point two places to the right in both the divisor and dividend.
- Multiplying by 1,000 moves decimal point three places to the right in both the divisor and dividend.

$.2\overline{)4.28}$ is rewritten and worked as $2\overline{)42.8}$ with quotient 21.4 check: 21.4 × 2 = 42.8

$1.25\overline{)5}$ is rewritten and worked as $125\overline{)500.}$ with quotient 4. check: 125 × 4 = 500

Rewrite and divide; then use the letters to solve the riddle on the next page.

r $.3\overline{).171}$

m $.8\overline{)7.04}$

a $.06\overline{).312}$

i $.09\overline{)1.71}$

b $.4\overline{)6}$

o $.005\overline{).0345}$

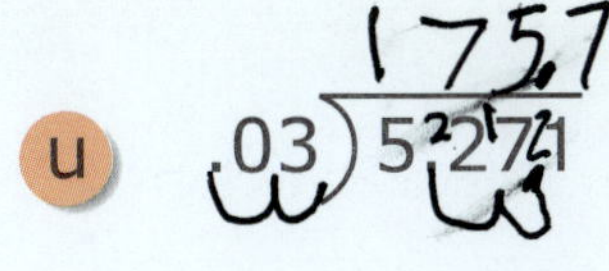

u .03) 5.271 3)

e .9) .00135 9)

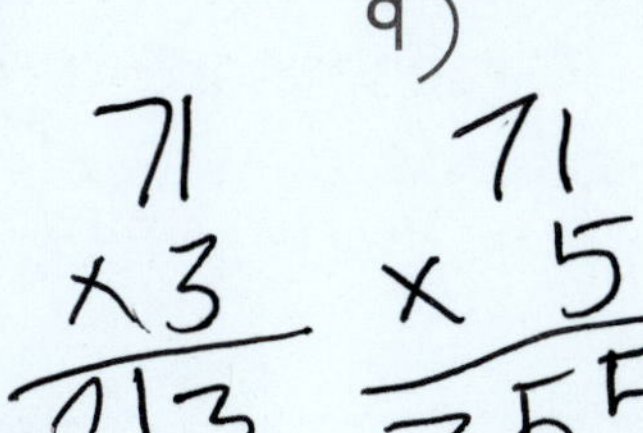

w 1.1) .33 11)

p .071) 2.485 71)

s .004) .21 4)

l 3.2) 5.12 32)

d How many 1.2 centimeter pieces can be cut from a piece of wire 6 centimeters long? _____

What loses its head every morning yet gets it back at night?

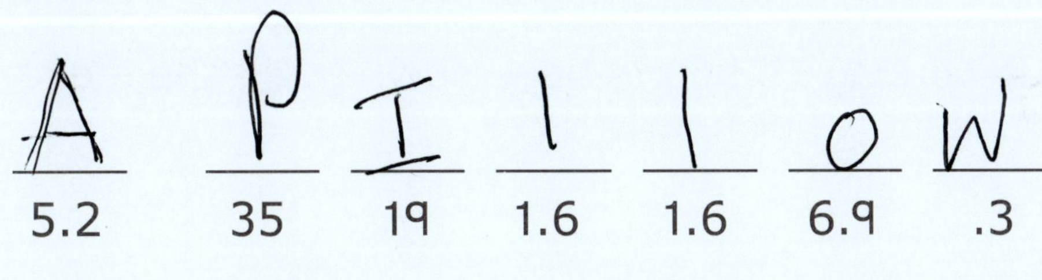

5.2	35	19	1.6	1.6	6.9	.3

A **rate** is a fixed ratio between two things.

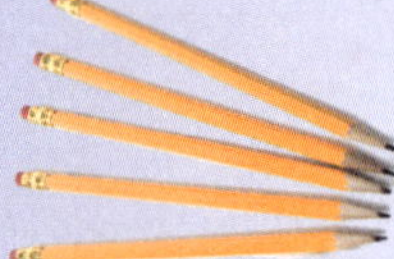

Five pencils costing \$2.50 is a fixed ratio.

$$\frac{5}{2.50} = 5 \text{ to } 2.50 = 5 : 2.50$$

If five pencils cost \$2.50, how much does one pencil cost? The price for one item is called the unit rate. This can be figured by dividing the cost of five pencils by 5 or by solving a proportion problem. Let n be the cost of one pencil.

$$\frac{\text{number of pencils}}{\text{cost of pencils}} \qquad \frac{5}{2.50} = \frac{1}{n}$$

product of extremes → $5 \bullet n = 2.50 \bullet 1$ ← product of means

$5n = 2.50$ ← divide each side by 5

$n = \$.50$

1. If five pencils cost \$2.50, how much would seven pencils cost?
   Hint: $\frac{5}{2.50} = \frac{7}{n}$

2. If a 24 ounce bag of candy cost \$6.00, what is the unit rate, which is the cost of 1 ounce of candy?

3. If Hana made \$112 working 14 hours, how much would she make working 20 hours? What is her hourly rate?

4. Ray travels 444 miles in 8 hours. At that rate, how many miles can he travel in a day? What is his unit rate of speed?

Which Is the Best Buy?

To decide which purchase is the best buy, first figure each unit price to compare.

$6.72

$9.90

Is 6 ounces of Brand X detergent or 9 ounces of Brand Y detergent the best buy?

$6.72 ÷ 6 = $1.12 per ounce

$9.90 ÷ 9 = $1.10 per ounce
Brand Y is the best buy.

Which is the best buy below?

	X	Y	Best Buy? (circle one)
1	4 tickets for $25	3 tickets for $18.45	X or Y
2	8 candy bars for $10	6 candy bars for $6.90	X or Y
3	10 apples for $7.50	a dozen apples for $9.96	X or Y
4	5 foot board for $8	9 foot board for $15.75	X or Y

1) The three intersecting circles below form seven areas. Place the numbers 1, 2, 3, 4, 5, 6, and 7 in the seven areas to make the sum in each of the three circles equal. Three of the numbers have been placed already.

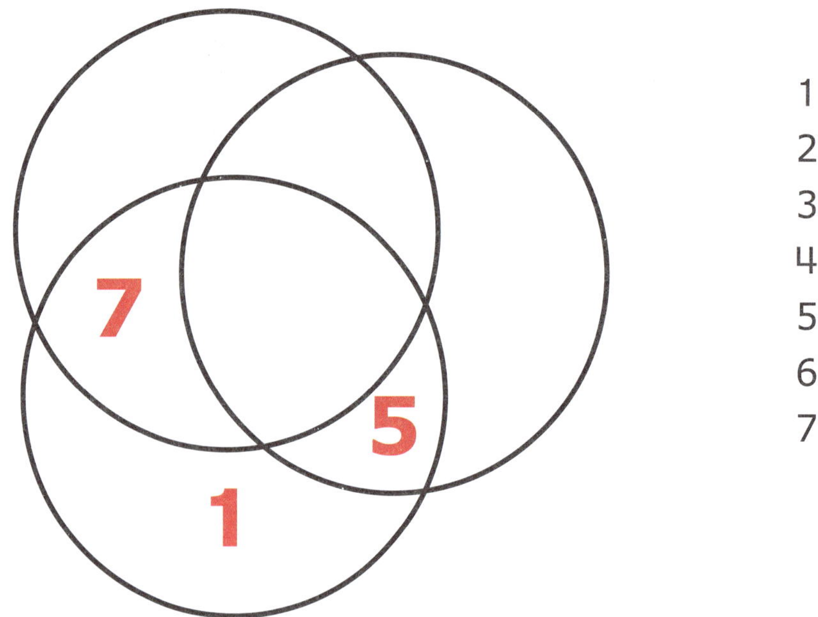

1
2
3
4
5
6
7

2) Place a math symbol between 5 and 9 to make the resulting number more than 5 and less than 9.

5 ___ 9

3) If you type the numbers 1 to 100, how many 9s will you type?

____

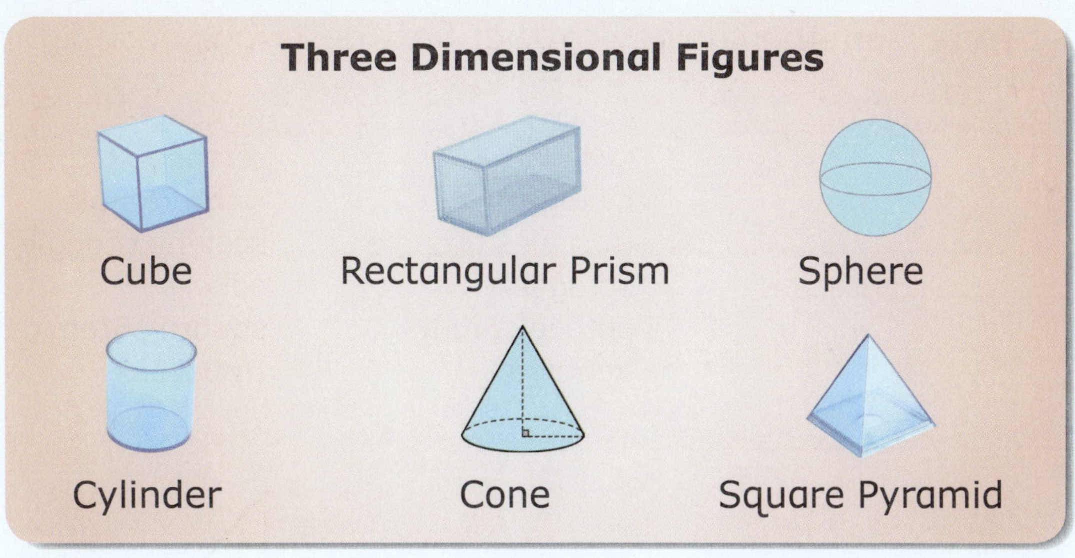

Write the letter of the object that matches the word the closest.

1) cube _____

2) cone _____

3) square pyramid _____

4) cylinder _____

5) rectangular prism _____

6) sphere _____

A. 

B. 

C. 

D. 

E. 

F. 

Name a common item that has the stated shape.

7) cylinder ______________________________

8) sphere ______________________________

9) rectangular prism ______________________________

Name the two shapes that combine to form the objects shown.

10) 

____

____

11) 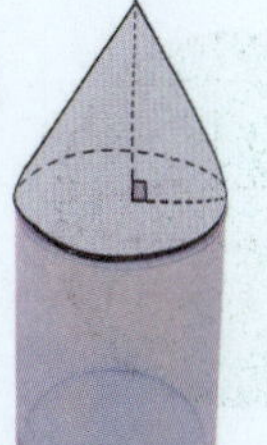

____

____

12) 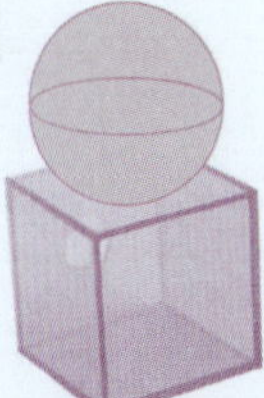

____

____

Write the term from the choice box that best describes each figure.

cube	rectangle
cylinder	rectangular prism
hexagon	right triangle
isosceles triangle	scalene triangle
octagon	sphere
parallelogram	square pyramid
pentagon	trapezoid

1 ______________________

2 ______________________

3 ______________________

4 ______________________

5 ______________________

6 ______________________

7 ______________________

8 ______________________

9 ______________________

10 ______________________

11 ______________________

12 ______________________

1 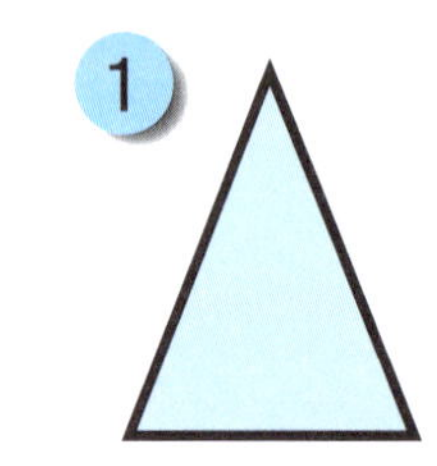

2 

3 

4 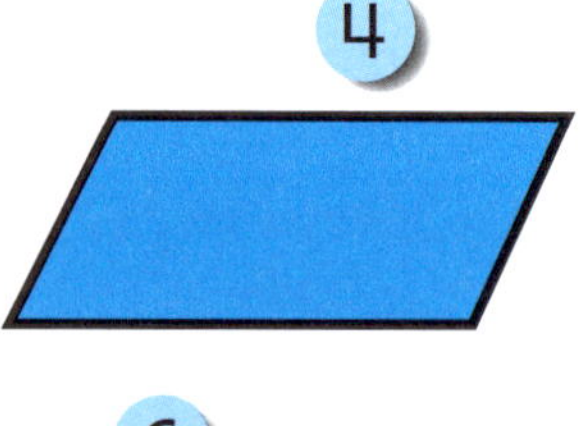

5 

6 

7 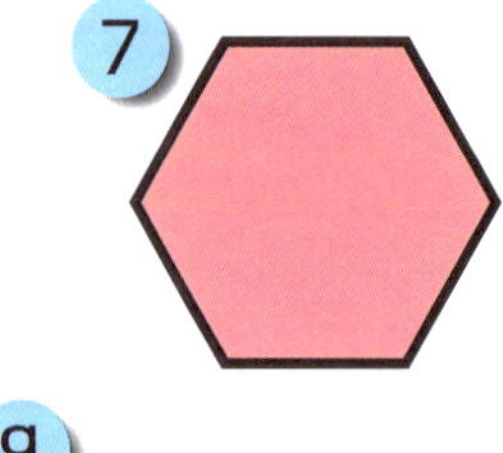

8 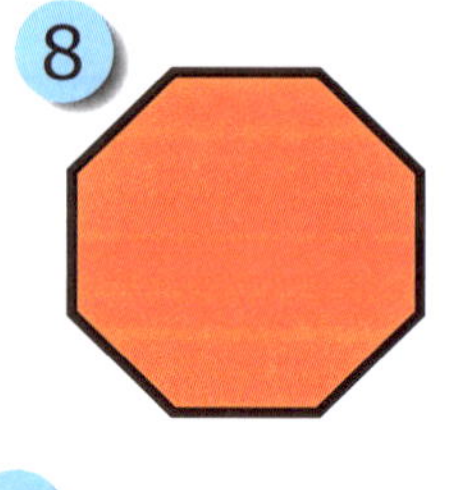

9 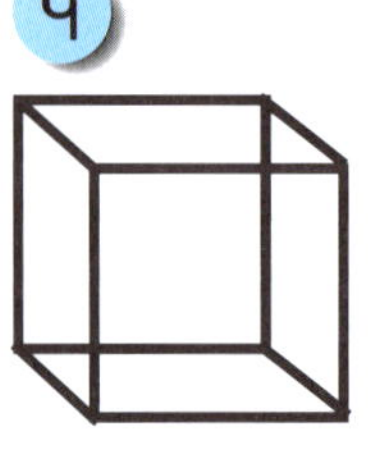

10 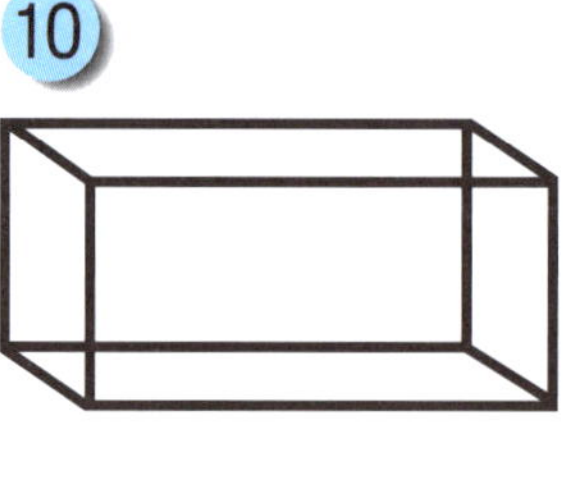

11 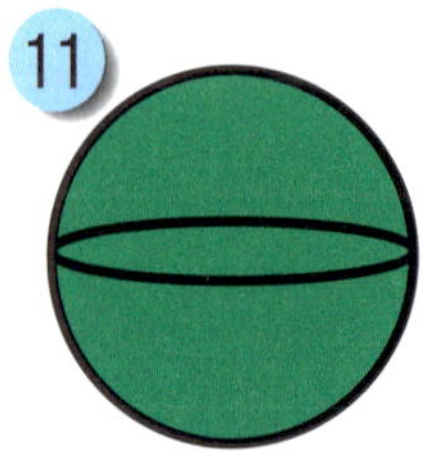

12 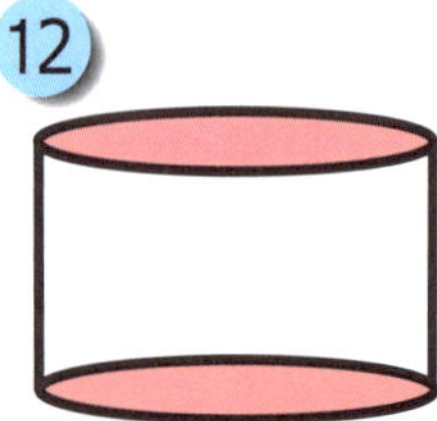

Slide, Flip, and Turn Transformation Message

1) Slide O to the right 3 units and draw.

2) Turn Z 90° counterclockwise and draw on the right.

3) Flip T ⁚ and draw on the right.

4) Slide H to the right 2 units and draw.

5) Flip Ǝ ⁚ and draw on the right.

6) Slide M to the right 3 units and draw.

7) Slide O down 6 units and then slide 3 units right and draw.

8) Flip ∧ ... and draw on the right.

9) Turn ш clockwise 90° and draw on the right.

				Message
1	O			
2			Z	
3			T	
4		H		
5			Ǝ	
6	M			
7				
8			∧	
9			ш	

1. In a **Magic Square**, the sum of each row, column, and main diagonal equals the same number. Fill in the blank areas to make the following a Magic Square.

3		14	0
	6		11
4		9	
15			12

2. Use only three 2s to make 16.

multiple	dot	factor	composite	prime	improper
commutative	absolute value	percent	lowest terms		

2, 4, 6, 8, ...

Write the correct term from the choice box for each blank. 1/8

1. A fraction with a numerator as large or larger than the denominator is called ________________. 3/4

2. A counting number greater than 1 that is only evenly divisible by 1 and itself is called ________________.

3. Another term for a fraction in simplest form is ________________.

4. A number is a ________________ of another number if it can evenly divide into it.

5. ________________ is the distance from a number to zero.

6. Multiplying a number by an integer makes it a ________________ of that number.

7. A ________________ represents multiplication.

8. The property that states that the order of multiplication does not matter is called ________________.

9. ________________ means per hundred.

10. A ________________ number is a counting number greater than 1 that is not prime.

Customary units for measuring weight are ounces and pounds. It is common to use a scale to measure weight.

1 ounce (oz) is the approximate weight of a handful of pretzels.

1 pound (lb) is the approximate weight of three medium-sized bananas.

 16 ounces = 1 pound 

Choose the best estimate for the weight of each item.

1) pencil
a. 2 ounces
b. 20 ounces
c. 20 pounds

2) bike
a. 15 ounces
b. 100 ounces
c. 15 pounds

3) adult
a. 150 ounces
b. 250 ounces
c. 150 pounds

4) 2 cans of pop
a. 1 ounce
b. 8 ounces
c. 1 pound

5) How many quarter-pound hamburgers does it take to make approximately one pound? ______

6) If one pound of peanuts costs $10, how much would 12 ounces of peanuts cost? ______

7) What is a common item around the house that weighs about one pound? ________________

In one year, a person can shed about 8 pounds of dead skin.

Metric units for measuring weight are grams and kilograms.

1 gram (g) is the approximate weight of a grape.

1 kilogram (kg) is the approximate weight of a textbook.

→ 1,000 grams = 1 kilogram ←

Choose the best estimate for the weight of each item.

1. lemon
   a. 10 grams
   b. 100 grams
   c. 10 kilograms

2. shoelace
   a. 2 grams
   b. 200 grams
   c. 2 kilograms

3. adult
   a. 150 grams
   b. 75 kilograms
   c. 150 kilograms

4. boot
   a. 1 gram
   b. 100 grams
   c. 1 kilogram

5. If a can of soda weighs 400 grams, how many kilograms does it weigh? ______

6. If a nickel weighs 5 grams, how many nickels does it take to weigh 100 grams? ______

7. What is a common item around the house that weighs about one gram. ____________

8. Find a common item around the house that weighs about one kilogram. ____________

Capacity is the amount a container can hold.

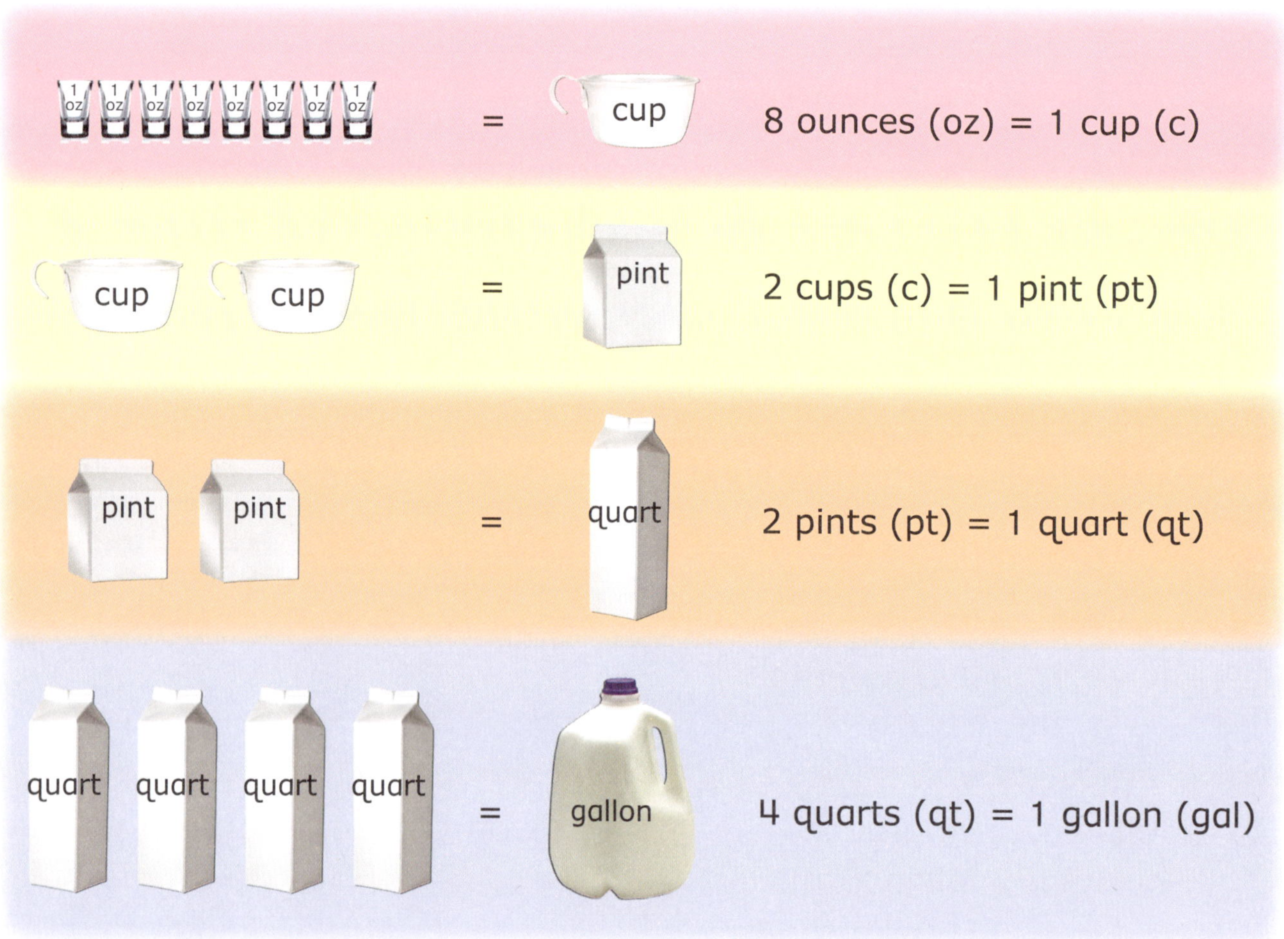

Dale drew the following four equal pictures to help him visualize the relationships between the different measurements.

cup	cup	cup	cup
cup	cup	cup	cup
cup	cup	cup	cup
cup	cup	cup	cup

pint	pint
pint	pint
pint	pint
pint	pint

quart	quart
quart	quart

gallon

1. Draw a picture showing the relationship between cup, pint, quart, and gallon.

2. How many cups of rice will fill a pint container? ______

3. How many cups of rice will fill a quart container? ______

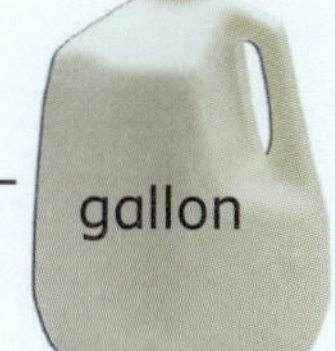

4. How many cups of rice will fill a gallon container? ______

5. How many ounces are in a cup? ______

6. How many ounces are in a pint? ______

7. How many ounces are in a quart? ______

8. How many ounces are in a gallon? ______

9. If a recipe calls for 2 pints of milk, how many cups would that be? ______

10. If a recipe calls for 2 pints of milk, how many ounces would that be? ______

11. If a pint of milk cost 64¢, how much is the price per ounce?

______

Capacity is the amount a container can hold. In the metric system, milliliters and liters are units of capacity.

1 milliliter (mL) is approximately the amount an eyedropper holds.

1 liter (L) is the amount a cube with length, width, and height of 10 centimeters holds.

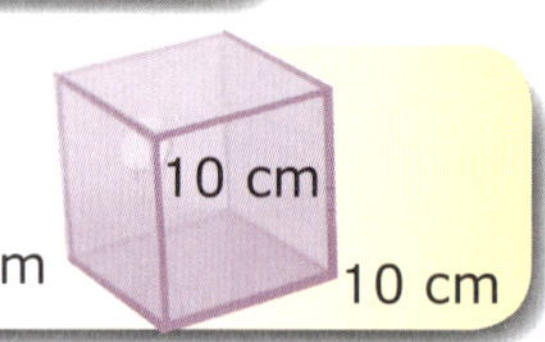

 1,000 milliliters = 1 liter 

Circle the best estimate for the capacity of each item.

1) gas tank
   a. 75 mL
   b. 75 L
   c. 750 L

2) gallon milk
   a. 4 mL
   b. 40 mL
   c. 4 L

3) cup
   a. 230 mL
   b. 23 mL
   c. 23 L

4) spoon
   a. 10 mL
   b. 100 mL
   c. 1 L

5) If a fish tank holds 5 liters of water, how many milliliters does it hold? ________

6) A can of soda pop holds about 350 milliliters. About how many cans does it take to get a liter of pop? ________

7) Which container holds more liquid detergent, a 1.090 liter container or a 1,100 milliliter container?

____

 Adults produce between one and two liters of saliva per day.

Rules for Divisibility

÷ by	evenly (no remainder) if ...
2	the ones place value is even.
3	the sum of the digits is divisible by 3.
4	the last two digits are divisible by 4.
5	the ones place value is 0 or 5.
6	the number is evenly divisible by 2 and 3.
8	the last three digits are divisible by 8.
9	the sum of the digits is divisible by 9.
10	the ones place value is 0.

156 divides by 2 evenly because the ones place value is even.

$$2\overline{)156} = 78$$

712 divides by 4 evenly because the last two place values divide by 4 evenly.

$$4\overline{)712} = 178$$

115 divides by 5 evenly because the ones place value is 5.

$$5\overline{)115} = 23$$

1. Circle four numbers that divide by 2 evenly.

4,016	5,100	8,001	4,444
397	949	10,243	600

2. Circle four numbers that divide by 3 evenly.

514	711	100	969
113	4,002	24,319	10,920

3. Circle four numbers that divide by 4 evenly.

512	917	1,000	7,040
8,215	736	114	5,009

4. Circle two numbers that divide by 6 evenly.

112	2,202	607	1,110

Prime numbers are whole numbers greater than 1 that are only evenly divisible by 1 and themselves. All other numbers are called composite. Notice 2 is the only even prime.

Examples of prime numbers: 2, 5, 7, 11, 23, 31, 37, 97
Examples of composite numbers: 6, 8, 10, 24, 32, 55

There are 25 prime numbers from 1-100 shown in green in the array.

1	2	3	4	5	6	7	8	9	10
11	12	13	14	15	16	17	18	19	20
21	22	23	24	25	26	27	28	29	30
31	32	33	34	35	36	37	38	39	40
41	42	43	44	45	46	47	48	49	50
51	52	53	54	55	56	57	58	59	60
61	62	63	64	65	66	67	68	69	70
71	72	73	74	75	76	77	78	79	80
81	82	83	84	85	86	87	88	89	90
91	92	93	94	95	96	97	98	99	100

From 100-150 there are 10 primes. Find and circle them.

101	102	103	104	105	106	107	108	109	110
111	112	113	114	115	116	117	118	119	120
121	122	123	124	125	126	127	128	129	130
131	132	133	134	135	136	137	138	139	140
141	142	143	144	145	146	147	148	149	150

A multiple of a number is a product of that number and another whole number factor.

$7 \times 0 = 0$
$7 \times 1 = 7$
$7 \times 2 = 14$
$7 \times 3 = 21$
$7 \times 4 = 28$
$7 \times 5 = 35$

Since 0, 7, 14, 21, 28, and 35 were formed using a factor of 7 and a whole number, they are multiples of 7. **A multiple of a number is always evenly divisible by that number.**

45	64	48	27	52
96	105	80	144	49

Use the table above to answer the questions.

1. Which numbers are multiples of 2? ____________________

2. Which numbers are multiples of 6? ____________________

3. Which numbers are multiples of 5? ____________________

4. Which numbers are multiples of 8? ____________________

5. Which numbers are multiples of 12? ____________________

1. Place the seven numbers 18, 24, 30, 50, 56, 60, and 80 in the seven areas such that only one number is placed per area and placed with the correct multiple.

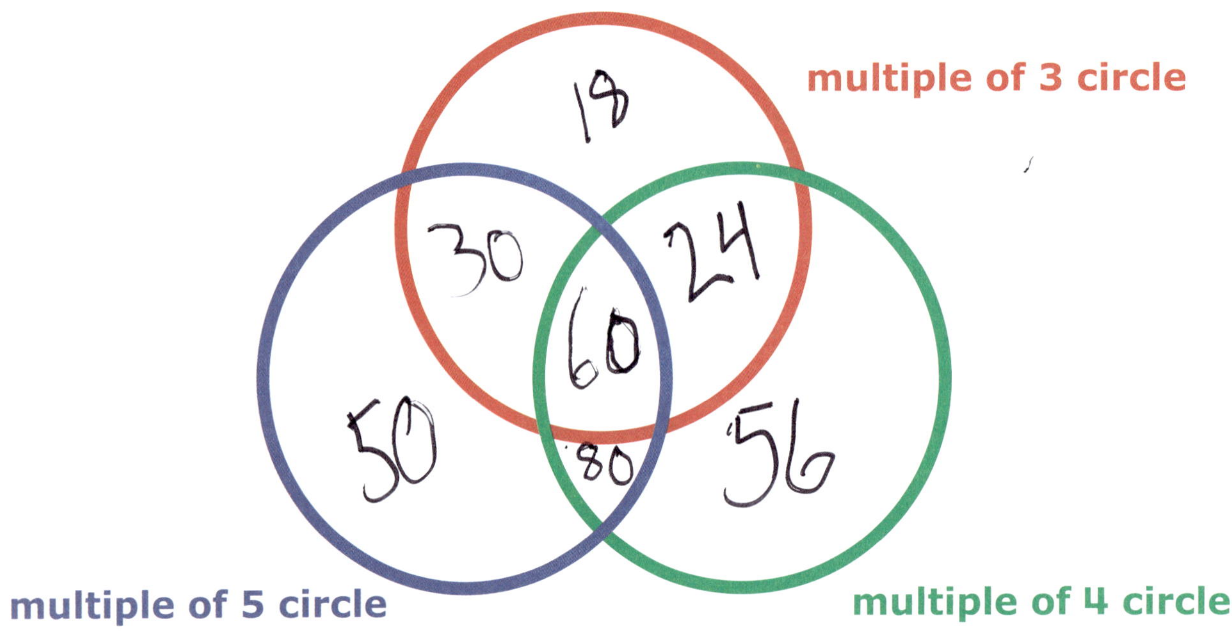

2. Which two of the four listed numbers makes a two-digit number that is a multiple of 17? ______

Multiples of 8 are formed by multiplying 8 by another whole number. Multiples of 8 are always evenly divisible by 8.

Find a path from the top row to the bottom row of the array by moving only left, right, up, or down and landing on multiples of 8.

START

35	408	18	54	32	56
234	191	64	123	168	206
62	45	81	252	96	72
144	24	48	63	80	90
432	42	0	88	592	156
184	40	742	406	308	328
106	208	352	65	800	124
16	658	712	54	526	304

FINISH

A **prime number** is only evenly divisible by 1 or itself.

The set of prime numbers includes: 2, 3, 5, 7, 11, 13, 17

Go through the maze, passing only prime numbers and your path should total 110.

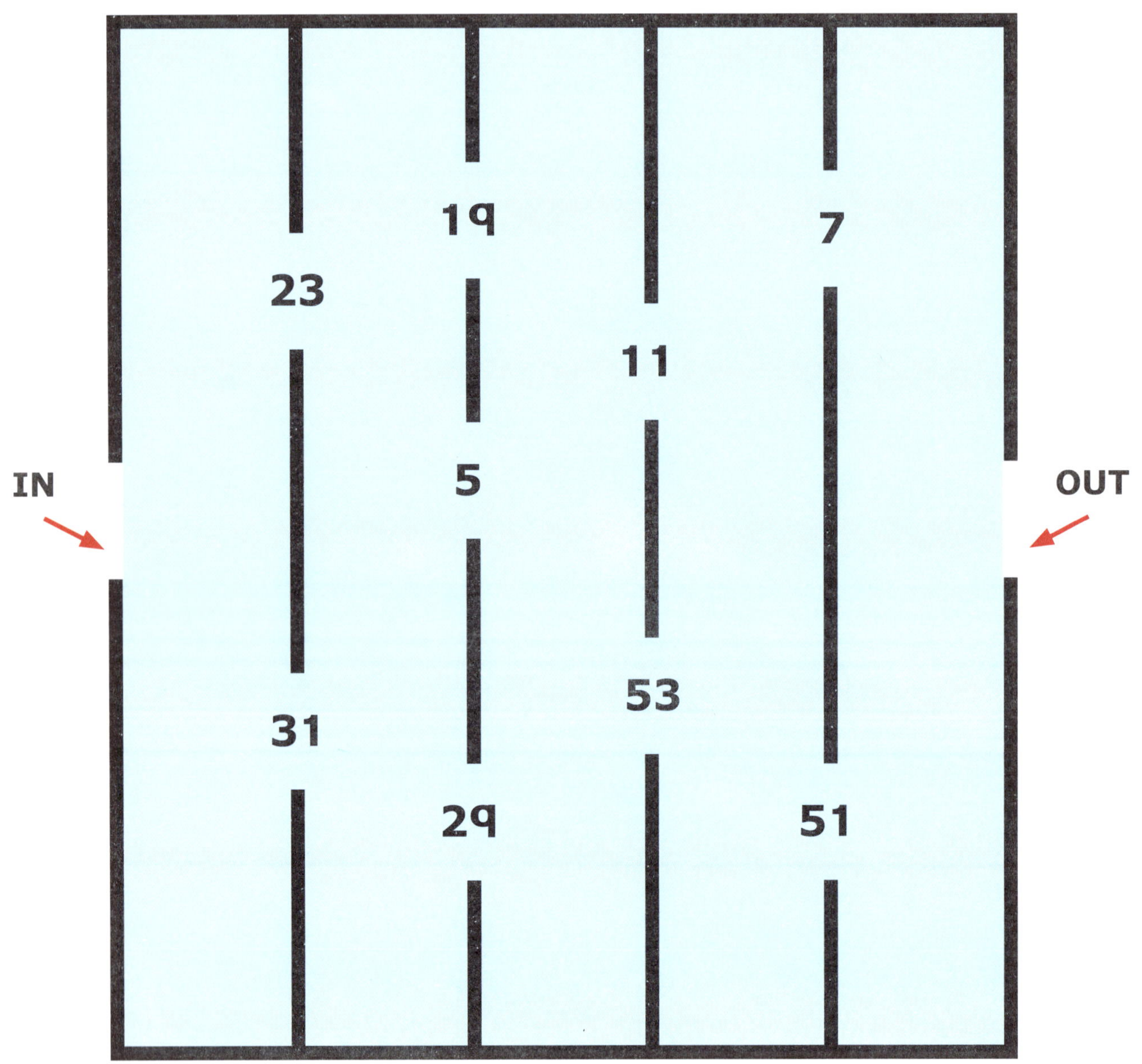

Any composite number can be expressed as a product of prime numbers.

$15 = 3 \times 5$
$36 = 2 \times 2 \times 3 \times 3$
$42 = 2 \times 3 \times 7$

A number is said to be written in prime factorization when it is written as a product of all prime numbers. The prime factorization of 15, 36, and 42 is shown above. It is customary to write the factors in increasing order. However, $2 \times 3 \times 5$ is the same as $5 \times 2 \times 3$. In multiplication, the order of the factors does not change the product, because of the commutative property of multiplication.

Write 54 as a product of prime numbers.

$54 = 6 \times 9$
$2 \times 3 \times 3 \times 3$

OR

$54 = 2 \times 27$
$2 \times 3 \times 9$
$2 \times 3 \times 3 \times 3$

The prime factorization of $54 = 2 \times 3 \times 3 \times 3$

Begin by thinking "what times what makes a number." Continue exchanging each composite number into a product of primes.

Write the following numbers as a product of primes.

1. 45 = ____________________
2. 81 = ____________________
3. 48 = ____________________
4. 60 = ____________________
5. 54 = ____________________
6. 72 = ____________________

A factor of a number divides the number evenly with no remainder. The greatest common factor (GCF) of two numbers is the greatest number that is a factor of both numbers. The GCF is used to put a fraction in simplest form or lowest terms.

factors of 12: 1, 2, 3, 4, 6, 12
factors of 16: 1, 2, 4, 8, 16
GCF: 4

Another way to find the greatest common factor is to write each number as a product of primes and the GCF is the product of all the common prime factors.

prime factorization of 12: $2 \times 2 \times 3$
prime factorization of 16: $2 \times 2 \times 2 \times 2$
GCF: $2 \times 2 = 4$

Find the greatest common factor (GCF) for each pair of numbers, then use the letters to solve the riddle on the next page.

d 6 and 10 = _____

t 20 and 50 = _____

s 9 and 12 = _____

u 16 and 32 = _____

f 18 and 24 = _____

i 36 and 48 = _____

y 40 and 60 = _____

a 42 and 105 = _____

e 64 and 96 = _____

n 5 and 7 = _____

Why did the shark spit out the clown?

___	___		___	___	___	___	___	___		___	___	___	___	___
12	10		10	21	3	10	32	2		6	16	1	1	20

Fill in the blanks using only prime numbers.

☐ × ☐ = 91

☐ × ☐ × ☐ = 154

The least common multiple (LCM) of a pair of numbers is the smallest common multiple. Zero is excluded when determining the least common multiple.

multiples of 6: 6, 12, 18, 24, 30, 36, ...
multiples of 10: 10, 20, 30, 40, 50, 60, ...

LCM: 30

Another way to find the LCM for a pair of numbers is to write each as a product of primes and form a product of the greatest number of times a factor appears in the factored form of any number.

$$6 = 2 \times 3$$
$$10 = 2 \times 5$$
$$\text{LCM} = 2 \times 3 \times 5 = 30$$

Find the least common multiple (LCM) for each pair of numbers; then use the letters to solve the riddle on the next page.

t
5 = __________
4 = __________
LCM = _____

r
6 = __________
4 = __________
LCM = _____

o
6 = __________
9 = __________
LCM = _____

c
10 = __________
15 = __________
LCM = _____

l
9 = __________
36 = __________________
LCM = _____

m
4 = __________
22 = __________
LCM = _____

(w) 35 = ________
14 = ________
LCM = _____

(u) 12 = ________
30 = ________
LCM = _____

(i) 9 = ________
15 = ________
LCM = _____

(a) 8 = ________
18 = ________
LCM = _____

What kind of car has a motor that purrs?

___	___	___	___	___	___	___	___
30	72	20	45	36	36	72	30

Find the multiple of 16 closest to 450. _____

State the rule and next 2 terms for each pattern.

1) 0 1 1 2 3 5 8 13 21 34 * . . .

Each term is formed by adding the two terms before it.

2) 80 71 62 53 44 35 26 ___ ___ . . .

___

3) $\frac{1}{5}$ $\frac{3}{5}$ 1 $1\frac{2}{5}$ ___ ___ . . .

___

4) 2 8 6 12 10 16 14 ___ ___ . . .

___

5) Originally, John was hired to help a neighbor for $32 a week. He was such a good worker he received a $1.35 raise in pay at the end of each week.

a) How much was he making a week after the 8th week? ___

b) What was his total earned after 8 weeks?

___

*named the Fibonacci Sequence

Complete the chart and graph showing the cost for parking at the City Parking Garage.

Time	Cost
up to 1 hour	free
over 1, up to 2 hours	$2.00
over 2, up to 3 hours	$3.50
over 3, up to 4 hours	$4.50
over 4, up to 5 hours	$5.00
over 5 hours	$5.25

Time In	Time Out	Cost
8:00 a.m.	11:25 a.m.	
9:30 a.m.	noon	
1:00 p.m.	5:30 p.m.	
7:35 a.m.	4:37 p.m.	

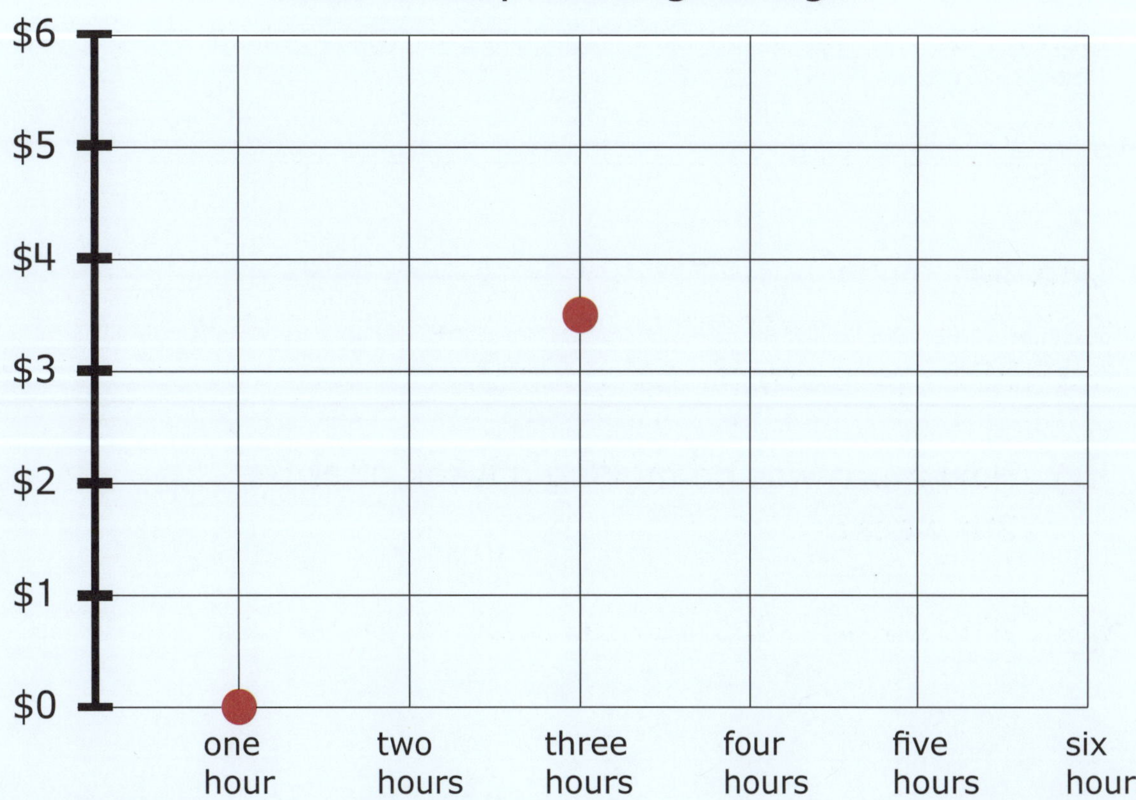

Rules for Adding Integers

same signs: Add and keep the same sign.

4 + 5 = 9 -3 + -2 = -5

different signs: Subtract as if whole numbers, then use the sign of the integer farther from zero.

9 + -11 = -2 8 + -5 = 3

$$\begin{array}{r} 11 \\ -\ 9 \\ \hline 2 \end{array} \qquad \begin{array}{r} 8 \\ -\ 5 \\ \hline 3 \end{array}$$

Find each result; then cross out the correct answers below to find the two false answers.

1. 12 + 3 = _____
2. -4 + -8 = _____
3. 8 + -4 = _____
4. -5 + -5 = _____
5. 5 + -2 = _____
6. -5 + -2 = _____
7. -1 + 6 = _____
8. 7 + -10 = _____
9. 10 + -2 = _____
10. -6 + -3 = _____

-12 -1 3
15 -3
-10 4 -7
2 8
5 -9

Find each result; then cross out the correct answers below to find the two false answers.

1) -40 + 50 = _____

2) -13 + -13 = _____

3) 25 + -37 = _____

4) 40 + 26 = _____

5) -11 + 25 = _____

6) -18 + -37 = _____

7) 43 + -35 = _____

8) 23 + -23 = _____

9) 121 and -131 = _____

10) -425 + 1,000 = _____

11) -45 and 37 = _____

12) -110 + 233 = _____

13) Today the high temperature for Los Angeles was 84°. If the temperature dropped 16°, what is the current temperature? _____

14) Tomas was playing football on the 18 yard line. He moved forward 25 yards and back 34 yards. What yard line is Tomas on now? _____

Rules for Adding Integers

same signs: Add and keep the same sign (-4 + -6 = -10)

different signs: Subtract the numbers as if they were both positive, then use the sign of the number farther from zero (-7 + 2 = -5 and -1 + 3 = 2)

Rules for Subtracting Integers

When subtracting integers, rewrite and use the addition of integers rules. If you are subtracting a negative integer (5 – -1), the two negatives are replaced by a positive sign because the opposite of negative is positive (5 + 1).

	Rewrite			Rewrite	
4 – 1 =	4 + -1 =	3	2 – -3 =	2 + 3 =	5
-6 – 5 =	-6 + -5 =	-11	-7 – -4 =	-7 + 4 =	-3

Solve; then cross out the correct answers below to find the two false answers.

1) -25 + 10 = ____

2) -43 + -86 = ____

3) 17 + -20 = ____

4) -63 + 0 = ____

5) -11 + -23 + -46 = ____

6) 28 + (-19) + (-9) = ____

7) 8 - -6 = ____

8) -9 - (-10) = ____

9) 15 - 85 = ____

10) 101 - (-101) = ____

11) 78 - 69 = ____

12) -200 - (-109)= ____

13) At 6 a.m. the temperature was -8°. By 6 p.m. the temperature had rose 17°. What is the temperature at 6 p.m. Write an equation for the situation.

____

-3	14	9	-129	-19	-91	-70
202	-309	-80	-15	1	0	-63

Rules for Multiplying and Dividing Integers

positive	×	positive	=	positive
positive	×	negative	=	negative
negative	×	positive	=	negative
negative	×	negative	=	positive

positive	÷	positive	=	positive
positive	÷	negative	=	negative
negative	÷	positive	=	negative
negative	÷	negative	=	positive

Solve each problem; then use the letters of the answers to solve the riddle below.

b) $56 \times (-30) =$

r) $-20 \cdot 10 =$

a) $(-12)(12) =$

u) $-18 \times 6 =$

s) $(-3)(-3)(-3) =$

m) $(-15)^2 =$

c) $(-30) \cdot (-30) =$

d) $(-15)(15) =$

y) $-1918 \times 0 =$

p) $-415 \div (-5) =$

q) $300 \div (-6) =$

n) $-50 \div (-.5) =$

x) $\frac{-1000}{10} =$

t) $\frac{308}{-22} =$

e) $\frac{(-4)^2}{8} =$

f) $-35 \div 5 \times 2 =$

o) $(-9)(-8) \div 6 =$

g) $(-8) \cdot 6 \div 12 =$

h) $-144 \div (-3) \div (-2) \div (-4) =$

What insect is good at numbers?

___	___		___	___	___	___	___	___	___	-	___	___	___
-144	100		-144	900	900	12	-108	100	-14		-144	100	-14

To locate a point on a plane, a horizontal line called the *x*-axis and a vertical line call the *y*-axis are used. Points are located by using an ordered pair (*x*, *y*) of numbers inside a parentheses separated by a comma. The *x* indicates the placement on the *x*-axis. The second number of the ordered pairs indicates to move that many units either up or down from that point on the *x*-axis.

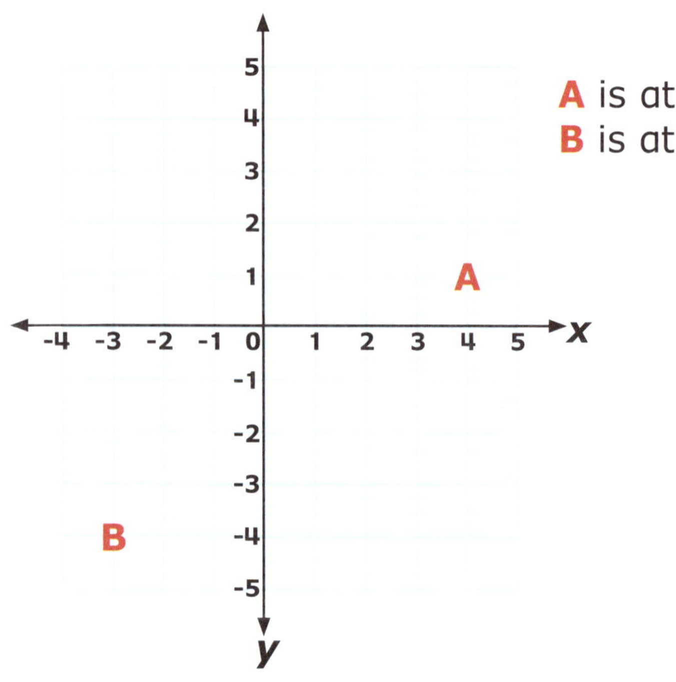

A is at (4,1)
B is at (-3,-4)

1 Circle the ordered pair that is not a point on line *m*.
(-2,-1) (2,-1) (-4,2) (4,-2)

2 Circle the ordered pair that is not a point on line *n*.
(2,-2) (0,0) (-3,-3) (1,1)

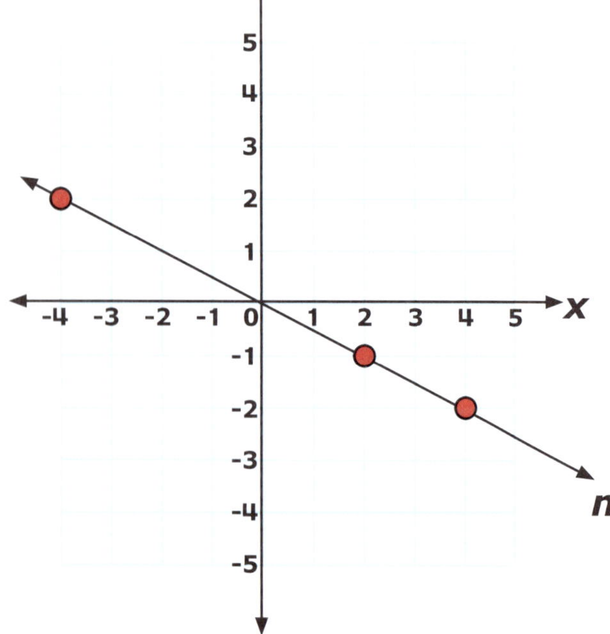

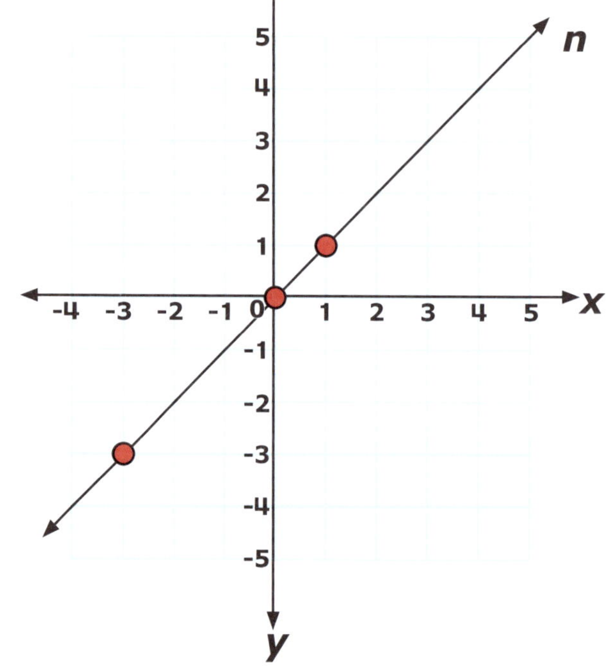

Connect the points in order to make a picture.

1. (5,5)
2. (5,4)
3. (4,4)
4. (4,0)
5. (5,0)
6. (5,-2)
7. (4,-2)
8. (4,-3)
9. (3,-4)
10. (1,-4)
11. (0,-3)
12. (-1,-3)
13. (-2,-4)
14. (-3,-4)
15. (-4,-3)
16. (-4,2)
17. (-3,2)
18. (-3,3)
19. (-2,3)
20. (-2,2)
21. (0,2)
22. (0,4)
23. (-1,4)
24. (-1,5)
25. (5,5)

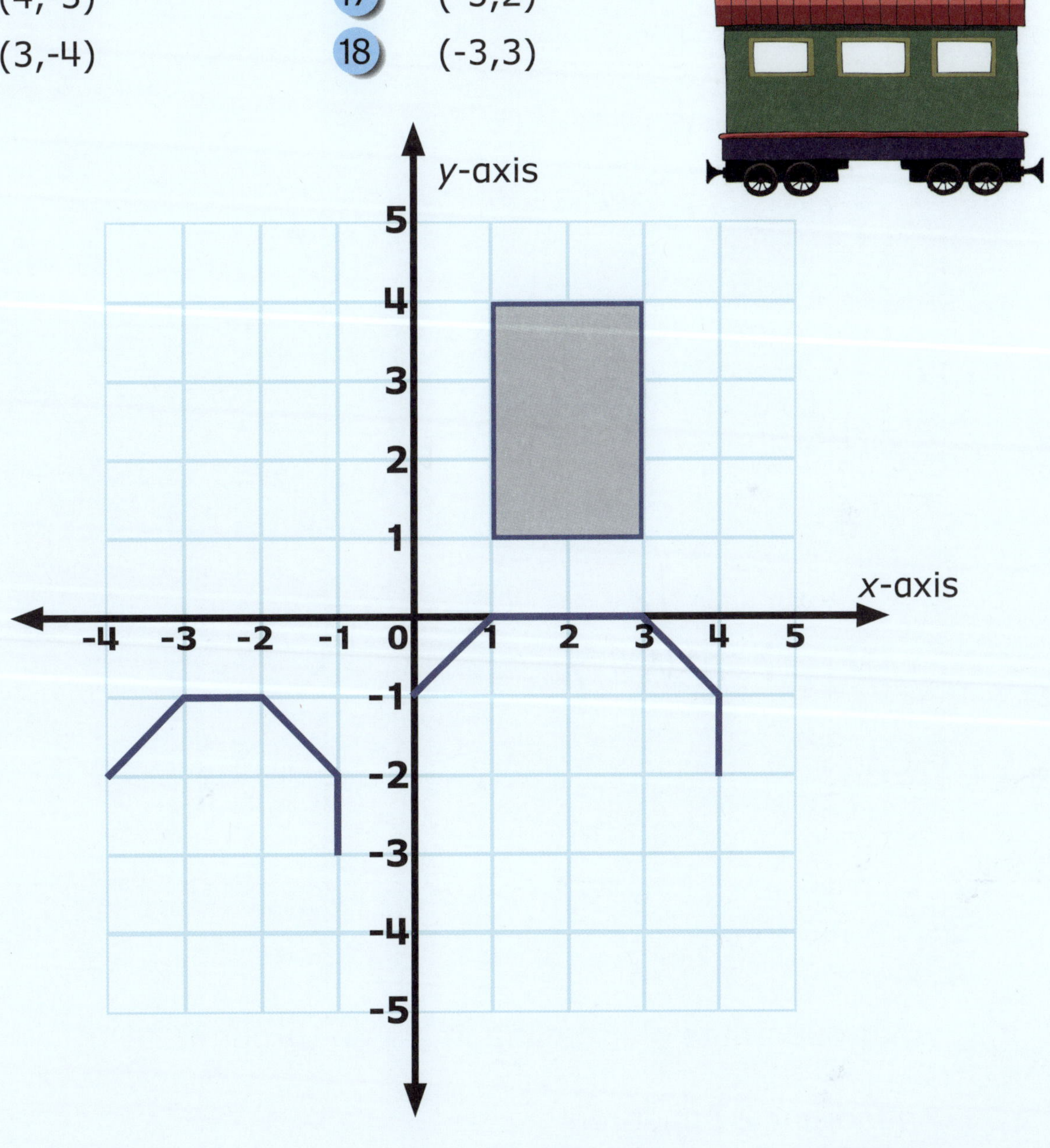

Replace x with the given value in the equation and determine what y would have to be to form a true equation. Graph and connect the ordered pairs of the solutions.

1 $y = x - 3$

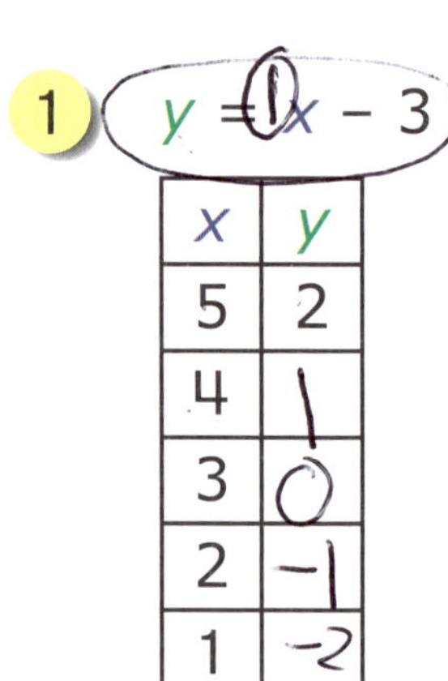

x	y
5	2
4	1
3	0
2	-1
1	-2

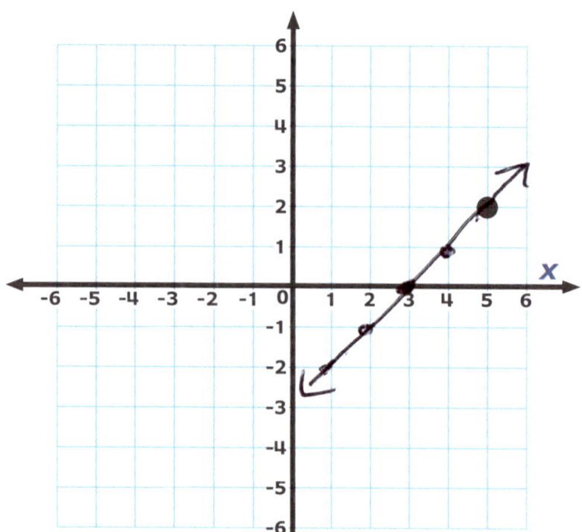

2 $y = 2x + 1$

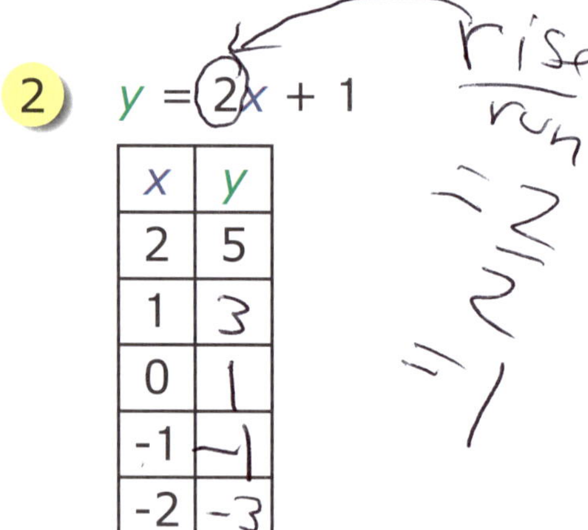

x	y
2	5
1	3
0	1
-1	-1
-2	-3

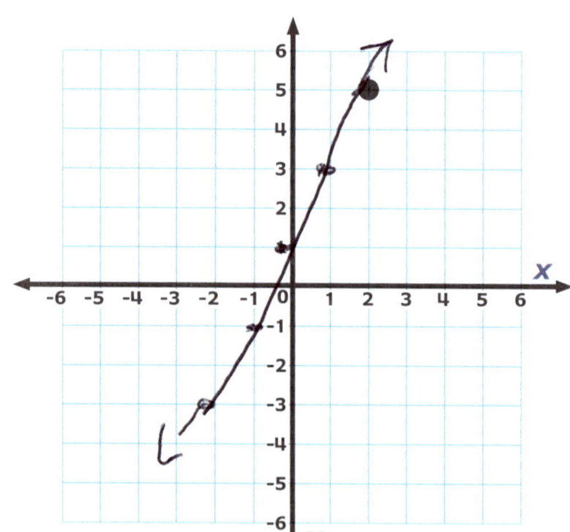

3 $y = 4 - x$

x	y
4	0
3	1
1	3
0	4
-2	

4 What quadrants did the line in #1 go through? ____________

quadrant 2 | quadrant 1

quadrant 3 | quadrant 4

Discover a pattern that relates the in value to the out value and write a rule for that relationship. The relationship is called a **function**.

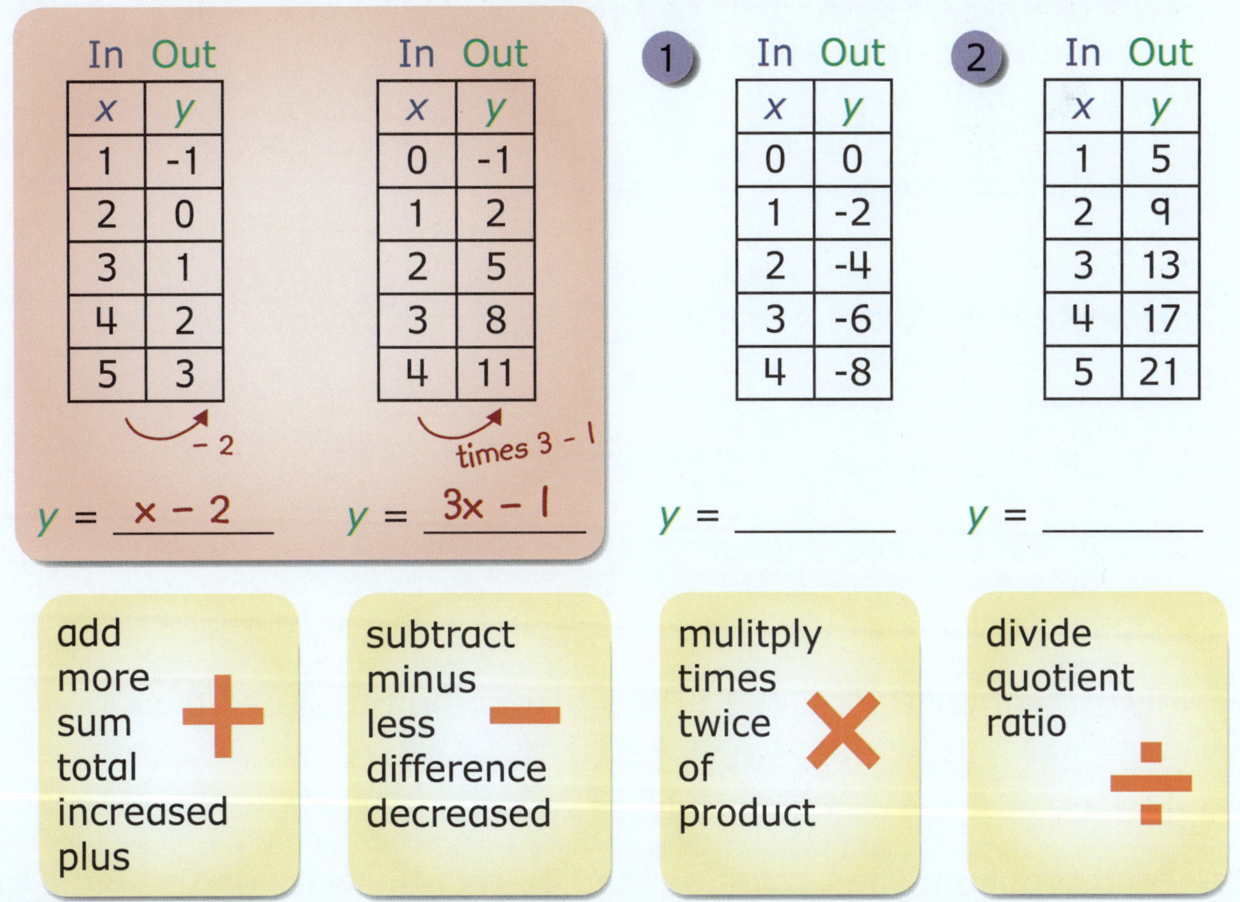

Use *n* as the number and write the following in math symbols.

3. 4 less than some number n − 4

4. 3 times some number 3n ← The coefficient is written first.

5. 5 more than a number ______

6. some number increased by 7 ______

7. the quotient of 6 and some number ______

8. the product of some number and 9 ______

9. twice the sum of some number and 3 ______

10. the difference between 8 and some number ______

11. three less than the product of 6 and some number ______

Math Communication

The use of ×, •, or no operation sign between numerical values indicates multiplication. $3 \times 4 = 3 \cdot 4 = 3(4) = 12$

$8n$ means 8 times the value of n. The numerical part, 8, is called the coefficient.

The absolute value of a number is its distance from zero and is represented by the symbol "| |." Distance is always positive.

$|3| = 3$ and $|-3| = 3$

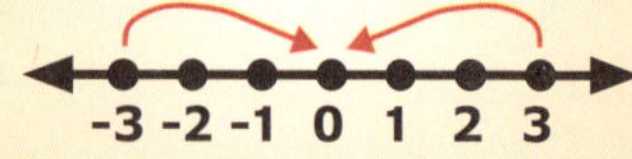

absolute value of 2.4 = $|2.4| = 2.4$

absolute value of the sum of $-5 + 1 = |-5 + 1| = |-4| = 4$

Always complete any operations inside the absolute value sign first. $|-4 + -3| = |(-4 + -3)| = |-7| = 7$

Solve each problem; then cross out the correct answers on the right to find the two false answers.

1) $-80 \cdot 12 =$

2) $30(1.5) =$

3) $\frac{1}{3} \cdot 6 =$

4) $\frac{8}{9} \cdot \frac{3}{2} \cdot \frac{3}{4} =$

Let $a = 4$, $n = -8$, and $w = .25$

5) $7an =$

6) $9a \cdot |n| =$

7) $|a - n| =$

8) $-2anw =$

9) $3|nw| =$

10) $-6 \cdot n^2 =$

11) $2 \cdot |n| \cdot |w| =$

12) $|-6 + n| =$

288
2
16
-384
-960
14
1
4
-4
45
6
-252
-224
12

The symbol = means equal to. (17 – 9 = 8)
The symbol < means less than. (21 < 24)
The symbol > means greater than. (13 > 8)

Write the symbol =, <, or > in the circle to make a true sentence. Always use the correct order of operations.*

1) $2 \times 14 - 1 \bigcirc 12 + 10$

2) $4 \times 2 \times 3 \bigcirc 100 \div 4$

3) $25 - 7 - 2 \bigcirc 8 + 3 + 5$

4) $18 + 6 - 19 \bigcirc 20 - (5 + 9)$

5) $2 \times (3 + 4) \bigcirc (9 - 7) \times 5$

6) $6.4 + 1.6 \bigcirc 8$

7) $3 \times 26 - 20 \bigcirc 150 \div 6$

8) $5.4 + .44 \bigcirc 9 - 4.4$

9) $1\frac{1}{2} + 1\frac{1}{2} + 1\frac{1}{2} \bigcirc 4.5$

10) $3 \bigcirc \frac{3}{4} + \frac{3}{4} + \frac{3}{4} + \frac{3}{4}$

***Order of Operations**

First: Work inside parentheses.

Second: Do multiplication and division from left to right.

Third: Do addition and subtraction from left to right.

Place parentheses to make each sentence true.

11) $8 - 2 \times 3 > 15$

$(8 - 2) \cdot 3 > 15$
$6 \cdot 3 > 15$
$18 > 15$

12) $64 \div 4 \times 2 < 10$

13) $20 - 10 \div 5 - 3 = 16 \div 4 + 4 + 3$

A Logic Problem

1) Ava, Ann, Sara, and Ripa have different last names. Use the clues below to find each child's last name.

	Johnson	Pine	Smith	Brown
Ava				
Ann				
Sara				
Ripa				

Clue #1: Ripa's last name is not the longest.

Clue #2: Ava's last name is not the shortest and does not end in "n".

Clue #3: Ann's last name has 5 letters.

Fill in the blanks in the following patterns.

2) 2, _____, 18, 54, _____, 486, ...

3) _____, 45, 37, _____, 21, 13, ...

4) 1, $\frac{1}{2}$, _____, $\frac{1}{8}$, _____, $\frac{1}{32}$, ...

Comparing and Ordering Decimals

For decimal numbers, a placeholder of one or more zeroes can be added to the right without changing the value of the number.

June ran the race in 21.5 seconds.

21.5
21.50
21.500

To order decimal numbers, line up the decimal points and add enough zero placeholders so all the numbers have the same number of decimal places and compare sizes.

order from least to greatest: .2, .04, .11. and .009

.2 = .200 largest
.04 = .040 second smallest
.11 = .110 second largest
.009 = .009 smallest .009, .04, .11, and .2

1. Place in order from least to greatest:

   .1, .01, .001, .011 ____ ____ ____ ____

2. Place in order from least to greatest:

   .21, .119, .4, .02 ____ ____ ____ ____

3. Place in order from least to greatest:

   50.2, 6.1, .05, .9 ____ ____ ____ ____

4. Is the statement 3.009 < 3.1 true or false? ______

5. Is the statement .6 > .39 true or false? ______

Review: Before adding or subtracting decimals, line up the decimals to align digits with like place values. Always fill in with necessary zeros.

$$2 + 1.2 = \begin{array}{r} 2.0 \\ +\ 1.2 \\ \hline 3.2 \end{array} \qquad 5.2 - 1.35 = \begin{array}{r} 5.20 \\ -\ 1.35 \\ \hline 3.85 \end{array}$$

Solve each problem; then cross out the correct answers on the next page to find the two false answers. Use the information on average hair growth given at the bottom of the page.

1. Troy's hair grows on average 1 cm faster per month than usual. How many centimeters per month does his hair grow? ______

2. Baret's hair average growth is 2.05 cm per month. How much faster than the average does his hair grow? ______

3. Ann's hair is 12.9 cm long now. How long can she expect it to be in 4 months at an average growth rate? ______

4. If Ali cuts 2 cm off her hair every 2 months, how much longer than now will it be in a year if it grows at an average rate? ______

5. John's hair grows on average .5 cm slower per month than usual. How many centimeters per month does his hair grow? ______

6. On average, how many centimeters does hair grow in a year?

   Draw a line that long on the margin of this page. ________

7. The thickness of hair varies depending on many factors. An average thickness would be around .01 centimeters. If Mary's hair is .0181 cm thick and Jan's hair is .009 cm thick, what is the difference in their hair thickness? _____

8. 23 + 1.2 + .85 = _______

9. 5.07 − 1.8 = _______

10. .12 + 65 + 5.5 = _______

11. 11 − 9.06 = _______

12. 5.695 + 1.005 = _______

13. 45.71 − 6.9 = _______

14. 36 + 3.6 + .36 = _______

15. 100 − .1 = _______

Review: In multiplying decimals, the total number of decimal places in the factors equals the total number of decimal places in the product. When dividing a decimal by a whole number, the decimal point is placed in the quotient above its placement in the dividend.

2.5 × .5 =

```
  2.5
× 0.5
 1.25
```

7.5 ÷ 5 =

```
   1.5
5)7.5
  5
  25
  25
```

Solve each problem; then cross out the correct answers on the next page to find the two false answers.

1. If six of the lumber boards as pictured below were placed on top of each other, how high would the stack be? ______

2. If 12 of the lumber boards were placed on the floor next to each other as pictured below, how wide would the set of boards be? ______

3. If the lumber board is 92.625 inches long, how long would each part be if the board was cut into five equal parts? ______

4. How long would each part be if the board be in #3 was cut into two equal parts? ______

A 2-by-4 board actually measures 1.5 inches by 3.5 inches.

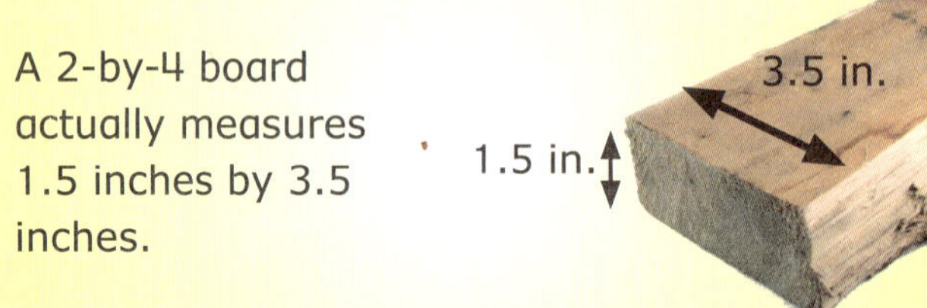

5) 4.23 × .8 = ______

6) .45 × .11 = ______

7) .09 × 707 = ______

8) 36.7 × 2.9 = ______

9) 4)9.28 = ______

10) 9).0126 = ______

11) 20)29.20 = ______

12) 63)466.2 = ______

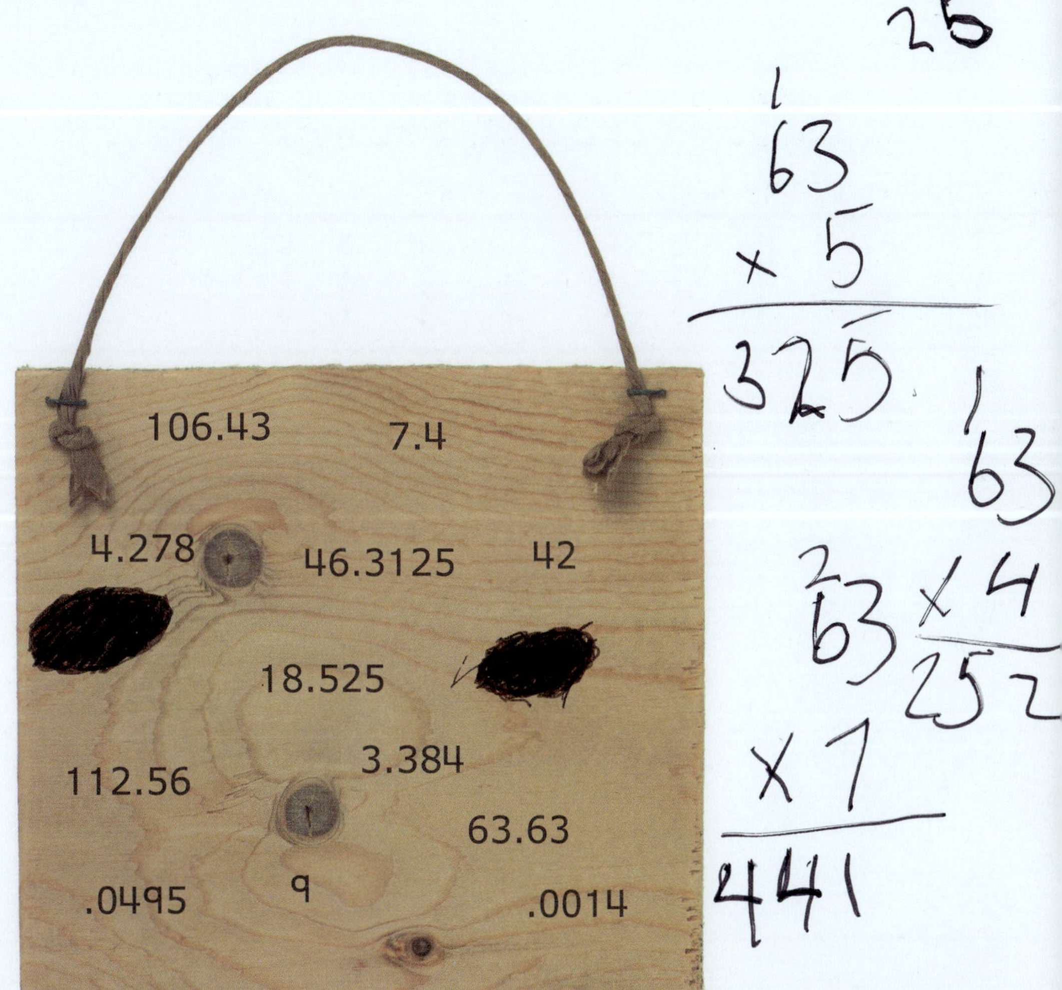

Customary Units

In the ruler below, each inch (in.) is cut into 16 equal parts. The marks between whole inches would be:

$\frac{1}{16}, \frac{2}{16}, \frac{3}{16}, \frac{4}{16}, \frac{5}{16}, \frac{6}{16}, \frac{7}{16}, \frac{8}{16}, \frac{9}{16}, \frac{10}{16}, \frac{11}{16}, \frac{12}{16}, \frac{13}{16}, \frac{14}{16}, \frac{15}{16}$

$\frac{2}{16} \rightarrow \frac{1}{8}$, $\frac{4}{16} \rightarrow \frac{1}{4}$, $\frac{6}{16} \rightarrow \frac{3}{8}$, $\frac{8}{16} \rightarrow \frac{1}{2}$, $\frac{10}{16} \rightarrow \frac{5}{8}$, $\frac{12}{16} \rightarrow \frac{3}{4}$, $\frac{14}{16} \rightarrow \frac{7}{8}$

$1\frac{13}{16}$ in.

$1\frac{1}{16}$ in.

0 in. 1 2 3 4

1) Use the letters of the measurements to solve the riddle below.

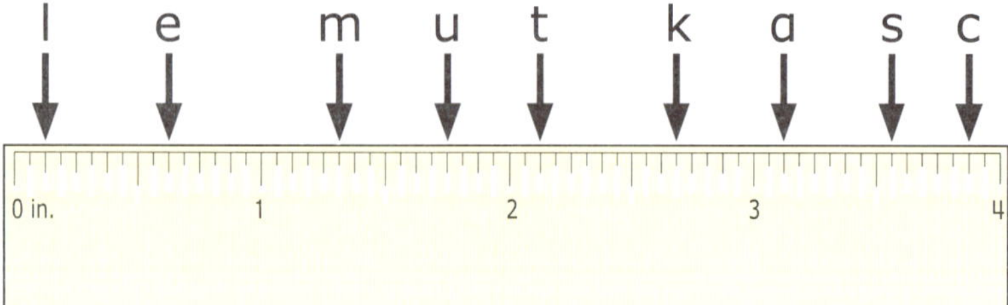

What do you get if you cross an addition problem with a rabbit's foot?

____ $3\frac{9}{16}$ ____ $1\frac{3}{4}$ ____ $1\frac{5}{16}$ ____ $\frac{1}{8}$ ____ $1\frac{3}{4}$ ____ $3\frac{7}{8}$ ____ $2\frac{11}{16}$

2) Use the letters of the measurements to solve the riddle below.

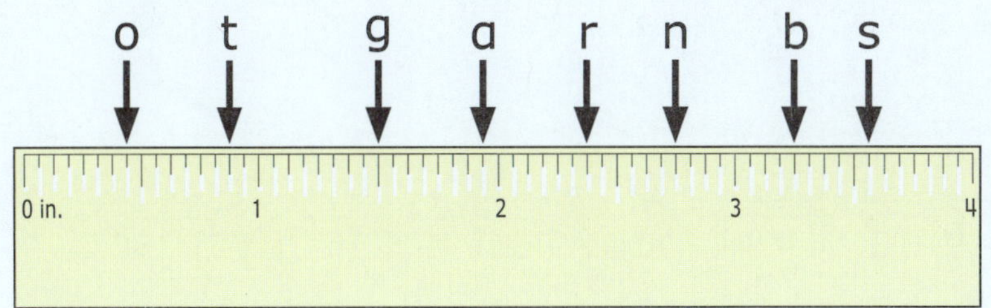

What is an empty gun hairdo?

_____ _____   _____ _____ _____ _____ _____

$2\frac{3}{4}$ $\frac{7}{16}$ $3\frac{1}{4}$ $1\frac{15}{16}$ $2\frac{3}{4}$ $1\frac{1}{2}$ $3\frac{9}{16}$

Write the letter for each item's closest measurement.

3) length of a sheet of notebook paper _____

4) width of a sheet of notebook paper _____

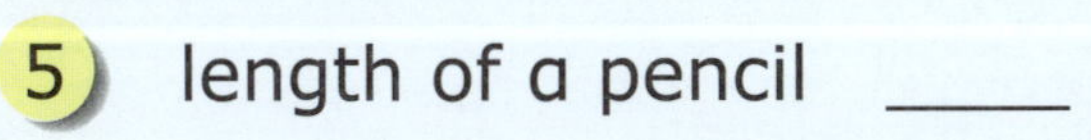

5) length of a pencil _____

6) height of a chair from floor to seat _____

a. 14 in.
b. $8\frac{1}{2}$ in.
c. $7\frac{1}{2}$ in.
d. $6\frac{1}{4}$ in.
e. 11 in.
f. $4\frac{1}{2}$ in.

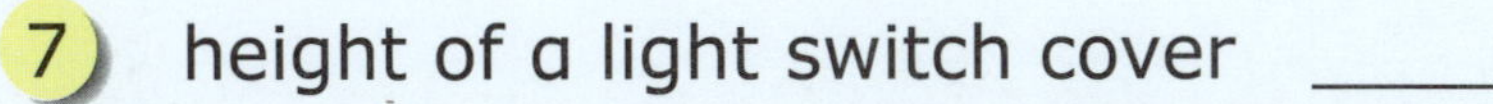

7) height of a light switch cover _____

Customary units for measuring length are inches, feet, yards, and miles.

12 inches (in.) = 1 foot (ft)
3 feet (ft) = 1 yard (yd)
5,280 feet = 1 mile (mi)

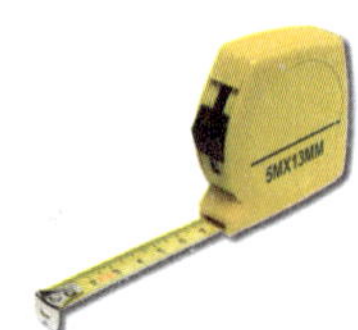

1. A yardstick is 36 inches long. How many feet are in a yardstick?

 ______

2. There are 5,280 feet in a mile. How many yards are in a mile?

 ______

3. A plane flying from Chicago to Los Angeles is averaging 412 miles per hour. How many feet per hour is the plane averaging? ______

4. Brad is 6 feet tall. How tall is Brad in inches? ______

5. A board is 96 inches long. How long is the board in feet? ______

6. 24 in. = _____ ft

7. 48 in. = ____ ft

8. 5 ft = _____ in.

9. 12 ft = ______ in.

10. 3 yd = ____ ft

11. 7 yd = ____ in.

Metric Units

In the ruler below, each centimeter (cm) is cut into 10 equal parts called millimeters (mm).   1 cm = 10 mm

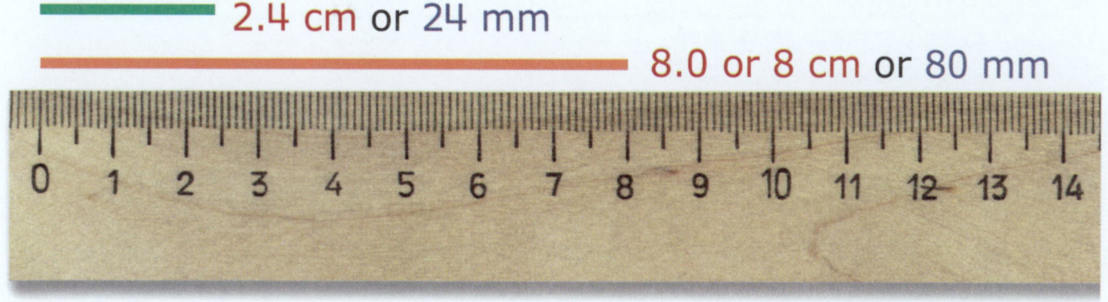

1. Use the letters of the measurements to solve the riddle below.

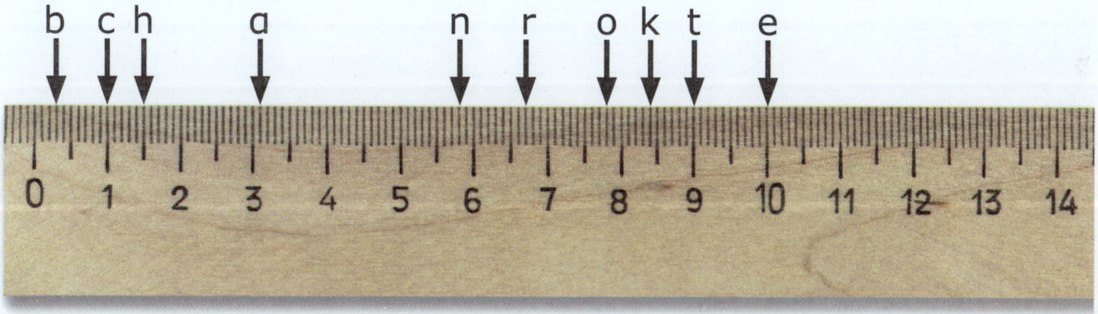

What kind of book should you bring to music class?

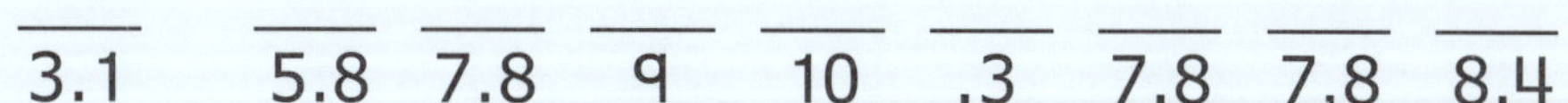

Write the letter for each item's closest measurement.

2. width of a sheet of notebook paper _____
3. length of a sheet of notebook paper _____
4. length of a pencil _____
5. width of your thumb _____

a. 24.3 cm
b. 19 cm
c. 1.5 cm
d. 27 cm
e. 20.5 cm

Parallel lines (||) are always an equal distance apart.

Perpendicular lines (⊥) meet at a right angle or 90°.

1) Below is a drawing of a rectangular prism and lines denoted *a*, *b*, *c*, *d*, *e*, *f*, *g*, *h*, *i* , *j*, *k*, and *m*.

Answer the questions "true" or "false".

Lines *a*, *b*, and c are ||. ________

Lines *b* and *f* are ⊥. ________

Lines *d* and *e* are ||. ________

Lines *a* and *e* are ⊥. ________

Lines *j* and *k* are ⊥. ________

Lines *m* and *k* are ⊥. ________

Lines *e* and *i* are ||. ________

Lines *k* and *b* are ||. ________

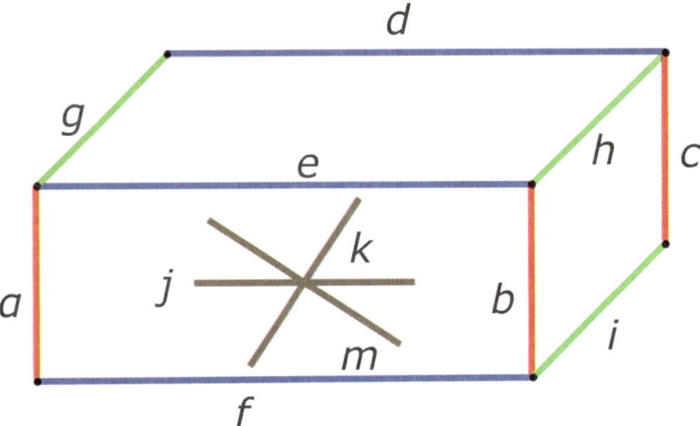

2) Draw a familiar picture with at least 3 parallel lines and 2 perpendicular lines.

Perimeter is the distance around a polygon. To find the perimeter, sum the sides. The measurements must be in the same units.

Find each perimeter.

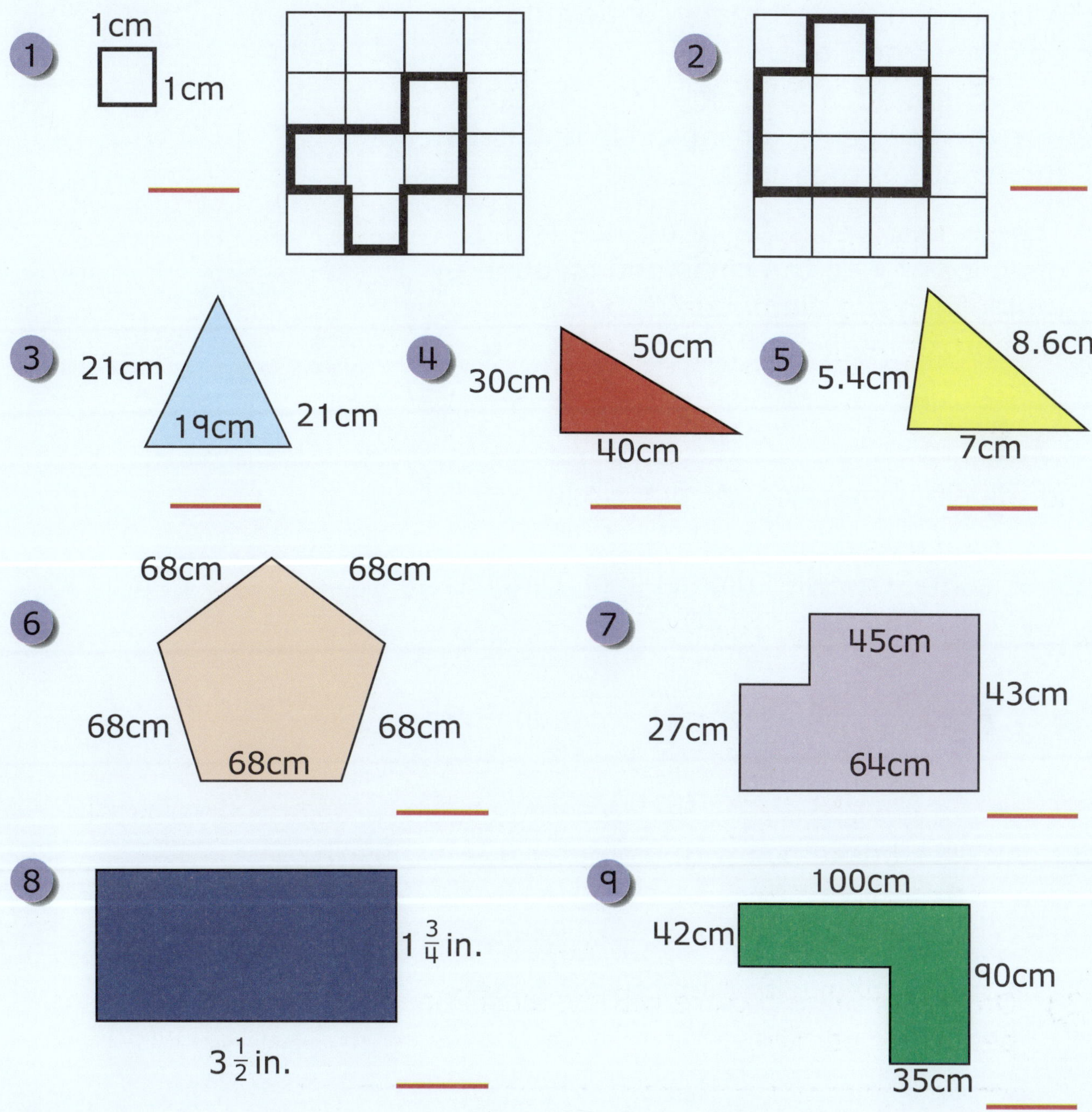

10. Ben decided to put a 20 ft by 25 ft pool in his backyard. His wife wanted a 24 ft by 25 ft pool. What is the difference in their perimeters? ______

A **circle** is a set of points an equal distance from a center point on a plane.

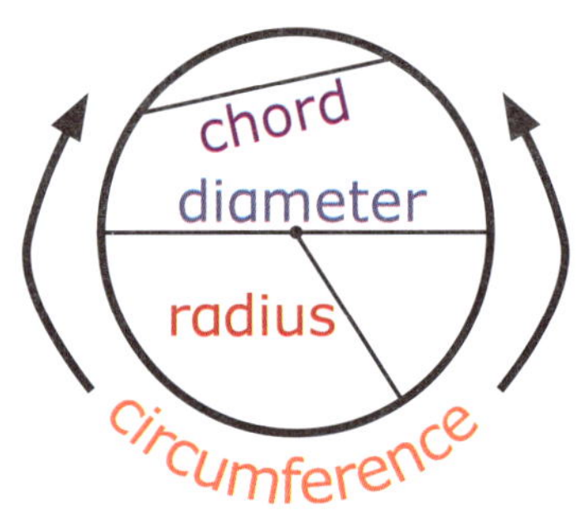

The radius (r) is a line segment that connects the center point to a point on the circle.

A chord is a line segment connecting two points on the circle.

The diameter (d) is a chord that passes through the center of the circle and is twice the length of the radius.

The circumference (C) of a circle is the distance around the circle and is found by multiplying the diameter (d) by pi (π), which is approximately 3.14. $C = \pi \times d$

$$C = \pi \times d$$
$$= 3.14 \times 7$$
$$= 21.98 \text{ in.}$$

Find the circumference of each circle.

1. A coffee can with diameter of 7 inches. _____

2. A ring with diameter of 1.5 centimeters. _____

3. An NBA basketball with diameter 9.4 inches. _____

4. A round table with diameter of 5 feet. _____

5. A car wheel with diameter of 1.25 feet. _____

6. A mile has 5,280 feet. How many times does the wheel in #5 have to go around to go a mile? _____

Area (A) is the number of square units in a figure. The area of a rectangle is equal to the length (l) times the width (w). Sometimes a shape needs to be broken into smaller shapes to find the area.

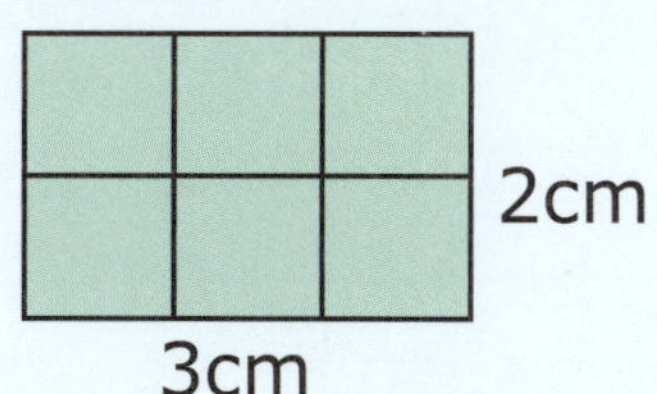

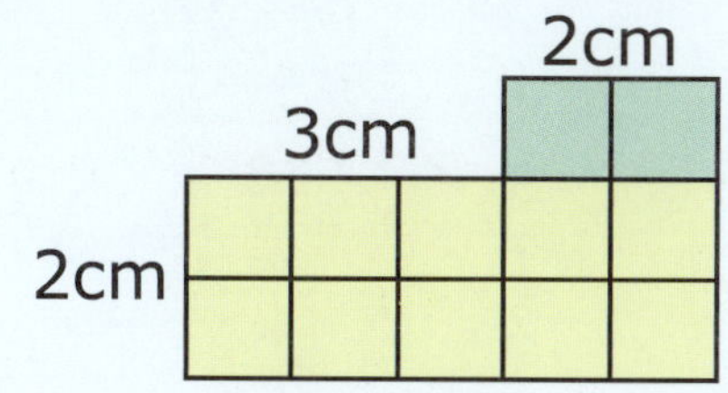

Area = length × width
$A = l \times w$
$= 3 \times 2$
= 6 sq cm

Area = (2 × 1) + (5 × 2)
= 2 + 10
= 12 sq cm

Find the area, then use the letters to solve the riddle below. All units are in *cm*.

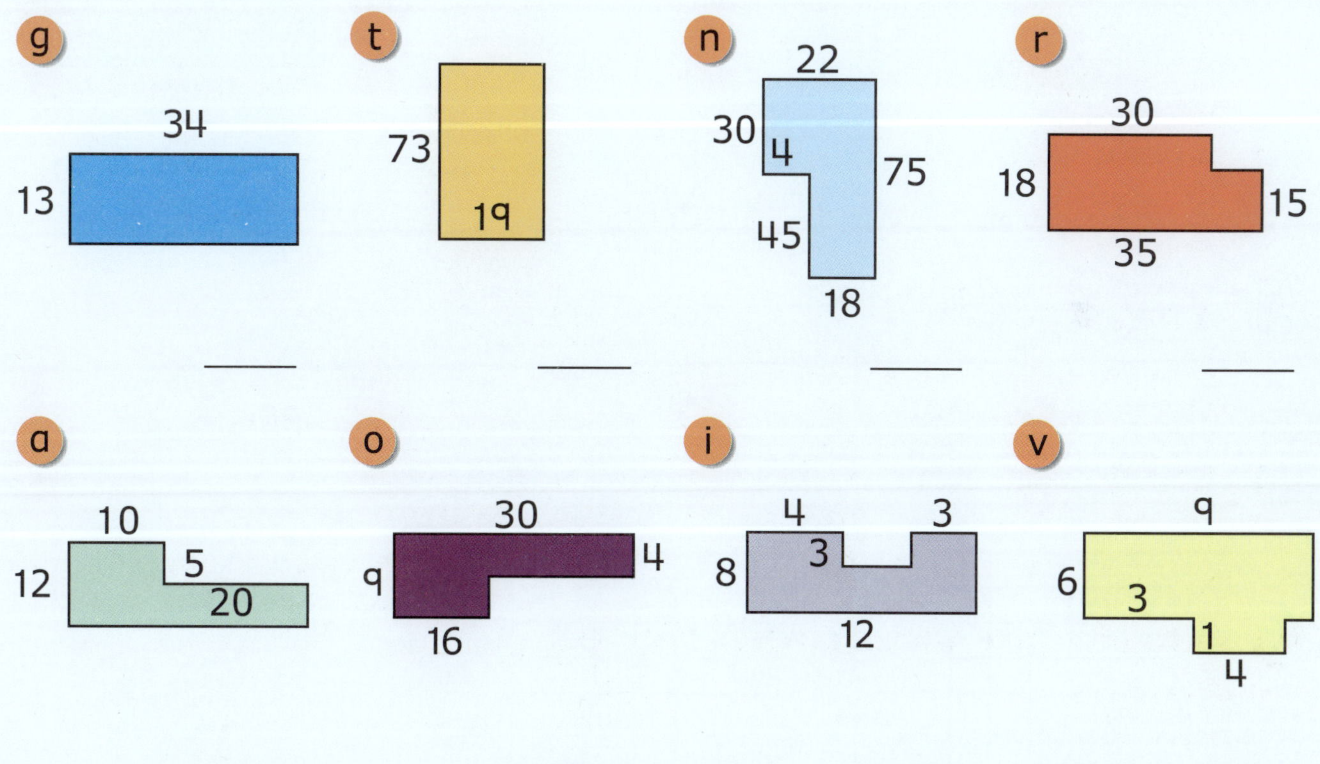

What reptile do you find on a Navy ship?

___ ___ ___ ___ - ___ ___ ___ ___ ___
1,470 260 58 81 442 260 1,387 200 615

The area (A) of a triangle is equal to half the base (b) times the height (h). The base is selected and the height is measured perpendicular from the base. Area is the number of square units in the figure.

$$\text{Area } (A) = \frac{1}{2} \times \text{base} \times \text{height}$$
$$A = \frac{1}{2} \times b \times h$$
$$A = \frac{1}{2} \times (4 \times 3)$$
$$A = 6 \text{ square cm}$$

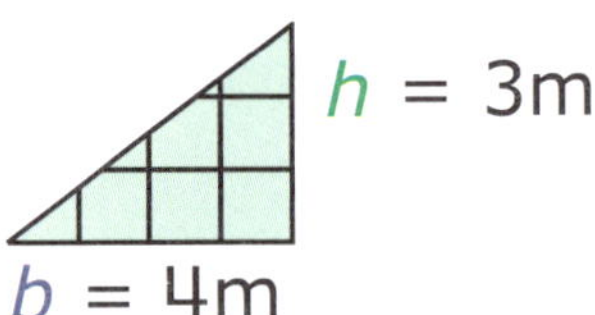

Find the area of each triangle, then use the letters to solve the riddle below.

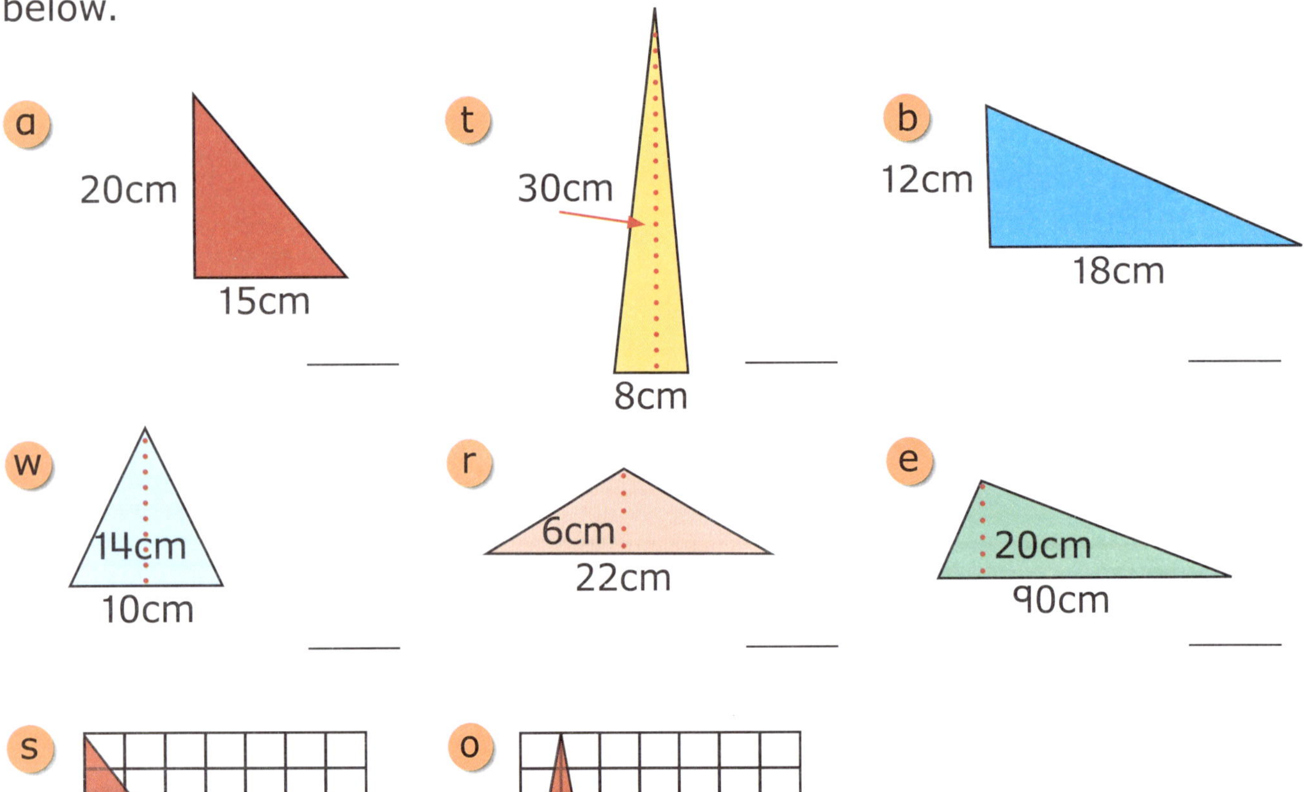

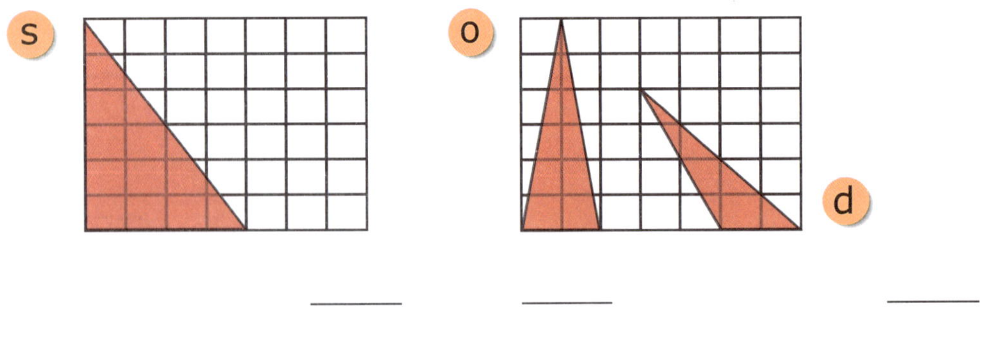

What do sea monsters sleep on?

____ ____ ____ ____ ____ ____ ____ ____ ____
70 150 120 900 66 108 900 4 12

The formula for finding the area (A) of a circle is π times the radius (r) squared. Use 3.14 for approximation of π.

radius = 2 units

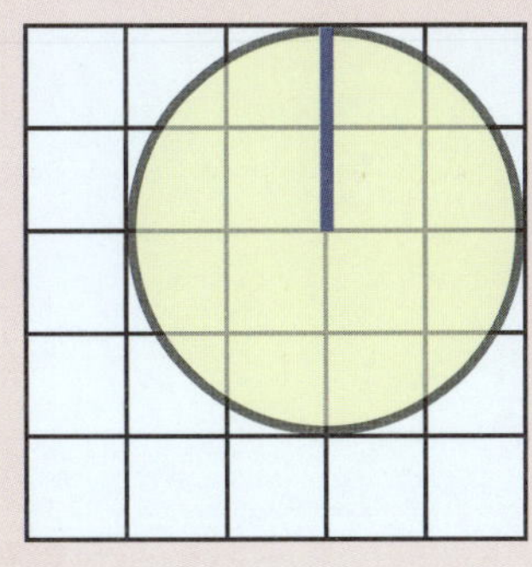

$$A = \pi \times r^2$$
$$= 3.14 \times 2 \times 2$$
$$= 12.56 \text{ square units}$$

Find the area of the following circles.

1 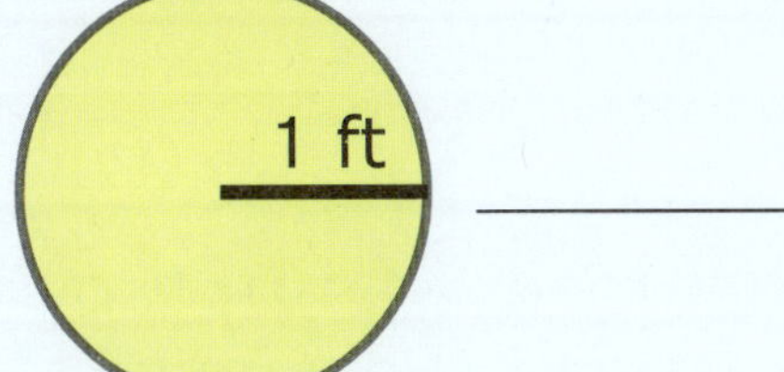

____

2 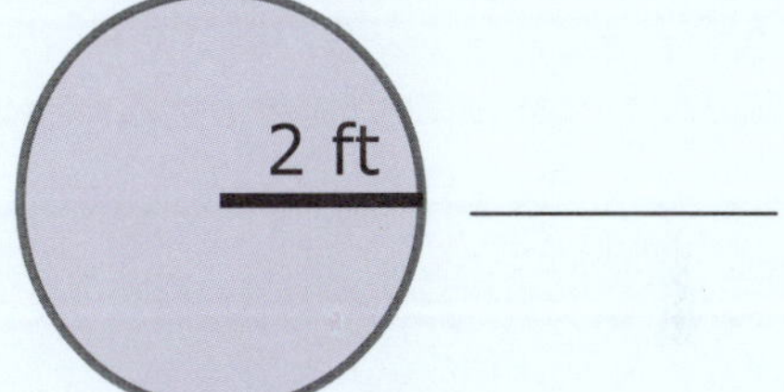

____

3 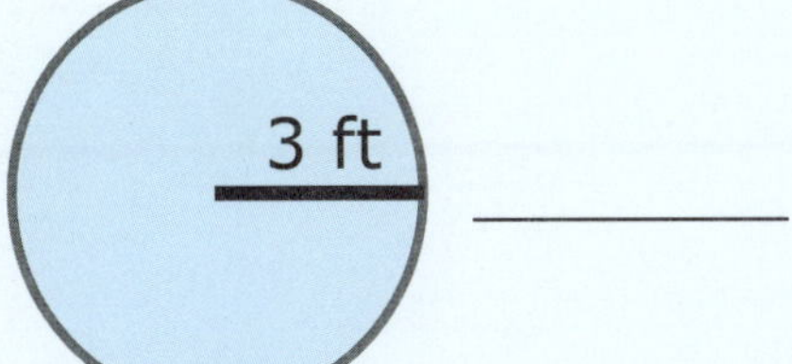

____

4 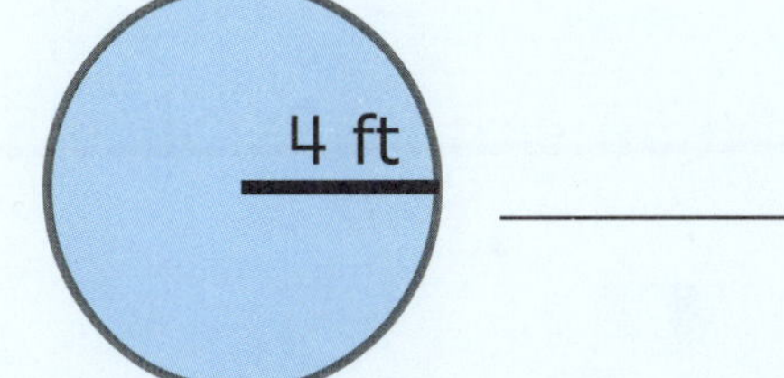

____

5 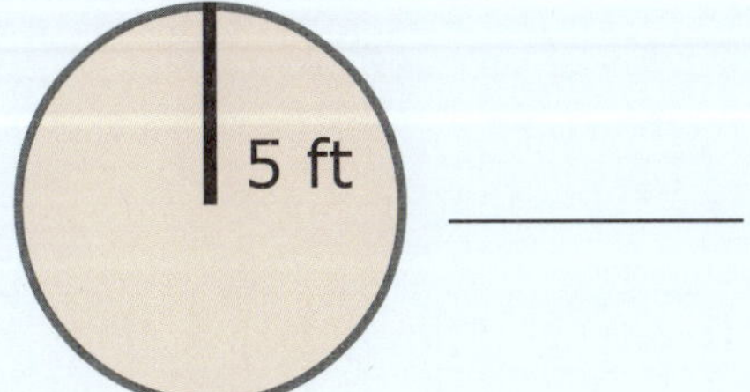

____

6 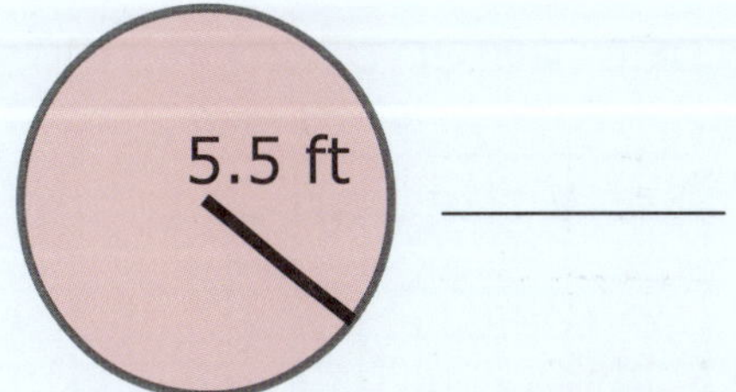

____

7 Carl built a deck around a circular pool. What is the area of the deck?

____

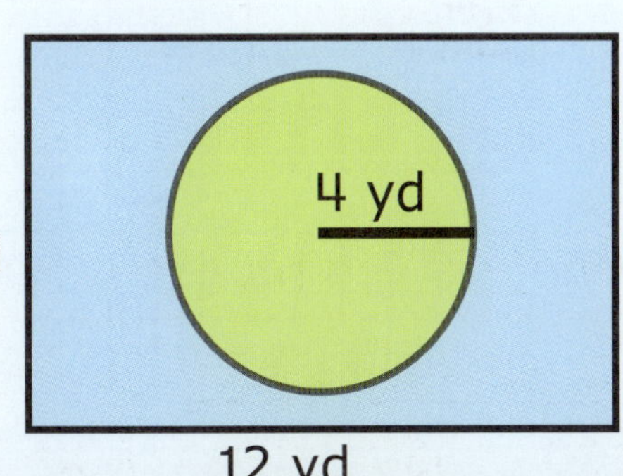

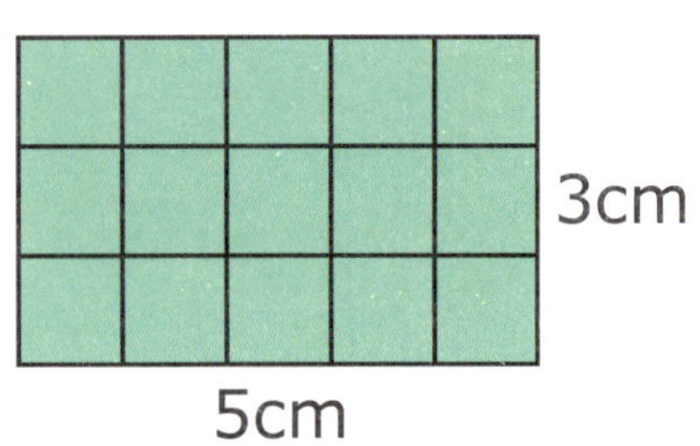

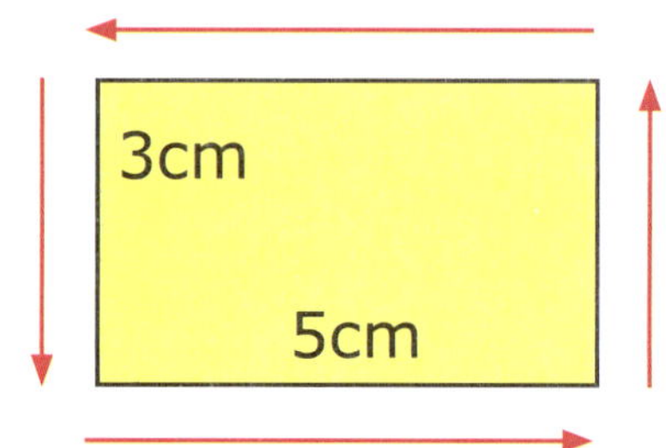

Area = length (l) × width (w)
= 5 × 3
= 15 square cm

Perimeter = $2l + 2w$
= 2 × 5 + 2 × 3
= 16 cm

1. Sal has a pool in his backyard that measures 16 ft by 20 ft. If Sal walks around the pool, how many feet has he walked? ______

2. Sal's neighbor John is building a pool that measures 24 ft by 30 ft. What will be the perimeter of this pool? How much farther is it around John's pool than Sal's? ______ ______

3. What is the difference in area of the pools? ______

4. Sal wants to build a kiddie pool with a perimeter of 20 ft and an area of 24 square ft. Draw the pool.

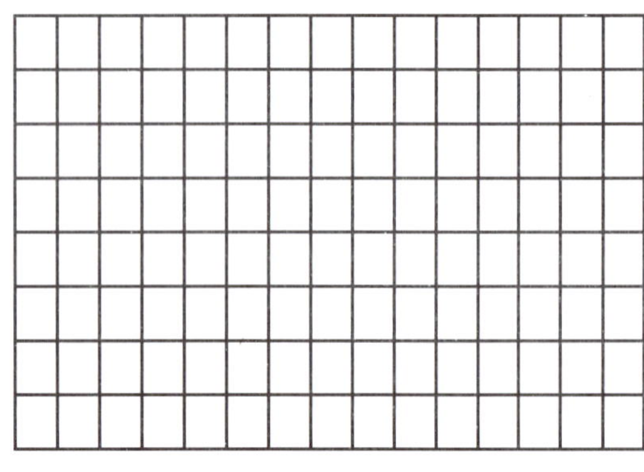

15 ft

5. John wants to build a kiddie pool with a perimeter of 24 ft and an area of 36 sq ft. Draw the pool.

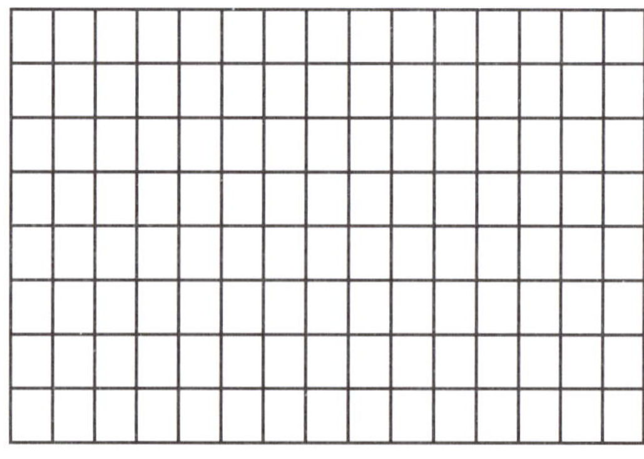

15 ft

Volume (V) is the amount of three-dimensional space inside a figure. The units are in terms of cubes. The volume (V) of a rectangular prism is found by multiplying the length (l) times the width (w) times the height (h).

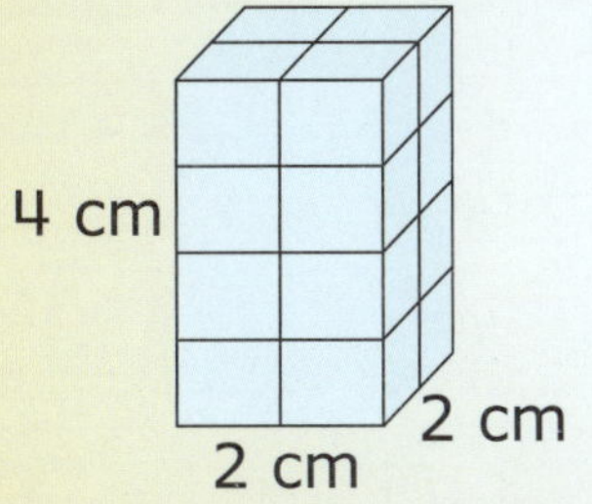

V = length (l) × width (w) × height (h)
= 2 × 2 × 4
= 16 cubic centimeters

Find the volume of each figure.

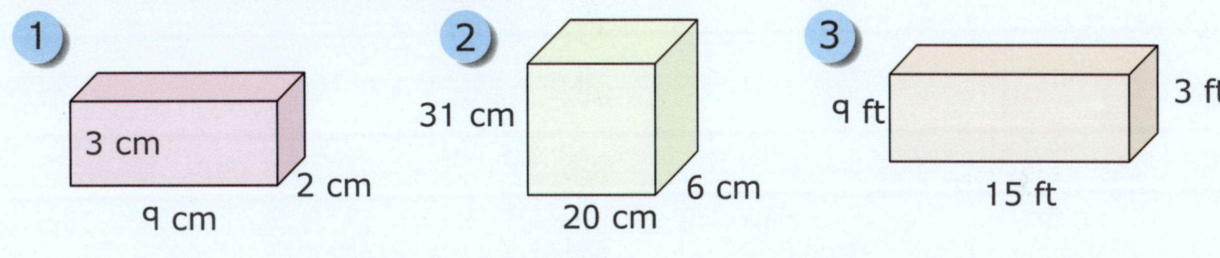

1. ________
2. ________
3. ________

Which figure has the most volume?

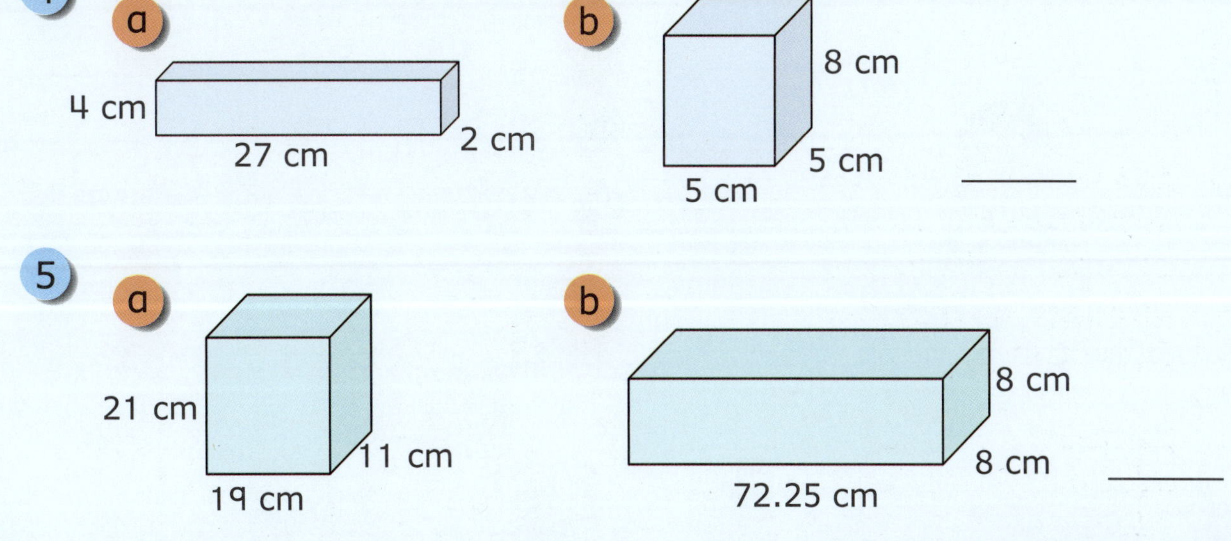

4. ________
5. ________

6. Measure the length, width, and height to the nearest centimeter and find the volume.

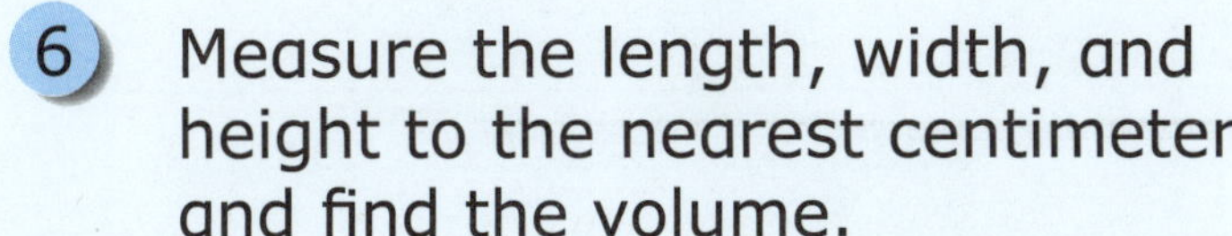

____

Write each answer in the crossword puzzle below. You may need a piece of paper to do your work.

Across

1. 100 − 12 = ______
3. 98 + 647 = ______
6. 7,001 − 286 = ______
10. 2,941 − 2,842 = ______
11. 3,126 + 5,183 = ______
12. 9 + 83 + 47 = ______
13. 4,021 − 1,362 = ______
14. 42 − 24 = ______
15. 86 + 39 + 5 = ______
20. 2,437 − 1,527 = ______
21. 253 + 458 = ______
23. 431 − 296 = ______
24. 2,143 + 674 = ______

Down

1. 745 + 147 = ______
2. 10,000 − 1,036 = ______
3. 7,243 + 648 = ______
4. 51 − 8 = ______
5. 60,000 − 9,099 = ______
7. 243 + 52 + 423 = ______
8. 1 + 4 + 8 = ______
9. 600 − 10 = ______
14. 32 − 15 = ______
16. 216 + 178 = ______
17. 526 − 115 = ______
18. 90 − 29 = ______
19. 21 + 9 + 5 = ______
21. 24 + 32 + 22 = ______
22. 100 − 83 = ______

1. 8	2. 8	■	3.	4.	5.	■	6.	7.	8.	9.
10.		■	11.				■	12.		
13.				■		■	14.		■	
■		■	15.	16.		■		■	17.	■
18.	■	19.	■	20.			■	21.		22.
23.			■		■	■	24.			

Write each answer in the crossword puzzle below. You may need a piece of paper to do your work.

Across

1. 8 × 9 = ______
3. 7 × 46 = ______
6. 72 × 49 = ______
10. 92 ÷ 4 = ______
11. 20 × 50 = ______
12. 2,608 ÷ 8 = ______
13. 24,670 ÷ 10 = ______
14. 1,248 ÷ 52 = ______
15. 41 × 23 = ______
20. 268 × 3 = ______
21. 624 ÷ 4 = ______
23. 32 × 18 = ______
24. 316 × 25 = ______

Down

1. 3,610 ÷ 5 = ______
2. 78 × 30 = ______
3. 31,790 ÷ 10 = ______
4. 600 ÷ 30 = ______
5. 1,342 × 15 = ______
7. 89 × 6 = ______
8. 242 ÷ 11 = ______
9. 108 × 8 = ______
14. 234 ÷ 9 = ______
16. 27 × 18 = ______
17. 700 ÷ 2 = ______
18. 45 ÷ 3 = ______
19. 12 × 8 = ______
21. 19 ÷ 1 = ______
22. 2 × 2 × 3 × 5 = ______

Multiple Step Problems

1. There are 7 boys and 9 girls in the 6th grade class. They were celebrating their teacher's birthday by filling the room with balloons. If each boy was holding 5 balloons and each girl had 4 balloons, how many balloons were at the party? ______

2. Trevor had 1,046 baseball cards. He decided to give 128 cards to his best friend. Then for his birthday, Trevor received 8 packs of baseball cards each containing 12 cards. How many baseball cards does Trevor have? ______

3. Joe, Bob, and Moe are saving their money. Joe has $14.56. Bob has $23 more than Joe. Moe has $1.95 less than Bob. How much does Bob have? ______

   How much money do they have altogether? ______

4. A cheetah can run at a top speed of 65 miles an hour. If a cheetah runs at top speed for two hours, how much less than 500 miles did he run? ______

5. America's population increases by five people every minute. What is the population increase every hour and every day?

______ ______

6.   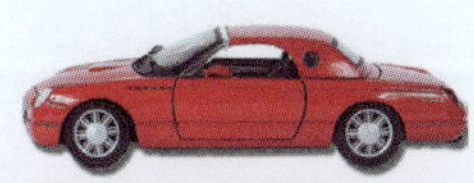 

truck	compact	car	SUV
15 miles per gallon	40 miles per gallon	24 miles per gallon	20 miles per gallon

Mark plans to buy one of the above vehicles. To help him make his decision, he figured what it would cost him in gas to drive 480 miles from San Diego to San Francisco.

a. Number of gallons used to drive 480 miles in the truck = _____
Cost if $5 per gallon = ______

b. Number of gallons used to drive 480 miles in the compact = _____
Cost if $5 per gallon = ______

c. Number of gallons used to drive 480 miles in the car = _____
Cost if $5 per gallon = ______

d. Number of gallons used to drive 480 miles in the SUV = _____
Cost if $5 per gallon = ______

Rounding is used to give an easy estimation of an amount. The population of a city may be 51,247. When people refer to the population, they may say 51,000 for a quick rounded number approximation.

Steps for rounding a number:

Step 1 To round a number to a certain place value, turn all digits to the right of that place value into zero.

Step 2 If the digit to the immediate right of the place value to be rounded had been a 5, 6, 7, 8, or 9, add 1 to that place value. Otherwise, the Step 1 result is the rounded number.

The population of Dallas is 1,209,468.

Round the population to the nearest hundred.

Step 1 1,209,468 ⟶ 1,209,400

Step 2 1,209,500

Rounded to the nearest hundred is 1,209,500

The population of Austin is 799,287.

Round the population to the nearest thousand.

Step 1 799,287 ⟶ 799,000

Step 2 799,000

Rounded to the nearest thousand is 799,000.

To the nearest tens, 13,951 is 13,950.

To the nearest thousand, 248,629 is 249,000.

Use the letters of the answers to write the message below.

1. Round 45,871 to the nearest ten.

   t = 45,900 e = 45,870 r = 45,880

2. Round 5,698 to the nearest thousand.

   a = 6,000 o = 5,000 s = 5,700

3. Round 595 to the nearest hundred.

   u = 500 e = 590 t = 600

4. Round 27,092 to the nearest thousand.

   r = 27,000 n = 28,000 a = 27,100

5. Round 8,149 to the nearest hundred.

   h = 8,200 i = 8,100 o = 8,000

6. Round 24,692 to the nearest ten-thousand.

   a = 24,000 n = 25,000 g = 20,000

7. Round 9,999 to the nearest ten.

   h = 10,000 i = 9,000 s = 9,990

8. Round $4 to the nearest ten.

   r = $10 e = $5 t = $0

Message:

___ ___ ___   ___ ___ ___ ___ ___
1 2 3   4 5 6 7 8

Rounding can be used to get a quick estimation of an answer.

Round each number to the nearest tens before performing the operation. Then work the actual problem to see how close the estimation came.

Actual	Estimate
34	30
+ 19	+ 20
53	50

Actual	Estimate
167	170
− 22	− 20
145	150

Actual	Estimate
56	60
× 14	×10
224	600
560	
784	

Actual	Estimate
31	37
12)372	10)370
36	30
12	70
12	70

Find the actual answer. For an estimate, round each number in the problem to the nearest tens before performing the operation. Then cross out the correct estimates on the next page to find the two false estimates.

1. | Actual | Estimate |
|---|---|
| 59 | |
| +17 | + ____ |

2. | Actual | Estimate |
|---|---|
| 245 | |
| − 78 | − ____ |

3. | Actual | Estimate |
|---|---|
| 21 | |
| × 32 | × ____ |

4. | Actual | Estimate |
|---|---|
| 24)504 |) ____ |

5

Actual	Estimate
259	
+145	+ ____

6

Actual	Estimate
160	
− 41	− ____

7

Actual	Estimate
89	
× 41	× ____

8

Actual	Estimate
$8\overline{)5,264}$	$\overline{)\quad\quad}$

9

Actual	Estimate
536	
+275	+ ____

10

Actual	Estimate
1,908	
− 1,000	− ____

11 A ticket to the play cost \$18. If 198 tickets were sold, how much money was collected? Find the actual and estimated amount.

Actual	Estimate
____	____

At Park School, each of the 6th grade classes sold boxes of cookies for a fund raiser. Listed below are the number of boxes that each class sold. Complete the following charts and bar graph to be displayed in each classroom. Charts and bar graphs are a good way to show information.

1 Boxes of Cookies Sold by Class

Teacher	Boxes Sold	Boxes Sold
Adams	12	1 2 3 4 5 6 / 1 2 3 4 5 6
Allen	27	1 2 3 4 5 6 / 1 2 3 4 5 6 / 1 2 3 4 5 6 / 1 2 3 4 5 6 / 1 2 3
Brown	21	
Jones	10	
Smith	17	

1 2 3 4 5 6 = 6 boxes

2 What is the total number of boxes sold by the 6th grade and how would it be drawn in a chart?

Boxes of Cookies Sold by Grade

Boxes Sold	Boxes Sold

1 2 3 4 5 6 = 6 boxes

3 Fill in the bar graph with the number of boxes each class sold.

4 If each box of cookies sold for $3, what was the total amount of money collected from selling cookies? ________

5 If each box of cookies cost them $1.20 to buy and they sold them for $3, how much profit did they make? ________

6 If they had bought each box for $1.20 and sold it for $4, how much profit would they make? ________

Miss Sara's 6th grade class made and sold 240 cupcakes to help fund a local charity. Read the statements below and find the number of cupcakes each student sold.

- Katie sold $\frac{1}{6}$ of the cupcakes.
- Allie sold 12 more than Katie.
- Dawn sold 18 less than Allie.
- Madi sold half as many as Allie.
- Deb sold as many as Madi and Dawn combined.

1. Complete the chart.

Student	Cupcakes Sold
Katie	
Allie	
Dawn	
Madi	
Deb	

2. How many cupcakes where sold by students other than the ones listed in problem 1? ______

3. How many dozen cupcakes did the class sell? (12 cupcakes = 1 dozen) ______

An equivalent fraction is formed by multiplying the numerator and denominator by the same nonzero number.

Examples: $\frac{1 \times 2}{4 \times 2} = \frac{2}{8}$

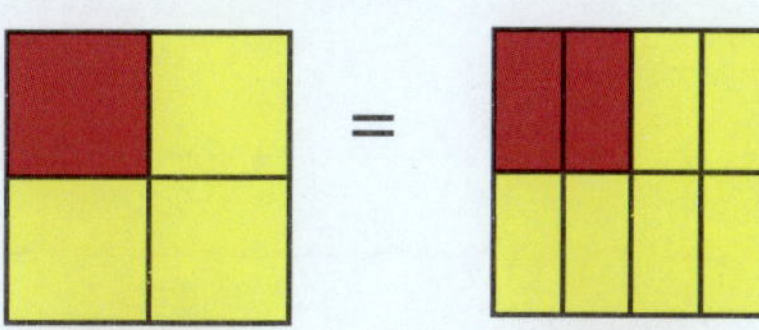

$\frac{2 \times 3}{3 \times 3} = \frac{6}{9}$

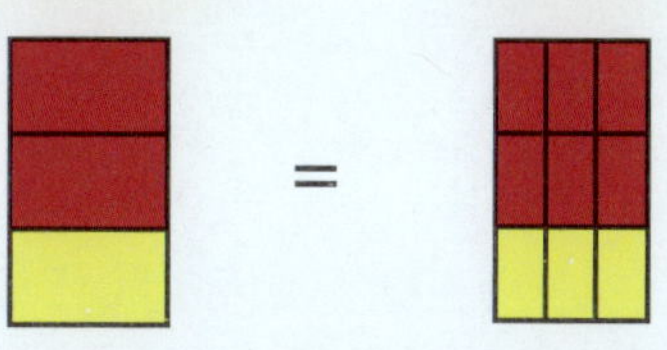

Multiply the numerator and denominator by the same number to find an equivalent fraction in the choice box below. Then cross out the correct answers below to find the two false answers.

1. $\frac{3}{4}$
2. $\frac{1}{2}$
3. $\frac{2}{5}$
4. $\frac{1}{3}$
5. $\frac{3}{8}$
6. $\frac{5}{6}$
7. $\frac{3}{5}$
8. $\frac{1}{6}$
9. $\frac{5}{12}$
10. $\frac{2}{3}$
11. $\frac{4}{9}$
12. $\frac{3}{7}$

$\frac{12}{32}$ $\frac{9}{12}$ $\frac{12}{20}$ $\frac{10}{12}$ $\frac{6}{36}$ $\frac{4}{10}$ $\frac{5}{15}$ $\frac{20}{32}$ $\frac{8}{18}$ $\frac{10}{24}$ $\frac{8}{10}$ $\frac{18}{42}$ $\frac{10}{15}$ $\frac{4}{8}$

Fractions are always written in simplest form (lowest terms). To place a fraction in simplest form, the greatest common factor (GCF) is divided out of the numerator and denominator.

The greatest common factor (GCF) is the largest number that can be evenly divided into the numbers.

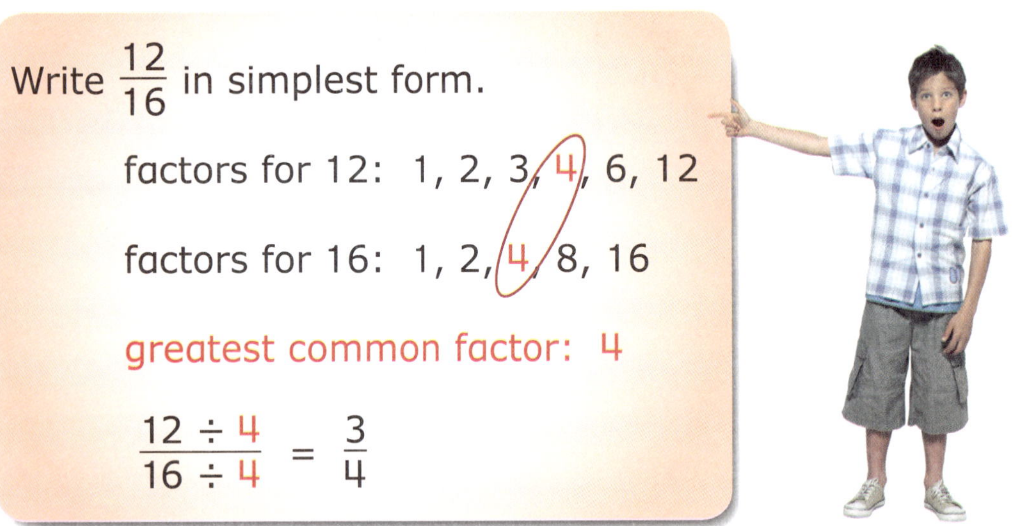

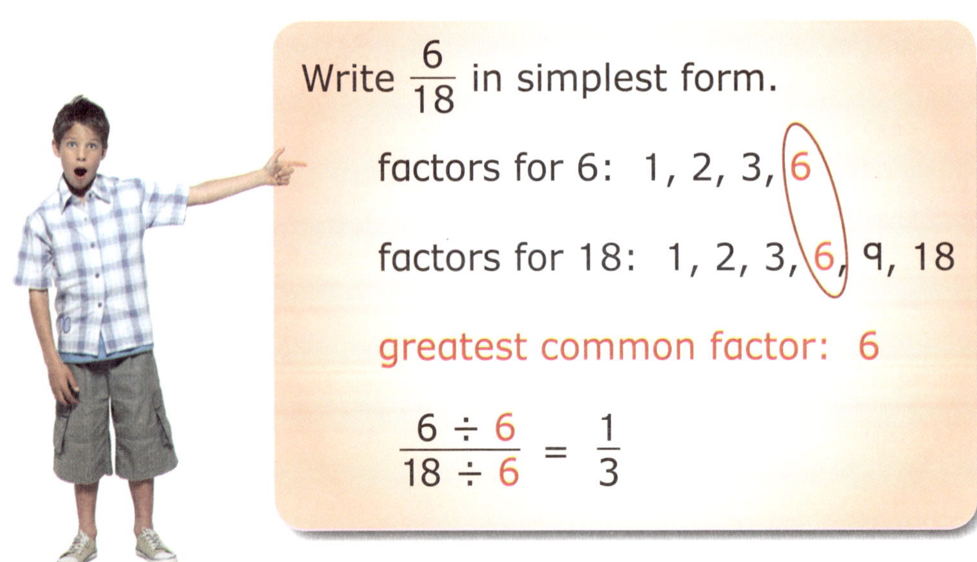

Write each fraction in simplest form; then cross out the correct answers on the next page to find the two false answers.

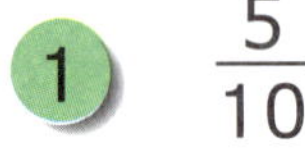 $\frac{5}{10}$

2 $\frac{4}{16}$

3 $\frac{12}{20}$

4 $\frac{45}{81}$

5 $\frac{9}{24}$

6 $\frac{3}{18}$

7 $\frac{20}{32}$

8 $\frac{4}{10}$

9 $\frac{12}{42}$

10 $\frac{42}{54}$

11 $\frac{2}{10}$

12 $\frac{32}{40}$

13 $\frac{10}{12}$

14 $\frac{21}{24}$

15 $\frac{18}{60}$

16 $\frac{27}{36}$

$\frac{1}{4}$ $\frac{1}{5}$ $\frac{1}{6}$ $\frac{5}{6}$ $\frac{3}{5}$ $\frac{3}{10}$ $\frac{1}{2}$ $\frac{5}{8}$ $\frac{7}{8}$ $\frac{2}{5}$ $\frac{2}{7}$ $\frac{7}{9}$ $\frac{2}{3}$ $\frac{3}{8}$ $\frac{5}{9}$ $\frac{7}{12}$ $\frac{4}{5}$ $\frac{3}{4}$

A construction worker was asked to cut a 146 inch board into 4 equal parts. How long was each part?

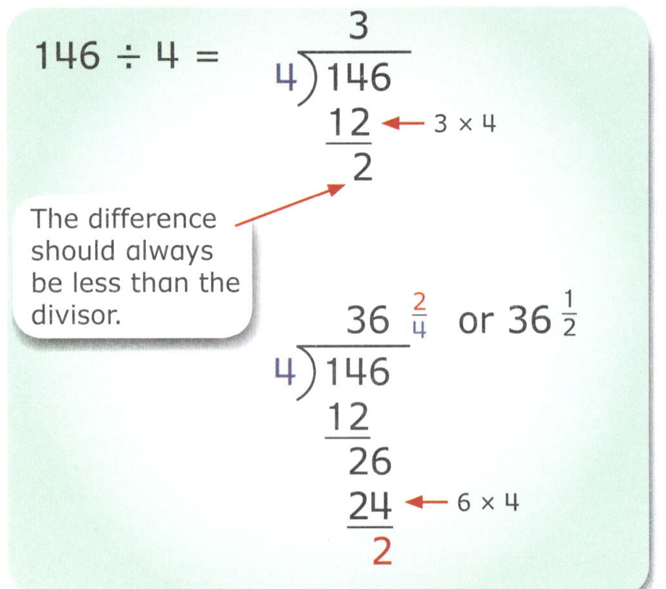

! Each part is $36\frac{1}{2}$ inches long.

Write remainders as a fraction part by placing the remainder in the numerator and the divisor in the denominator.

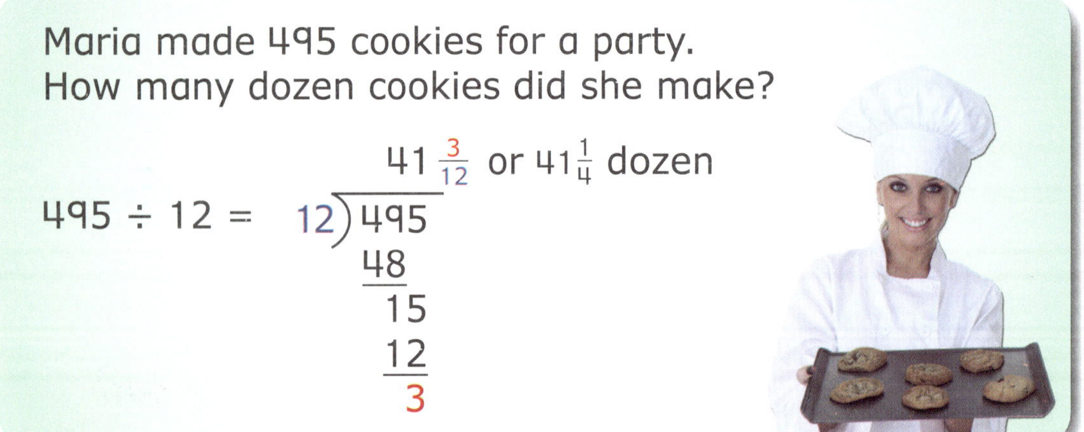

Divide, then use the letters to solve the riddle on the next page.

l 5)137

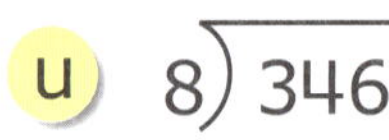
u 8)346

a 9)505

r) $4\overline{)134}$

e) $6\overline{)946}$

j) $3\overline{)740}$

y) $2\overline{)591}$

m) $8\overline{)510}$

g) $7\overline{)394}$

n) Bella had 525 inches of red ribbon to gift wrap boxes of candy. If she uses 20 inches of ribbon on each box, how many complete boxes can she wrap? ________

w) Joe drove 616 miles in 12 hours. What was his average hourly speed? ________

Where do lions go to work out?

___	___	___	___	___	___		___	___	___
$246\frac{2}{3}$	$43\frac{1}{4}$	26	$56\frac{2}{7}$	$27\frac{2}{5}$	$157\frac{2}{3}$		$56\frac{2}{7}$	$295\frac{1}{2}$	$63\frac{3}{4}$

Either a fraction or decimal can represent part of a whole.

fraction $\frac{\text{numerator}}{\text{denominator}} = \frac{\text{number of parts used}}{\text{total number of equal parts}}$

decimal place values • ______ tenths ______ hundredths . . .

Write each amount using a fraction and a decimal.

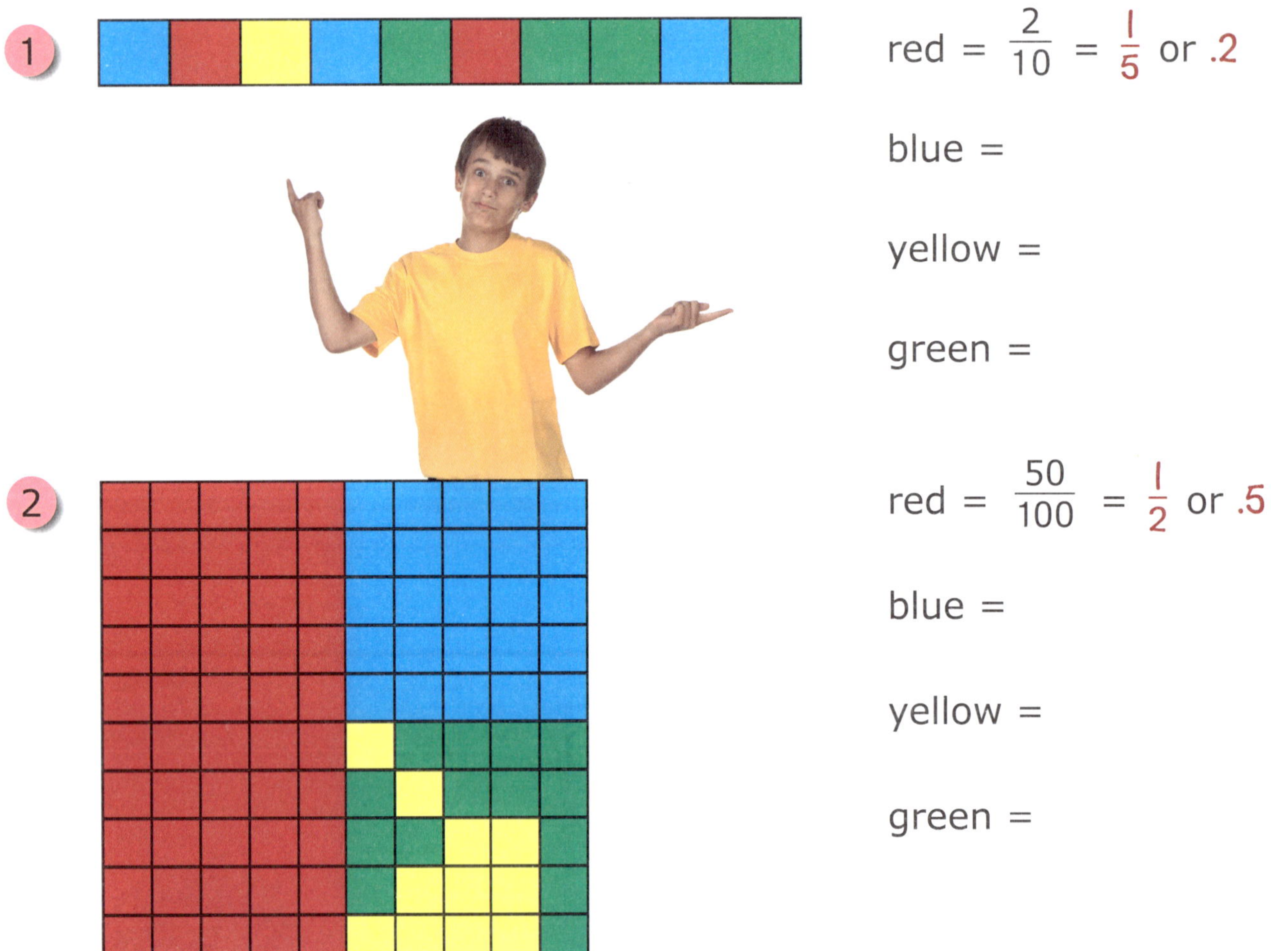

1 red = $\frac{2}{10} = \frac{1}{5}$ or .2

blue =

yellow =

green =

2 red = $\frac{50}{100} = \frac{1}{2}$ or .5

blue =

yellow =

green =

Terminating Decimals

To change a fraction into an equivalent decimal number, divide. Continue adding a zero in place values to the right of the decimal point as needed.

$\frac{1}{2} = .5$

$\frac{1}{2} = 1 \div 2 = 2\overline{)1.} = 2\overline{)1.0}$; quotient $.5$; $\underline{10}$

$\frac{1}{4} = .25$

$\frac{1}{4} = 1 \div 4 = 4\overline{)1.} = 4\overline{)1.00}$; quotient $.25$; $\underline{8}$, 20, $\underline{20}$

$\frac{3}{8} = .375$

$\frac{3}{8} = 3 \div 8 = 8\overline{)3.} = 8\overline{)3.000}$; quotient $.375$; $\underline{24}$, 60, $\underline{56}$, 40, $\underline{40}$

Complete the conversion chart.

$\frac{1}{2} =$	$\frac{3}{8} =$	$\frac{2}{5} =$
$\frac{1}{4} =$	$\frac{5}{8} =$	$\frac{1}{10} =$
$\frac{3}{4} =$	$\frac{7}{8} =$	$\frac{1}{100} =$
$\frac{1}{8} =$	$\frac{1}{5} =$	$\frac{1}{16} =$

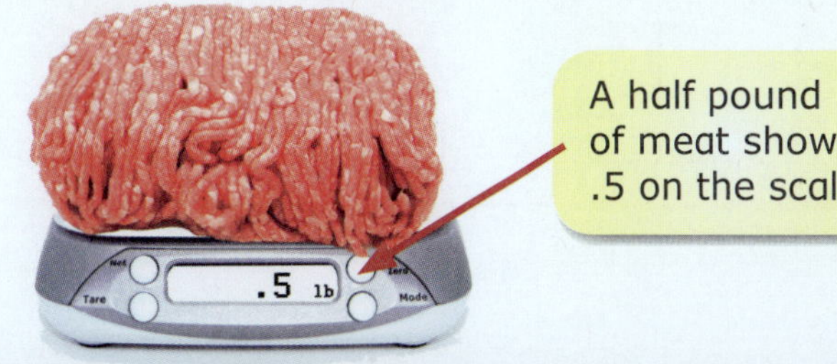

A half pound of meat shows .5 on the scale.

Repeating Decimals

To change a fraction into an equivalent decimal number, divide. Continue adding a zero in place values to the right of the decimal point as needed. If the fraction does not change to an exact decimal number, it will always repeat a pattern. The pattern can repeat one or more digits and may not immediately be observed.

$\frac{1}{3} = 1 \div 3 = 3\overline{)1.} = 3\overline{)1.000}$ = .333 . . .

Long division steps: 1.000; − 9; 10; − 9; 10; − 9; 1

$\frac{1}{3} = .\overline{3}$

Look at the difference to find when a pattern is starting to repeat.

Once the pattern has been discovered, write a bar over the repeating pattern indicating what will be repeating forever.

$.7777777\ldots = .\overline{7}$

$.67123123123\ldots = .67\overline{123}$

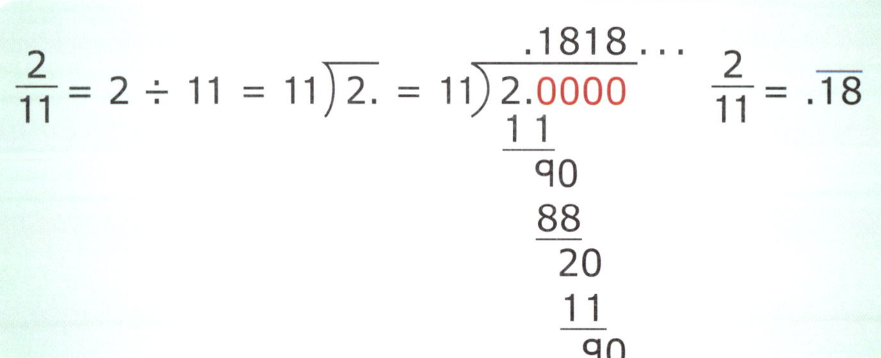

$\frac{2}{11} = 2 \div 11 = 11\overline{)2.} = 11\overline{)2.0000}$ = .1818 . . .

Long division steps: 2.0000; − 11; 90; − 88; 20; − 11; 90

$\frac{2}{11} = .\overline{18}$

$\frac{5}{6} = 5 \div 6 = 6\overline{)5.} = 6\overline{)5.000}$ = .833 . . .

Long division steps: 5.000; − 48; 20; − 18; 20; − 18; 2

$\frac{5}{6} = .8\overline{3}$

Write the following fractions in decimal form, then use the letters to solve the riddle below.

s $\frac{1}{3}$ = ______

n $\frac{2}{3}$ = ______

t $\frac{4}{9}$ = ______

o $\frac{7}{9}$ = ______

m $\frac{1}{6}$ = ______

r $\frac{3}{11}$ = ______

a $\frac{8}{11}$ = ______

e $\frac{5}{12}$ = ______

b $\frac{1}{12}$ = ______

d $\frac{7}{24}$ = ______

What is a lion's favorite street?

___ ___ ___ ___ ___ ___ ___ ___ ___ ___

$.1\overline{6}$ $.\overline{72}$ $.\overline{6}$ $.41\overline{6}$ $.\overline{3}$ $.\overline{4}$ $.\overline{27}$ $.41\overline{6}$ $.41\overline{6}$ $.\overline{4}$

Percent (%) means per hundred. A 9% unemployment rate means 9 out of every 100 workers can not find a job.

$$9\% = \frac{9}{100} = .09$$

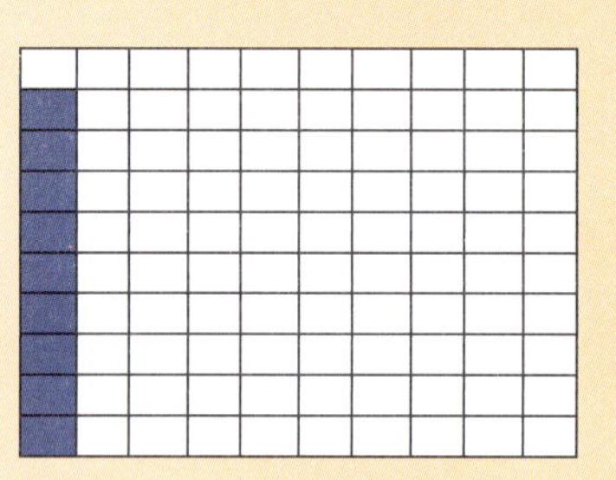

Write $\frac{3}{4}$ as a percent.

Multiply the numerator and denominator by the same number to get an equivalent fraction with a denominator of 100.

$$\frac{3 \times 25}{4 \times 25} = \frac{75}{100} = .75 = 75\%$$

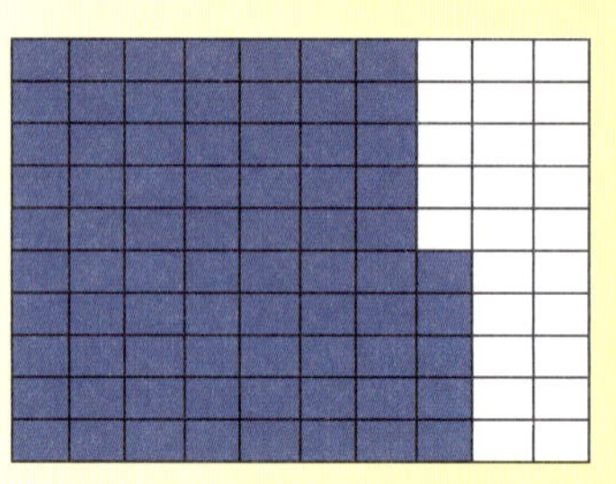

Complete each activity to show the fraction, decimal amount, percent, and graph.

1. 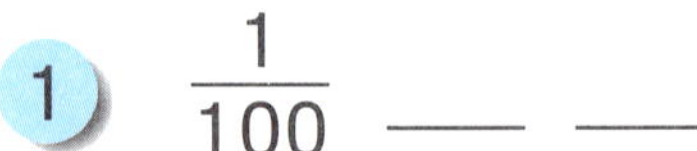 $\frac{1}{100}$ ____ ____

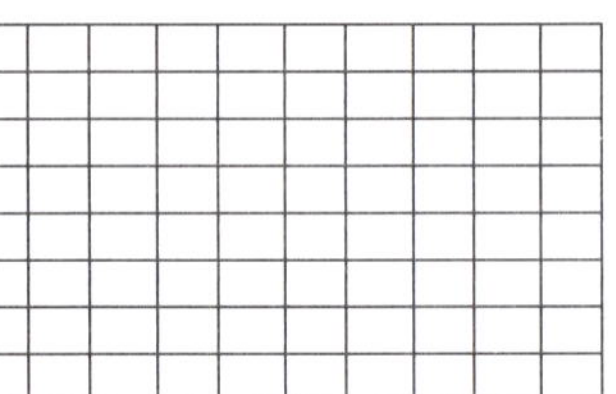

2. ____ .19 ____

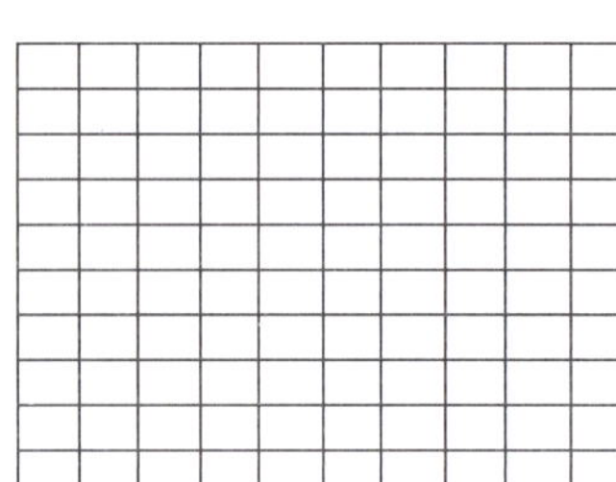

3.  ____ ____ 50%

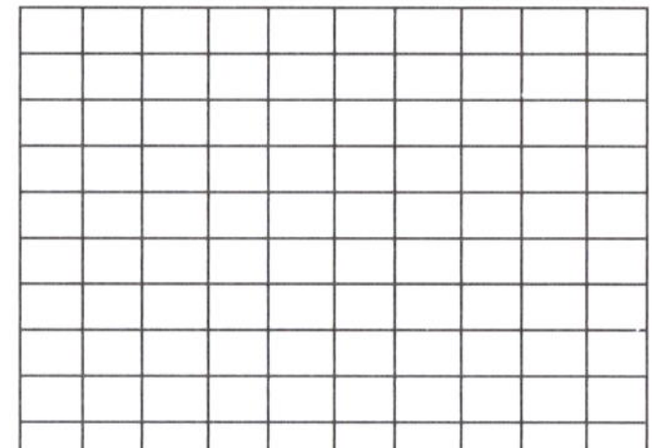

4.  $\frac{3}{10}$ ____ ____

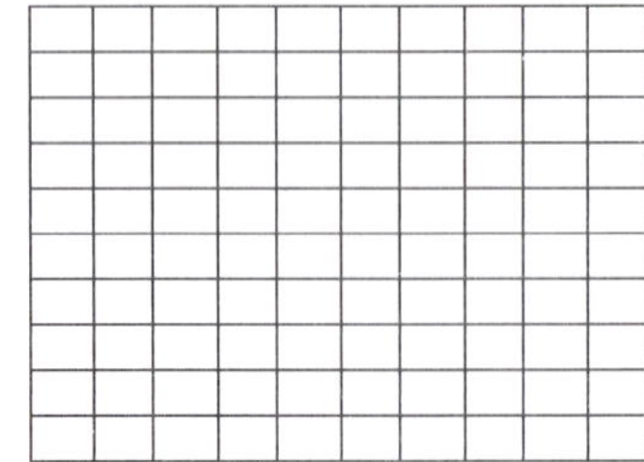

5.  ____ .25 ____

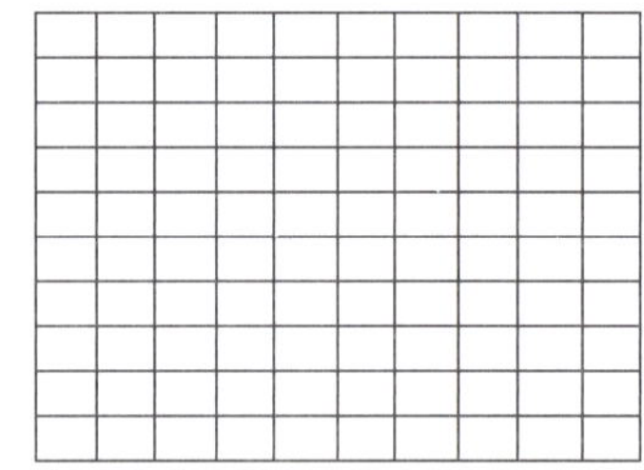

6.  ____ ____ 64%

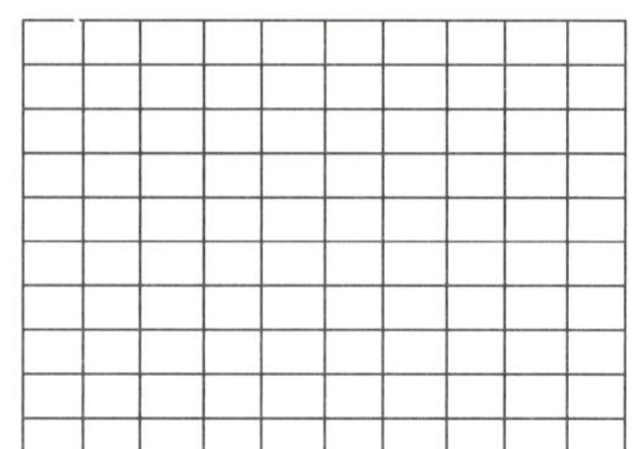

Hints:

To change a fraction to a decimal, divide.	$\frac{1}{2} = 1 \div 2 = 2\overline{)1.0}$ quotient .5, 10
To change a decimal to a fraction, write it as a fraction and simplify.	$.5 = \frac{5}{10} = \frac{1}{2}$
To change a percent to a decimal, drop the percent sign and move the decimal point two places to the left.	18% = .18

Find and circle a bingo in each array. A bingo has equal quantities in an entire row, column, or main diagonal.

2.5%	$\frac{2}{5}$	$\frac{1}{4}$
$\frac{25}{100}$	.25	.25%
25%	2.5	25

$\frac{3}{4}$	75	$\frac{75}{100}$
.75	75%	$\frac{9}{12}$
7.5	$\frac{15}{24}$	.75%

Tic Tac Total!

Fill in the blanks so that the sum of all rows, columns, and two main diagonals add to the same sum.

1

13		11
	10	
		7

2

		15
		22
21		17

For more activities like this, please see our *Balance Math™ and More!* series.

Probability tells the likelihood that an event will happen. Probability can be written as a ratio of favorable outcomes to the total possibilities.

The probability of getting a head when a coin is tossed is $\frac{1}{2}$. Heads is one choice out of two possible choices.

Below are three spinners. Figure the probability of each possible spin.

1. 

Probability of landing on a 1 = $\frac{5}{8}$

Probability of landing on a 2 = ____

Probability of landing on a 3 = ____

2. 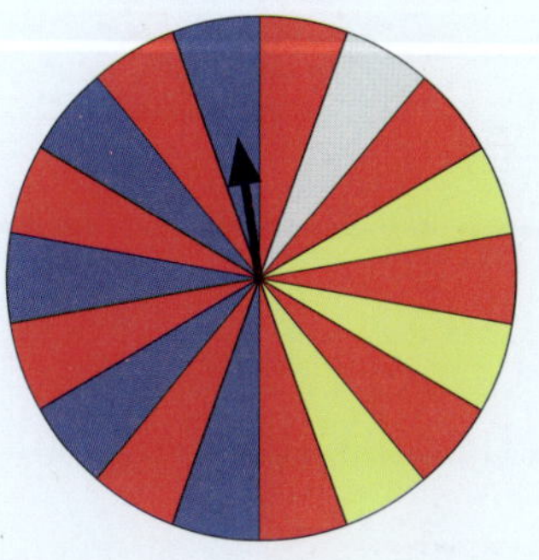

Probability of landing on red = ____

Probability of landing on blue = ____

Probability of landing on yellow = ____

Probability of landing on white = ____

3. 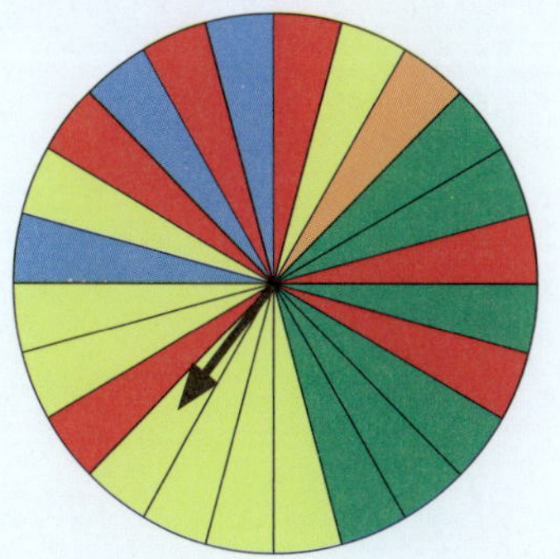

Probability of landing on orange = ____

Probability of landing on red = ____

Probability of landing on blue = ____

Probability of landing on green = ____

Probability of landing on yellow = ____

1. Find and circle two numbers next to each other in a row, column, or diagonal that sum to 256.

214	312	112	239	37
146	46	150	37	149
210	138	122	201	95
126	134	118	125	171
138	172	94	121	155

2. Find and circle two numbers next to each other in a row, column, or diagonal whose difference is 194.

342	128	506	292	376
136	300	514	370	534
422	214	508	215	400
207	401	297	374	184
433	155	183	108	390

3. Find and circle two numbers next to each other in a row, column, or diagonal that multiply to 864.

27	34	32	19
29	26	54	16
37	39	18	43
44	56	26	18

A whole number is prime if it is greater than 1 and only evenly divisible by itself and 1. Numbers that are not prime are called composite.

2, 3, 5, 7, 11, 13, 17, 19, 23, ... are primes
4, 6, 8, 9, 10, 12, 14, 15, 16, ... are composites

Using primes only, fill in the blanks with either a 1-digit or 2-digit prime that makes the equation true. Answers are not unique.

1. ______ + ______ = 80

2. ______ − ______ = 60

3. ______ + ______ + ______ = 57

4. ______ + ______ − ______ = 56

5. ______ × ______ = 65

6. ______ × ______ × ______ = 1,001

A **tree diagram** can be used to show all **combinations** possible from a set of choices. An entire branch shows one unique choice.

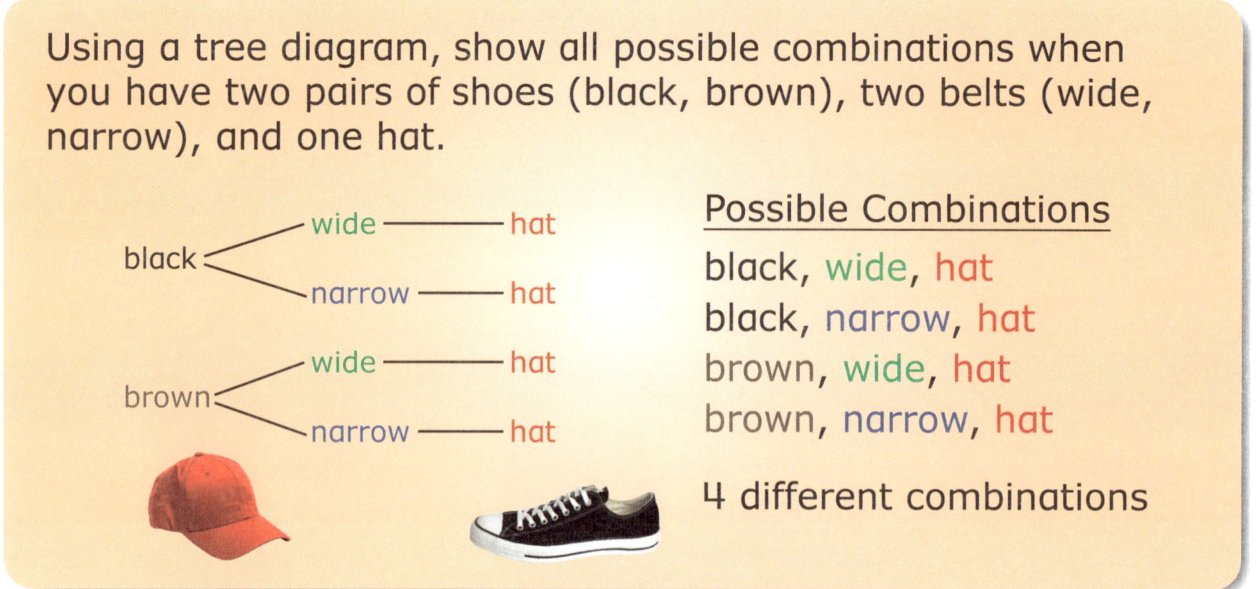

1. To represent their school at the assembly, the students had to pick one girl of out three (Lia, Ann, Sue), one boy out of two (Bob, Joe), and one teacher out of a list of two (Miss Jones, Mr. Smith). Use a separate sheet of paper to make a tree diagram showing all the different combinations.

2. With 2 pairs of jeans (A, B), 4 shirts (C, D, E, F), and 2 pairs of shoes (G, H), how many different outfits are possible? _____ Use a separate sheet of paper to make a tree diagram showing the possibilities.

3. How many different combinations are possible with 8 shirts, 2 pairs of jeans, and 3 pairs of shoes? _____

Students of the Month

At Franklin Elementary School, they are interested in celebrating and rewarding good students. They consider students who always work harder and do more work than necessary on their assignments to be ones that they should reward. After having a meeting, the teachers and principal came up with a way to reward their outstanding students. They will select two boys and two girls each month to be rewarded for being model students. The students will get to eat their favorite snack and play their favorite game during a recess.

The reward winners in May were Steve, Stan, Mary, and Maria. Stan told everyone how he hates bananas but loves playing chess. One of the other winners loves checkers and eating apples. Another student loves pears but hates to play cards. Mary loves jacks but hates pears. Maria stated she doesn't ever play cards and Steve said he never eats oranges.

The following are the students, snacks, and games selected for May.

Students: Stan, Steve, Mary, Maria
Snacks: bananas, apples, oranges, pears
Games: chess, checkers, cards, jacks

Match the students with their favorite snack and game using the above mentioned facts.

	bananas	apples	oranges	pears	chess	checkers	cards	jacks
Stan								
Steve								
Mary								
Maria								
chess								
checkers								
cards								
jacks								

A **Stem-and-Leaf Plot** places data quickly in a least to greatest form. The left column (stems) dislays the tens and the right column (leaves) show the ones of the data.

data: 21, 19, 23, 17, 8, 5, 19

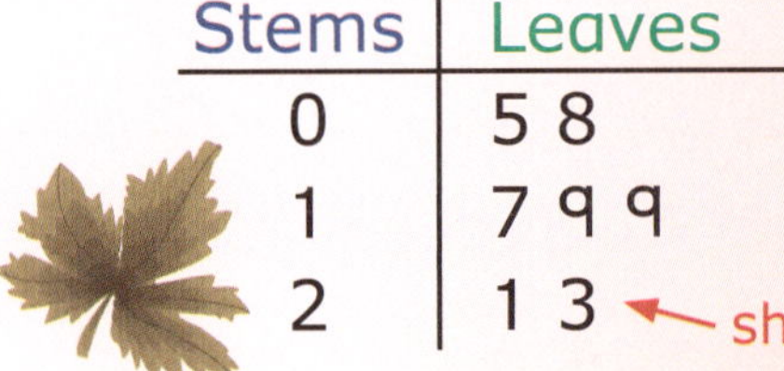

Stems	Leaves
0	5 8
1	7 9 9
2	1 3 ← shows 21 & 23

A **Scatter Plot** shows the relationship between two sets of data shown on horizontal and vertical scales. It might show that both increase together or relate differently.

Average Height	Average Weight
72 in.	150 lbs
68 in.	120 lbs
64 in.	110 lbs
60 in.	105 lbs

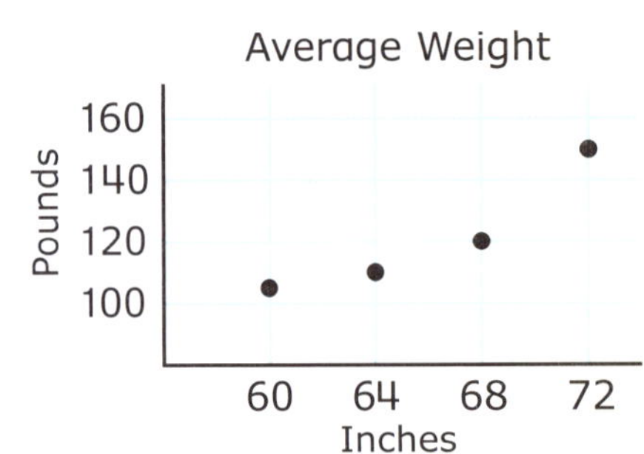

The range is the difference between the smallest data number and the largest data number. The range of pounds is 45.

150 – 105 = 45

1 Make a stem-and-leaf plot using eight student heart rates (103, 112, 109, 129, 127, 112, 126, & 128) after a minute run.

2 Make a scatter plot using the information below.

Age	Number at Party
15	8
16	20
17	15
18	6

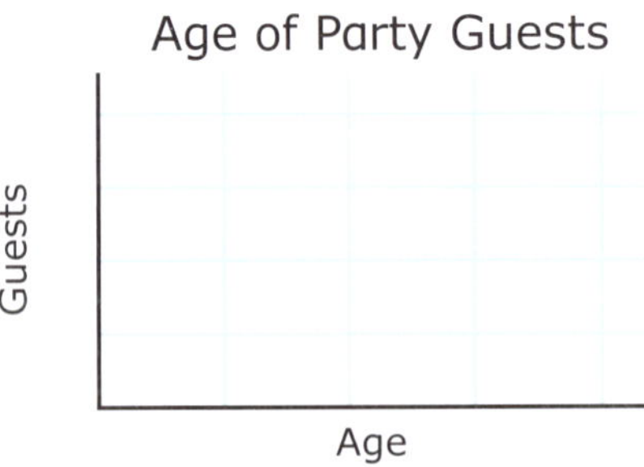

What does the plot show? ______________________________

3 Find the range for the data in #1. ______

The mean, median, and mode help describe data.

Data: 4, 1, 4, 6, 5

The mean is found by adding all the values and dividing by the number of values. Mean = $(4 + 1 + 4 + 6 + 5) \div 5 = 4$

The median is the middle value after placing from smallest to largest. The median for the data 1, 4, 4, 5, 6 is 4.

The mode is the value that occurs the most. There is no mode if all values are different. The mode is 4.

New York
Week of July 4th

Day	High	Low
Mon.	93°	71°
Tues.	90°	71°
Wed.	85°	71°
Thurs.	92°	73°
Fri.	80°	69°
Sat.	90°	73°
Sun.	86°	69°

1. Mean for temperature highs = _____

2. Mean for temperature lows = _____

3. Median for temperature highs = _____

4. Median for temperature lows = _____

5. Mode for temperature highs = _____

6. Mode for temperature lows = _____

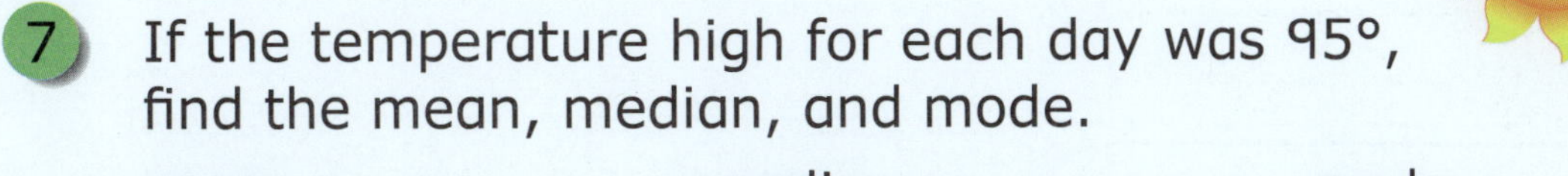

7. If the temperature high for each day was 95°, find the mean, median, and mode.

mean = _______ median = _______ mode = _______

The sun's surface temperature is about 10,000°!

Everyone wanted to know who the best hitter on the team was at this point in the season. The coach figured the batting average for each of his players to find the top three players.

To figure a player's batting average, make a fraction comparing the number of hits to the times at bat. Then divide to write it as a decimal rounded to the nearest thousandths.

Divide out to the ten-thousandth place to be able to round to the nearest thousandth.

Ralph = $\frac{7}{25}$

$$\begin{array}{r} .2800 \\ 25\overline{)7.0000} \\ \underline{5\,0} \\ 2\,00 \\ \underline{2\,00} \\ 00 \end{array}$$

Juan = $\frac{5}{32}$

$$\begin{array}{r} .1562 \\ 32\overline{)5.0000} \\ \underline{3\,2} \\ 1\,80 \\ \underline{1\,60} \\ 200 \\ \underline{192} \\ 80 \\ \underline{64} \end{array}$$

Tom = $\frac{6}{21}$

$$\begin{array}{r} .2857 \\ 21\overline{)6.0000} \\ \underline{4\,2} \\ 1\,80 \\ \underline{1\,68} \\ 120 \\ \underline{105} \\ 150 \\ \underline{147} \end{array}$$

Figure the batting averages for each player to fill in the chart on the next page. Then answer the questions below the chart.

Brett = _____

$40\overline{)10.}$

Al = _____

$22\overline{)5.}$

Lou = _____

$20\overline{)7.}$

Jim = _____

$\_\_\overline{)\_\_.}$

Eddy = _____

$\_\_\overline{)\_\_.}$

Ned = _____

$\_\_\overline{)\_\_.}$

Player	Hits	Times at Bat	Batting Average to Nearest Thousandth
Ralph	7	25	.280
Juan	5	32	.156
Tom	6	21	.286
Brett	10	40	
Al	5	22	
Lou	7	20	
Jim	10	30	
Eddy	7	24	
Ned	6	15	

1. Which player has the best batting average and deserves the 1st place award? ______

2. Which player has the 2nd best batting average and deserves the 2nd place award? ______

3. Which player has the 3rd best batting average and deserves the 3rd place award? ______

4. What was the mean of the batting averages for the top three hitters? ______

Percent (%) means "parts per hundred."

$25\% = \frac{25}{100} = .25 \qquad 7\% = \frac{7}{100} = .07 \qquad 100\% = \frac{100}{100} = 1$

To change a percent directly to a decimal, drop the % sign and move the decimal point to the left two places.

$25\% = 25 = .25$

To find the percent of a number, change the percent to a decimal and multiply.

At a sale, Brent got 15% off a $20 shirt. How much did he get off the shirt?

15% of 20 = .15 × 20 = $3.00

Solve each problem; then cross out the correct answers below to find the two false answers.

1. 10% of $6 = ______
2. 40% of $28 = ______
3. 25% of $36 = ______
4. 50% of $75 = ______
5. 38% of $85 = ______
6. 8% of $125 = ______
7. 20% of $5.50 = ______
8. 45% of $120 = ______
9. Lyne bought a $39 jacket at 25% off. How much did she pay for the jacket before adding tax? ______

Rapid Multiplication Tricks to Do in Your Head

A. To multiply a two-digit number by 11, write the tens and ones place values with their sum in the tens place.

$43 \times 11 = 4\_3 = 473$

$4 + 3$

$76 \times 11 = 7\_6 = 836$

$7 + 6$

Be a human calculator!

B. To multiply two identical two-digit numbers ending in 5, multiply the tens place value by the tens place value increased by one and place 25 to the right.

$35 \times 35 = 12\ 25 = 1{,}225$

$(3 + 1) \times 3$

$75 \times 75 = 56\ 25 = 5{,}625$

$(7 + 1) \times 7$

Multiply each problem in your head.

1. $23 \times 11 =$ ______
2. $41 \times 11 =$ ______
3. $56 \times 11 =$ ______
4. $87 \times 11 =$ ______
5. $64 \times 11 =$ ______
6. $11 \times 11 =$ ______
7. $25 \times 25 =$ ______
8. $15 \times 15 =$ ______
9. $85 \times 85 =$ ______
10. $65 \times 65 =$ ______
11. $95 \times 95 =$ ______
12. $55 \times 55 =$ ______

An exponent tells the number of factors of a base number.

base → $2^4 = 2 \times 2 \times 2 \times 2 = 16$
read as "base to the exponent power"
" two to the fourth power"

$5^3 = 5 \times 5 \times 5 = 125$
read as "five to the third power" or "five cubed"

$7^2 = 7 \times 7 = 49$
read as "seven to the second power" or "seven squared"

Exponents are used to write formulas in simplest form.

Area of circle = 3.14 × radius × radius
$A = \pi r^2$

Write the answers in the crossword puzzle.

1. 6^3
2. 36^2
3. twelve squared
4. four cubed
5. 25^2
6. 2^9
7. 3^3
8. 9^3
9. 7^2
10. 21^2

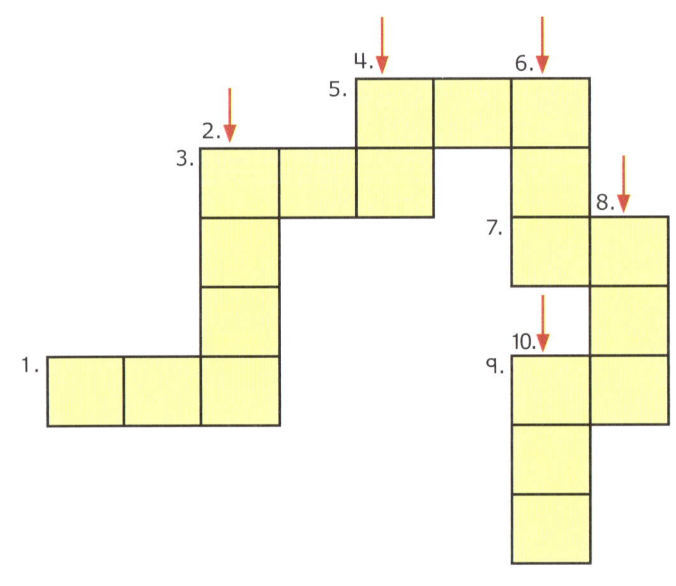

Use the **order of operations** steps to solve a problem involving several operations.

Step 1: Work within the parentheses.
Step 2: Figure exponents.
Step 3: Do multiplication and division from left to right.
Step 4: Do addition and subtraction from left to right.

$8^2 - (6 + 3) + 8 \div 4 =$
$8^2 - 9 + 8 \div 4 =$
$64 - 9 + 8 \div 4 =$
$64 - 9 + 2 = 57$

Solve each problem; then cross out the correct answers on the right to find the two false answers.

1. $1 + 5(8 - 2) - 1 =$

2. $(12 - 9)^2(3 + 4)^2 =$

3. $2(12 \div 2 - 1) - 4 \div 2 =$

4. $10^2 - 5 \times 2 + 2 \div 2 =$

5. $2(27 - 19)^2 - 8 \times 2 =$

6. $32\left(\frac{1}{2}\right)^2 - 16 \div 4 \times 2 =$

8
6
91
1,296
30
0
112
441

Some Math Terms

+, add, sum, total

−, subtract, minus, less, difference

÷, divide, quotient, ratio

×, times, multiply, product, of

Solve each problem.

1. Missy had a plate full of cookies. She ate 3 and gave her mother 4. After putting 37 cookies in a box for her soccer team, she had 14 left. How many cookies did Missy start with? ______

2. Michael bought 4 large and 3 medium pizzas for a party. If the large pizzas had 12 slices and the medium pizzas have 8 slices, how many total slices did Michael have? ______

3. Griffin decided to drive a 2,722 mile trip across the United States from Los Angeles to New York City. The first day he drove 8 hours of the trip and averaged 55 miles per hour. After the first day, how many miles did he have left to drive? ______

4. Sam gave $\frac{1}{2}$ of his baseball cards to Bowie. Bowie gave $\frac{1}{8}$ of the cards Sam gave him to Roger. If Sam started with 384 cards, how many of those did Roger get? ______

5. In Death Valley, California, the record high temperature for July is 134° and the record low for July is 67°. What is the difference between the record high and low temperatures for July? ______

Solve each problem.

1. Gabby has 156 pennies, 37 nickels, 18 dimes, and 12 quarters in her piggy bank. What is the total amount of money in Gabby's piggy bank? _______

2. Joline has 519 nickels she has collected. She puts them in paper rolls to take to the bank. How many rolls of nickels can she fill if there are 20 coins in a roll? What is the total amount of money she has? _______ _______

3. Each one of the 21 students in the 6th grade class bought 2 dozen pencils for the school supply cabinet. What was the total number of pencils they brought? _______

4. Usain Bolt ran a record 100 meter dash in 9.58 seconds while Florence Griffith-Joyner ran it in 10.49 seconds. What is the difference in time between the men's and women's record time? _______

5. Madi has $36. If she gets $19 more, she will have exactly half as much as Anne. How much money does Anne have? _______

A **polygon** is a closed figure made from line segments.

The number of line segments determines a polygon's name.

3-sided	triangle
4-sided	quadrilateral
5-sided	pentagon
6-sided	hexagon
7-sided	heptagon*
8-sided	octagon
10-sided	decagon

*also called septagon

1. Color a triangle in the figure.

2. Color a quadrilateral in the figure.

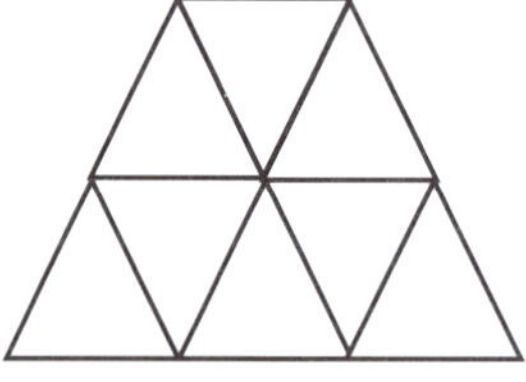

3. Color a pentagon in the figure.

4. Color a hexagon in the figure.

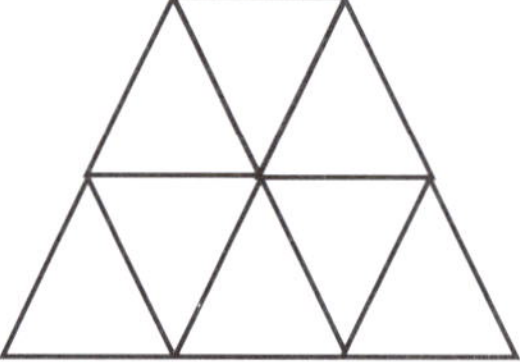

5. Color a heptagon in the figure.

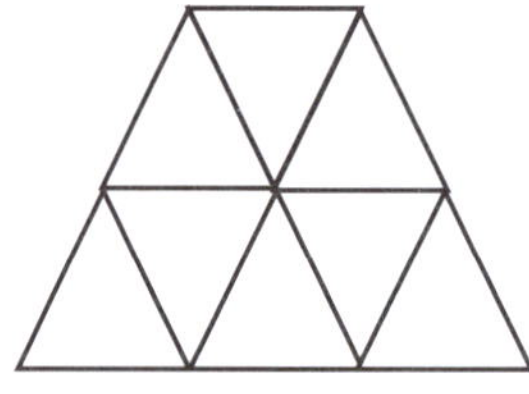

6. Draw a decagon.

Angles are measured in degrees (°) with a protractor. To measure an angle, place the center of the protractor on the vertex of the angle. When one side of the angle is on the 0° edge, read the degrees of the angle from where the other side of the angle touches the scale.

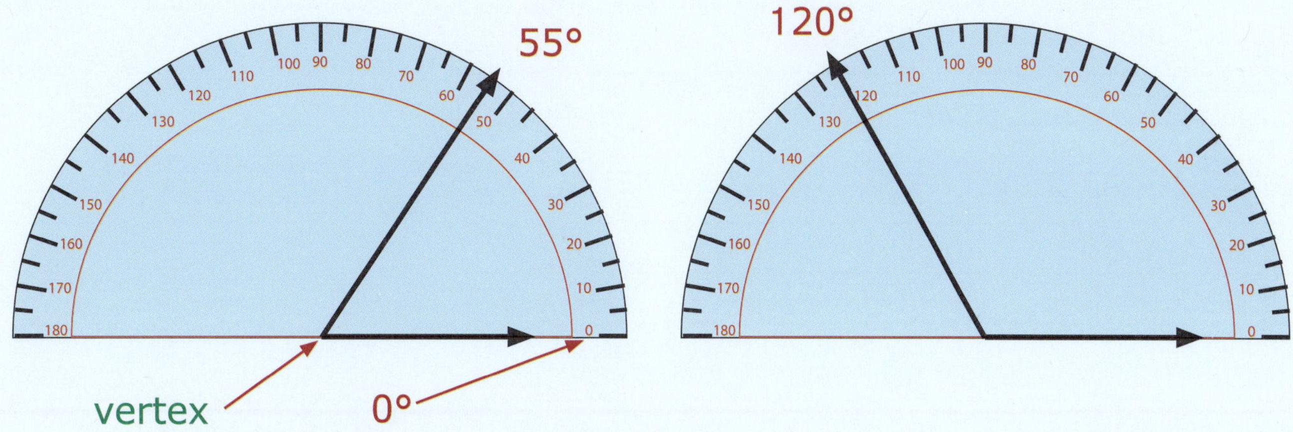

Measure each angle, then use the letters to solve the riddle below.

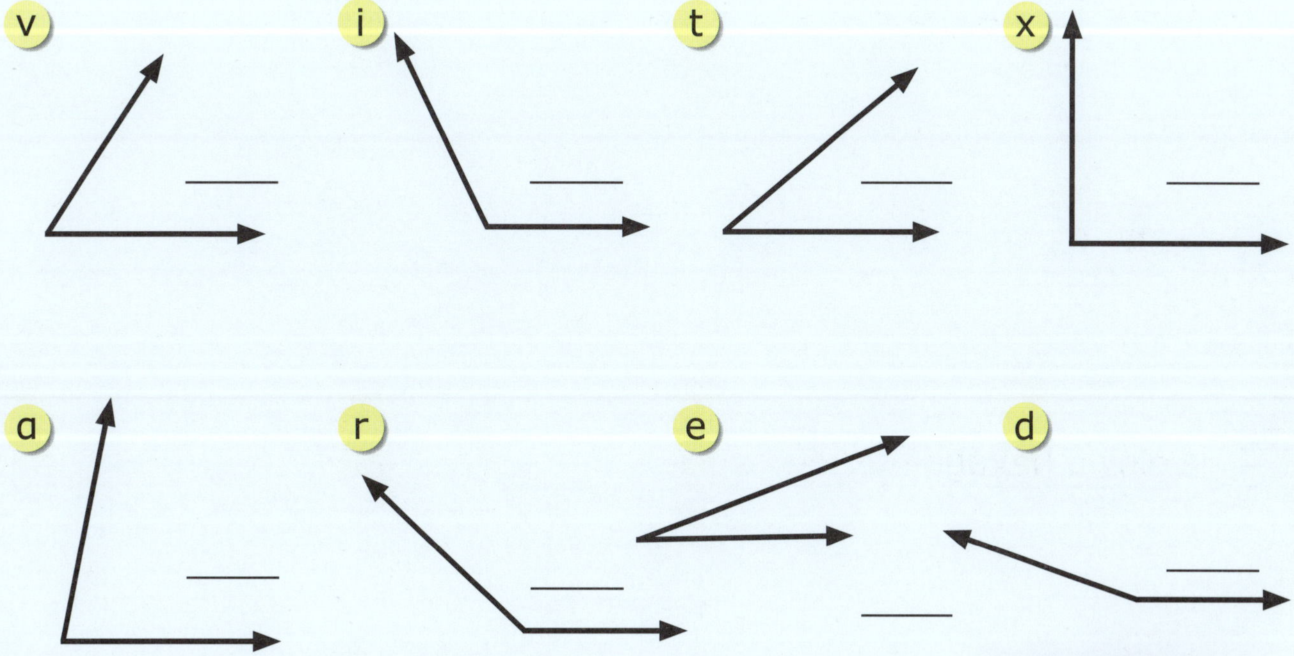

v ____

i ____

t ____

x ____

a ____

r ____

e ____

d ____

Who makes a living while driving customers away?

____ ____ ____ ____
40° 79° 90° 115°

____ ____ ____ ____ ____ ____
160° 135° 115° 58° 20° 135°

The sum of the three angles in a triangle always adds to 180°.

78° + 63° + 39° = 180°

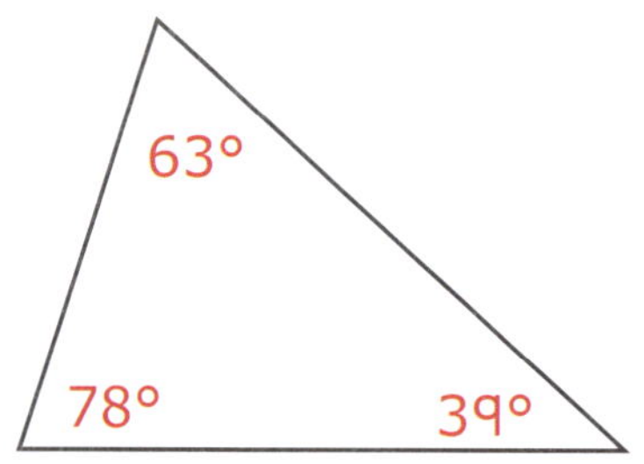

Polygon	Sum of the Angles
triangle	180°
quadrilateral	360°
pentagon	540°
hexagon	720°

adding a side adds 180° to the total

Find each missing angle using the given angles by adding the given angles and subtracting from the total for the polygon.

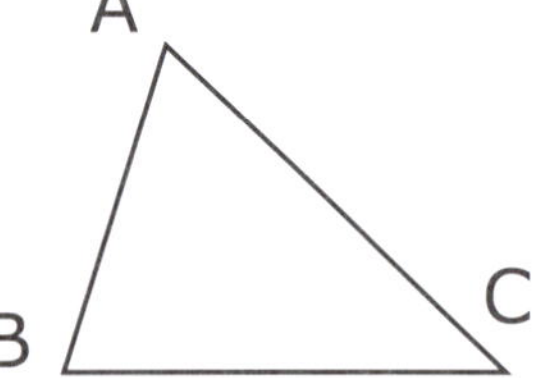

∠A = 70°
∠B = 73°
∠C = ____

2

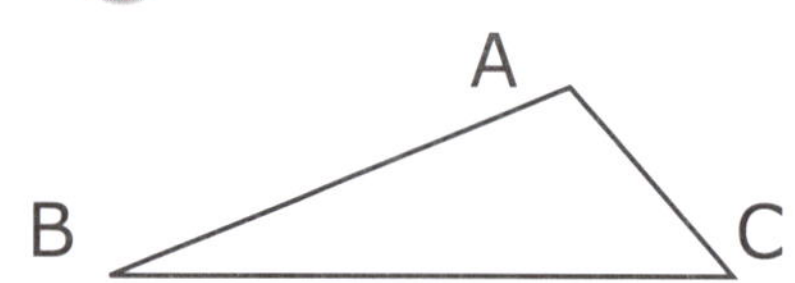

∠A = ____
∠B = 28°
∠C = 46°

3

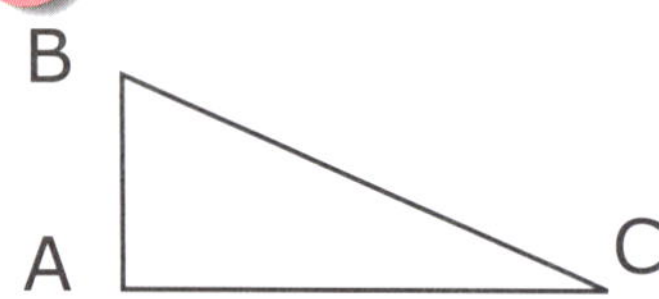

∠A = 90°
∠B = 60°
∠C = ____

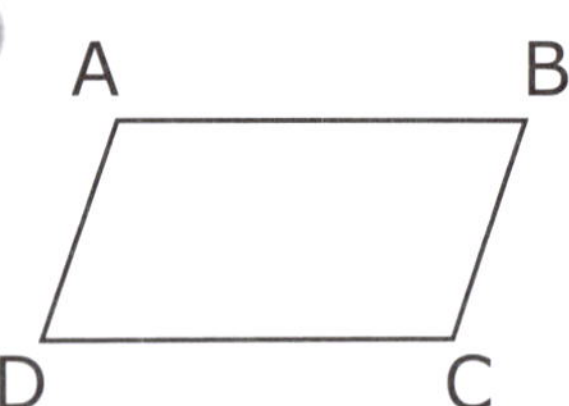

∠A = 115°
∠B = ____
∠C = 115°
∠D = 65°

5

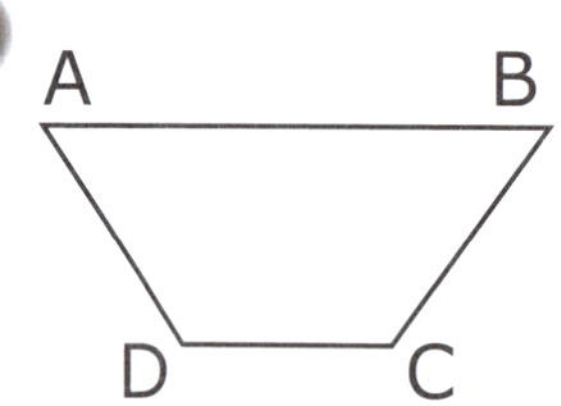

∠A = 58°
∠B = 58°
∠C = ____
∠D = 122°

6

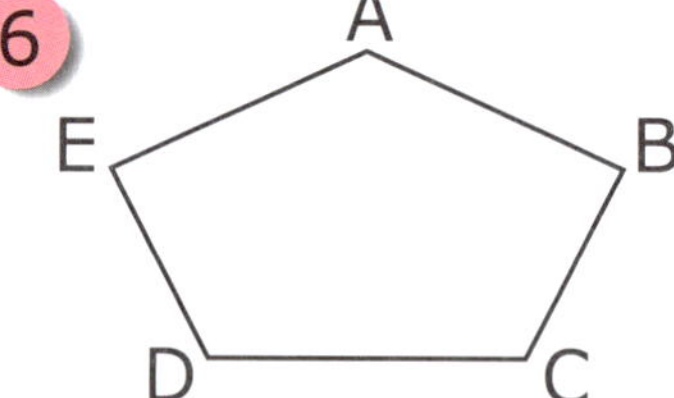

∠A = ____
∠B = 76°
∠C = 118°
∠D = 118°
∠E = 76°

Area of a rectangle = length × width, or simply $A = lw$.

Find the area of each room in square feet.

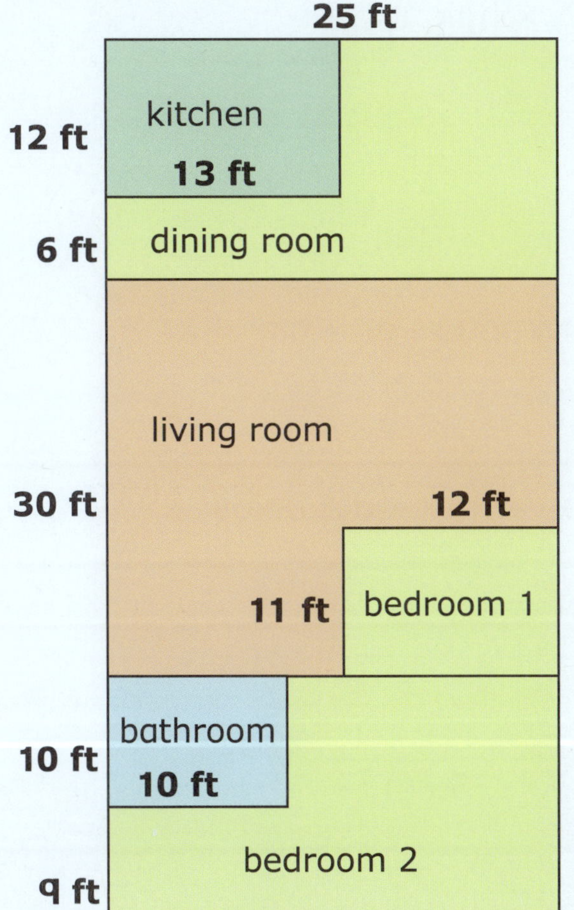

1. kitchen = ______
2. dining room = ______
3. bedroom 1 = ______
4. living room = ______
5. bathroom = ______
6. bedroom 2 = ______

7. Carpeting costs $4 per square foot. How much would it cost to carpet the living room? ______

8. Wood flooring costs $5 per square foot. How much would it cost to put a wood floor in the kitchen? ______

9. Would $500 be enough to carpet bedroom 1 if the carpet is $4 per square foot? ______

For a rectangular prism, volume (V) is the number of cubic units it contains and is found by multiplying the length (l), width (w), and height (h) together. The measurements must be in the same units.

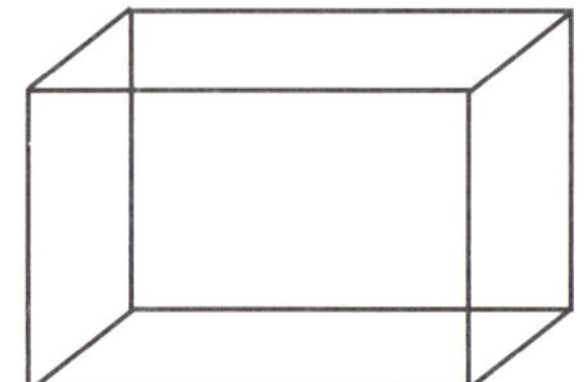

Volume = length × width × height

$V = l \times w \times h$

$V = lwh$

$V = 2 \times 2 \times 1$

V = 4 cubic centimeters or 4 cm^3

Find the volume and use the letters to solve the riddle below.

e

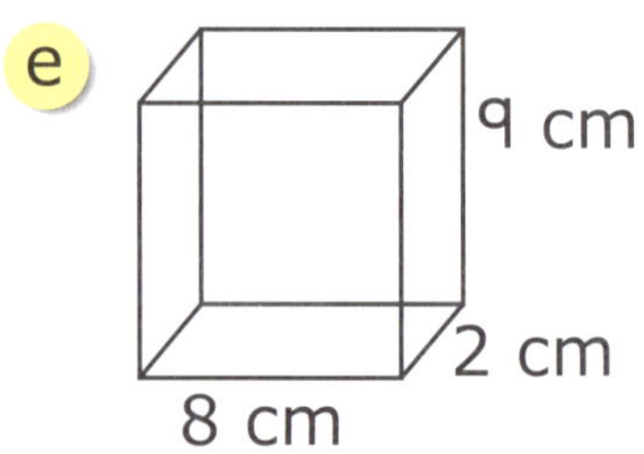

r

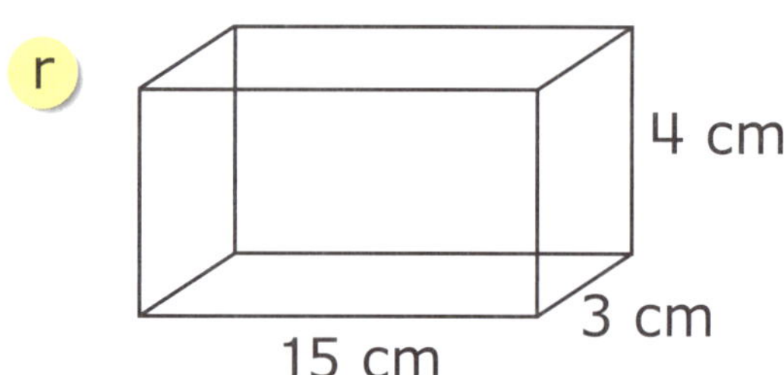

a

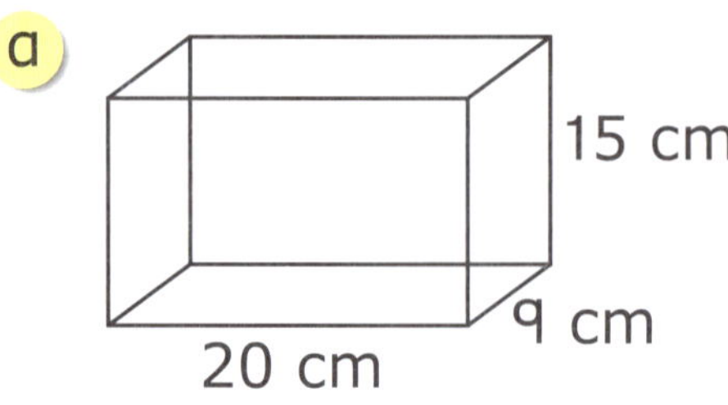

v

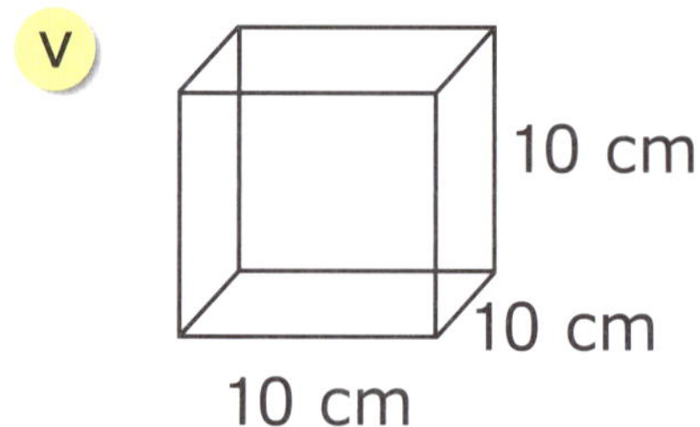

s

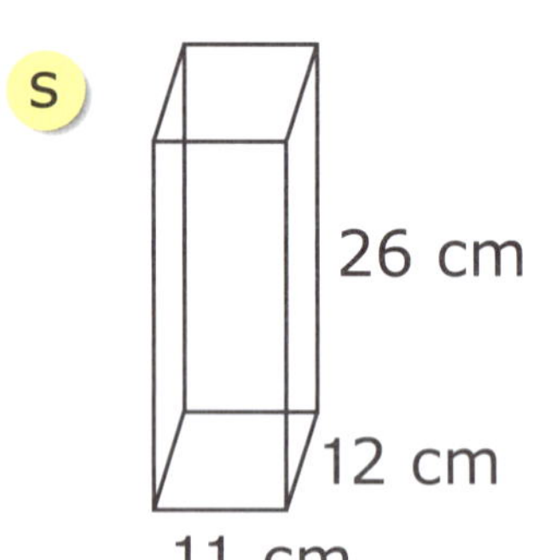

i

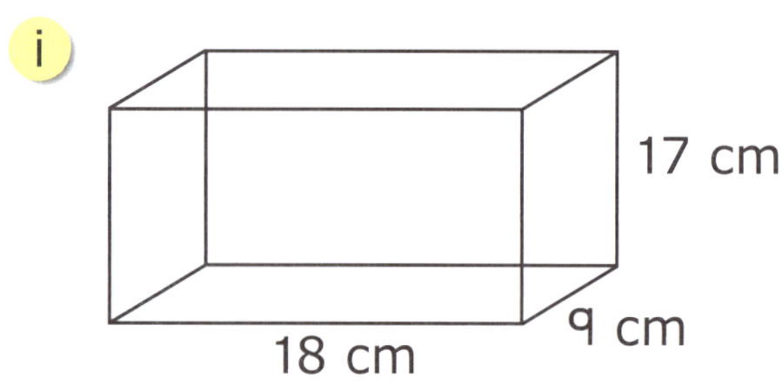

What has a big mouth but doesn't speak?

____	____	____	____	____	____
2,700 cm^3	180 cm^3	2,754 cm^3	1,000 cm^3	144 cm^3	180 cm^3

Complete each analogy.

1. 7 is to 49 **as** 8 is to ______.

2. 15% is to .15 **as** 6% is to ______.

3. $\frac{1}{2}$ is to .5 **as** $\frac{1}{4}$ is to ______.

4. 2^3 is to 8 **as** 4^3 is to ______.

5. 3 is to triangle **as** 6 is to ______.

6. cm^2 is to area **as** cm^3 is to ______.

7. 36 is to 6 **as** 81 is to ______.

8. 10 mm is to cm **as** 12 in. is to ______.

9. 124 is to 31 **as** 200 is to ______.

10. 81 & 27 is to 3 **as** 256 & 64 is to ______.

11. $\frac{51}{8}$ is to $6\frac{3}{8}$ **as** $\frac{31}{7}$ is to ______.

12. $\frac{20}{24}$ is to $\frac{5}{6}$ **as** $\frac{36}{40}$ is to ______.

Equations of the Form $n + a = b$

Below are the steps to follow when solving for an unknown quantity (n) when a number (a) has been added to it.

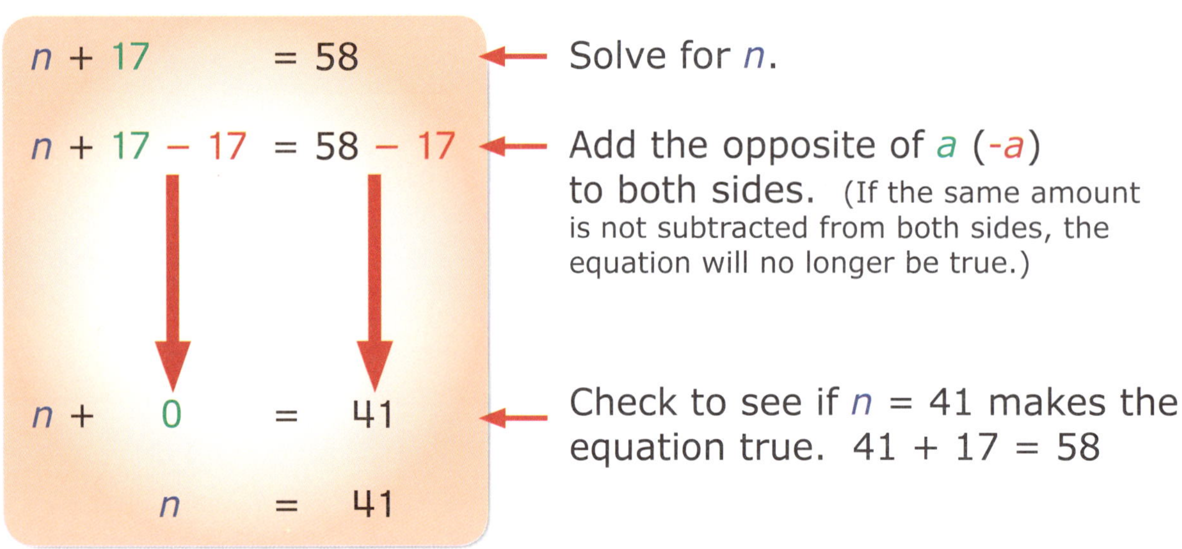

Use the steps above to solve the following equations for n.

1) $n + 51 = 94$

2) $n + 67 = 100$

3) $n + 38 = 135$

4) $n + 17 = 75$

5) $n + 1.4 = 5.6$

6) $n + 18.45 = 20$

7) How much more does Ana need with the $48 she has saved to buy a $55 game? Write an equation and solve.

Equations of the Form $n - a = b$

Below are the steps to follow when solving for an unknown quantity (n) when a number (a) has been subtracted from it.

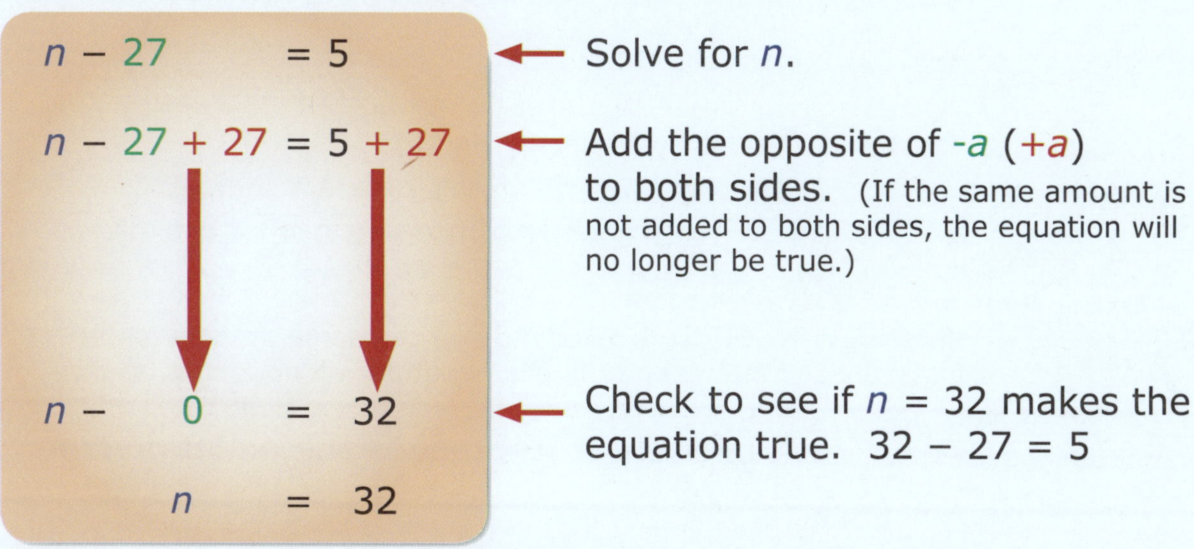

Use the steps above to solve the following equations for n.

1. $n - 14 = 20$
2. $n - 25 = 15$
3. $n - 18 = 57$
4. $n - 50 = 7$
5. $n - 1.8 = 2.4$
6. $n - 2.35 = 5$
7. How much will William need to be able to spend \$8 at the movies and still have \$15 left? Write an equation and solve.

Equations of the Form $a \times n = b$

Below are the steps to follow when solving for an unknown quantity (n) when a number (a) has been multiplied to it.

$3 \times n = 24$	← Solve for n.
$3n = 24$	← $3 \times n$ can be written as $3n$.
$\frac{3n}{3} = \frac{24}{3}$	← Undo $\times$ by 3 with the inverse operation of $\div$ by 3.
$\frac{\cancel{3}n}{\cancel{3}} = \frac{24}{3}$	← Divide each side by 3. (If the same amount is not divided into each side, the equation will no longer be true.)
$n = 8$	← Check to see if $n = 8$ makes the equation true. $3 \times 8 = 24$

Use the steps above to solve the following equations for n.

1. $5n = 40$

2. $9n = 72$

3. $3n = 102$

4. $8n = 648$

5. $20n = 200$

6. $2.4n = 48$

7. Reba paid $108 for 4 tickets. How much was one ticket? Write an equation and solve.

Equations of the Form $n \div a = b$

Below are the steps to follow when solving for an unknown quantity (n) when a number (a) has been divided into it.

$n \div 6 = 8$ ← Solve for n.

$\frac{n}{6} = 8$ ← $n \div 6$ can be written as $\frac{n}{6}$

$\frac{n}{6} \times 6 = 8 \times 6$ ← Undo ÷ by 6 with the inverse operation × by 6. (If the same amount is not multiplied to each side of the equation, the equation will no longer be true.)

$\frac{n}{\cancel{6}} \times \cancel{6} = 8 \times 6$

$n = 48$ ← Check to see if $n = 48$ makes the equation true. $48 \div 6 = 8$

Use the steps above to solve the following equations for n.

1. $\frac{n}{4} = 9$

2. $\frac{n}{7} = 10$

3. $\frac{n}{9} = 102$

4. $\frac{n}{3} = 59$

5. $\frac{n}{5} = 6.8$

6. $\frac{n}{1.4} = 21$

7. Maria and her two sisters were each given \$11.25 by their father. What was the total amount he gave them? Write an equation and solve.

Formulas

Notes
"lw" means "l" × "w"

Use 3.14 for π.

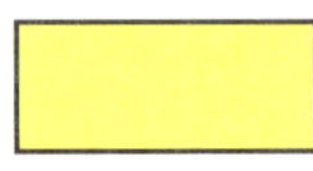

Area of a rectangle = length × width.
$A = lw$

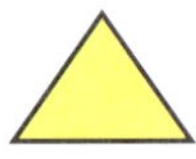

Area of a triangle = $\frac{1}{2}$ × base × height. $A = \frac{1}{2}bh$

Area of a circle = pi × radius × radius. $A = \pi r^2$

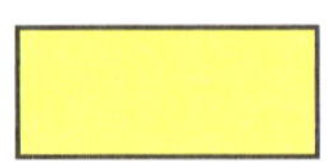

Perimeter of a rectangle = 2 × length + 2 × width.
$P = 2l + 2w$

Circumference of a circle = π × diameter. $C = \pi d$

Find the values with all units in feet; then cross out the correct answers below to find the two false answers.

1. area of a rectangle with $l = 40$ and $w = 25$ ______
2. area of a triangle with $b = 20$ and $h = 16$ ______
3. area of a circle with $r = 8$ ______
4. perimeter of a rectangle with $l = 12$ and $w = 9$ ______
5. circumference of a circle with $d = 32$ ______
6. area of rectangle with $l = 4.2$ and $w = 3$ ______

160 sq ft
42 ft
84 ft
12.6 sq ft
100.48 ft
1,000 sq ft
15.4 sq ft
200.96 sq ft

Write the letter of the closest match.

1. boiling point for Celsius ____
2. freezing point for Fahrenheit ____
3. area of a rectangle ____
4. area of a triangle ____
5. area of a circle ____
6. parallel ____
7. perpendicular ____
8. flip ____
9. slide ____
10. turn ____
11. 10 mm ____
12. 1 inch ____
13. radius ____
14. diameter ____
15. less than ____
16. greater than ____

a. <

b. $A = lw$

c. ———

d. (two crossing double-headed arrows)

e. $A = \frac{1}{2}bh$

f. (triangle turned)

g. 100°

h. (circle with radius)

i. (two parallel double-headed arrows)

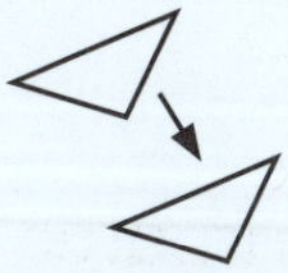

j. $A = \pi r^2$

k. (triangle slid)

l. ——————

m. (circle with diameter)

n. >

o. 32°

p. (triangle flipped over dotted line)

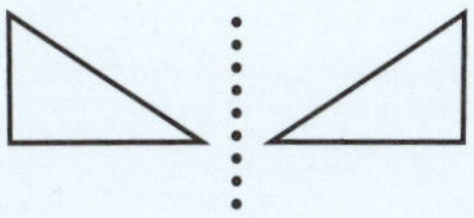

Solve each problem and write the answer in the puzzle.

1. 4,235 + 426 + 67 = ______

2. 8,023 − 145 = ______

3. 28 × 136 = ______

4. 26,976 ÷ 32 = ______

5. 4.3 + .1 + 30 = ______

6. 2.41 − .982 = ______

7. 6,400 × .125 = ______

8. 1024 ÷ .5 = ______

9. $\frac{1}{2}$ of 1,618 = ______

10. 33 ÷ $\frac{1}{3}$ = ______

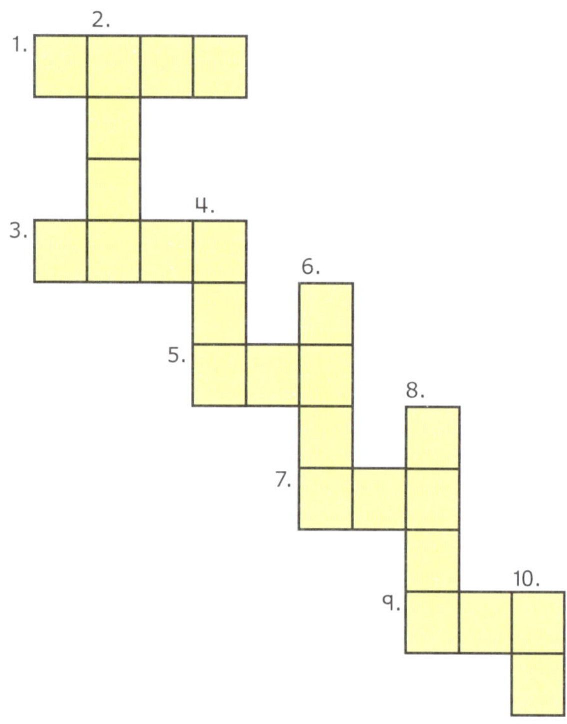

Answers

Page 1 — 1. fourteen; 2. hundred; 3. thousand; 4. million; 5. thousand; 6. hundred

Page 2

									7. 1		9. 6	
						5. 7	6. 3	0	7	3	0	
		1. 2		4. 1			3		4		2	
	2. 4	7	0	0	0	0	3		2		0	
		0		0			3		10. 5	0	0	5
		1		0			0		6		0	
3. 5	0	4	0	3	0		8. 3	2	1	0	4	

Page 3 — #4

Page 4 — 2. 7,500,000; 3. 2,016; 4. 897; 5. 1,500; 6. 60

Page 5 — 5,013; 5,200; 6,006; 8,088; 12,047; 17,100; 50,020; 100,059; 900,001; 1,005,000

Page 6 — 1. 352; 2. 294; 3. 251; 4. 718; 5. 728; 6. 532; 7. 940; 8. 627; 9. 777; 10. 956; 11. 133; 12. 78; 13. 400; 14. 583; 820

Page 7 — 1. 55 mph; 2. 35 mph; 3. 200 mph; 4. 132 students; 5. 2,878 miles

Page 8

1. 8	2. 8		3. 2	4. 4	5. 7		6. 1	7. 3	8. 8	9. 7
10. 7	5		11. 6	2	3	0		12. 5	8	8
13. 9	1	5	1		0		14. 9	1		4
	7		15. 3	16. 2	3		6		17. 1	
18. 8		19. 7		20. 5	6	3		21. 8	5	22. 2
23. 9	0	8		1			24. 8	1	5	3

Page 9 — 1. 561; 2. 364; 3. 867; 4. 96; 5. 29; 6. 1,460; 7. 974; 8. 402; 9. 639; 10. 4,629; 11. 18,947; 12. 10,081; 13. 924; 14. 1,186; 1,236

Page 10 — a. 782; h. 116; w. 173; s. 547; i. 4,339; n. 4,299; o. 3,751; l. 709; g. 5,009; u. 862; t. 768; p. 49,198; hogspital

Page 11 — 1. 1903; 2. 1924; 3. 1946; 4. 1997; 5. 1,250 − 605 = 645 feet

Page 12

1.

14	0	10
4	8	12
6	16	2

or

6	16	2
4	8	12
14	0	10

; 2.

10	25	4
7	13	9
22	1	16

or

16	19	4
1	13	25
22	7	10

Page 13

1. Sides: $\overline{AB}$, $\overline{BC}$, $\overline{AC}$; Vertices: A, B, C
2. Sides: $\overline{DE}$, $\overline{EF}$, $\overline{FG}$, $\overline{DG}$; Vertices: D, E, F, G
3. Sides: $\overline{HI}$, $\overline{IJ}$, $\overline{JK}$, $\overline{KL}$, $\overline{HL}$; Vertices: H, I, J, K, L
4. Answers will vary. Example:

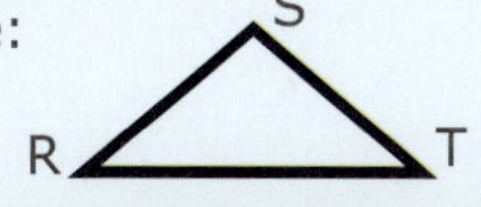

Page 14 1. isosceles; 2. equilateral; 3. scalene; 4. ; 5. 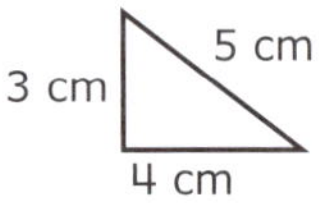

Page 15 apple

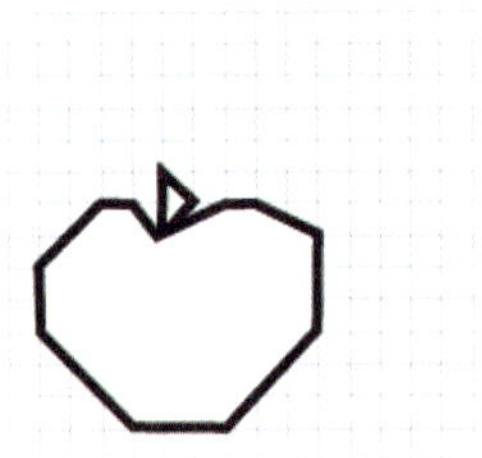

Page 16

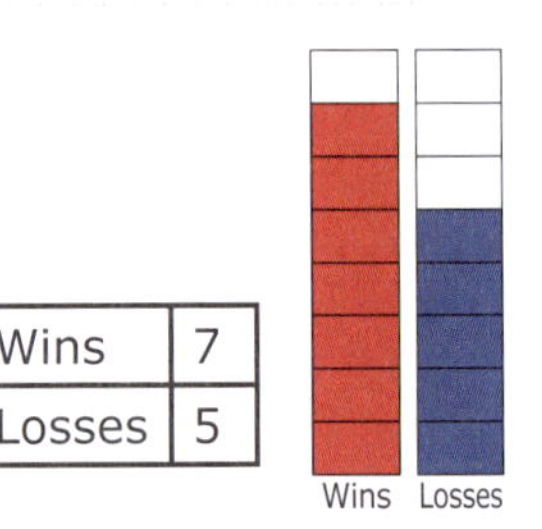

Wins	7
Losses	5

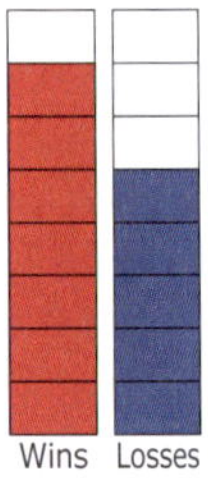

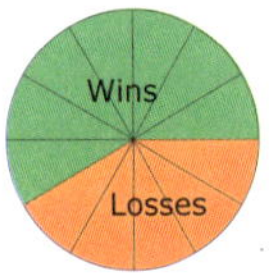

Page 17

×	1	2	3	4	5	6	7	8	9
1	1	2	3	4	5	6	7	8	9
2	2	4	6	8	10	12	14	16	18
3	3	6	9	12	15	18	21	24	27
4	4	8	12	16	20	24	28	32	36
5	5	10	15	20	25	30	35	40	45
6	6	12	18	24	30	36	42	48	54
7	7	14	21	28	35	42	49	56	63
8	8	16	24	32	40	48	56	64	72
9	9	18	27	36	45	54	63	72	81

Page 18 1. 144; 2. 747; 3. 370; 4. 552;
5. 1,058; 6. 2,844; 7. 3,060; 8. 8,265; 474; 3,458

Page 19 h. 68,694; c. 97,578; a. 46,698; o. 63,612;
r. 259,168; n. 86,528; an anchor

Page 20

1. 8	2. 8		3. 4	4. 7	5. 6		6. 4	7. 4	8. 1	9. 6
10. 8	1		11. 2	1	4	6		12. 5	0	4
13. 4	3	0	7		0		14. 6	3		8
	0		15. 6	16. 2	5		0		17. 1	
18. 2		19. 8		20. 5	3	2		21. 8	5	22. 8
23. 1	4	4		2			24. 9	1	0	2

Page 21 1. 1,440 minutes; 2. 840 breaths; 3. 20,160 breaths; 4. Answers will vary.
5. number of breaths per minute × 60; 6. number of breaths per hour × 24

Page 23
1. Zero Property for Multiplication; 2. Commutative Property of Multiplication;
3. Associative Property of Addition; 4. Distributive Property;
5. Identity Property for Multiplication; 6. Associative Property of Multiplication;
7. Zero Property for Multiplication; 8. Identity Property for Addition;
9. Commutative Property of Addition; 10. Distributive Property;
11. Commutative Property of Addition, Associative Property of Addition, Distributive Property
12. Commutative Property of Multiplication, Zero Property for Multiplication

Page 24
1. c; 2. b

Page 25
1. $\overrightarrow{YX}$ and $\overrightarrow{YZ}$; vertex Y; ∠XYZ, ∠Y, ∠ZYX
2. $\overrightarrow{RS}$ and $\overrightarrow{RT}$; vertex R; ∠SRT, ∠R, ∠TRS
3., 4., 5.

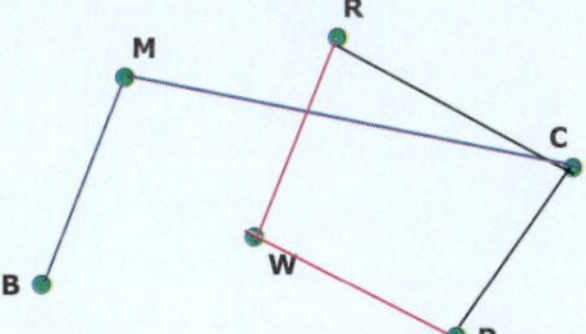

Page 26
1. 44° acute; 2. 111° obtuse; 3. 90° right; 4. 62° acute
5. 134° obtuse; 6. 42° acute; 7. 25° acute; 8. 90° right

Page 27
2. 145°; 3. 90°; 4. 60°; 5. 35°; 6. 30°; 7. 25°; 8. 70°;
9. house; 10. 100°, 50°, 30°

Page 28
1. 256, 1024; 2. 52, 40; 3. 64, 77; 4. 693, 812; 5. 604, 505;
6. 9, $4\frac{1}{2}$; 7. 32, 31; 8. 256, 128; 9. $3\frac{1}{4}$, 4; 10.

Page 29
1. 26; 2. 42; 3. 65; 4. 19; 5. 37; 6. 66;
7. 46; 8. 28; 9. 17; 10. 18; 11. 67; 12. 69; 25; 38

Page 30
u. 128; t. 564; n. 859; b. 502; l. 834; a. 137; h. 415; m. 508; thumbnail

Page 31

1. 8	2. 8	■	3. 1	4. 2	5. 4	■	6. 1	7. 6	8. 3	9. 5
10. 9	4	■	11. 2	3	1	6	■	12. 6	7	8
13. 1	5	5	5	■	5	■	14. 3	6	■	6
■	6	■	15. 2	16. 1	7	■	7	■	17. 1	■
18. 5	■	19. 7	■	20. 4	3	8	■	21. 9	3	22. 1
23. 8	3	4	■	6	■	■	24. 1	0	2	6

Page 32
1. 200; 2. 240; 3. 2,400; 4. 20,000; 5. 2,000; 6. 4,000;
7. 40; 8. 400; 9. 400,000; 10. 10,000; 11. 24,000; 12. 1,000
1,100; 100,000; 200,000; 240,000

Page 33
e. 3,500; t. 1,200; n. 460; p. 450; g. 1,260; c. 6,300; w. 2,800;
r. 63,000; l. 62,000; o. 2,520; a. 28,000; s. 7,200; clogs

Page 34 1. 3; 2. 5; 3. 9; 4. 4; 5. 7; 6. 4; 7. 6; 8. 7; 9. 6; 10. 4; 11. 9; 12. 3; 13. 48 doughnuts = 4 dozen (48 ÷ 12 = 4)

Page 35 1. 32; 2. 45; 3. 64; 4. 83; 5. 97; 6. 57; 7. 96; 8. 87

Page 36 1. 108 ÷ 9 = $12; 2. 1,040 ÷ 20= 52 miles; 3. 39 ÷ 13 = $3; 4. 1,183 ÷ 7= 169 blocks; 5. 200 ÷ 2 = 100 words; 6. Answers will vary.

Page 37 1. b; 2. c

Page 38

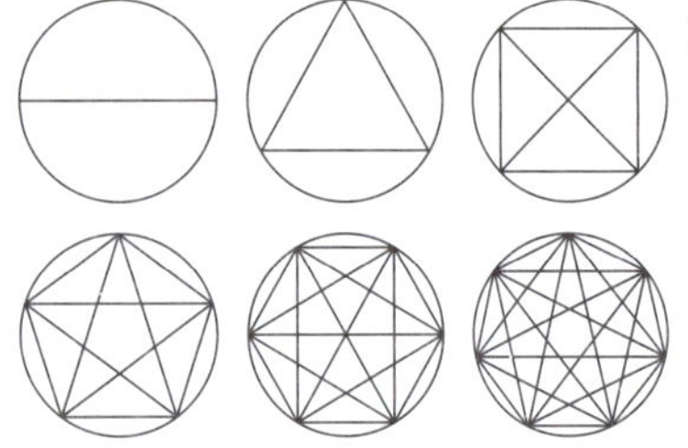

;

Points on a Circle	Number of Possible Chords
2	1
3	3
4	6
5	10
6	15
7	21
8	28

;

For every additional point, there are the number of points minus one additional possible chords. The number of possible chords for any given number of points is the sum of all lower whole numbers.

Page 39 1. 1, 2, 4, 8, 16; 2. 1, 2, 3, 4, 6, 8, 12, 24; 3. 1, 2, 4, 7, 14, 28;
4. 1, 5, 7, 35; 5. 1, 2, 3, 6, 9, 18, 27, 54;
6. factors for 8: 1, 2, 4, 8; factors for 12: 1, 2, 3, 4, 6, 12; GCF is 4;
7. factors for 20: 1, 2, 4, 5, 10, 20; factors for 25; 1, 5, 25; GCF is 5;
8. factors for 40: 1, 2, 4, 5, 8, 10, 20, 40;
factors for 60: 1, 2, 3, 4, 5, 6, 10, 12, 15, 20, 30, 60; GCF is 20

Page 40 1. 8; 2. $\frac{4}{4}$, 12; 3. $\frac{8}{8}$, 40; 4. $\frac{7}{7}$, 35; 5. $\frac{6}{6}$, 6; 6. $\frac{9}{9}$, 36; 7. $\frac{9}{9}$, 18;
8. $\frac{9}{9}$, 27; 9. $\frac{3}{3}$, 15; 10. $\frac{7}{7}$, 14; 11. $\frac{3}{3}$, 3; 12. $\frac{10}{10}$, 90

Page 41 f. $\frac{1}{2}$; t. $\frac{3}{3}$, $\frac{2}{3}$; c. $\frac{2}{2}$, $\frac{1}{4}$; m. $\frac{2}{2}$, $\frac{5}{6}$; a. $\frac{5}{5}$, $\frac{4}{5}$; n. $\frac{2}{2}$, $\frac{1}{8}$;
l. $\frac{5}{5}$, $\frac{2}{9}$; r. $\frac{3}{3}$, $\frac{3}{4}$; e. $\frac{2}{2}$, $\frac{1}{5}$; p. $\frac{4}{4}$, $\frac{5}{6}$; u. $\frac{4}{4}$, $\frac{5}{8}$; i. $\frac{7}{7}$, $\frac{2}{7}$; calfeteria

Page 42 orange= $\frac{1}{4}$; blue = $\frac{1}{12}$; red = $\frac{1}{2}$

green = $\frac{1}{12}$; orange = $\frac{1}{8}$; black = $\frac{5}{24}$; blue = $\frac{1}{4}$; red = $\frac{1}{3}$

Coloring may vary. Example:

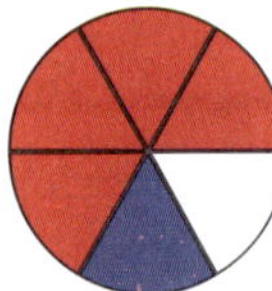

Page 43 green = $\frac{1}{8}$; orange = $\frac{1}{4}$; blue = $\frac{1}{2}$; red = $\frac{1}{8}$

green = $\frac{1}{8}$; orange = $\frac{1}{4}$; blue = $\frac{3}{8}$; red = $\frac{1}{4}$

Coloring may vary. Example:

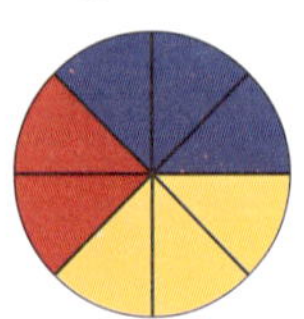

Page 44 — 2. ; 3. ; 4. ;

5. ; 6. ; 7. Inches 1 2

Page 45 — 1. red: $1\frac{1}{4}$ in.; blue: 2 in.; green: $2\frac{1}{2}$ in.; orange: $2\frac{7}{8}$ in.

2. red: $\frac{7}{8}$ in.; blue: $4\frac{3}{4}$ in.; green: $1\frac{5}{8}$ in.; orange: $5\frac{1}{4}$ in.; brown: $3\frac{3}{8}$ in.

Page 46 — 1. r. $\frac{1}{2}$; o. $\frac{7}{8}$; w. $1\frac{1}{4}$; s. $1\frac{1}{2}$; a. $2\frac{3}{4}$; b. $3\frac{3}{8}$; t. $3\frac{3}{4}$; i. $4\frac{1}{4}$; e. $4\frac{5}{8}$; l. $4\frac{7}{8}$; towel

2. Length = $1\frac{1}{2}$ in.; Width = $\frac{5}{8}$ in.

Page 47 — 1. c; 2. b; 3. a

Page 48 — 1. red: 2.7 cm; blue: 12.1 cm; green: 5.5 cm; orange: 8.4 cm

2. red: 3.4 cm; blue: 7.3 cm; green: 11.6 cm; orange: 12.6 cm

Page 49 — 1. t. 1; c. 2.1; b. 3.6; n. 4.6; o. 5.5; a. 7; i. 7.8; r. 8.3; m. 9; e. 9.4; ocean

2. Height = 5.2 cm, Width = 2.7 cm

Page 50 — 2. 14 cm; 3. 16 cm; 4. 24 cm; 5. 72 in.; 6. Answers will vary.

Examples (14cm): , ; (12 cm): , ,

Page 51 — 1. 8 sq cm; 2. 11 sq cm; 3. 12 sq cm; 4. 594 sq ft; 5. 1,620 sq ft;

6. 1 by 24, 2 by 12, 3 by 8, 4 by 6 (any 3 of the 4)

Page 52

E	L	G	N	A	I	R	T	R	O	H	A	S
O	N	T	A	G	R	O	A	B	S	E	T	U
A	N	T	H	E	X	A	G	O	N	P	E	D
R	O	D	P	N	O	G	A	T	N	T	P	O
R	G	N	O	G	A	T	C	O	R	A	C	T
T	A	P	O	S	R	A	G	O	N	G	O	A
O	N	P	E	N	T	A	G	O	N	O	G	O
T	O	T	R	I	C	O	N	A	W	N	T	A
N	N	R	T	E	O	N	T	S	R	D	E	C
Q	U	A	D	R	I	L	A	T	E	R	A	L

Page 53 — 1. \$20, \$5, \$25, \$12.50; 2. \$20 more; 3. \$7.50 less; 4. \$62.50 total;

5. ; 6.

Page 54 — 1. ; 2. 135 mph; 3. 182 mph

F5
F4
F3
F2
F1
F0
1st 2nd 3rd 4th 5th 6th 7th

Page 55

Amount
$8.58
$12.02
$9.50
$15.91
$8.20
$11.61
$6.03
$8.58
$12.26
$8.92

; sun scream

Page 56 2. $5.88; 3. $5.94; 4. $13.29; 5. $8.16; 6. 2 drinks, hotdog; 7. burger, cheeseburger, hotdog; 8. hotdog, 2 fries, drink

Page 57

Change	Match
$8.61	D
$7.75	J
$.91	B
$40.99	K
$19.11	C
$5.21	F
$.95	E
$19.99	G
$.16	H
$6.20	I
$8.44	A
$32.95	L

Page 58 1. Empty the coin in the second glass into the fifth glass. 2. 6 chickens and 4 goats; 3. 8 + 8 + 8 + 88 + 888 = 1,000

Page 59 1. 111,111; 2. 222,222; 3. 333,333; 4. 444,444; 5. 555,555; 6. 666,666; The products contain repeat digits 1-6, which are the numbers on a die.

Page 60 1. 1,257; 2. 958; 3. 4,173; 4. 294; 5. 6,928; 6. 22,131; 7. 1,750; 8. 77,184; 9. 46,893; 10. 289; 11. 15; 12. 62; 437; 7,653

Page 61 1. 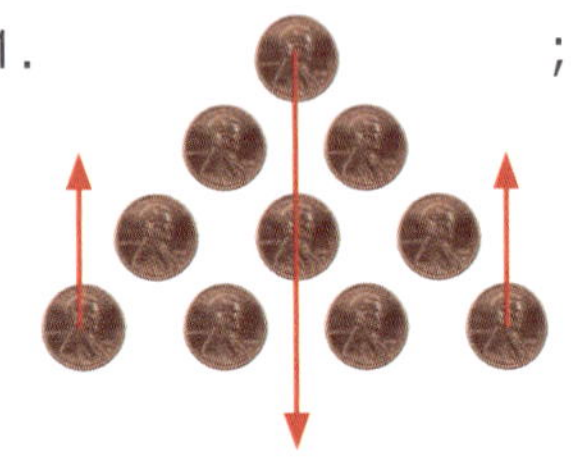 ; 2. 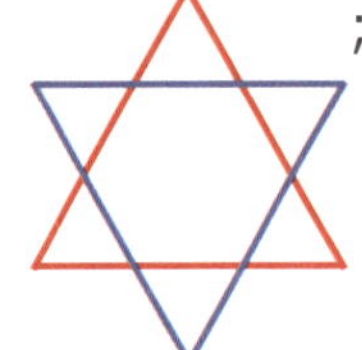 ; 3. 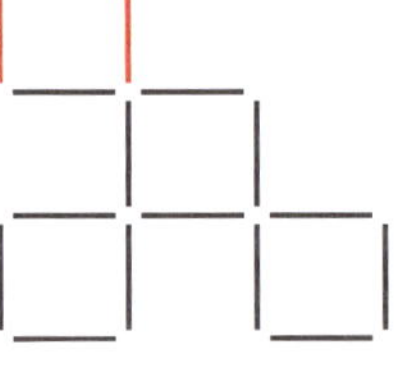

Page 62 1. 47; 2. 40; 3. 173; 4. 105; 5. 4; 6. 33; 52; 154
7. 20 − 10 − (10 − 5) = 5; 8. 24 ÷ (3 + 2 ÷ 2) × 2 = 12

Page 63 2. (4 + 8) ÷ (8 − 4) = 3; 3. 20 − 12 ÷ (2 × 3) = 18;
4. 24 ÷ (4 + 2 × 2) = 3; 5. 12 − (6 − 4) − 2 = 8;
6. 4 + (8 − 4 + 2) × 2 = 16; 7. (24 − 12) ÷ (2 + 8 ÷ 2) = 2;
8. 4 × (2 + 2) × 2 ÷ 2 = 16; 9. 100 − (48 + 24) − (12 + 6) = 10

Page 64 1.

Celsius	Fahrenheit
0° C	32° F
5° C	41° F
10° C	50° F
15° C	59° F
20° C	68° F
25° C	77° F
30° C	86° F
35° C	95° F
40° C	104° F
45° C	113° F
50° C	122° F

Celsius	Fahrenheit
55° C	131° F
60° C	140° F
65° C	149° F
70° C	158° F
75° C	167° F
80° C	176° F
85° C	185° F
90° C	194° F
95° C	203° F
100° C	212° F

; 2. 122°F = 50°C

Page 65 2. 15 sec., 14 sec., 14 sec.; 3. 59 mm, 57 mm, 57 mm; Answers will vary.

Page 66 1. 74°; 2. 78°; 3. 76°; 4. 73°; 5. 80°; 6. 81°; 7. 80°

Page 67 1.

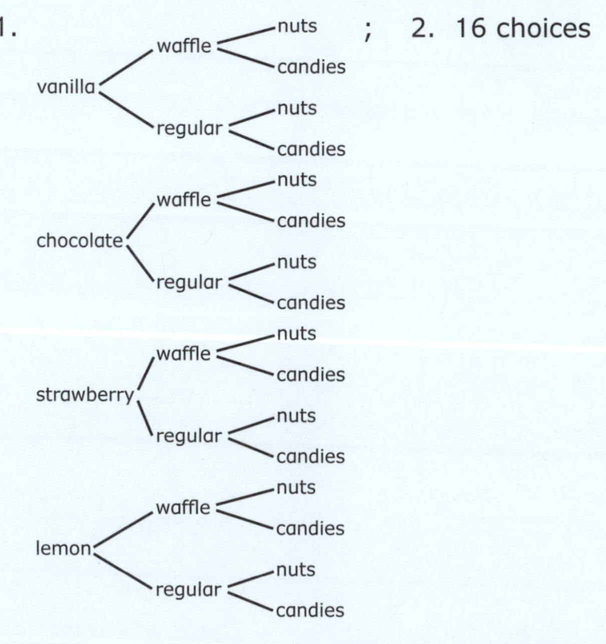

; 2. 16 choices

Page 68 1. 180; 2. 1,400; 3. 44; 4. 2,880; 5. 1,020; 6. 2,400; 7. 1,512; 8. 720; 9. 650; 10. 4,968; 11. 1,000,000; 12. same number of zeroes; 92; 1,640

Page 69 1. 120; 2. 360; 3. 168; 4. 95; 5. 50; 6. 40; 7. 2,500; 8. 144; 9. 80; 10. 168; 11. 1,120; 12. 160; 13. 980; 14. 6,720

Page 70 1. 1,246; 8,888; 2. 111; 216; 30,111; 3. 924; 1,000; 88; 132; 4. 75; 810; 5. 120; 96; 6. 800; 5,040; 7. 99; 711; 10,800; 8. 20,170; 90; 3,100

Page 71 2. $2 \times 2 \times 2 \times 3$; 3. $3 \times 3 \times 3$; 4. $2 \times 3 \times 5$; 5. $2 \times 3 \times 3$; 6. $3 \times 3 \times 5$; 7. $3 \times 3 \times 7$; 8. $2 \times 2 \times 7$; 9. $2 \times 2 \times 2 \times 5$; 10. $2 \times 2 \times 3 \times 3$; 11. $2 \times 2 \times 2 \times 2$; 12. $2 \times 3 \times 3 \times 5$; 13. $3 \times 3 \times 3 \times 3$; 14. $2 \times 2 \times 3 \times 7$; 15. $2 \times 2 \times 5 \times 5$; 16. $2 \times 2 \times 3 \times 3 \times 5$

Page 72

5 squared	5^2	25	s
3 cubed	3^3	27	e
7 squared	7^2	49	o
2 to the fourth power	2^4	16	m
9 squared	9^2	81	w
4 cubed	4^3	64	a
10 squared	10^2	100	b
5 cubed	5^3	125	t
6 to the fourth power	6^4	1,296	i
8 squared	8^2	64	a
2 to the fifth power	2^5	32	p
11 cubed	11^3	1,331	r

; tap water

Page 73

1. 8	2. 1		3. 1	4. 2	5		5. 6	6. 4		7. 1
8. 3	6		9. 6	4				10. 2	1	6
11. 2	4	3			12. 9		13. 4	9		9
	0		14. 1	15. 2	1		9		16. 8	
17. 6		18. 8		19. 1	0	0		20. 1	4	4
21. 4	0	0		9			22. 2	5	6	

Page 74

1.

Length (*l*)	Width (*w*)	Area (*A*)
20 cm	30 cm	600 sq cm
14 in.	15 in.	210 sq in.
9 m	114 m	1,026 sq m
17 ft	20 ft	340 sq ft
25 mm	9 mm	225 sq mm
124 in.	65 in.	8,060 sq in.
15 in.	1 ft	180 sq in.
6 ft	25 in.	1,800 sq in.

; 2. 30 sq cm;
3. $l = 41$; $w = 2$
or $l = 2$; $w = 41$
or $l = 82$; $w = 1$

Page 75

1.

Base (*b*)	Height (*h*)	Area (*A*)
45 cm	6 cm	270 sq cm
12 in.	12 in.	144 sq in.
8 m	589 m	4,712 sq m
19 ft	30 ft	570 sq ft
107 mm	39 mm	4,173 sq mm
10 in.	90 in.	900 sq in.
9 in.	2 ft	216 sq in.
4 ft	20 in.	960 sq in.

; 2. Answers will vary.
Examples:
$b = 17$ cm; $h = 5$ cm
$b = 1$ cm; $h = 85$ cm

Page 76

1. 120 square cm; 2. 1,200 square cm; 3. 399 square cm;
4. 154 square cm; 5. 600 square cm; 6. 495 square cm;
7. height = 16 ft

Page 77

1.

Length (*l*)	Width (*w*)	Perimeter (*P*)
20 cm	25 cm	90 cm
15 in.	15 in.	60 in.
9 m	145 m	308 m
18 ft	30 ft	96 ft
206 mm	34 mm	480 mm
30 in.	50 in.	160 in.
10 in.	1 ft	44 in.
3 ft	11 in.	94 in.

; 2. Perimeter = 44 ft;
Answers will vary.

Page 78 1. true; 2. true; 3. false; 4. true;

P	O	R	E	F	O	L	S	Q	P	E	C	T	R	S
R	L	A	R	E	T	A	L	I	R	D	A	U	Q	E
R	E	C	T	R	A	P	E	Z	O	I	D	U	P	A
R	T	P	A	O	S	Q	U	A	R	W	A	T	R	E
P	A	R	A	L	L	E	L	O	G	R	A	M	S	Q
E	R	E	L	G	N	A	T	C	E	R	R	E	C	T

Page 79 Answers will vary. Examples:

2. 3.

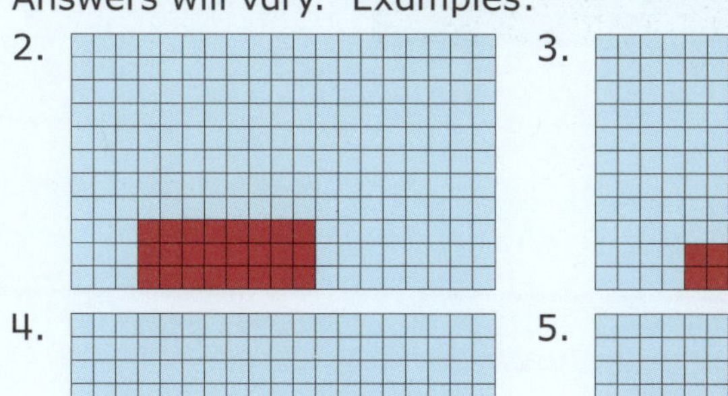

4. 5.

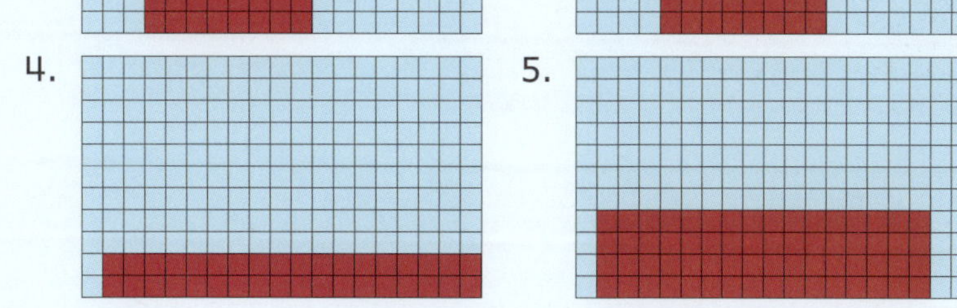

Page 80 1. triangle; 2. prime; 3. lowest; 4. area; 5. numerator; 6. sum; 7. vertex; 8. quadrilateral; 9. product; 10. perimeter; 11. polygon; 12. quotient; great student

Page 81 19 + 23 + 29 + 29 = 100

Page 82 Answers will vary. Examples:

1. ; 2. ; 3.

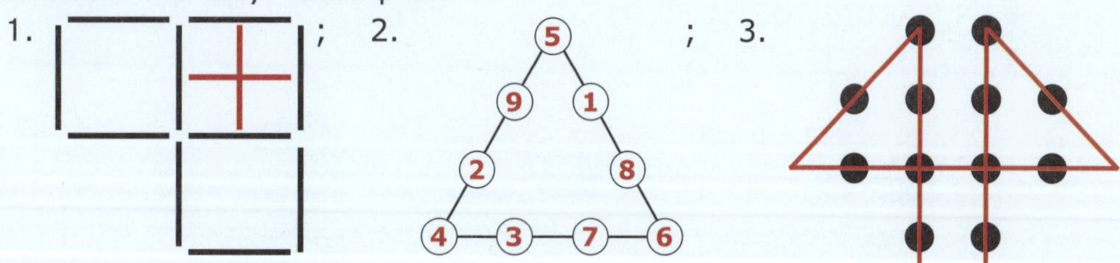

Page 83 1. 10; 2. 50; 3. 56 4. 6

5. Answers will vary. Example: Count the number of pieces of cereal your spoon holds and multiply it by an estimate of the number of spoonfuls your bowl contains.
6. Answers will vary. Example: Estimate the number of left-handed students in a school by counting one classroom and multiplying by the number of classrooms.

Pages 84-85 1. 20; 2. 300; 3. 3,000; 4. 60; 5. 600; 6. 2,000; 7. 900; 8. 1,000; 9. 0; 10. 100; 11. 560; 12. 2,000; 13. 660; 14. 16,000; 15. 2,000; to a lunch counter

Page 86 1. 130; 2. 50; 3. 400; 4. 120; 5. 20; 6. 900; 7. 290; 8. 80; 9. 600; 10. 10,000; 11. 1,500; 12. 4,900; 13. yes; 150; 5,300

Page 87 1. Main Field; 2. $4.40; 3. $1.60; 4. ($25.70 ÷ 5) = $5.14;
5. Answers will vary. Examples: Cost of hot dog and bun varies, price fans willing to pay is different, profit concerns, wages, etc.

Page 88

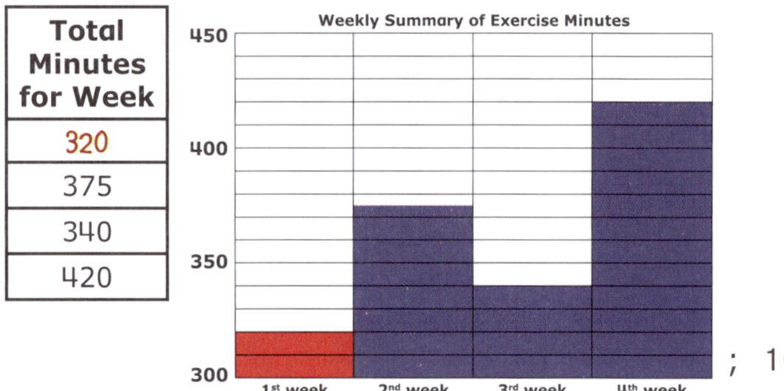

; 100 minutes

Page 89 1.

Stems	Leaves
7	5 8
8	3 8 9
9	2 2

; 2.

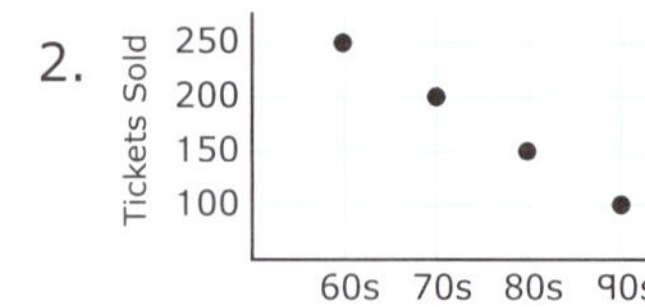

Ticket sales decrease as the temperature increases.;

3. 92 – 75 = 17

Page 90

	11:30	11:45	12:00	12:15	12:30
Grade	4th	1st	2nd	5th	3rd

Page 91 1. $64; 2. $100; 3. $198; 4. $31; 5. $80; 6. $25; 7. $154; 8. $217;
9. $248; 10. $20; 11. $235; 12. $129; swallow the leader

Page 92 1. 30°; 2. 60°; 3. 45°; 4. 59°; 5. 61°; 6. 22°

Page 93 1. 44° + 74° + 62° = 180°; 2. 90° + 32° + 58° = 180°; 3. No, this is impossible.

Page 94 1. 9,814,072,356; 2. 0, 1, 2, 3, 4, 5, 6, 7, 8, 9; 3. All digits 0-9 are in the product.

Page 95

1. 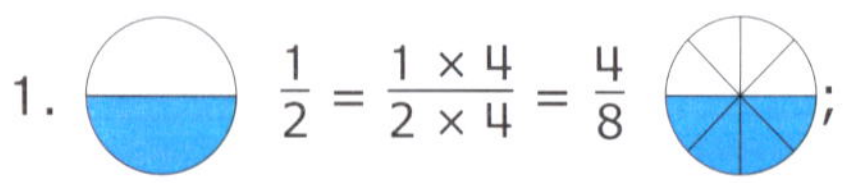 $\frac{1}{2} = \frac{1 \times 4}{2 \times 4} = \frac{4}{8}$;

2. 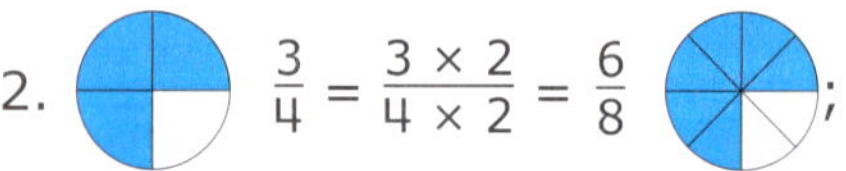 $\frac{3}{4} = \frac{3 \times 2}{4 \times 2} = \frac{6}{8}$;

3.  $\frac{1}{6} = \frac{1 \times 2}{6 \times 2} = \frac{2}{12}$;

4. 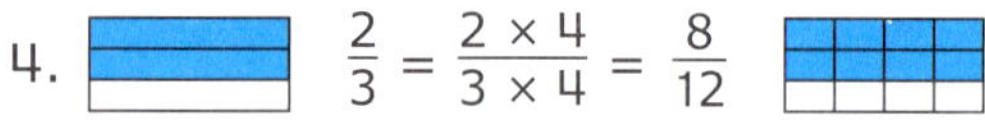 $\frac{2}{3} = \frac{2 \times 4}{3 \times 4} = \frac{8}{12}$;

5.  $\frac{3}{5} = \frac{3 \times 2}{5 \times 2} = \frac{6}{10}$ 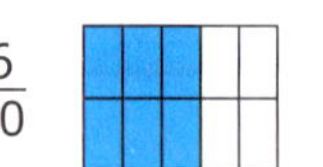

Page 96 2. $\frac{4}{6}$; 3. $\frac{6}{12}$; 4. $\frac{15}{18}$; 5. $\frac{2}{8}$; 6. $\frac{10}{25}$; 7. $\frac{6}{18}$; 8. $\frac{4}{24}$; 9. $\frac{3}{27}$;
10. $\frac{21}{24}$; 11. $\frac{2}{20}$; 12. $\frac{12}{80}$; 13. $\frac{21}{54}$; 14. $\frac{16}{36}$; 15. $\frac{16}{20}$; 16. $\frac{22}{24}$; $\frac{5}{8}$; $\frac{14}{24}$

Page 97 1. 6, 12; 2. 6, 9, 18; 3. 3, 4, 6, 8, 12, 24; 4. 1, 3, 17, 51;
5. 1, 2, 4, 7, 8, 14, 28, 56;

43	21	101	57	17
20	11	45	1	99
56	72	31	81	29
59	88	91	97	42

Page 98 1. $\frac{6}{8} = \frac{6 \div 2}{8 \div 2} = \frac{3}{4}$; 2. $\frac{2}{8} = \frac{2 \div 2}{8 \div 2} = \frac{1}{4}$; 3. $\frac{8}{12} = \frac{8 \div 4}{12 \div 4} = \frac{2}{3}$

Page 99 r. $\frac{1}{7}$; a. $\frac{5}{8}$; s. $\frac{3}{4}$; o. $\frac{5}{6}$; w. $\frac{1}{3}$; t. $\frac{1}{9}$; u. $\frac{3}{5}$; e. $\frac{4}{9}$;
x. $\frac{8}{9}$; g. $\frac{9}{16}$; t. $\frac{3}{7}$; ewe are out

Page 100 1. $\frac{1}{6}$; 2. $\frac{6}{5}$

Page 101 1. $\frac{2}{5}$; 2. 2; 3. $\frac{1}{6}$; 4. $\frac{5}{4}$; 5. 6; 6. $\frac{-1}{6}$; 7. 1; 8. 0; 9. $\frac{2}{3}$

Page 102 1. 3; 2. 4

Page 103 1. Celsius; 2. mode; 3. degrees; 4. ordered pair; 5. inch; 6. mean
7. range; 8. slope; 9. median; 10. Fahrenheit; 11. millimeter

Page 104

5	10	3
4	6	8
9	2	7

8	15	10
13	11	9
12	7	14

20	13	18
15	17	19
16	21	14

22	29	24
27	25	23
26	21	28

Page 105 1. 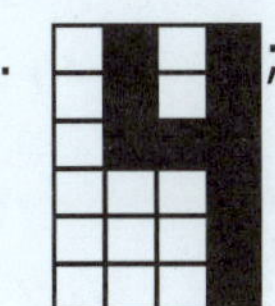; 2. 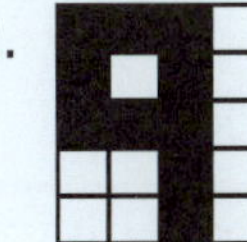

Pages 106-107 a. $1\frac{2}{5}$; b. $1\frac{2}{3}$; c. $2\frac{1}{4}$; d. $3\frac{1}{3}$; e. $4\frac{1}{2}$; f. $2\frac{1}{8}$; g. $3\frac{1}{6}$; h. $4\frac{1}{5}$;
i. $2\frac{3}{4}$; j. $1\frac{1}{10}$; k. 4; l. $3\frac{1}{2}$; m. $3\frac{2}{7}$; n. $1\frac{3}{5}$; o. $6\frac{2}{3}$; p. $1\frac{1}{9}$;
q. $2\frac{4}{5}$; r. $8\frac{1}{8}$; s. $3\frac{3}{4}$; t. $3\frac{3}{7}$; u. 10; y. $2\frac{1}{2}$; day scare centers

Page 108 1. $\frac{2}{3}$, g; 2. $\frac{5}{6}$, d; 3. $1\frac{1}{8}$, a; 4. $1\frac{1}{4}$, h; 5. $1\frac{1}{2}$, b; 6. 1, f; 7. $\frac{1}{2}$, c; 8. 2 cups, e

Page 109 25 pairs of 102, 25 × 102 = 2,550

Pages 110-111 r. $3\frac{4}{5}$; m. $2\frac{2}{3}$; a. $5\frac{1}{3}$; w. $4\frac{3}{5}$; e. $5\frac{3}{4}$; s. 6; o. $2\frac{1}{3}$; t. $3\frac{2}{5}$;
h. $5\frac{1}{2}$; c. $5\frac{2}{3}$; x. $4\frac{1}{7}$; u. $3\frac{1}{2}$; b. $3\frac{3}{4}$ ft; watch me

Page 112 Mystery number is 60.

Page 113

1. multiples of 6: 6, 12, 18, ...; multiples of 9: 9, 18, ...; LCM 18
2. multiples of 4: 4, 8, 12, ...; multiples of 6: 6, 12, ...; LCM 12
3. multiples of 15: 15, 30, ...; multiples of 10: 10, 20, 30, ...; LCM 30
4. multiples of 6: 6, 12, 18, 24, ...; multiples of 8: 8, 16, 24, ...; LCM 24
5. multiples of 3: 3, 6, 9, 12, 15, 18, 21, ...; multiples of 7: 7, 14, 21, ...; LCM 21
6. multiples of 9: 9, 18, 27, 36, ...; multiples of 12: 12, 24, 36, ...; multiples of 4: 4, 8, 12, 16, 20, 24, 28, 32, 36, ...; LCD 36
7. LCD 24

Pages 114-115

1. $\frac{3}{4}$; 2. $\frac{5}{6}$; 3. $\frac{7}{12}$; 4. $\frac{5}{12}$; 5. $\frac{7}{10}$; 6. $\frac{7}{18}$; 7. $\frac{5}{8}$; 8. $\frac{5}{9}$; 9. $\frac{20}{21}$; 10. $\frac{11}{16}$ in.; $\frac{5}{18}$; $\frac{9}{16}$

Page 116

1. $\frac{1}{3}$, e; 2. $\frac{1}{8}$, h; 3. $\frac{1}{4}$, f; 4. $\frac{2}{3}$, b; 5. $\frac{5}{8}$, c; 6. $\frac{1}{6}$, g; 7. $\frac{1}{2}$ hour, a; 8. $\frac{3}{4}$ cup, d

Page 117

1. $\frac{5}{8}$; 2. $\frac{1}{4}$; 3. $\frac{2}{3}$; 4. $\frac{1}{3}$; 5. $\frac{5}{6}$; 6. $\frac{3}{8}$; 7. $\frac{3}{4}$; 8. $\frac{1}{2}$; 9. $\frac{1}{6}$; $\frac{7}{8}$; $\frac{5}{12}$

Pages 118-119

s. $2\frac{2}{3}$; e. $1\frac{1}{4}$; b. $2\frac{1}{4}$; m. $2\frac{3}{5}$; v. $2\frac{3}{4}$; u. $1\frac{1}{3}$; g. $1\frac{2}{5}$; o. $2\frac{1}{2}$;
t. 3; r. $2\frac{4}{5}$; l. 1; a. $\frac{2}{3}$; w. $1\frac{1}{2}$ hour; vegetables

Pages 120-121

p. $\frac{1}{4}$; u. $\frac{1}{8}$; l. $\frac{1}{6}$; t. $\frac{7}{12}$; h. $\frac{4}{9}$; w. $\frac{7}{18}$; o. $\frac{2}{15}$; a. $\frac{1}{12}$; m. $\frac{3}{14}$;
r. $\frac{3}{4}$; e. $\frac{1}{20}$; s. $\frac{19}{36}$; b. $\frac{29}{60}$ (29 minutes); home plate

Page 122

2. $78 \div 6 = 13$; 3. $45 \times 8 = 360$; 4. $48 \times 6 + 7 = 295$;
5. $4 \times 5 \times 7 = 140$; 6. $68 \div 4 = 17$; 7. $468 \div 9 = 52$;
8. $69 \times 7 = 483$; 9. $5 \times 8 \div 4 = 10$ 10. $65 \times 48 = 3{,}120$

Page 123

1. >; 2. >; 3. >; 4. <; 5. <; 6. >

Page 124

	Decimal	Fraction
1	.3	$\frac{3}{10}$
2	.4	$\frac{2}{5}$
3	.5	$\frac{1}{2}$
4	.6	$\frac{3}{5}$
5	.7	$\frac{7}{10}$
6	.8	$\frac{4}{5}$
7	.9	$\frac{9}{10}$
8	1.0	1

Page 125

	Decimal	Fraction
1	.41	$\frac{41}{100}$
2	.25	$\frac{1}{4}$
3	.2	$\frac{1}{5}$
4	.55	$\frac{11}{20}$
5	.07	$\frac{7}{100}$
6	1.1	$1\frac{1}{10}$

Page 126 Row 1: .9, 1.2, 1.9, 2.7; Row 2: 3.15, 3.83, 4.5, 5, 5.8; Row 3: 7, 8.3; Row 4: 9.25, 9.7, 10.5, 11.05

Page 127

1. 2 5 . 1 4	2. 1 0 0 0 . 2
3. . 1 6	4. 5 0 1 . 0 1
5. 2 0 0 3	6. 3 . 0 3
7. 8 0 1 7 . 1	8. 1 0 0 . 0 1
9. 2 2 0 0 . 0 2	10. 6 0 . 6 0

Pages 128-129 c. 11:55; h. 4:50; i. 1:32; e. 4:05; w. 2:50; a. 2:52; s. 10:09; b. 4:10; y. 5:05; r. 4:45; u. 12:15; o. 1:10;
hareobics 5:45 a.m.

Page 130 1. 48"; 2. 33"; 3. 120"; 4. 66"; 5. 72"; 6. 59"; 7. 63,360 inches;
53"; 84"

Page 131

Three-Dimensional figure	Faces	Edges	Vertices
rectangular prism	6	12	8
cube	6	12	8
square-based pyramid	5	8	5

Page 132 1. true; 2. true; 3. false; 4. true; 5. true; 6. false;
7. line *c*; 8. line *d*

Page 133 1.

2	3	1	4
4	1	3	2
3	2	4	1
1	4	2	3

;

2. Answers will vary. Example:

一	(四)	二	三
三	二	(四)	一
(四)	一	三	二
二	三	一	(四)

Page 134 1. 3; 2. 7

Page 135 1. $\frac{3}{5}$; 2. $\frac{1}{5}$; 3. $\frac{1}{5}$; 4. $\frac{1}{8}$; 5. $\frac{1}{4}$; 6. $\frac{1}{2}$

Page 136

1. 123, 132, 213, 231, 312, 321;
2. 1234, 1243, 1324, 1342, 1423, 1432,
   2134, 2143, 2314, 2341, 2413, 2431,
   3124, 3142, 3214, 3241, 3412, 3421,
   4123, 4132, 4213, 4231, 4312, 4321;
3. 120 different numbers;
4. for 1 digit, 1 choice
   for 2 digits, 2 × 1 choices
   for 3 digits, 3 × 2 × 1 choices
   for 4 digits, 4 × 3 × 2 × 1 choices
   for 5 digits, 5 × 4 × 3 × 2 × 1 choices
   for 6 digits, 6 × 5 × 4 × 3 × 2 × 1 choices

Page 137

Date	Amount Added	Total
		$0.00
6/15	$15.25	+$15.25
		$15.25
6/22	$15.25	+$15.25
		$30.50
6/29	$15.25	+$15.25
		$45.75
7/6	$15.25	+$15.25
		$61.00
7/13	$15.25	+$15.25
		$76.25
7/20	$15.25	+$15.25
		$91.50
7/27	$15.25	+$15.25
		$106.75
8/3	$15.25	+$15.25
		$122.00

; 1. $15.25 × 8 = $122.00 ; 2. $16.75 × 8 = $134.00

Page 138

Date	Amount
	$1000.00
1/31	-$65.39
	$934.61
2/28	- $65.39
	$869.22
3/31	- $65.39
	$803.83
4/30	- $65.39
	$738.44
5/31	- $65.39
	$673.05
6/30	- $65.39
	$607.66
7/31	- $65.39
	$542.27
8/31	- $65.39
	$476.88
9/30	- $65.39
	$411.49
10/31	- $65.39
	$346.10
11/30	- $65.39
	$280.71
12/31	- $65.39
	$215.32

; $215.32

Page 139

1. banana, tomato, potato;
2. apple, carrot, red pepper;
3. banana, tomato, broccoli;
4. apple, carrot, potato, onion;
5. four red peppers

Page 140

Day	Pay
1st Monday	$.01
1st Tuesday	$.02
1st Wednesday	$.04
1st Thursday	$.08
1st Friday	$.16
1st Saturday	$.32
1st Sunday	$.64

Day	Pay
2nd Monday	$1.28
2nd Tuesday	$2.56
2nd Wednesday	$5.12
2nd Thursday	$10.24
2nd Friday	$20.48
2nd Saturday	$40.96
2nd Sunday	$81.92

; $163.83

Page 141 1. 8.91; 2. 4.65; 3. 4.3; 4. 13.11; 5. 1.19; 6. 5.9; 7. 6.1; 8. 8.18;
7.64; 12.41

Pages 142-143 r. 20.58; w. 2.456; e. 19.00; c. 8.409; m. 6.35; k. 15.234;
p. 19.05; a. 14.10; h. 73.2; s. 10.01; u. 12.638; b. 8.884;
n. 100.9 + 1.1 = 102.0 mph; cheesecake

Page 144 1. Jim, 2, 3, 1; 2. Ben, 3, 2, 1; 3. Fairbanks, 2, 1, 3; 4. 40 cm, 2, 1, 3

Page 145 1. .44; 2. 2.37; 3. 15.95; 4. 3.44; 5. 19.29; 6. 23.03;
7. .999; 8. 101.755; 9. .905; 4.63; 22.37

Pages 146-147 e. 3.79; p. 4.13; q. 6.19; t. 3.118; n. 1.792; o. 60.958; h. 49.4;
m. 1.412; c. .952; d. .091; w. 1.24; r. 1.147; b. 3.99; a. 103.55;
y. .9; u. 82.971; l. 101.1° – 98° = 3.1°; the crane

Page 148

1. .8	2. 8		3. 3	4. .1	5. 7		6. 2	7. 6	8. .0	9. 1
10. 3	1		11. 4	5	7	.6		12. .8	9	4
13. 9	.2	3	4		.0		14. .0	1		.5
	4		15. .8	16. 1	8		1		17. 9	
				18. .8	3	9		19. 9	.8	6

Page 149 1. $87.96; 2. $71.58; 3. $32.00; 4. $94.50; 5. $22.74;
6. $89.91; 7. $40.80; 8. $32.95; $34.00; $72.36

Page 150 1. No, total = $106.88; 2. No, total = $32.85; 3. Yes, total = $11.06

Page 151

1. .8	2. 8		3. 8	4. .8	5. 9		6. 9	7. 7	8. .0	9. 2
10. 9	0		11. 1	5	2	.9		12. .3	9	6
13. 4	.3	0	3		.1		14. .4	2		.4
	5		15. .3	16. 6	9		2		17. 8	
				18. .1	8	4		19. 9	.7	5

Pages 152-153 r. 5; g. -4; o. -2; u. -3; d. -7; t. 1; p. 4; y. 0; i. 3;
e. -6; z. 2; s. -5; f. -9; n. 6; b. -1; a. 8; q. -12; v. 9;
l. 10; c. 12; h. -10; w. -8; m. 7; z. -11; j. 11; x. 14; k. -15;
fryday

Page 154 1. 3; 2. -7; 3. 10; 4. -1; 5. -3; 6. -6; 7. 11; 8. -23;
9. 52; 10. -82; 11. 14; 12. 6; 13. -350; 14. -51; 15. -164; 16. -305;
131; -144

Page 155 1. 5; 2. -3; 3. -4; 4. -9; 5. 9; 6. 10; 7. 28;
8. -18; 9. -16; 10. -14; 11. 88 – -11 = 99°; -12; 26; -40

Page 156 1. 84; 2. -36; 3. -375; 4. 1; 5. 0; 6. 64; 7. -264; 8. 81;
9. -280; 10. 102; 11. -567; 12. 9; 13. 51; 14. 30; 15. -6; 16. 144;
-84; 36; 375; -1; -64; 264; -81; 280; -102; 567; -9; -51; -30; 6; -144;
-216; 216; 45; -45

Page 157 1. 5; 2. -5; 3. 5; 4. -7; 5. -37; 6. 42; 7. 8; 8. 6;
9. -25; 10. -125 11. -19; 12. 4; 13. -20; 14. 24; 15. -12; 16. 8;
17. 560; -8; -24

Page 159

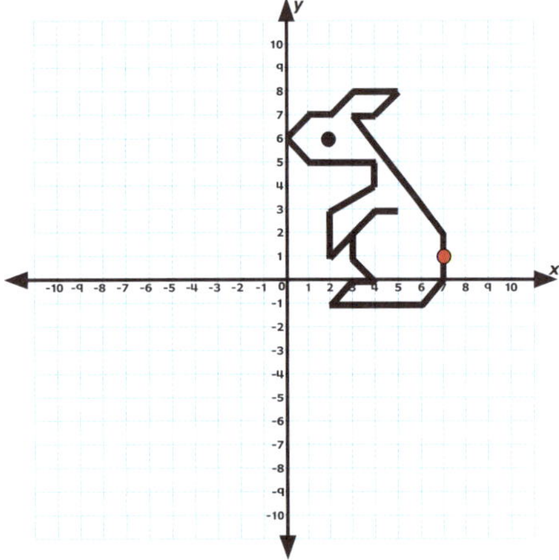

Page 160

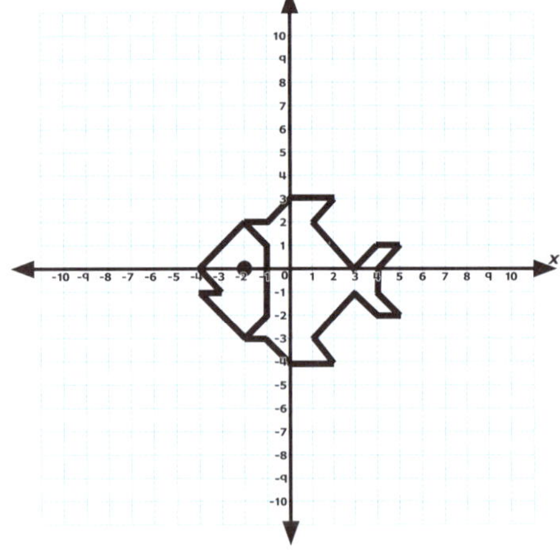

Page 161

1.

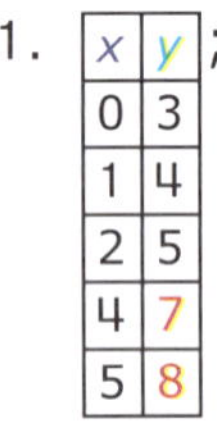

x	y
0	3
1	4
2	5
4	7
5	8

;

2.

x	y
8	6
6	4
5	3
3	1
2	0

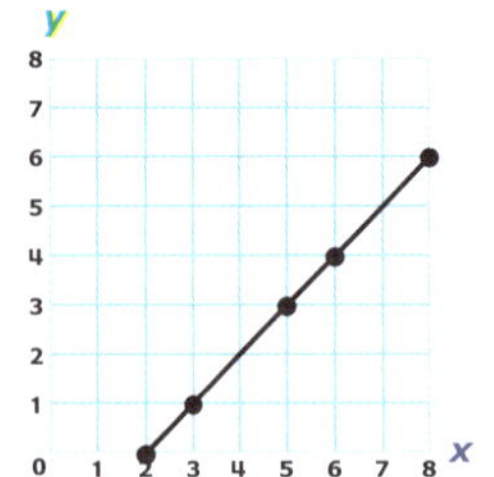

Page 162

1.

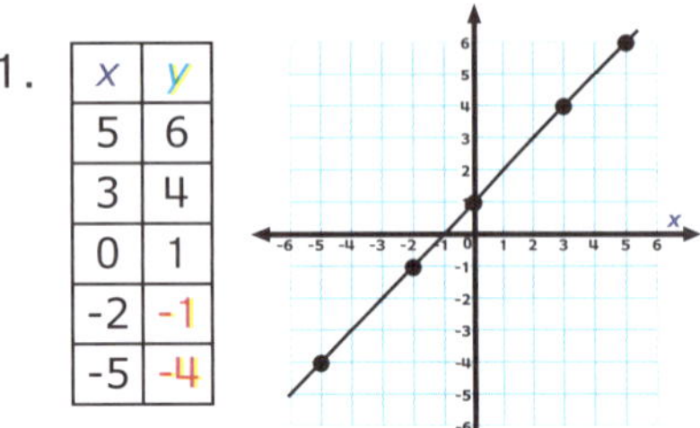

x	y
5	6
3	4
0	1
-2	-1
-5	-4

;

2.

x	y
6	4
3	1
2	0
0	-2
-4	-6

Page 163

1. $y = 3x$; 2. $y = x - 2$; 3. $y = 2x - 1$; 4. $b = \frac{1}{2}a$;
5. $n = 5m$; 6. $d = 2c - 3$

Page 164

1. 165 ; + 49 214	2. 448 ; + 57 505	3. 69 ; + 29 98	4. 286 ; 38 + 61 385
5. 789 ; 36 + 45 870	6. 92 ; 75 + 68 235	7. 51 ; 18 36 + 186 291	8. 26 ; 49 58 + 672 805
9. 79 ; 91 82 + 45 297	10. 23 ; 36 56 + 242 357	11. 4 ; 134 17 + 65 220	12. 123 242 95 + 68 528

Page 165

1. 573 ; − 86 487	2. 404 ; − 76 328	3. 161 ; − 85 76	4. 500 ; − 13 487	5. 202 ; − 146 56
6. 425 ; − 179 246	7. 5,800 ; − 3,945 1,855	8. 2,063 ; − 1,290 773	9. 3,428 ; − 1,783 1,645	

10. 31 + 19 + 25 + 25 = 100; 11. 8 + 21 + 37 + 18 + 16 = 100;
12. 120 + 2,452 + 1,709 = 4,281 13. 2,135 + 2,865 = 5,000

Page 166

1. 74 ; × 4 296	2. 164 ; × 4 656	3. 745 ; × 9 6,705	4. 84 ; × 9 756	5. 252 ; × 6 1,512
6. 276 ; × 2 552	7. 23 ; × 52 46 + 1,150 1,196	8. 223 ; × 43 669 + 8,920 9,589	9. 94 ; × 94 376 + 8,460 8,836	

10. 10 × 10 × 10 × 70 = 70,000; 11. 2 × 3 × 4 × 5 × 6 × 7 = 5,040;
12. 4 × 5 × 2 × 3 × 5 × 6 = 3,600

Page 167

1. 36 7) 252 ; 21 42 42	2. 67 8) 536 ; 48 56 56	3. 48 9) 432 ; 36 72 72	4. 92 3) 276 ; 27 6 6
5. 91 4) 364 ; 36 4 4	6. 76 8) 608 ; 56 48 48	7. 35 50) 1,750 ; 150 250 250	8. 42 42) 1,764 ; 168 84 84
9. 37 86) 3,182 ; 258 602 602	10. 63 25) 1,575 ; 150 75 75	11. 32 63) 2,016 ; 189 126 126	12. 75 46) 3,450 322 230 230

Page 168

1. $\begin{array}{r} 13 \\ \times\ 4 \\ \hline 52 \end{array}$;

2. $\begin{array}{r} 17 \\ \times\ 4 \\ \hline 68 \end{array}$ $\begin{array}{r} 68 \\ +\ 25 \\ \hline 93 \end{array}$

Page 169

1. 11; 2. 49; 3. 10; 4. 110; 5. 541; 6. 209; 7. 13; 8. 224; 9. 901; 10. 46; 334; 892

Page 170

1. flip; 2. slide; 3. turn; 4. turn; 5. slide; 6. flip; 7. Answers will vary. Example:

Page 171

1.

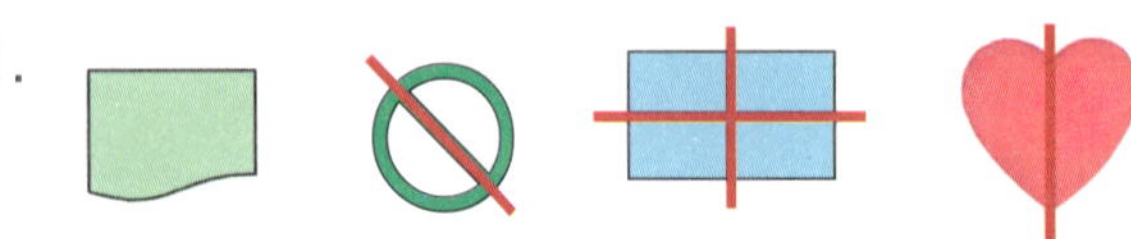

2.

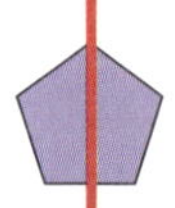

3.

Page 172

1. c; 2. b; 3. a; 4. a; 5. b; 6. a; 7. 1,600 oz; 8. 5 lbs;
9. Answers will vary. Example: $\frac{1}{2}$ cup chips;
10. Answers will vary. Example: 4 sticks of butter

Page 173

1. a; 2. c; 3. c; 4. b; 5. a; 6. c; 7. 45,000 g; 8. 2 kg;
9. Answers will vary. Example: $\frac{1}{4}$ teaspoon of sugar;
10. Answers will vary. Example: whole pineapple

Page 174

1. 5; 2. 4

Page 175

1. category 3; 2. 37 mph; 3. category 2;

4.

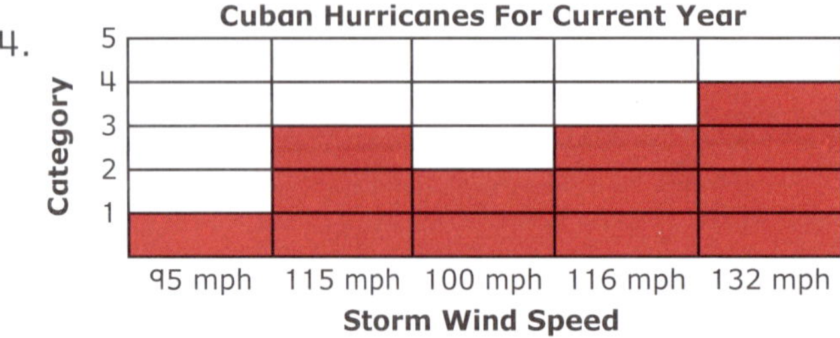

Page 176

Date	Described	Diameter (in.)
April 4	penny	$\frac{3}{4}$
May 2	quarter	1
May 9	golf ball	$1\frac{3}{4}$
June 11	pea	$\frac{1}{4}$
June 15	hen egg	2
July 18	marble	$\frac{1}{2}$
August 1	ping-pong ball	$1\frac{1}{2}$
August 28	half dollar	$1\frac{1}{4}$

Page 177

1. Descriptions will vary. Examples given.
a. $\frac{3}{4}$ in., penny; b. $1\frac{1}{4}$ in., half-dollar; c. $\frac{1}{4}$ in., pea;
d. 1 in., quarter; e. $1\frac{1}{2}$ in., ping-pong ball; f. $\frac{1}{2}$ in., marble;
2. should measure $\frac{3}{4}$ in.; should measure $1\frac{3}{4}$ in.

Pages 178-179

1. 200 min; 2. 100 min; 3. 40 - 10 = 30 min;
4. 40 × 15 = 600 min; 10 hours; 5. 400 calories; 6. 200 calories;
7. 150 calories; 8. 35 hours; 9. 150 min, $2\frac{1}{2}$ hours; 10. 14,000 calories

Page 180

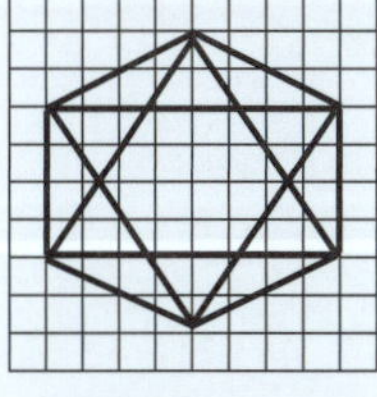

; Challenge: 48 square centimeters

Page 181

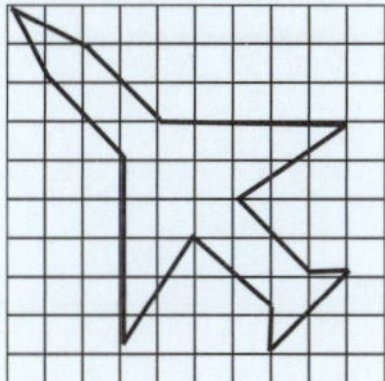

Page 182

Drawings will vary.

Page 183

1. $\frac{1}{3}$; 2. $\frac{3}{4}$; 3. $\frac{1}{4}$; $\frac{1}{2}$; $\frac{4}{3}$

Page 184

1.

miles	55	110	165	220	275	330
hours	1	2	3	4	5	6

2.

dollars	$3.50	$7	$10.50	$14	$17.50	$21
gallons	1	2	3	4	5	6

3.

dollars	$5.15	$10.30	$15.45	$20.60	$25.75	$30.90
tickets	1	2	3	4	5	6

4.

pounds	1	2	3	4	5	6
dollars	$.30	$.60	$.90	$1.20	$1.50	$1.80

Page 185 — 1. true; 2. true; 3. false; 4. true; 5. true; 6. true; 7. true; 8. false

Page 186

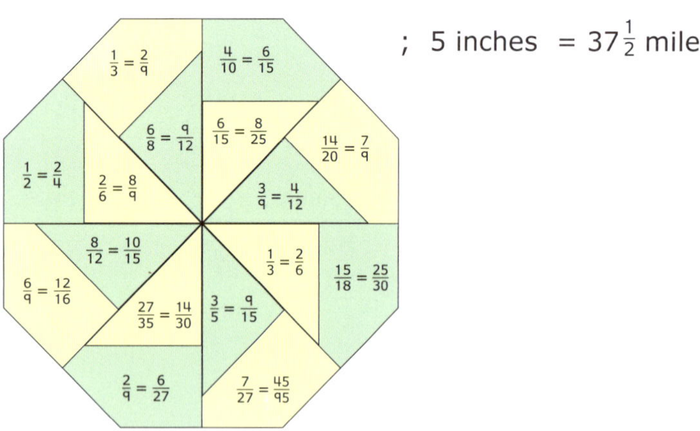

; 5 inches = $37\frac{1}{2}$ miles

Page 187 — 1. s; 2. t; 3. n; 4. e; 5. a; 6. r; 7. p; 8. t; patterns

Pages 188-189 — h. 18; a. 15; r. 21; t. 8; s. 14; i. 20; n. 60; c. 24; w. 40;
d. $\frac{8}{50} = \frac{12}{n}$, n = \$75; e. $\frac{5,000}{n} = \frac{12,500}{n}$, n = 25 min.; f. $\frac{1}{4} = \frac{n}{48}$, n = 12 in.
sandwitch

Page 190 — 1. 5 days, \$27; 2. 20 minutes, 440 feet per minute;
3. 54 minutes, 3:36 per page (3.6 minutes)

Page 191 — 1.

- 1
  - 1 — 1, 2, 3
  - 2 — 1, 2, 3
  - 3 — 1, 2, 3
- 2
  - 1 — 1, 2, 3
  - 2 — 1, 2, 3
  - 3 — 1, 2, 3
- 3
  - 1 — 1, 2, 3
  - 2 — 1, 2, 3
  - 3 — 1, 2, 3

; 2. 27 outcomes

Page 192 — 1. d, $\frac{1}{16}$; 2. a, $\frac{1}{8}$; 3. f, $\frac{3}{16}$; 4. b, $\frac{1}{4}$; 5. c, $\frac{3}{8}$; 6. e, 0

Page 193 — 1. $\frac{1}{2}$; 2. $\frac{1}{6}$; 3. $\frac{1}{3}$; 4. $\frac{4}{52} = \frac{1}{13}$; 5. $\frac{3}{52}$; 6. 75 made

Page 194 — 1. 1 red, 2 blue, 3 yellow; 2. 1 red, 2 green, 3 blue, 4 yellow, 2 purple

Page 195

45% =	y .45	t 4.5	r 45
.15 =	r 1.5%	m .15%	o 15%
.09 =	a 90%	u 9%	t .9%
60% =	a .6	c .06	o 600
5% =	s .5	m 50	r .05
.72 =	t 7.2%	s .72%	e 72%
.3 =	n 3%	a 30%	b 300%
2% =	m .02	y 20	r 200
25% =	s 2.5	n 25	a .25
.81 =	t 81%	u .81%	o 8.1%
1% =	b .1	h .01	d 10
.111 =	e 1.11%	a 111%	w 11.1%
34.5% =	o 34.5	h .345	n 3.45
.005 =	i .5%	s 5%	a 50%
100% =	n .10	t .1	z 1

; You are a math whiz!

Page 196

Decimal	Fraction	Percent
.27	$\frac{27}{100}$	27%
.89	$\frac{89}{100}$	89%
.07	$\frac{7}{100}$	7%
.25	$\frac{25}{100} = \frac{1}{4}$	25%
.5 (.50)	$\frac{50}{100} = \frac{1}{2}$	50%
.75	$\frac{75}{100} = \frac{3}{4}$	75%

Page 197

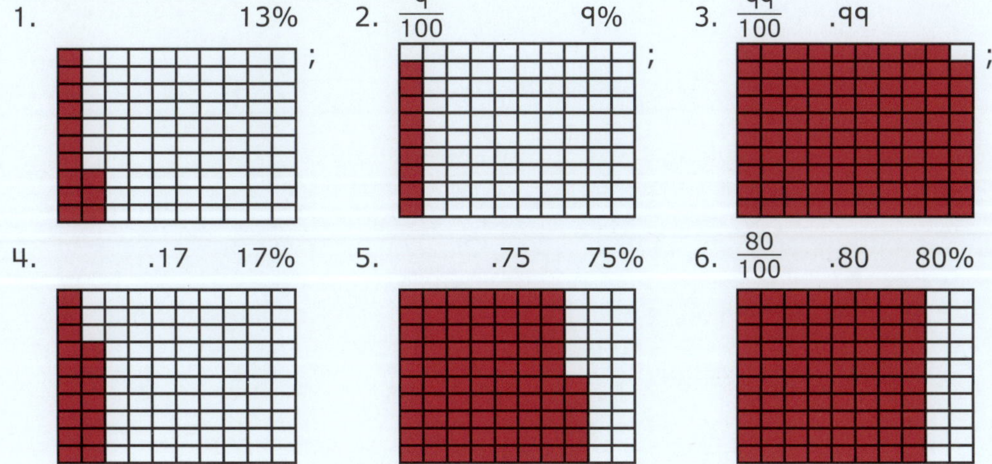

Page 198

e. \$12; h. \$6; r. \$2.10; s. \$6.30; t. \$28.80; n. \$7.20; u. \$3.60; w. \$3.50 c. \$29.40; i. \$12.80; a. \$19.20; g. \$42; it gets an earache

Page 199

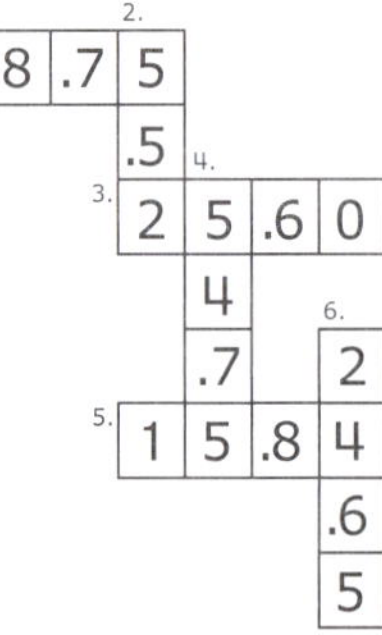

Page 200

1.

number of dimes	number of nickels	number of pennies	total amount
5	2	1	$.61

; 2.

number of dimes	number of nickels	number of pennies	total amount
4	3	1	$.56

Page 201

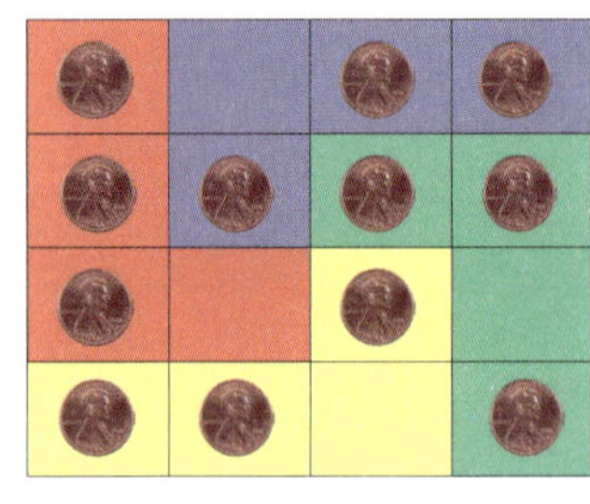 ; 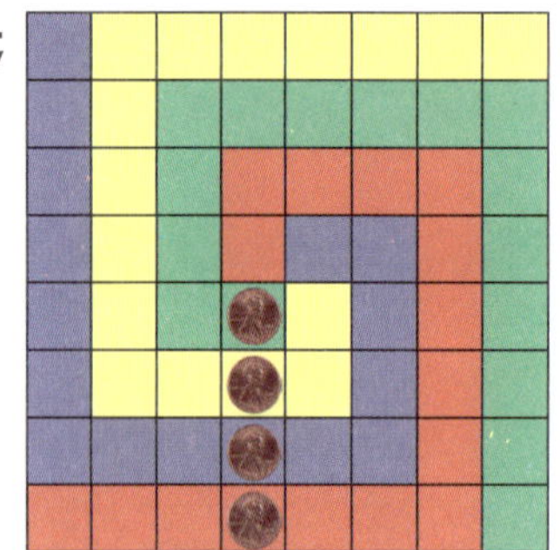

Page 202

1. quadrants; 2. ratio; 3. probability; 4. diameter; 5. integers; 6. exponent; 7. rate; 8. proportion; 9. origin; 10. negative

Page 203

1. b; 2. f; 3. c; 4. h; 5. a; 6. m; 7. k; 8. i; 9. g; 10. l; 11. d; 12. e; 13. j; 14. n; 15. o

Page 204

1. ≥; 2. quotient; 3. decagon; 4. right angle; 5. divisor; 6. $\frac{39}{100}$; 7. million; 8. composite

Page 205

1. 1,688; 2. 211; 3. 214; 4. 214; 5. 161; 6. The largest number was omitted.

Pages 206-207

1. 5,000,020,014; 2. 400,300,002; 3. 2,002,002,002; 4. 730,601,401; 5. 8,030,011,009; 6. 42,308; 7. 1,001,001,001; 8. 407,209,039; 9. 8,050,050,008; 10. 203,622,430;
11. six million, nine hundred ninety-eight thousand, six hundred eighty-one;
12. six billion, nine hundred twenty-eight million, one hundred ninety-eight thousand, two hundred fifty-three;
13. $1,000,000,000

Page 208

2. 7,369,093; 3. 57,743; 4. 41,295; 5. 296,172; 6. 2,714,138; 7. 713,121; 8. 40,641; 9. 737,826;
41,641; 396,172; 727,826

Page 209

2. 59,549; 3. 15,087; 4. 397,495; 5. 12,176; 6. 565,596; 7. 392,927; 8. 818,000; 9. 116,305; 10. 1,495;
22,176; 297,495; 718,000

Page 210

2. 2,494; 3. 2,291; 4. 4,096; 5. 10,075; 6. 4,644; 7. 45,760; 8. 72,192; 73,192

Page 211 — 2. 165; 3. 254; 4. 725; 5. 2,433; 6. 174; 7. 582; 8. 2,405 308; 1,564

Page 212 — 2. 31; 3. 52; 4. 74; 5. 63; 6. 35; 7. 67; 8. 82; 43; 89

Page 213 — (row number)^3; seventh row sum = 7^3 = 343

Pages 214-215 — t. 36; o. 81; m. 16; b. 10; l. 54; p. 11; y. 38; w. 12; i. 15; u. 10; s. 4; n. 41; put it on my bill;
Challenge: 1. $(16 - 8) \div (4 \times 2) = 1$; 2. $24 - (18 - 12 \div 2) + 1 = 13$

Pages 216-217 — 1. 36; 2. 39; 3. 44; 4. 43; 5. 355; 6. 99; 7. 373; 8. 193; 9. 364; 10. 64; 11. 4; 12. 4; 13. 131; 14. 198; 15. 75; 16. 343; 17. 298; 18. 875; 19. 38; 20. 17; 21. 93; 22. 290; 23. 63; 24. 150; 25. 440; 26. 225; 27. 95; 28. 710; 29. 1,047; 30. 4,091; 31. 21+ ___ = 90, 69 minutes; 32. 34 + ___ = 125, $91

Pages 218-219 — 1. $n = 3$; 2. $n = 8$; 3. $n = 28$; 4. $n = 94$; 5. $n = 15$; 6. $n = 46$; 7. $n = 35$; 8. $n = 51$; 9. $n = 24$; 10. $n = 21$; 11. $n = 69$; 12. $n = \frac{1}{3}$; 13. n = $3.05; 14. n = $4.45; 15. n + $16 = $40, n = $24; 16. n + $25 = $54, n = $29

Pages 220-221 — 1. 44; 2. 49; 3. 9; 4. 7; 5. 9; 6. 19; 7. 53; 8. 95; 9. 22; 10. 45; 11. 15; 12. 47; 13. 53; 14. 69; 15. 39; 16. 85; 17. 175; 18. 26; 19. 430; 20. 99; 21. 125; 22. 103; 23. 99; 24. 295; 25. 950; 26. 70; 27. 1,800; 28. 899; 29. 950; 30. 991; 31. 42 – ___ = 25, $17; 32. 440 – ___ = 156, 284 words

Pages 222-223 — 1. $n = 19$; 2. $n = 17$; 3. $n = 61$; 4. $n = 69$; 5. $n = 76$; 6. $n = 122$; 7. $n = 82$; 8. $n = 82$; 9. $n = 18$; 10. $n = 204$; 11. $n = 1.63$; 12. $n = \frac{5}{6}$; 13. n = $2.62; 14. n = $27.01; 15. n – $6 = $8, n = $14; 16. n – $9.99 = $12.45, n = $22.44

Pages 224-225 — 1. 6; 2. 8; 3. 9; 4. 9; 5. 15; 6. 24; 7. 21; 8. 29; 9. 50; 10. 30; 11. 400; 12. 20; 13. 15; 14. 48; 15. 45; 16. 75; 17. 27; 18. 150; 19. 100; 20. 40; 21. 35; 22. 25; 23. 20; 24. 16; 25. 20; 26. 20; 27. 12; 28. 30; 29. 50; 30. 13; 31. 8 × ___ = 56, $7; 32. 55 × ___ = 165, 3 hours

Pages 226-227 — 1. $n = 4$; 2. $n = 9$; 3. $n = 22$; 4. $n = 7$; 5. $n = 9$; 6. $n = 13$; 7. $n = 39$; 8. $n = 52$; 9. $n = 49$; 10. $n = 47$; 11. $n = 97$; 12. $n = 100$; 13. n = $.50; 14. n = $1.65; 15. $3n$ = $78, n = $26; 16. $8n$ = $10.80, n = $1.35

Pages 228-229 — 1. 45; 2. 24; 3. 27; 4. 40; 5. 56; 6. 90; 7. 200; 8. 55; 9. 72; 10. 60; 11. 135; 12. 630; 13. 372; 14. 5,400; 15. 200; 16. 750; 17. 245; 18. 432; 19. 400; 20. 1,300; 21. 77; 22. 192; 23. 258; 24. 145; 25. 270; 26. 570; 27. 300; 28. 5,880; 29. 1,600; 30. 3,240;
31. ___ ÷ 12 = 8 or ___ ÷ 8 = 12, 96 tokens;
32. ___ ÷ 23 = 4 or ___ ÷ 4 = 23, $92

Pages 230-231　1. $n = 30$　2. $n = 72$　3. $n = 360$　4. $n = 276$;　5. $n = 812$;
6. $n = 413$　7. $n = 96$　8. $n = 600$;　9. $n = 234$;　10. $n = 144$;
11. $n = \$4.35$　12. $n = 125$;　13. $n = 375$　14. $n = 0$;
15. $\frac{n}{4} = \$3.35$, $n = \$13.40$　16. $\frac{n}{6} = \$5.50$, $n = \$33.00$

Page 232　3. 79°;　4. 68°;　5. 45°;　6. 117°

Page 233　1. 30°, 150°, 30°;　2. 52°, 128°, 52°;　3. 132°, 48°, 132°;　4. 73°, 107°, 73°;
67°;　120°

Page 234　2. 11 triangles

Page 235　1. 20°;　2. 60°;　3. 65°;　4. 50°;　5. 55°;　6. 70°;　45°;　75°

Page 236　1. 16 ft, 8 ft; 248 ft;　2. 256 mm, 128 mm, 64 mm; 1,984 mm;
3. 10 in., 5 in., $2\frac{1}{2}$ in., $1\frac{1}{4}$ in.; $38\frac{3}{4}$ in.

Page 237　1. 18;　2. 11;　3. 0;　4. $\frac{3}{8}$;　5. 4.75;　6. 1
7. 20;　8. 20;　9. 375;　10. 375;　11. -23;　12. 800
13. 77;　14. 10;　15. 144;　16. 0　17. 46

Page 238

5	4	9
9	6	2
3	8	7

; 5 + 9 + 6 + 8 + 7 = 35

Page 239　s. $\frac{4}{5}$;　b. $\frac{3}{4}$;　d. $\frac{1}{3}$;　j. $\frac{1}{4}$;　n. $\frac{1}{5}$;　l. $\frac{2}{3}$;　r. $\frac{3}{8}$;　o. $\frac{1}{2}$;　w. $\frac{3}{5}$;　m. $\frac{5}{8}$;
u. $\frac{1}{10}$;　t. $\frac{2}{5}$;　a. $\frac{5}{6}$;　z. $\frac{1}{8}$;　c. $\frac{2}{7}$;　e. $\frac{5}{9}$;　blue jeans

Page 240　1. $\frac{5}{6}$;　2. 3;　3. 1;　4. $\frac{5}{6}$;　5. 3;　6. $\frac{3}{4}$

Page 241　2. $\frac{10}{3}$;　3. 2;　4. $\frac{3}{2}$;　5. 1;　6. $\frac{11}{17}$;　7. $\frac{1}{3}$;　8. 0

Page 242　1. g, $\frac{4}{6}$;　2. o, $\frac{1}{3}$;　3. o, $\frac{6}{8}$;　4. d, $\frac{12}{18}$;　5. j, $\frac{10}{14}$;　6. o, $\frac{15}{32}$;　7. b, $\frac{32}{45}$;　good job

Page 243　1. $\frac{1}{2}$;　2. $\frac{1}{2}$;　3. 1;　4. $\frac{1}{2}$;　5. 1;　6. $\frac{1}{3}$;　7. True;　8. True;　9. True

Pages 244-245　m. $1\frac{5}{6}$;　s. $1\frac{1}{4}$;　o. $1\frac{1}{2}$;　b. $1\frac{2}{3}$;　r. $1\frac{1}{5}$;　a. $4\frac{1}{8}$;　u. $4\frac{3}{4}$;　n. $4\frac{1}{3}$;　x. 1;
j. $3\frac{2}{3}$;　i. $5\frac{1}{3}$;　g. $5\frac{1}{4}$;　v. $1\frac{1}{5}$;　w. $9\frac{1}{2}$;　c. $2\frac{5}{6}$;　d. $6\frac{3}{4}$;　z. $4\frac{1}{2}$;　t. $3\frac{1}{2}$;
p. $2\frac{1}{4}$;　a jumpsuit

Pages 246-247　1. $\frac{5}{8}$;　2. $\frac{3}{4}$;　3. $1\frac{1}{4}$;　4. $1\frac{2}{9}$;　5. $1\frac{2}{5}$;　6. $\frac{7}{8}$;　7. $3\frac{8}{9}$;
8. $4\frac{1}{4}$;　9. $5\frac{7}{12}$;　10. $\frac{1}{3}$;　11. $\frac{7}{10}$;　12. $\frac{6}{7}$;　13. $\frac{4}{5}$;　14. $5\frac{2}{5}$;
15. $5\frac{1}{2}$;　16. $4\frac{1}{12}$;　17. $3\frac{1}{2}$;　$\frac{3}{8}$;　$4\frac{1}{2}$

Page 248　1. a;　2. c

Page 249　1. 21;　2. 24;　3. 36;　4. 50;　5. 18;　6. 6;　7. 20;　8. 12;　8;　22;　9. LCD =10

Pages 250-251 a. $1\frac{1}{3}$; g. $\frac{7}{8}$; e. $1\frac{1}{6}$; h. $\frac{1}{2}$; b. $\frac{7}{12}$; t. $1\frac{7}{18}$; m. $\frac{14}{15}$; i. $1\frac{5}{24}$;
l. $\frac{17}{21}$; o. $1\frac{1}{2}$; s. $\frac{11}{15}$; z. $\frac{43}{72}$; n. $\frac{5}{8}$ in.; p. $\frac{3}{4}$; he logs on

Page 252 1. b; 2. c

Page 253 1. $2\frac{3}{4}$; 2. $3\frac{5}{8}$; 3. $2\frac{9}{10}$; 4. $3\frac{5}{6}$; 5. $5\frac{1}{12}$; 6. $4\frac{3}{8}$; 7. $4\frac{43}{45}$; 8. $5\frac{7}{12}$; $1\frac{2}{3}$; $3\frac{1}{4}$

Pages 254-255 1. a; 2. c; 3. b; 4. c; 5. a; 6. c; 7. a; 8. c;
9. c; 10. b; 11. c; 12. b; 13. a

Page 257 1. $1\frac{1}{4}$; 2. $4\frac{5}{8}$; 3. $3\frac{1}{12}$; 4. $4\frac{4}{9}$; 5. $2\frac{5}{6}$; 6. $3\frac{3}{4}$; 7. $1\frac{7}{8}$; 8. $\frac{17}{21}$;
9. $3\frac{1}{4}$; 10. $2\frac{1}{6}$; 11. $1\frac{5}{8}$; 12. $3\frac{11}{12}$; $3\frac{1}{6}$; $4\frac{1}{12}$; $4\frac{3}{8}$

Page 258 1. g; 2. f; 3. a; 4. j; 5. b; 6. d; 7. c; 8. i; 9. e; 10. h

Page 259 1. $1\frac{1}{2}$ cups; 2. $3\frac{1}{4}$ cups; 3. $\frac{1}{2}$ hour; 4. $\frac{5}{6}$ cup; 5. $3\frac{1}{4}$ cups

Pages 260-261 1. 64 in.; 2. 1 in.; 3. 66 ft; 4. 1.2 mm; 5. 472 m; 6. 9.6 mm;
7. 36 in.; 8. $22\frac{1}{2}$ yds; 9. 22 mm, 44 mm; 10. 29 mm, 58 mm;
11. 11 mm, 22 mm; 12. 15 mm, 30 mm

Page 262 Answers will vary. Example:

Object	Circumference (C)	Diameter (d)	$C \div d$
soda can	22 cm	7 cm	3.14
glass	27 cm	8.6 cm	3.14
clock	96 cm	30.6 cm	3.14
tire	208 cm	66.2 cm	3.14

Page 263 b. 15.7 m; i. 9.42 m; t. 3.14 m; g. 31.4 m; n. 21.98 m;
a. 34.54 m; s. 25.12 m; u. 113.04 m; giant

Page 265

3.

1	4	1	5	9	2	6	5	3	5
8	9	7	9	3	2	3	8	4	6
2	6	4	3	3	8	3	2	7	9
5	0	2	8	8	4	1	9	7	1
6	9	3	9	9	3	7	5	1	0
5	8	2	0	9	7	4	9	4	4
5	9	2	3	0	7	8	1	6	4
0	6	2	8	6	2	0	8	9	9
8	6	2	8	0	3	4	8	2	5
3	4	2	1	1	7	0	6	7	9
8	2	1	4	8	0	8	6	5	1

Page 266

Celsius	Fahrenheit
100°	212°
95°	203°
90°	194°
85°	185°
80°	176°
75°	167°
70°	158°
65°	149°
60°	140°
55°	131°
50°	122°
45°	113°
40°	104°
35°	95°
30°	86°
25°	77°
20°	68°
15°	59°
10°	50°
5°	42°
0°	32°

; For every 5°C rise there is a 9°F rise.

Page 267 1. 100°C; 2. 0°F; 3. 30°F; 4. 37.5°C; 5. 100°; 6. 180°; 7. 60°F; 8. 63°F

Pages 268-269 1. 16 ounces; 2. 32 ounces; 3. 56 ounces; 4. 2 pints; 5. 4 pints; 6. 32 ounces; 7. 2 quarts; 8. 40 ounces; 9. 3 quarts

Page 270 1. b; 2. a; 3. c; 4. b; 5. 2,000 mL; 6. 3 L; 7. 1 L; 8. 19,000 mL; 9. 45 L; 10. 8.1 L

Page 271 1. 4 + 4 = 8; 2. 8 + 8 + 2 = 18; 3. 2 + 8 = 10

Page 273 1. 9; 2. 14; 3. 3; 4. 2

Page 274 1. moderate; 2. 2 .5 to 5.4; 3. major; 4. 100 earthquakes; 5. about 30,620 earthquakes

Page 275 1. 4 packages, 2 left over; 2. \$6.50 (4 × .50 + 2 × 1 + 2 × 1.25); 3. 3 × 4 + 2 × 3 = \$18

Page 276 green path

Page 277 1. 4,466; 2. 25,849; 3. 1,568; 4. 7,480; 5. 671; 6. 74,029; 7. 39,191; 8. 2,028 9. 21,906; 10. 918; 11. 5,658; 12. 28,080; 13. 19; 14. 647; 15. 83; 16. 24; 781; 75,350

Page 278 Shading will vary. Examples: 1. ; 2. ; 3.

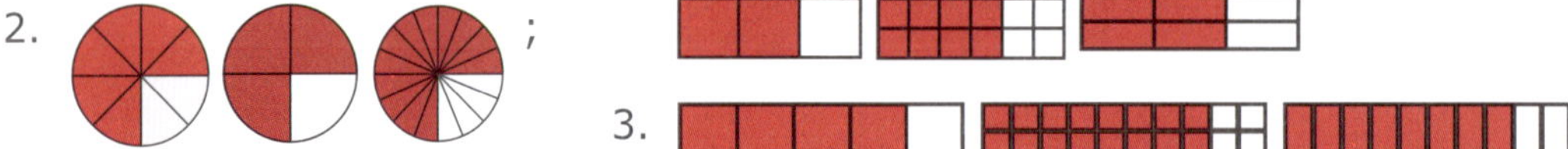

Page 279 r. $\frac{3}{5}$; n. $\frac{3}{4}$; e. $\frac{2}{3}$; t. $\frac{1}{2}$; i. $\frac{5}{8}$; s. $\frac{1}{6}$; b. $\frac{13}{15}$; a. $\frac{5}{12}$; beets

Pages 280-281 1. 4 balls; 2. 3 pennies; 3. 4 candies; 4. 2 dollars; 5. \$14; 6. \$32; 7. \$37; 8. \$56; 9. \$64; 10. \$30; 11. \$122.20; 12. \$14; 13. \$8; 14. 2 cups; 15. \$250,000

Pages 282-283 1. $\frac{1}{6}$; 2. $\frac{3}{16}$; 3. $\frac{1}{9}$; 4. 3; 5. $\frac{4}{15}$; 6. 4 7. 3; 8. $\frac{3}{5}$; 9. 6; 10. $\frac{1}{6}$; 11. $\frac{1}{5}$; 12. $\frac{1}{12}$; 13. $\frac{1}{4}$ cup; 14. 8 cookies

Pages 284-285 y. $\frac{1}{6}$; d. 9; i. $\frac{4}{9}$; o. 10; c. $\frac{1}{2}$; t. $\frac{3}{7}$; w. $\frac{3}{4}$; a. $\frac{5}{8}$; u. $1\frac{1}{4}$; g. $\frac{10}{27}$; r. $3\frac{1}{3}$; b. $1\frac{7}{8}$; h. $\frac{5}{16}$; z. 1; l. 3; x. 12; e. \$8; m. $7\frac{1}{2}$ yards; a drizzly bear

Page 286 r. $\frac{6}{5}$; n. $\frac{4}{3}$; e. 2; h. $\frac{3}{5}$; m. $\frac{1}{3}$; p. $\frac{1}{5}$; u. $\frac{2}{3}$; t. $\frac{5}{12}$; o. $\frac{3}{2}$; l. $\frac{4}{5}$; s. $\frac{20}{19}$; x. $\frac{3}{10}$; w. $\frac{1}{6}$; a. 1; f. $\frac{2}{9}$; the flea

Page 287 1. 3; 2. $\frac{1}{8}$; 3. $\frac{6}{7}$; 4. 20; 5. 2; 6. 10; 7. $\frac{5}{16}$; 8. 5; $\frac{1}{4}$; 4

Page 288 1. \$15; 2. 4 batches; 3. $2\frac{1}{2}$ ft; 4. \$52.50

Page 289 1. F; 2. A; 3. D; 4. E; 5. B; 6. C

Page 290 1. 8.18; 2. 3.98; 3. 12.2; 4. 2.69; 5. 5.4; 6. 3.02; 7. 57.72; 8. .187; 9. 3; 10. 6.71; 2.96; 7.33

Page 291 1. \$45.51; 2. \$144.16; 3. \$311.31; 4. \$11.88; 5. \$119.80; 6. \$16.25; 7. \$451.80; 8. \$413.10; 9. \$38.61

Page 293 1. 14.4; 2. 1.44; 3. 14.4; 4. .0144 5. 58.4; 6. 5.84; 7. .0584; 8. 5.84 9. 19.68; 10. 1.02; 11. 74.2; 12. .968; 13. 12.88; 14. 15.257; 15. .02116; 16. .00266

Pages 294-295 o. .172; r. 1.72; h. 7.74; g. .00774; e. .774; a. 17.94; l. 179.4; w. 1.794; v. 369.46; p. 3,694.6; i. 36.946; k. .0616; m. .09; s. 129.6; x. 18.48; q. .0009; c. 17.885; b. 14.925 kg; z. 63.2 cm; n. 16.875 miles; peek-a-moo

Page 296 1. .077; 2. 6.4; 3. .0195; 4. 1.83 5. 31.6; 6. .0057; 7. 1.326; 8. 1.28 9. .002; 10. .52; 11. 1.4; 12. .0121

Page 297 1. 3.38; 2. .0086; 3. 87; 4. .48; 5. .0005; 6. 1.12; 7. 2.34; 8. .205; 9. 15.05; 10. .3; 11. .042; 12. .5; 12.32; .7

Pages 298-299 r. .57; m. 8.8; a. 5.2; i. 19; b. 15; o. 6.9; u. 175.7; e. .0015; w. .3; p. 35; s. 52.5; l. 1.6; d. 5 pieces; a pillow

Page 300 1. \$3.50; 2. \$.25; 3. \$160, \$8 per hour; 4. 1,332 miles, 55.5 mph

Page 301 1. Y; 2. Y; 3. X; 4. X

Page 302 1. 4 2 7 3 6 5 1 ; 2. 5.9; 3. 20

Page 303

1. C; 2. B; 3. F; 4. D; 5. A; 6. E;
7-9. Answers will vary. Examples: 7. soda can; 8. basketball; 9. juice box;
10. square pyramid, rectangular prism; 11. cone, cylinder; 12. sphere, cube

Page 304

1. isosceles triangle; 2. right triangle; 3. rectangle;
4. parallelogram; 5. trapezoid; 6. pentagon;
7. hexagon; 8. octagon; 9. cube;
10. rectangular prism; 11. sphere; 12. cylinder

Page 305

O
N
T
H
E
M
O
V
E

; on the move

Page 306

3	13	14	0
8	6	5	11
4	10	9	7
15	1	2	12

; $2^{2^{2}}$

Page 307

1. improper; 2. prime; 3. lowest terms; 4. factor; 5. absolute value;
6. multiple; 7. dot; 8. commutative; 9. percent; 10. composite

Page 308

1. a; 2. c; 3. c; 4. c; 5. 4; 6. $7.50;
7. Answers will vary. Example: a loaf of bread

Page 309

1. b; 2. a; 3. b; 4. c; 5. $\frac{400}{1,000}$; 6. 20 nickels;
7-8. Answers will vary. Examples: 7. a shoelace; 8. a liter of soda.

Page 311

1. Pictures will vary. Example:

cup
cup
pint
quart
gallon

2. 2 cups; 3. 4 cups; 4. 16 cups; 5. 8 oz; 6. 16 oz;
7. 32 oz; 8. 128 oz; 9. 4 cups; 10. 32 oz; 11. 4¢ per oz

Page 312

1. b; 2. c; 3. a; 4. a; 5. 5,000 mL; 6. 3 cans; 7. 1,100 mL

Page 313

1. 4,016, 5,100, 4,444, 600; 2. 711, 969, 4,002, 10,920;
3. 512, 1,000, 7,040, 736; 4. 2,202, 1,110

Page 314

101	102	**103**	104	105	106	**107**	108	**109**	110
111	112	**113**	114	115	116	117	118	119	120
121	122	123	124	125	126	**127**	128	129	130
131	132	133	134	135	136	**137**	138	**139**	140
141	142	143	144	145	146	147	148	**149**	150

Page 315 1. 64, 48, 52, 96, 80, 144; 2. 48, 96, 144; 3. 45, 80, 105; 4. 64, 48, 96, 80, 144; 5. 48, 96, 144

Page 316 1. 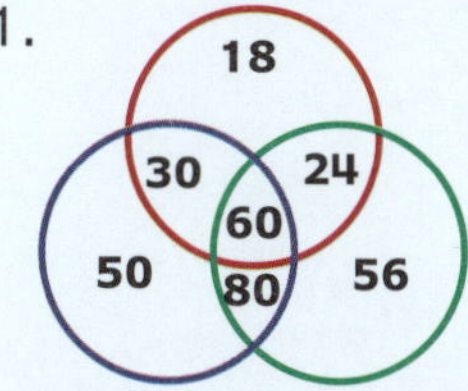

; 2. 68

Page 317

35	408	18	54	32	56
234	191	64	123	168	206
62	45	81	252	96	72
144	24	48	63	80	90
432	42	0	88	592	156
184	40	742	406	308	328
106	208	352	65	800	124
16	658	712	54	526	304

Page 318

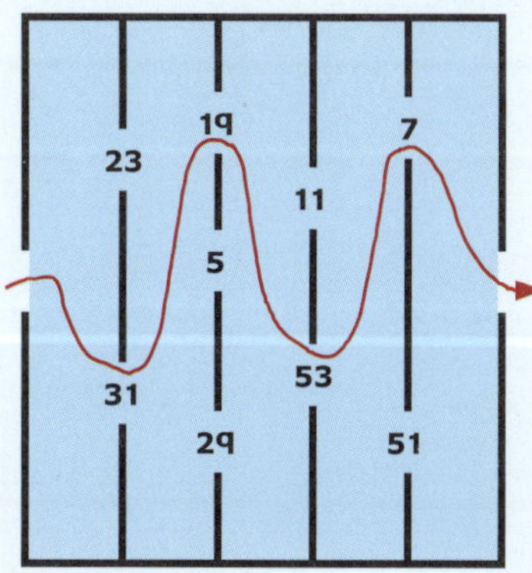

Page 319 1. 3 × 3 × 5; 2. 3 × 3 × 3 × 3; 3. 2 × 2 × 2 × 2 × 3; 4. 2 × 2 × 3 × 5; 5. 2 × 3 × 3 × 3; 6. 2 × 2 × 2 × 3 × 3

Pages 320-321 d. 2; t. 10; s. 3; u. 16; f. 6; i. 12; y. 20; a. 21; e. 32; n. 1; it tasted funny; 7 × 13 = 91; 2 × 7 × 11 = 154

Pages 322-323 t. 20; r. 12; o. 18; c. 30; l. 36; m. 44; w. 70; u. 60; i. 45; a. 72; catillac; 448

Page 324 2. -9 from prior term; 17, 8; 3. $+\frac{2}{5}$ to prior term; $1\frac{4}{5}$, $2\frac{1}{5}$; 4. + 6 then -2; 20, 18; 5a. $41.45; b. $293.80

Page 325

Time In	Time Out	Cost
8:00 a.m.	11:25 a.m.	$4.50
9:30 a.m.	noon	$3.50
1:00 p.m.	5:30 p.m.	$5.00
7:35 a.m.	4:37 p.m.	$5.25

;

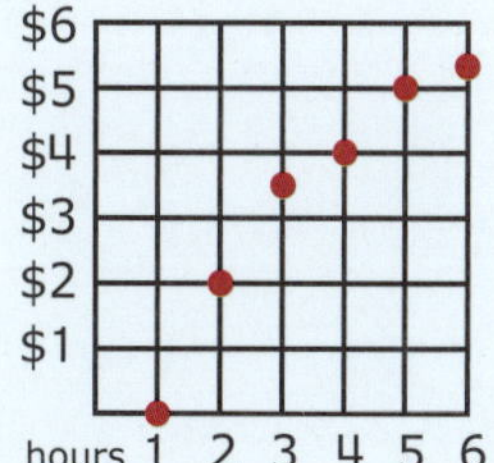

Page 326 1. 15; 2. -12; 3. 4; 4. -10; 5. 3; 6. -7; 7. 5; 8. -3; 9. 8; 10. -9; -1; 2

Page 327 1. 10; 2. -26; 3. -12; 4. 66; 5. 14; 6. -55; 7. 8; 8. 0; 9. -10; 10. 575; 11. -8; 12. 123; 13. 68°; 14. 9 yd; 7; -35

Page 328 1. -15; 2. -129; 3. -3; 4. -63; 5. -80; 6. 0; 7. 14; 8. 1; 9. -70; 10. 202; 11. 9; 12. -91; 13. -8 + 17 = 9; -19; -309

Page 329 b. -1680; r. -200; a. -144; u. -108; s. -27; m. 225; c. 900; d. -225; y. 0; p. 83; q. -50; n. 100; x. -100; t. -14; e. 2; f. -14; o. 12; g. -4; h. 6 an account-ant

Page 330 1. (-2,-1); 2. (2,-2)

Page 331

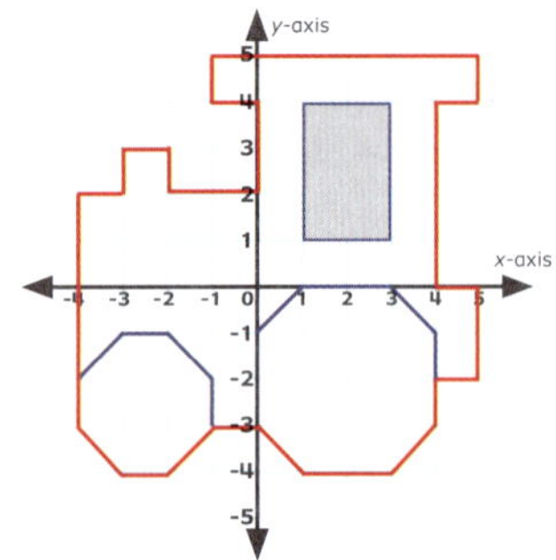

Page 332

1.

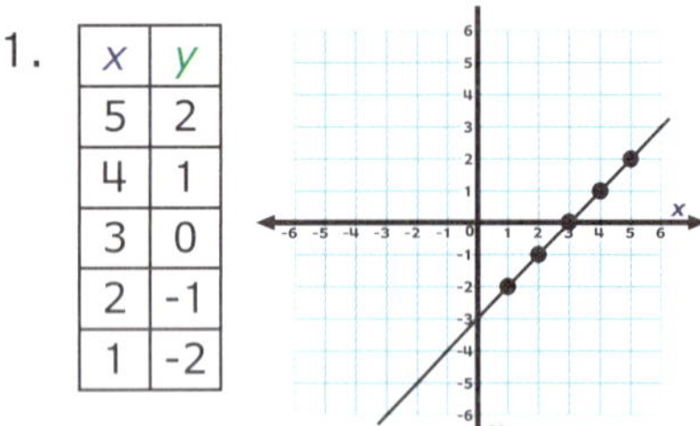

x	y
5	2
4	1
3	0
2	-1
1	-2

;

2.

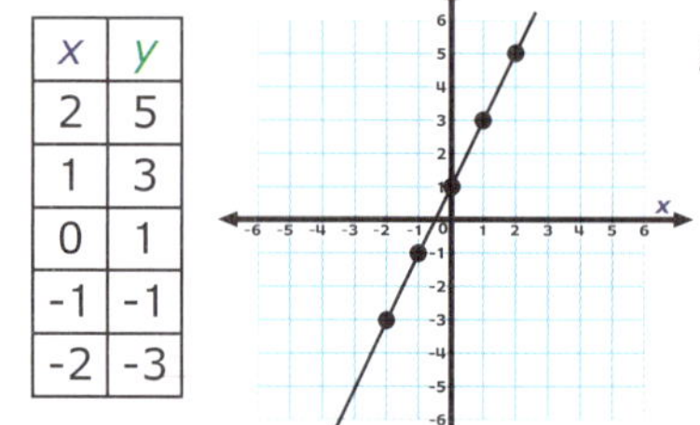

x	y
2	5
1	3
0	1
-1	-1
-2	-3

;

3.

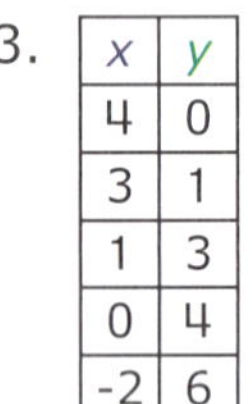

x	y
4	0
3	1
1	3
0	4
-2	6

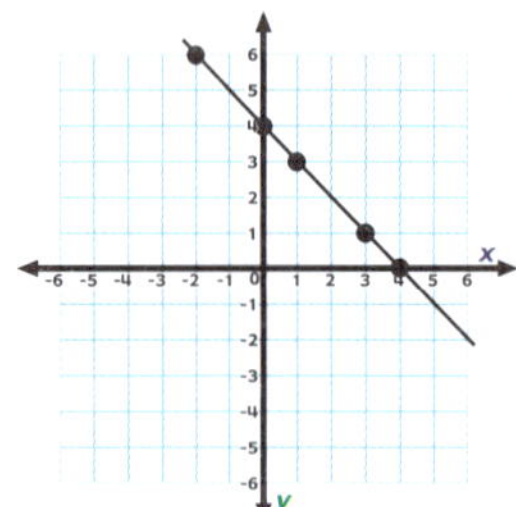

; 4. quadrants 1, 4, 3

Page 333 1. $y = -2x$; 2. $y = 4x + 1$; 3. $n - 4$; 4. $3n$; 5. $n + 5$; 6. $n + 7$; 7. $\frac{6}{n}$; 8. $9n$; 9. $2(n + 3)$; 10. $8 - n$ 11. $6n - 3$

Page 334 1. -960; 2. 45; 3. 2; 4. 1; 5. -224; 6. 288; 7. 12; 8. 16; 9. 6; 10. -384; 11. 4; 12. 14; -4; -252

Page 335 1. >; 2. <; 3. =; 4. <; 5. >; 6. =; 7. >; 8. >; 9. =; 10. =
11. (8 − 2) × 3 > 15; 12. 64 ÷ (4 × 2) < 10
13. (20 − 10) ÷ (5 − 3) = 16 ÷ (4 + 4) + 3

Page 336 — 1. Ava Smith, Ann Brown, Sara Johnson, and Ripa Pine; 2. 6, 162; 3. 53, 29; 4. $\frac{1}{4}$, $\frac{1}{16}$

Page 337 — 1. .001, .01, .011, .1; 2. .02, .119, .21, .4; 3. .05, .9, 6.1, 50.2; 4. true; 5. true

Pages 338-339 — 1. 2.25 cm; 2. .8 cm; 3. 17.9 cm; 4. 3 cm; 5. .75 cm; 6. 15 cm; 7. .0091 cm; 8. 25.05; 9. 3.27; 10. 70.62; 11. 1.94; 12. 6.7; 13. 38.81; 14. 39.96; 15. 99.9; 24.87; 51.6

Pages 340-341 — 1. 9 in.; 2. 42 in.; 3. 18.525 in.; 4. 46.3125 in.; 5. 3.384; 6. .0495; 7. 63.63; 8. 106.43; 9. 2.32; 10. .0014; 11. 1.46; 12. 7.4; 4.278; 112.56

Pages 342-343 — 1. sum luck; 2. no bangs; 3. e; 4. b; 5. c; 6. a; 7. f

Page 344 — 1. 3 ft.; 2. 1,760 yd; 3. 2,175,360 ft; 4. 72 in.; 5. 8 ft; 6. 2 ft; 7. 4 ft; 8. 60 in.; 9. 144 in.; 10. 9 ft; 11. 252 in.

Page 345 — 1. a notebook; 2. e; 3. d; 4. b; 5. c

Page 346 — 1. true; true; true; true; false; true; false; false; 2. Drawings will vary. Example: shoe box

Page 347 — 1. 12 cm; 2. 12 cm; 3. 61 cm; 4. 120 cm; 5. 21 cm; 6. 340 cm; 7. 214 cm; 8. $10\frac{1}{2}$ in.; 9. 380 cm; 10. 8 ft

Page 348 — 1. 21.98 in.; 2. 4.71 cm; 3. 29.516 in.; 4. 15.7 ft; 5. 3.925 ft; 6. 1,345 times

Page 349 — g. 442 sq cm; t. 1387 sq cm; n. 1470 sq cm; r. 615 sq cm; a. 260 sq cm; o. 200 sq cm; i. 81 sq cm; v. 58 sq cm; navi-gator

Page 350 — a. 150 sq cm; t. 120 sq cm; b. 108 sq cm; w. 70 sq cm; r. 66 sq cm; e. 900 sq cm; s. 12 sq cm; o. 6 sq cm; d. 4 sq cm; waterbeds

Page 351 — 1. 3.14 sq ft; 2. 12.56 sq ft; 3. 28.26 sq ft; 4. 50.24 sq ft; 5. 78.5 sq ft; 6. 94.985 sq ft; 7. 69.76 sq ft (120 − 50.24)

Page 352 — 1. 72 ft; 2. 108 ft, 36 ft; 3. 400 sq ft (720 − 320); 4. 6 ft by 4 ft; 5. 6 ft by 6 ft

Page 353 — 1. 54 cubic cm; 2. 3,720 cubic cm; 3. 405 cubic cm; 4. a; 5. b; 6. 6 cubic cm

Page 354

1. 8	2. 8	■	3. 7	4. 4	5. 5	■	6. 6	7. 7	8. 1	9. 5
10. 9	9	■	11. 8	3	0	9	■	12. 1	3	9
13. 2	6	5	9	■	9	■	14. 1	8	■	0
■	4	■	15. 1	16. 3	0	■	7	■	17. 4	■
18. 6	■	19. 3	■	20. 9	1	0	■	21. 7	1	22. 1
23. 1	3	5	■	4	■	■	24. 2	8	1	7

Page 355

<table>
<tr><td>1. 7</td><td>2. 2</td><td></td><td>3. 3</td><td>4. 2</td><td>5. 2</td><td></td><td>6. 3</td><td>7. 5</td><td>8. 2</td><td>9. 8</td></tr>
<tr><td>10. 2</td><td>3</td><td></td><td>11. 1</td><td>0</td><td>0</td><td>0</td><td></td><td>12. 3</td><td>2</td><td>6</td></tr>
<tr><td>13. 2</td><td>4</td><td>6</td><td>7</td><td></td><td>1</td><td></td><td>14. 2</td><td>4</td><td></td><td>4</td></tr>
<tr><td></td><td>0</td><td></td><td>15. 9</td><td>16. 4</td><td>3</td><td></td><td>6</td><td></td><td>17. 3</td><td></td></tr>
<tr><td>18. 1</td><td></td><td>19. 9</td><td></td><td>20. 8</td><td>0</td><td>4</td><td></td><td>21. 1</td><td>5</td><td>22. 6</td></tr>
<tr><td>23. 5</td><td>7</td><td>6</td><td></td><td>6</td><td></td><td></td><td>24. 7</td><td>9</td><td>0</td><td>0</td></tr>
</table>

Pages 356-357

1. 7 × 5 + 9 × 4 = 71 balloons; 2. 1,046 − 128 + 8 × 12 = 1,014 cards;
3. Bob = $14.56 + $23.00 = $37.56; Moe = $37.56 − $1.95 = $35.61;
Total = $14.56 + $37.56 + $35.61 = $87.73;
4. 500 − 130 = 370 miles;
5. 5 × 60 = 300 people per hour; 300 × 24 = 7,200 people per day;
6a. 480 ÷ 15 = 32 gallons at $160; b. 480 ÷ 40 = 12 gallons at $60;
c. 480 ÷ 24 = 20 gallons at $100; d. 480 ÷ 20 = 24 gallons at $120

Page 359

1. e; 2. a; 3. t; 4. r; 5. i; 6. g; 7. h; 8. t; eat right

Pages 360-361

1. 76(A), 80(E); 2. 167(A), 170(E); 3. 672(A), 600(E);
4. 21(A), 25(E); 5. 404(A), 410(E); 6. 119(A), 120(E);
7. 3,649(A), 3,600(E); 8. 658(A), 526(E); 9. 811(A), 820(E);
10. 908(A), 910(E); 11. 3,564(A), 4,000(E) 35; 2,400

Pages 362-363

1.

Teacher	Boxes Sold	Boxes Sold
Adams	12	1 2 3 4 5 6 / 1 2 3 4 5 6
Allen	27	1 2 3 4 5 6 / 1 2 3 4 5 6 / 1 2 3 4 5 6 / 1 2 3 4 5 6 / 1 2 3
Brown	21	1 2 3 4 5 6 / 1 2 3 4 5 6 / 1 2 3 4 5 6 / 1 2 3
Jones	10	1 2 3 4 5 6 / 1 2 3 4
Smith	17	1 2 3 4 5 6 / 1 2 3 4 5 6 / 1 2 3 4 5

2.

Boxes Sold	Boxes Sold
87	1 2 3 4 5 6 / 1 2 3 4 5 6 / 1 2 3 4 5 6 / 1 2 3 4 5 6 / 1 2 3 4 5 6 / 1 2 3 4 5 6 / 1 2 3 4 5 6 / 1 2 3 4 5 6 / 1 2 3 4 5 6 / 1 2 3 4 5 6 / 1 2 3 4 5 6 / 1 2 3 4 5 6 / 1 2 3 4 5 6 / 1 2 3 4 5 6 / 1 2 3

3.

4. $3 × 87 = $261; 5. $261 − 1.20 × 87 = $156.60;
6. $156.60 + 87 = $243.60

Page 364

1.

Student	Cupcakes Sold
Katie	40 cupcakes
Allie	52 cupcakes
Dawn	34 cupcakes
Madi	26 cupcakes
Deb	60 cupcakes

; 2. 240 − 212 = 28 cupcakes;
3. 240 ÷ 12 = 20 dozen cupcakes

Page 365

1. $\frac{9}{12}$; 2. $\frac{4}{8}$; 3. $\frac{4}{10}$; 4. $\frac{5}{15}$; 5. $\frac{12}{32}$; 6. $\frac{10}{12}$; 7. $\frac{12}{20}$;
8. $\frac{6}{36}$; 9. $\frac{10}{24}$; 10. $\frac{10}{15}$; 11. $\frac{8}{18}$; 12. $\frac{18}{42}$; $\frac{8}{10}$; $\frac{20}{32}$

Pages 366-367

1. $\frac{1}{2}$; 2. $\frac{1}{4}$; 3. $\frac{3}{5}$; 4. $\frac{5}{9}$; 5. $\frac{3}{8}$; 6. $\frac{1}{6}$;
7. $\frac{5}{8}$; 8. $\frac{2}{5}$; 9. $\frac{2}{7}$; 10. $\frac{7}{9}$; 11. $\frac{1}{5}$; 12. $\frac{4}{5}$;
13. $\frac{5}{6}$; 14. $\frac{7}{8}$; 15. $\frac{3}{10}$; 16. $\frac{3}{4}$; $\frac{2}{3}$; $\frac{7}{12}$

Pages 368-369

l. $27\frac{2}{5}$; u. $43\frac{1}{4}$; a. $56\frac{1}{9}$; r. $33\frac{1}{2}$; e. $157\frac{2}{3}$; j. $246\frac{2}{3}$;
y. $295\frac{1}{2}$; m. $63\frac{3}{4}$; g. $56\frac{2}{7}$; n. 26; w. $51\frac{1}{3}$; jungle gym

Page 370

1. blue = $\frac{3}{10}$ or .3;
yellow = $\frac{1}{10}$ or .1;
green = $\frac{2}{5}$ or .4;

2. blue = $\frac{1}{4}$ or .25;
yellow = $\frac{11}{100}$ or .11;
green = $\frac{7}{50}$ or .14

Page 371

$\frac{1}{2}$ = .5	$\frac{3}{8}$ = .375	$\frac{2}{5}$ = .4
$\frac{1}{4}$ = .25	$\frac{5}{8}$ = .625	$\frac{1}{10}$ = .1
$\frac{3}{4}$ = .75	$\frac{7}{8}$ = .875	$\frac{1}{100}$ = .01
$\frac{1}{8}$ = .125	$\frac{1}{5}$ = .2	$\frac{1}{16}$ = .0625

Page 373

s. $.\overline{3}$; n. $.\overline{6}$; t. $.\overline{4}$; o. $.\overline{7}$; m. $.1\overline{6}$; r. $.\overline{27}$; a. $.\overline{72}$;
e. $.41\overline{6}$; b. $.08\overline{3}$; d. $.291\overline{6}$; mane street

Page 374

1. .01 1%

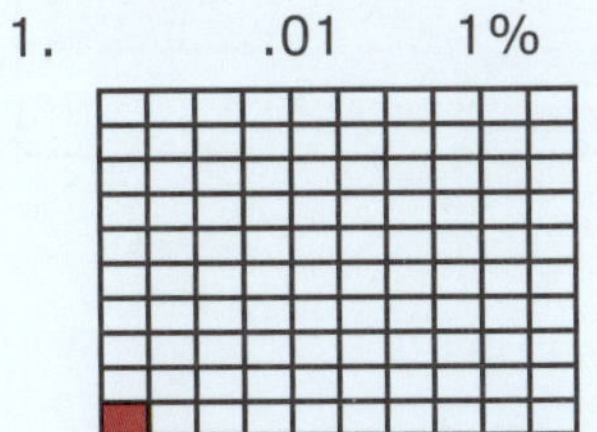

;

2. $\frac{19}{100}$ 19%

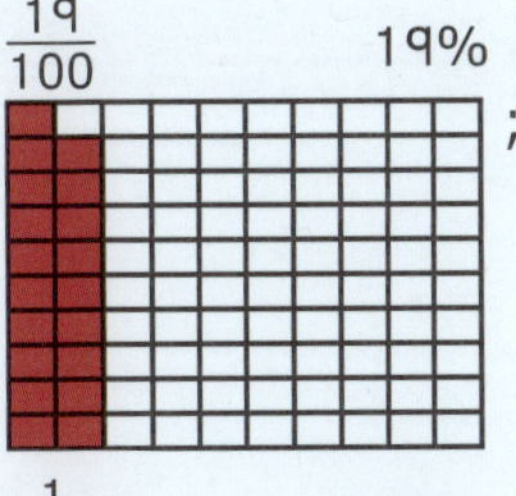

;

3. $\frac{1}{2}$ .50

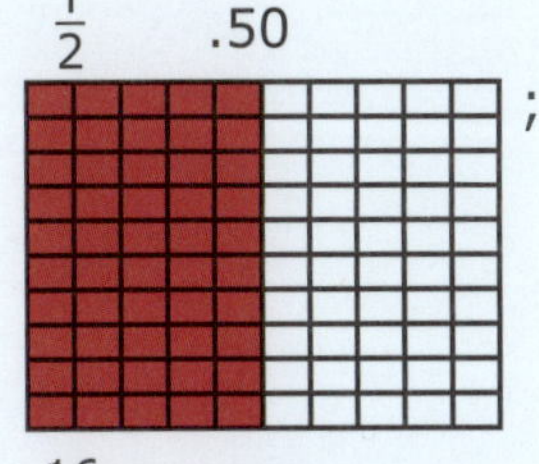
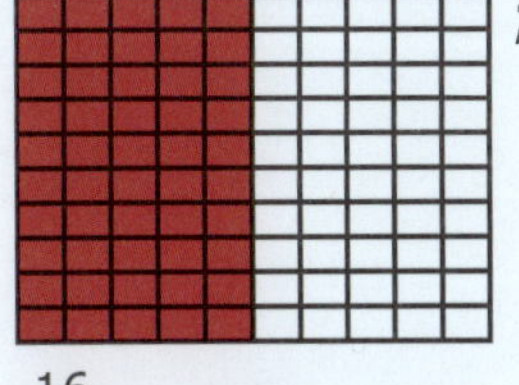

;

4. .30 30%

5. $\frac{1}{4}$ 25%

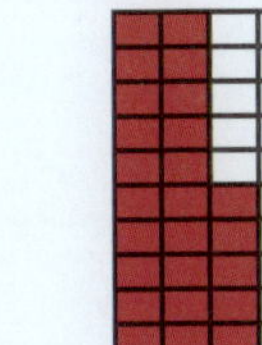
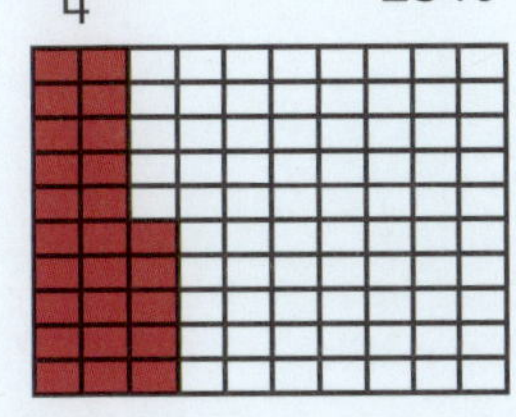

6. $\frac{16}{25}$ .64

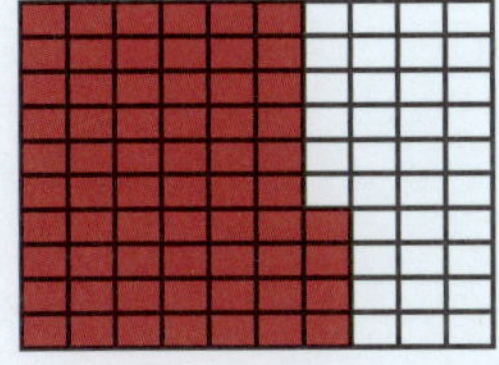

Page 375

1.

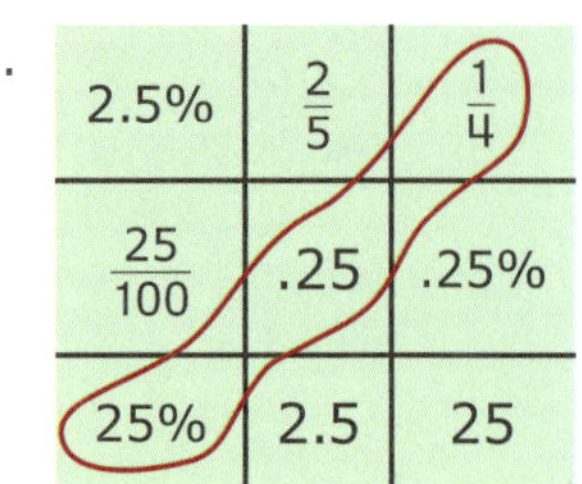

2.5%	$\frac{2}{5}$	$\frac{1}{4}$
$\frac{25}{100}$	.25	.25%
25%	2.5	25

;

2.

$\frac{3}{4}$	75	$\frac{75}{100}$
.75	75%	$\frac{9}{12}$
7.5	$\frac{15}{24}$	.75%

Page 376

1.

13	6	11
8	10	12
9	14	7

2.

19	20	15
14	18	22
21	16	17

Page 377

1. $\frac{5}{8}$, $\frac{1}{8}$, $\frac{1}{4}$; 2. $\frac{1}{2}$, $\frac{5}{18}$, $\frac{1}{6}$, $\frac{1}{18}$; 3. $\frac{1}{24}$, $\frac{1}{4}$, $\frac{1}{8}$, $\frac{1}{4}$, $\frac{1}{3}$

Page 378

1.

214	312	112	239	37
146	46	150	37	149
210	138	122	201	95
126	134	118	125	171
138	172	94	121	155

; 2.

342	128	506	292	376
136	300	514	370	534
422	214	508	215	400
207	401	297	374	184
433	155	183	108	390

;

3.

27	34	32	19
29	26	54	16
37	39	18	43
44	56	26	18

Page 379

Answers will vary. Examples:
1. 19 + 61 = 80; 2. 97 − 37 = 60; 3. 17 + 17 + 23 = 57;
4. 47 + 11 − 2 = 56; 5. 13 × 5 = 65; 6. 7 × 11 × 13 = 1,001

Page 380

1.

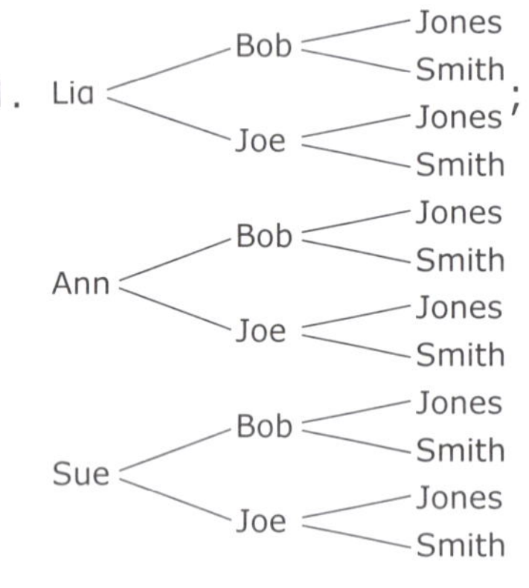

; 2.

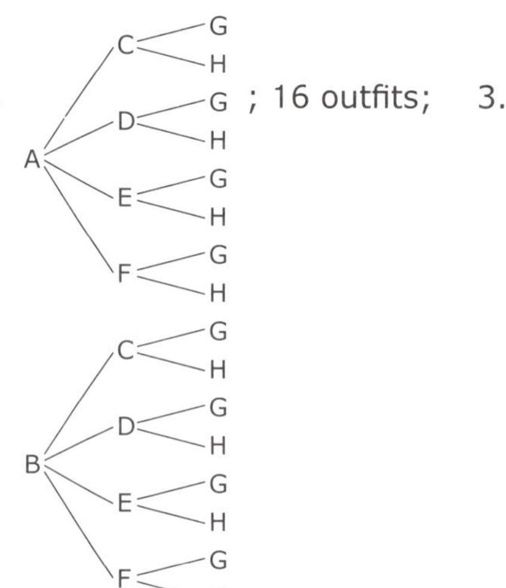

; 16 outfits; 3. 48 choices

Page 381

Stan: pears, chess;
Steve: bananas, cards;
Mary: oranges, jacks;
Maria: apples, checkers

Page 382

1.

Stems	Leaves
10	3 9
11	2 2
12	6 7 8 9

;

2. There are more 16-year-olds than any other age group.;

3. 129 – 103 = 26

Page 383

1. 88°; 2. 71°; 3. 90°; 4. 71°; 5. 90°; 6. 71°; 7. 95°, 95°, 95°

Pages 384-385

Player	Hits	Times at Bat	Batting Average
Ralph	7	25	.280
Juan	5	32	.156
Tom	6	21	.286
Brett	10	40	.250
Al	5	22	.227
Lou	7	20	.350
Jim	10	30	.333
Eddy	7	24	.292
Ned	6	15	.400

1. Ned
2. Lou
3. Jim
4. .361 (1.083 ÷ 3)

Page 386

1. $.60; 2. $11.20; 3. $9; 4. $37.50; 5. $32.30;
6. $10; 7. $1.10; 8. $54; 9. $29.25; $11; $12.70

Page 387

1. 253; 2. 451; 3. 616; 4. 957; 5. 704; 6. 121;
7. 625; 8. 225; 9. 7,225; 10. 4,225; 11. 9,025; 12. 3,025

Page 388

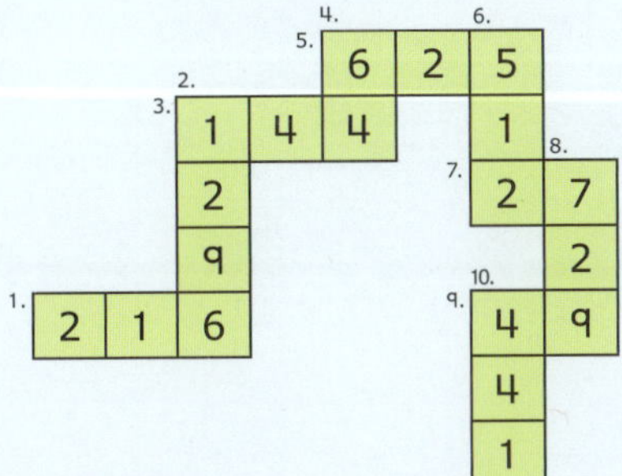

Page 389

1. 30; 2. 441; 3. 8; 4. 91; 5. 112; 6. 0; 6; 1,296

Page 390

1. 58 cookies; 2. 72 slices; 3. 2,282 miles;
4. 24 cards; 5. 67°

Page 391

1. $8.21; 2. 25 rolls, $25.95; 3. 504 pencils;
4. .91 seconds; 5. $110

Page 392

Drawings will vary. Examples:

2. ; 3. ; 4. ; 5. ; 6.

Page 393

v. 58°; i. 115°; t. 40°; x. 90°; a. 79°; r. 135°; e. 20°;
d. 160°; taxi driver

Page 394

1. 37°; 2. 106°; 3. 30° 4. 65°; 5. 122°; 6. 152°

Page 395
1. 156 sq ft; 2. 450 – 156 = 294 sq ft;
3. 132 sq ft; 4. 750 – 132 = 618 sq ft;
5. 100 sq ft; 6. 475 – 100 = 375 sq ft;
7. $2,472; 8. $780; 9. No, $528

Page 396
e. 144 cm^3; r. 180 cm^3; a. 2,700 cm^3; v. 1,000 cm^3; s. 3,432 cm^3;
i. 2,754 cm^3; a river

Page 397
1. 64; 2. .06; 3. .25; 4. 64;
5. hexagon; 6. volume; 7. 9; 8. foot;
9. 50; 10. 4; 11. $4\frac{3}{7}$; 12. $\frac{9}{10}$

Page 398
1. 43; 2. 33; 3. 97; 4. 58;
5. 4.2; 6. 1.55; 7. $n + 48 = 55$, n = $7

Page 399
1. 34; 2. 40; 3. 75; 4. 57;
5. 4.2; 6. 7.35; 7. $n - 8 = 15$, n = $23

Page 400
1. 8; 2. 8; 3. 34; 4. 81;
5. 10; 6. 20; 7. $4n = 108$, n = $27

Page 401
1. 36; 2. 70; 3. 918; 4. 177;
5. 34; 6. 29.4; 7. $\frac{n}{3} = 11.25$, n = $33.75

Page 402
1. 1,000 sq ft; 2. 160 sq. ft; 3. 200.96 sq ft; 4. 42 ft;
5. 100.48 ft; 6. 12.6 sq ft; 15.4 sq ft; 84 ft

Page 403
1. g; 2. o; 3. b; 4. e; 5. j; 6. i;
7. d; 8. p; 9. k; 10. f; 11. c; 12. l;
13. h; 14. m; 15. a; 16. n

Page 404

1. 4	2. 7	2	8						
	8								
	7								
3. 3	8	0	4. 8						
			4		6. 1				
			5. 3	4	.4				
					2		8. 2		
					7. 8	0	0		
							4		
							9. 8	0	10. 9
									9